VOICE
AND
DICTION

VOICE

AND

DICTION

A PROGRAM FOR IMPROVEMENT

SIXTH EDITION

JON EISENSON

PROFESSOR EMERITUS
STANFORD UNIVERSITY

WITH THE ASSISTANCE OF
ARTHUR M. EISENSON

Macmillan Publishing Company
New York
Maxwell Macmillan Canada
Toronto

To Eileen
and
To Art and Sara
and
To Rosanne and James
and
Their parents

Editors: David Chodoff and Patrick Shriner
Production Supervisor: Betsy Keefer
Production Manager: Aliza Greenblatt
Cover Designer: S. Goodman
This book was set in 10/12 Berkeley Book by V & M Graphics
and was printed and bound by Hamilton Press.

Macmillan Publishing Company
866 Third Avenue, New York, New York 10022

Macmillan Publishing Company is part of the
Maxwell Communication Group of Companies.

Maxwell Macmillan Canada, Inc.
1200 Eglinton Avenue East
Suite 200
Don Mills, Ontario M3C 3N1

Library of Congress Cataloging-in-Publication Data

Eisenson, Jon, 1907–
    Voice and diction : a program for improvement / Jon Eisenson.
      p. cm.
    Includes bibliographical references and index.
    ISBN 0-02-332105-9
    1. Voice culture—Exercises.   2. English language—United States—
Pronunciation.   I. Title.
PN4197.E46   1992
808.5—dc20   91-4401
                                    CIP

Printing: 1 2 3 4 5 6 7   Year: 2 3 4 5 6 7 8

PREFACE

The present sixth edition of *Voice and Diction* is updated to reflect contemporary information about voice production and diction (articulation, pronunciation, and intonation). For those who are motivated, this body of knowledge should enhance their effectiveness as communicators. As in the previous editions, the body of knowledge includes relevant information from the related disciplines of speech and hearing sciences, linguistics, and phonetics.

This edition is organized along the following lines: Part One is concerned with basic topics that include an expanded chapter, "Our Changing Speech Patterns," and a separate chapter, "American-English Pronunciation." These chapters trace the origins of American English and highlight some of the major dialect "differences" within the United States as well as some of the rapidly ongoing contributions to language generated in the computer age.

The seven chapters of Part Two deal with aspects of voice improvement, for which I have provided additional practice materials, including new dialogues.

Part Three — "Diction" — has been reorganized and now has eleven chapters. The new organization expresses my own preference for order of presentation and is by no means to be considered a prescription. The chapters in Part Three also have additional practice materials and new dialogues.

In addition, Part Three is concerned with likely "errors" of articulation and intonation that are usually carryovers from first (native) languages. Especially emphasized are the "errors" we find and may anticipate in Hispanic and Asian persons — both adolescents and adults — who are learning or have learned American English as a second language. In some instances, though American born, such persons' first language exposure was to the native language of their parents; thus American English was learned as a second language.

The appendixes have been revised and extended with the glossary considerably expanded.

As in earlier editions, I have in this edition resisted the temptation to be prescriptive, to recommend any one standard of pronunciation and language usage. A possible exception is my position on what in the way of content and manner of presentation may be appropriate and so desirable for effective communication. I do present "functional standards" that relate to specific situations and regional expectations. Thus some persons may choose to be bidialectal or even tridialectal according to given situations and use a "homey" turn of phrase in particular instances and for particular listeners. Some of our politicians have developed an aptitude, for their special purposes, for speaking as they judge they would like to be heard. Others are more comfortable in presenting themselves as they think they are and maintain what is for them a standard dialect. The choice is an individual one.

Whenever we speak, we employ a complex set of long-established habits. Most often these habits are appropriate to the speaking situation; sometimes they are not. When they are not appropriate, they should and can be changed, even though change requires considerable effort and a strong and persistent drive. In some instances, external imposition may bring about a change, but only with the cooperation of the speaker who accepts the imposition as being in her or his own interest. Usually, identification and emulation are more effective motivators than external imposition.

If this book is used in an academic or technical school course, it is likely that the students will fall into one of two major groups. The first will probably include persons who are self-motivated to use their voices comfortably and effectively and to improve their diction. This goal may be pursued as one worthwhile in itself or as a vocational asset. The five preceding editions of this book have, in fact, been used in courses for students who are preparing to teach, practice law, enter the ministry, or work in the mass media or in the theater, as well as for students who are already in these professions.

A second group is composed of students who may not have been initially self-motivated, but who were advised by a teacher, a counselor, or a friend to take a course in voice and/or diction. Even though such advice may have been accepted with some reluctance and the motivation "external," mature students will avail themselves of the opportunity to learn more about the mechanisms for the human behavior called *speech* and to learn as well how to use the mechanisms for voice and oral language proficiently and effectively.

This book has also been used by persons who, without specific vocational goals, were nevertheless interested in improving their voice and diction. These persons, through the use of tape recordings and, in some instances, videocassettes, were their own teachers. I have learned that these motivated speakers used the practice materials in the book to record the speech of friends whom they admired as models worthy of emulation. Their own recordings were then compared with those of their models.

Though speaking—the ability to learn and to use an oral language system—is a human-specific behavior, how well we speak is an individual achievement. I hope that the sixth edition of *Voice and Diction* will help to make the achievement and the effort to bring it about pleasant and, if possible, enjoyable. It was so in my writing.

For this edition of *Voice and Diction* I have incurred several debts. I continue to be deeply indebted to the reviewers and the instructors who have offered positive and constructive suggestions for updating materials and making them relevant to the students and the times. I am indebted to the readers who have sent me thoughtful notes about what they liked in the book and would like even more if their suggestions were followed. Many of these suggestions were indeed accepted and incorporated in this revision. I wish also to acknowledge my appreciation to Arthur Eisenson for the insights, research, and gentle suggestions that only a professional writer could express. To Sara Krane, I am grateful for several creative dialogues that enhance the practice materials. And, not just "of course," I am grateful to Eileen, who was considerably more than a patient wife in her willingness to read the pages of the manuscript to help me make certain that I wrote what I intended to communicate. She also smiled at the right places.

J. E.

CONTENTS

APPENDIXES   **395**

INDEX   **403**

PART ONE

BASIC CONSIDERATIONS

The music that can deepest reach,
And cure all ill, is cordial speech.

—Ralph Waldo Emerson, *Merlin's Song*

Speech is civilization itself. The word, even the
most contradictory word, preserves contact. It is
silence which isolates.

—Thomas Mann, *The Magic Mountain*

CHAPTER 1

VOICE, DICTION, AND EFFECTIVE COMMUNICATION

With gift of language
And articulate voice,
What we make of them
Is much our choice.

Although this book is not concerned with communication in its broadest sense, which includes public speaking, it is concerned with the effective use of voice and with diction[1] and, therefore, with oral (speech) production.

Whatever a speaker's purpose may be at a given occasion, whether it is to share ideas or feelings, to provide information, or to provoke thinking or emotions, the purpose or purposes will be most readily achieved with the effective use of voice and easily intelligible diction. However, this is not to say that in some instances a person may not be an effective communicator despite negative qualities of voice and or diction, or despite an overall speech output that suggests either a narrow regional influence or a strong foreign background. We who live in a democratic society will continue and even be privileged to hear speakers whose messages may be of such importance that we will be willing to expend effort in adjusting to their speech differences. But such speakers are the exceptions. Henry Kissinger may be cited as one of those exceptions. Few of our outstanding communicators make such demands on us for adjusting our expectations to their variations. It is true that among recent effective communicators, including a few whom we may consider outstanding—Winston Churchill, Franklin Delano Roosevelt, John F. Kennedy, and Martin Luther King, Jr.—all had some aspect of speech that was not quite "standard" or expressed strong regional influence or local dialect. However, what identified each of these speakers was a positive, attractive, and felicitous use of

[1] We shall use the term *diction* as synonymous with *pronunciation*, that is, with the human behavior of producing the sounds (vowels and consonants) of our language. Pronunciation also includes accent (syllable stress) and inflection (the intonation or "melody" of language). There is an underlying assumption that the speaker's productions are expressed with some reference or awareness of a standard of correctness or *acceptability*.

3

voice and clear diction. Each of these speakers conveyed thoughts and feelings with voice, words, and diction appropriate to the occasion and with particular attention to the listeners.[2]

However, most of us may have neither the aspiration nor the occasion to become "great communicators." Still, we probably do wish to be effective in our communicative efforts, even if they are limited to conversation or to the few times when we are engaged as public speakers and wish to say a few words particularly well. Those of us who teach, or who plan to become teachers, will find that the occasions for saying a few words well occur every day. We believe that to be able to use the voice easily and effectively, and to articulate intelligibly with a minimum of dialectal influence, will help toward this end.

Part One of this book is intended to provide information that should help the student to become aware of what constitutes an effective voice and what and how the voice expresses the speaker and is perceived by the listeners as suggesting personality and states of health. One of the objectives in Part One is to provide information about the mechanisms of the voice and articulation on the assumption that intelligent persons wish to understand the functioning of the "specialized equipment" that makes human beings unique in both the manner in which they communicate and the content they are able to communicate.

We will begin with some preliminary considerations relative to vocalization and articulation.

═══ EFFECTIVE COMMUNICATION ═══

Responsiveness

Above all else, an effective voice is responsive to your intentions as a speaker. Through awareness and responsiveness, you as a speaker are able to share attitudes and feelings as well as nuances of thought. Thus a listener knows not only what you wish to have him or her think, but also how you feel about the essential thoughts of your communicative effort.

Appropriateness of Attributes

An effective voice is intimately associated with what the speaker is saying and attracts no attention to itself; it therefore does not distract from what the speaker is trying to communicate. Distraction may result from either the attributes of the voice or the manner in which the voice is produced. If the duration, quality, pitch, loudness, or any combination of these vocal characteristics is faulty or in some way not consonant with the contents of the speech, an element of distraction is introduced. For example, matters of importance are usually spoken slowly rather than hurriedly. Unless secrecy is to be suggested, important content is uttered more loudly than content of lesser importance.

---

[2] We may add the name of Sharron Pratt Dixon, mayor of Washington, D.C. (elected November, 1990), as a likely candidate for a superior communicator.

Solemn utterances are usually associated with relatively low pitch and lighter remarks with relatively higher pitch. A reversal of these pitch-contents relationships is likely to be either distracting or misleading. Excessive nasality, huskiness, or any other vocal characteristic that is striking and culturally undesirable may serve as a distraction. In contrast, a very fine voice may also be momentarily distracting if it directs the listener's attention to its unusual qualities. Most listeners, however, soon accept the fine voice and respond to the contents of the speech. On the other hand, a voice that includes a constant element of irritation may continue to distract and may thus impair the speaker's ability to communicate.

We respond negatively to a speaker who, with loud voice and flashing eyes, insists, "I am not angry." We respond both negatively and with disbelief to a speaker whose voice level is just above that of a whisper, seeming by manner to suggest that he or she is about to share a secret, but who says something of little value, even if not a secret. On the other hand, if a speaker has a message of some importance that he or she wishes to communicate to listeners, a monotonous voice, even though readily heard, is unattractive and belittles the message. In sharp contrast is the stentorian-voiced speaker who is constantly testing the limits of his or her decibelic output. Unhappily for the listeners, the output shows little regard for the sensitivities of listeners and frequently no relationship to the content of the message.

Manner of Production

A voice may have acceptable characteristics and still be ineffective if the speaker's manner of producing the voice attracts attention. If the speaker is obviously straining to be heard, or if the external throat muscles appear tense or the jaw tight, the listeners may be distracted by what they observe. If listeners must force themselves to be attentive, the effort may be unpleasant. Some listeners may also become tense as a result of what they see and, through empathy, feel. On the other hand, overly relaxed speakers who seem to be too tired to vocalize and articulate with enough energy to be heard may fatigue their listener-observers. The stentorian-voiced speaker may also cause listener fatigue and a wish, as well, to withdraw, at least psychologically, from the excessive and unvarying decibelic output.

Appropriateness Related to Sex, Age, and Physique

Another area of vocal appropriateness is related to the sex, age, and physical build of the speaker. We expect men's voices to be different from those of women. We expect the voice of a mature person to sound different from that of a child, and we expect big persons to have "big" voices. A high-pitched, "thin" voice may be acceptable from a small, delicate child, but it is not likely to be acceptable from either a man, a physically mature-looking woman, or a large boy.

Listeners' Criteria of Effectiveness

From the viewpoint of the listener, an effective voice is one that can be heard without conscious effort or strain. It is consistent with the speaker's message and helps to make the message readily audible and intelligible. An effective voice is pleasant to hear, but the pleasure should be unconscious and should not dominate the listeners' reactions, as it might if they were listening to a good singer. To be effective, the voice should be as loud as the specific speaking situation demands. If the speaker is talking to a group, the voice should be heard with ease by every listener, but none should be disturbed because of its loudness. In a conversational situation, the listener with normal hearing and a normal power of concentration should not have to ask a speaker to repeat because of a failure to hear, nor should anyone wish to move away to avoid discomfort from over-loudness. In summary, the listener, if inclined to be analytic, should be able to conclude that the speaker's voice, as well as her or his actions, suits the words, the overall situation, and the speaker as an individual. However, a word of caution is in order. Just as speakers should adjust their vocal efforts to the occasion, listeners should adjust their expectations and demands. The public orator may be an autocrat at the breakfast table, but he or she should refrain from orating not only at breakfast with the family but also when dining with friends. His or her companions should make clear their demands, that they prefer conversational speaking to orating.

OBJECTIVE SELF-LISTENING: TO HEAR OURSELVES AS OTHERS HEAR US

It is now readily possible to hear ourselves almost as others hear us. We say *almost* as a concession to instrumentation that may be "high-fi" but nevertheless does not have the fidelity of the normal hearing apparatus. However, close enough will do for the time being. For those of us so inclined, it is also possible to see ourselves as, perhaps, others see us. Audiotapes and videotapes, the first at little expense and the latter at no great expense, have made these reflections possible. Tape or cassette recordings of reasonable fidelity can be made with inexpensive home equipment. Recordings with greater fidelity can be made at commercial studios or college speech-hearing clinics. Remember to make certain that the fidelity of the playback equipment is at least equal to that of the record-ing equipment.

When you make your first recording with the intention of playing it back for objec-tive listening, be prepared for something of a surprise that may border on shock. You may wish to deny that what you sound like and articulate can possibly be coming from you: "The fault must be in the recording or in the playback equipment." It is true that no one hears herself or himself as does a listener. This phenomenon will be explained later.

If your recording is "candid" because you have arranged with a friend to record your voice without telling you just when, it would be best if it were done in an informal setting, at a group gathering, or sometime in the course of a conversation. This will provide the best opportunity to hear yourself as others hear you. If the recording is staged rather than candid, it should include conversational speaking as well as content read in a conversational voice and material spoken as if to a small audience. If you are one who makes speeches or aspires to public speaking, you should include content presented as you would for an anticipated audience. You should then play back the recordings on equipment that is, as indicated earlier, in good condition and with fidelity capacity at least equal to that of your recording. While listening, you should respond to the following questions:

1. Is my voice pleasant to hear?
2. Does my voice have any characteristics that I would consider undesirable in another speaker?
3. Does my voice reflect what I intended to convey in thought and in feeling?
4. Were the changes in pitch, loudness, duration, and quality appropriate to the changes of thought and/or feeling that I was trying to convey?[3]
5. Would I listen to this voice if I were not the speaker?
6. Does the voice reflect me as a personality?
7. Is it the personality I want to express?
8. Is my articulation (diction) up to the standard of my own expectations? Are there any sounds or sound combinations that need improvement?

If as a speaker-listener you are completely satisfied with all of the answers to the questions just posed, then you are among the fortunate persons who are making the most of the gift of a good, effective voice. If you are not entirely satisfied and you recognize the need for improvement, then you should also be ready and willing to do whatever is necessary to bring about the required changes. An important step in this direction is to learn to hear yourself as others hear you.

Normally, the voice and the articulatory productions you hear when you speak — what you hear if you try to tune in to yourself while you are speaking — is different from what other listeners hear. If you wish to hear yourself as if you were a listener, make a high-fidelity voice recording of something you might read aloud to a friend to emphasize a point, or record about a hundred words of conversation with a friend. Both of you may be in for an interesting experience. Each of you will probably recognize the other's voice more readily than your own. Because you are so close to the source of your own voice, you cannot hear it as does a listener who is at even a small distance from you. You hear your voice through the tissues of your body, especially the bones of the head, as these tissues directly conduct the sounds you produce to your hearing mechanism. You also hear yourself by way of the sound waves you produce in the air, which simultaneously stimulate the hearing mechanism. The listener, however, hears you only through these air-laden sound waves.

---

[3] Quality will be considered in the next chapter in some detail. For the present, let us regard quality as the complex of voice features that enable us to identify an individual speaker. Voice quality may also be characterized as nasal, harsh, and orotund (full, "rounded," resonant). The last — orotund — may make a speaker sound pompous if the quality is not appropriate to the occasion. On the positive side, we may use such terms as *pleasant, clean, flexible, responsive, smooth, rich, mature,* and *strong.* These terms are obviously subjective. The inventory of words that we use to describe vocal quality is limited only by the lexicon of the listener.

You can appreciate some of the differences between the two avenues of stimulation if you plug up your ears while you talk. You then hear more nearly through bone conduction than you do with your ears "open." Your voice sounds different and somewhat strange. For immediate contrast, repeat what you have said with your ears unstopped. If at all possible, you should then immediately listen to a high-fidelity recording of your voice. Only then, making allowance for subjective reactions, will you be able to hear yourself as others hear you. Among the important differences resulting from our multiple-conduction feedback system of listening to ourselves is that we may misjudge the pitch, range, loudness, and quality, and possibly the rate, of our speech. Because we cannot hear ourselves as others hear us, we must accept the evaluation of others, especially if they are objective and professionally trained voice teachers or therapists. Fortunately, despite the limitations of our self-monitoring system, we have considerable evidence to show that learning to listen to our own voices is helpful in the improvement of both voice and diction.

The Process of Self-Monitoring: The Normal Feedback Loop

Although we cannot hear ourselves as others hear us, it may be of help to understand how we do hear ourselves, and how we feel when we talk and about what we are saying. If we have normal sensory mechanisms for hearing, seeing, feeling, and movement, our vocal efforts are sent back to us for *monitoring* as we speak. In the act of talking (or for any other learned behavior) we are engaged in producing and responding to the products of our ongoing productions. This is the feedback response. By virtue of these back-flow responses to sound (auditory), feeling (tactile), and articulatory movement (kinesthetic), we become the receivers (responders) to the flow of sensory information that we produce. If we are able to see ourselves in a mirror as we speak we can add the *visual*, although this is seldom possible in normal speaking situations. The feedback process is, of course, neither unique nor peculiar to speaking. Self-monitoring through feedback tells us whether we are walking as we should, throwing a ball as we would like, or swinging a racket, a bat, or a golf club according to instruction. Feedback functions in any learned activity over which we can exercise control.

If you are fortunate enough to be able to talk in a quiet environment, you may normally be able to have feedback control of sound, feeling, and articulatory action. If, however, you must do some of your talking with competition from noise — human, animal, or mechanical — you suffer a reduction in the amount of reliable information about the sound of your voice and articulation and so must rely, more than you might like and more than is usually necessary, on tactile and kinesthetic feedback. Some of us are much better at this than others. Some of us may say little, except for conventional acknowledgments, at noisy social gatherings because we lack adequate feedback and therefore do not feel in control of our speech.

Normally, feedback involves two ongoing, simultaneous processes, and, when needed, a third. The simultaneous processes are *self-inspection* and *evaluation* (comparison with an assumed standard or level of performance). For example in sports activity, you might ask, are you swinging the bat or golf club or tennis racket according to your intended plan? In speaking, are you vocalizing at the anticipated level of loudness and within the desired pitch range? Is your articulation correct? If all is going according to plan, you continue; if it is not, your goal is, or should be, to adjust and correct. On occasion, your decision may be not to make an obvious correction of the immediate past effort, but to make adjustments for future occasions. In any event, to adjust and/or to correct, you as a speaker must have a model in mind, a target or goal toward which to move.

When, after years of habitual but no longer desirable vocal or articulatory behavior, you are persuaded to make changes, two assumptions are in order: first, unless you have an organic problem, a change in a desired direction is realistic — it can be done; second, target behaviors (changes) will not come without concentrated effort. Even after new speech behaviors are established, you may experience temporary disruptions. Excessive fatigue, stage fright, or another highly emotional state or stress may produce disruption. However, such lapses can be overcome, as in the case of Eliza Doolittle in Shaw's *Pygmalion* (or in the musical version, *My Fair Lady*). When calm and the opportunity to resume practice were restored, so were Eliza's "new" voice and pronunciation.

═══ LISTENING TO OTHERS ═══

In addition to turning the audio reflection toward yourself, it should help for you to do some directed listening to the voices that are part of your everyday living. These are the voices of your close relatives, your friends and associates, teachers, media persons, and even shopkeepers. You may find that you have positive feelings toward some of these voices, negative feelings toward others, and reservations about a few. Do you suspect that any one of the people you listen to has a practiced, public voice that meets the requirements (expectations) of a public situation, yet is not the voice you hear and know in private life? Following are a few projects that should be useful to you in becoming a sophisticated listener.

EXERCISES FOR LISTENING TO OTHERS

1. Tune in to a daytime television "soap opera" and listen to the voices of the performers with your eyes closed. Can you identify the hero or the heroine through the medium of voice alone? Can you detect the likely role of other characters by their initial utterances? Can you pick out the family friend? The pseudofriend? A person whom you would like to like? One whom you instantly trust or distrust? What are the specific vocal attributes of each character that influenced your decision? Try to imitate these attributes.

2. Compare the newscaster you habitually listen to with one you seldom hear or even avoid. Do the vocal characteristics of the newscasters have anything

to do with your choice? For each of them, list the vocal characteristics that you like and dislike. Which of the two has a more favorable balance? Are there any television or radio personalities who intentionally use an unusual quality of voice to attract attention? Are these people whom you would accept as entertainers? Do you have the same expectations and "standards" for the voice of a newscaster and that of a commentator on the news? For a person who is regarded as an authority on a particular subject or issue? For a sportscaster or someone who gives the weather report? For a weather forecaster who is also identified as a meteorologist?

3. Listen critically to two or three of your friends. Are there any characteristics of their voices that you particularly like? Are there any that you would like to have modified? Why?

4. Listen critically to some persons whom you do not particularly like. Do you hear any vocal characteristics that might account for your reactions to them? Do they remind you of anyone you disliked as a child?

5. Recall a teacher, present or past, whom you consider especially effective. Is the voice of the teacher an important factor in your judgment? Describe the teacher's vocal attributes. Contrast this teacher with one you consider ineffective. Describe the voice of this teacher and determine whether it was a factor in your evaluation.

6. Tune in to a radio or television round-table discussion on a controversial topic. Do you find yourself inclined to the point of view of any of the speakers because of the way they sound? Do you find yourself disinclined to any of them for the same reason? List as specifically as you can the attributes and their effects on you. How would the following terms suit the individual speakers: *agreeable, irritable, pompous, antagonistic, aggressive, negativistic, soft-spoken, firm, tired, energetic, pedantic, indecisive, weak, complaining, congenial, authoritative, warm, cultured, charming, indifferent, conciliatory, nonconforming, rigid*? Any others?

7. Listen to a radio or television network program on which there are a professional moderator and two or more participants. Compare the vocal tones of the moderator with those of the participants. Observe whether the moderator reveals any partiality or personal prejudices through her or his voice.

8. Listen to a group of friends or acquaintances engaged in a conversation or discussion on a controversial topic. Do the participants reveal their personalities as well as their viewpoints through their voices? What terms listed in Project 6, or terms of your own choosing, would you apply to them?

9. Do you know any public figures who have had voice training? (Many public figures have had such training, and some prepare specifically for each important address.) Can you recall any changes resulting from this training? Are there any who have changed in a direction you consider undesirable? Are there any whose voices are so obviously "trained" that they no longer seem to be themselves? Are there any who might benefit from voice training? What vocal characteristics would you like to have improved?

Listening to Diction: Articulation

Let us turn our attention to diction (articulation) in our role as listeners and evaluate the production of friends, acquaintances, and mass media personalities. Do any of these people make obvious and/or habitual articulatory errors such as lisping, lalling (substituting a *w* sound for an *r* or *l*)? Do any of them slur syllables or sounds in unstressed positions? Do any stress or accent the wrong syllable, or give equal stress to all syllables in multiple-syllable words? Do any "mouth too much" and make their articulation both effortful and unpleasant to observe? Do any articulate so rapidly as to make you uncomfortable because you prefer not to listen that fast?

Are there any politicians or mass media personalities who seem to attack the language rather than articulate it with respect? In contrast, are there any speakers you look forward to hearing because of their respect for the language; a respect they share with their listeners? What characteristics of their speech evokes this response?

What did Hamlet mean when he advised his players to "Speak the speech, I pray you, as I pronounced it to you, trippingly on the tongue; but if you mouth it, as many of your players do, I had as lief the town-crier spoke my lines"?

Listen to a British Broadcasting Corporation (BBC) program and note some differences between BBC "standard" diction and that of an American broadcaster. Is there an American "standard" for diction?

$$=== \text{PHYSICAL HEALTH} ===$$

The voices of most speakers who are not especially aware of their speaking habits and who are not trained self-listeners are likely to reflect states and changes in physical health. In the absence of any specific, chronic condition affecting health or attitude, vocalization is adversely affected by such conditions as fatigue, involvements of the respiratory tract, and conditions that produce either hypertense of hypotense muscle tone.

Perhaps the single cause that most frequently affects our voices is the common cold, which, because it directly involves the nose and throat, impairs normal vocal reinforcement. In addition, if the larynx is involved, the vibrators (vocal bands)[4] may be temporarily thickened and so may produce tones that are not adequately reinforced. If there is a significant amount of inflammation, we tend to avoid laryngeal pain by keeping our vocal bands apart, and as a result, we produce breathy and husky tones.

Similar to the effects of the common cold are those produced by allergies that involve the respiratory tract. These may include nasal congestion, irritation of the throat and larynx, and coughing. If the coughing is persistent and severe, the vocal bands may become involved.

You may be one of the fortunate persons who are able to produce voice effectively despite the physical abuse to which vocal bands are subjected with violent coughing.

---

[4] Note that I have avoided using the misleading term *vocal cords*. *Vocal bands* or *vocal folds* are terms descriptive of the voice-generating mechanism which lies within the structure of the larynx (voice box).

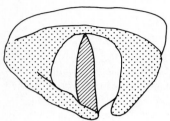

Figure 1–1 Diagram, adapted from a high-speed photo-
graph, showing vocal bands not sufficiently approximated for
good voice production, and too closely approximated for
normal breathing. [Courtesy AT&T Archives, New Jersey.]

Such coughing may result in the propulsion of air through the vocal bands and larynx
at supersonic speed, estimated at above 700 miles per hour. Most of us, however,
cannot be energetic and chronic hacking coughers without suffering ill effects.

Figure 1–1 is a diagram that shows the vocal bands in a position too far apart for
efficient vocalization. In this position, the voice becomes husky and suggests, at best, a
partially voiced whisper. Swollen vocal bands, usually associated with laryngitis, may be
a temporary cause of this condition because there may be pain if the bands are brought
together as in normal vocal effort. Intentional and prolonged "whispering" or the voluntary and habitual production of a husky voice may be associated with thickened vocal
bands and so may constitute both the cause and the effect of a chronic condition.

Figure 1–2 shows nodules on the vocal bands. This condition is often associated
with high-pitched shouting and may develop at any age.

Good vocal hygiene requires that you either avoid the conditions that are conducive
to poor vocalization or reduce vocal efforts if such conditions cannot be avoided. If your
obligations demand that you must speak often, then you have a duty to practice good
vocal hygiene. This calls for avoiding or at least minimizing talking under conditions
that involve competition with excessive noise. Beyond this, good vocal hygiene entails
doing whatever you need to do to keep physically healthy. This includes observing the
rules for both exercise and rest and doing whatever else good sense and your doctor
may advise to stay in good health.

Personality and Mental Health

Mentally healthy persons are aware of what is going on about them and respond, without violence to their own integrity, to the demands of their environment. Mental health[5]
and a healthy, well-adjusting personality are attained through continuous effort. Speech
and voice are both the tools and the result of this process.

Young infants respond to their environment and express themselves almost entirely
through the voice and reflexive body movements. Babies who cry much of their waking
time may be colicky. Those who whine or are almost always on the verge of crying are
probably unhappy. If they do little crying, but coo for self-amusement, as well as for
the amusement of those who surround them, they may be considered happy, or at least
normal, babies. Whatever the condition, whether it is temporary or chronic, babies

---

[5] In this discussion of mental health, the reference is to conditions that suggest anxiety, mild depression
(indifference), and neurotic states, rather than to psychotic conditions. Sometimes speakers are not aware that
their vocalizations express their attitudes. Occasionally, vocal habits persist even when the condition is no
longer present. The voice may then be a mirror that reflects the past as well as the present.

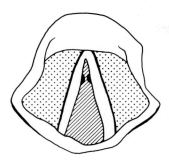

Figure 1–2 Vocal nodules, often associated with high-pitched shouting. Note the typical paired formation in the upper part (middle third) of the vocal folds.

express themselves mostly through the voice. At each successive stage of development, from infancy to maturity, a child's voice continues to express — to reveal or to betray — both personality and mental health.

Earlier in this chapter, I suggested that you become an objective self-listener and decide whether the voice you hear reflects you as a personality. Another question to be answered is whether your voice has any characteristic that you would consider undesirable in another speaker. Here are some further questions that we hope you can answer in the negative. Does your voice suggest a whine when no whine is intended? Do you sound as if you are complaining about something when you intend only to state a fact? Do you sound defeated? Do you sound aggressive or hostile rather than poised and secure? Do you sound chronically tired, bored, annoyed, or just too, too sophisticated for this mundane world in general and your associates in particular? If the answer is "yes" to any of these questions and you have no intention of suggesting the trait that is expressed, insight and recognition should be of help in motivating a change.

Among the more frequent vocal problems associated with maturation is the failure of the voice to become lower in pitch during physiological adolescence. Occasionally, we meet chronological adolescents and postadolescents who still speak in their childhood pitch range. Sometimes we even find the habitual pitch level raised above that of preadolescence. Although in rare instances this vocal problem may be related to disturbances in motor control or in the glands, more often the cause is emotional. The chronological adolescent, whether boy or girl, who wants to continue to be mother's or daddy's child, or who is, for other reasons, apprehensive about growing up and assuming grown-up responsibilities, may be announcing the wish or the fear through an infantile voice.

Another adolescent problem frequently associated with vocal disturbance may arise from a strong identification with an older person. As a result of such an identification, an adolescent girl, for example, may imitate the pitch and other vocal characteristics of an idolized adult. Unfortunately, the voice of the adult may be the product of a vocal mechanism unlike that of the imitator. The woman teacher on whom the high school girl has a "crush" may properly be a contralto with a pitch range too low for the vocal apparatus of the imitator. The effect may be a strained, husky voice. The problem for the boy in high school may be even more acute if he is intended by nature to be a tenor and his role model is a person with a bass voice.

I have had several male students who might have had good tenor voices, and may possibly even have been effective speakers within the upper part of their baritone range, but who wanted very much to speak like bassos. Within the bass range, unfortunately, they were constantly hoarse and could not be heard beyond the first two or three rows of a classroom. Psychological investigation strongly suggested that the young men were overanxious to be recognized as men—and fearful that they might not be so regarded. I have also had several middle-aged male voice patients with much the same problems of voice and associated psychodynamics. I have also had a number of women voice patients who were referred by laryngologists because of thickened vocal bands resulting from habitual vocalization in a pitch range that was too low. In several instances, the women were working in professional areas that until recently had been considered the province of males. The suspicion of "masculine protest" was supported by the psychodiagnostic evaluation. Fortunately, this type of protest is now less often needed than in the past twenty years.

Sometimes, to the misfortune of the speaker, habits of voice may persist and so reveal the maladjustments, personality, and mental health of a past period. Voice production is a motor act, and motor acts that are repeated tend to become habitual. Thus, once-dependent persons may still sound dependent, and once-aggressive, "chip-on-the-shoulder" individuals may still sound as if they are obviously hostile. With conscious effort, vocal habits can be modified so that we reveal ourselves as we are presently rather than as we once were during a past period of adjustment difficulties. However, if such difficulties are ongoing, an effective voice may not be achieved unless therapy includes resolution of the problems of which the voice is a symptom.

THE EFFECTIVE VOCALIZER

If we examine our reactions to individuals who have effective voices, we are likely to conclude that by and large they are also effective as persons. The voice, or any other attribute of human behavior, is not the free-floating essence of a blithe, disembodied spirit. It is, on the contrary, an essential product and aspect of human behavior. It may sometimes be possible for a mentally or physically sick individual who has had considerable professional training to produce voice effectively for a specific purpose and for a limited time, as actors and some public speakers may be required to do. Even professional performers, however, cannot continue to vocalize effectively, act effectively, or in general pretend effectively for an indefinite period. In our discussion in subsequent chapters, let us assume that we are addressing ourselves to essentially healthy persons. This assumption permits leeway for the expression of a little bit of neuroticism that is or should be the privilege of all. It also allows for occasionally physical ailments—even those that may be classified as psychosomatic, because the body does protest what the mind sometimes must accept.

If you are at any time in doubt as to whether your lack of an effective voice may be associated with either a temporary or chronic state of below par physical or mental well-being, proper medical consultation is in order. Certainly, any person who has been suffering from chronic hoarseness, or who has a disturbance centered in the larynx, should not undertake vocal training without first obtaining clearance from a physician, preferably a laryngologist. Although voice training can improve most persons' vocal efforts, such training should not be undertaken if your physician prescribes vocal rest. I also urge that you do not accept the advice of a friend as a substitute for a physician, even if the friend has had symptoms much like yours. There is serious danger in using a friend's prescription for what to do about your voice problem. If you would be an effective vocalizer, you deserve a personal examination by your own physician.

In general, you should engage in vocal practice only when you feel rested. If vocal fatigue sets in after a short period of practice, check with your physician, who may in turn refer you to a laryngologist. Practice distributed in short periods throughout a day is better than long periods of practice that may produce fatigue or boredom. Specific suggestions for voice improvement and practice are provided in the chapters that follow.

It is wise to remember, too, that except for possible rhetorical style, there is rarely any need for cultivating a loud speaking voice. The stentorian voice is seldom necessary when amplification is available. Incidentally, Stentor, a mythical loud-speaking Grecian creation—a herald in the Iliad—did not have the advantages of amplification. You do, and you are not a mythical creation. In our real world, unless there is an emergency that includes a power failure or you are in an open field, an adequate and easily heard voice seldom calls for loudness levels much above those for communication in areas of classroom size.

CHAPTER 2

THE MECHANISMS FOR SPEECH (VOICE AND ARTICULATION)

This chapter — on the mechanisms that process and control speech production — relies on the initial assumption that speech is a unique, species-specific achievement. This assumption acknowledges that a few psychologists and linguists have made some progress in their efforts to teach selected higher, but still-subhuman, primates to learn a few rudiments of a visual language system. However, we are in no immediate danger of having these primates take over and teach us what they think we need to know about how to communicate more effectively with them.

The human mechanisms for speech enable us to express and communicate our thoughts, feelings, and emotions; our attitudes and intentions, according to our needs. Conversely, when it suits our purpose we are usually able to conceal that, which under most circumstances, we share and reveal. Most of us, perhaps all of us, know persons who are highly efficient in revealing as well as concealing what they wish in their utterances. A few may even practice deception. All of these achievements in communication imply that there are differences in the degree to which we have control over the various mechanisms for speech. Acting — speaking in another person's words — demands a high level of voluntary control over how and what we say.

We first consider how voice is produced. For our purposes, *voice* is defined as the tones that are generated by the actions (pulsations) of the vocal folds or bands, which are immediately modified and reinforced by the cavities of the throat and the mouth. We use the terms *vocal folds* and *vocal bands* interchangeably; we avoid the term *vocal cords*, however frequently it is used as a lay term, simply because it gives an erroneous impression of this laryngeal apparatus. Whatever else this apparatus is, it certainly does not resemble cords.

Articulation refers to modifications — the narrowing or "opening" of the air passage, the partial or momentarily complete obstruction of the breath stream — to produce the sounds of a language system. In the act of articulating, we exercise control of a sequence or flow of sounds to produce *articulate speech*. Speaking, of course, implies the use of a *symbol system* that includes words and rules (grammar) that govern their usage.

For the present, we will address ourselves to the human voice-producing part of the speech mechanism. The human vocal mechanism deserves both respect and understanding for what it is: a highly sensitive and responsive instrument capable of permitting us to produce a type of sound of distinctive quality, range of pitch, and changes in loudness—to produce *voice*. Any direct comparison with a mechanical instrument tends to minimize the potential and the attributes of the human voice mechanism and its products. There are, however, a few parallels between the human vocal apparatus and some musical wind instruments. Considering them may help us to have at least an intellectual appreciation of how each functions.

VOICE PRODUCTION AND WIND INSTRUMENT SOUNDS

In most wind instruments, sound is produced when air (breath) is blown over a reed or through vibrating lips, as in the case of a trumpeter. The reed, or the reed substitute (the lips), is usually at the blowing end of an elongated tube. The quality of the sound of a wind instrument is determined partly by the size, shape, and nature of the material; partly by the length, thickness (mass), and type of reed, and partly by the ability of the person who is blowing.

Compared with a wind instrument, the potential of the human voice-producing mechanism enables even an average speaker to be a virtuoso. Without conscious practice, most of us become skilled in making our voice mechanisms produce sounds that respond to our wishes. We play our vocal apparatus through ranges of pitch, loudness, and quality possible only by combinations of instruments. The extreme flexibility of the vocal mechanism is the basis for its superiority over most musical wind instruments.

Basic Definitions

I have used the terms *pitch*, *loudness*, and *quality* with the assumption that the meaning of each is clear. Nevertheless, I will offer technical definitions for the terms so that their meanings will be understood throughout the discussions in Part One of this book.

Pitch is the result of the frequency of vibration of a sound source. In voice production, pitch is the attribute or "dimension" of sound that results primarily from the rapidity of the movement of the vocal bands. We perceive vocal pitch as levels and ranges in speaking; in singing and in listening to a single wind instrument—a flute—we may perceive pitch as notes on a musical scale.

Loudness is related physically to the amplitude of the movement of the vocal bands, that is, to the amount of force or energy that is applied to the vocal bands as they are set and maintained in pulsating motion.

Quality is produced by the complexity of the sound waves and their reinforcement by the speaker's resonating cavities. From your point of view as a listener, quality is your auditory impression of the effects of the sound wave activity. "Vocal quality is the audible feature of a voice that distinguishes it from another when both are at the same pitch and loudness" (Moore, 1982). (See Boone, 1983, and Zemlin, 1981, for expanded explanations of *quality*.)

The definition for *quality*, less technical than for pitch or loudness, reflects the ambiguity with which authorities on voice offer their explanations and near definitions of the terms. In general terms, *quality* refers to our subjective perception of such features as *smoothness* and *clarity* of the voice to which we are listening. On the positive side, we may use such terms as *velvety*, *rich*, *mature*, *sweet*, *cheerful*, *smiling*, and *cordial*. On the negative side, we may use such terms as *aggressive*, *grating*, *metallic*, *raspy*, *hoarse*, *nasal*, *stuffy*, *breathy*, *weak*, and *thin*. As a reader-listener, you may decide whether a *sultry*, *sexy* voice has positive or negative connotations.

What these terms imply is that vocal quality is a subjective listener reaction and, unlike pitch and loudness, is not readily and objectively measurable. We do know what we mean by the terms when we use them. We recognize these vocal qualities even over the telephone, an instrument of limited sound fidelity. Unless your friend has a cold or is suffering from a stuffy-nose allergy, you recognize her or him by the essential vocal quality. In brief, vocal quality is a subjective response, very much in your ear and mind as a listener.

===== REQUISITES FOR SOUND PRODUCTION =====

To produce sound, whether it be music, noise, or voice, three essential conditions must prevail: (1) there must be a body capable of being set into vibration; (2) there must be an available force that may be applied to the body to set it into vibration; and (3) there must be a medium for transmitting the results of the vibration to individuals who are capable of awareness and response. The first two requisites are provided in the human mechanism for breathing and are discussed subsequently. The third requisite is air.

When necessary, a normal person is readily able to modify and control breathing to produce voice while sustaining the necessary biological function of respiration. In the discussion that follows, we shall understand how voice production is accomplished through a study of the nature and structure of the vocal mechanism. The objective of the discussion is an overall view of the sound-producing mechanism rather than a detailed consideration of its component parts. For those who may wish for such consideration, I recommend Zemlin (1981).

===== THE HUMAN VOICE MECHANISM =====

The Vocal Bands

The vocal bands, or vocal folds, are bodies capable of vibration (pulsation); thus, they meet the first requirement for sound production. Biologically, the potential vibrators function as part of a valve mechanism to prevent foreign matter from entering the windpipe (trachea) and the lungs. The vocal bands are two small, tough folds of connective, or ligamentous, tissue situated in the larynx, or voice box, at the top of the trachea (see Figures 2–1 and 2–2). The bands are continuous with folds of muscle tissue and are connected to cartilages of the larynx.

The *trachea* is a tube, or a "pipe," about four inches in length and an inch in diameter that is continuous between the pharynx and the lungs. In construction, the trachea is a series of incomplete rings of cartilage and membranous tissue (see Figures 2–1 and 2–2). This construction provides form and elasticity so that there is no danger of tube constriction or collapse when air is drawn into the lungs. The elasticity of the trachea also permits movement in swallowing and in speaking. These movements may be felt with the finger and may also be observed in a mirror. In swallowing, the top of the trachea moves upward and slightly forward toward the chin. These movements are

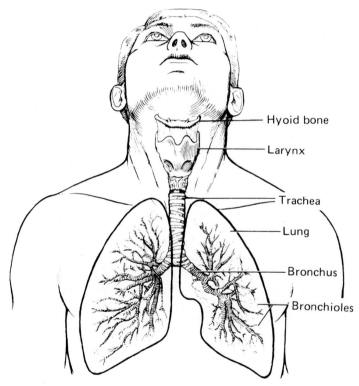

                                              — Hyoid bone

           — Larynx

           — Trachea

           — Lung

           — Bronchus

           — Bronchioles

Figure 2–1   Front upright view of the larynx, trachea, and lungs.
    The larynx is a structure of cartilage, muscles, and membranous tissue at the top of the trachea. The largest cartilage of the larynx is the *thyroid* cartilage, consisting of two fused shieldlike parts. The vocal bands are attached to the inner curved walls of the thyroid cartilage laterally, and in front to the angle of the two fused parts of the thyroid. At the back, the vocal bands are attached to the arytenoid cartilages.
    The trachea divides into two *bronchi*. Each *bronchus* divides into tubes of decreasing size known as *bronchioles* which terminate in the tiny air sacs (alveoli) of the lungs.

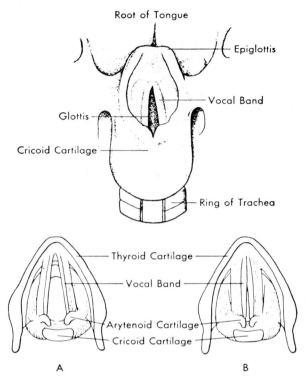

Root of Tongue

Epiglottis

Vocal Band

Glottis

Cricoid Cartilage

Ring of Trachea

Thyroid Cartilage

Vocal Band

Arytenoid Cartilage

Cricoid Cartilage

A   B

Figure 2–2   View and diagram-matic representation of the larynx and the vocal bands, showing attachments to cartilages and larynx.

Upper diagram: The larynx viewed from above and behind (posterior aspect).

Lower diagrams: (A) Vocal bands shown in position for quiet breathing; (B) Vocal bands in posi-tion for vocalization.

usually more apparent in men than in women, especially in those men who have a conspicuous Adam's apple.

The trachea subdivides into two tubes known as *bronchi*. Each *bronchus* further di-vides and subdivides into smaller tubes within the lungs. These smaller-sized tubes are known as *bronchioles*. The bronchioles, after many divisions, terminate in tiny air sacs (alveoli) of the lungs which function to exchange carbon dioxide for oxygen.

If we could view the vocal bands from above, as in Figure 2–2, they would appear as flat folds of muscle that have inner edges of connective tissue. The vocal bands are attached to the inner curved walls of the thyroid cartilage at either side. At the midline, the bands are attached to the angle formed by the fusion of the two shields of the thyroid cartilage. At the back of the larynx, each band is attached to a pyramid-shaped cartilage called the *arytenoid*.

Because of their shape and their muscular connections, the arytenoid cartilages can move in several directions. In doing so, they directly influence the position and state of tension of the vocal bands. The arytenoid cartilages can pivot or rotate and tilt backward and sidewise. As a result of these movements, the vocal bands can be brought into a straight line along the midline position so that there is only a narrow opening between them (B in Figure 2–2), or they can be separated for quiet breathing (A in Figure 2–2). If the bands are brought together in a narrow **V**, as in the upper part of Figure 2–2, noisy whispering or possibly a breathy voice would be produced if an effort were made to vocalize.

The small, tough vocal bands, ranging in length from seven-eighths of an inch to one and one-fourth inches in adult males, and from less than one-half to seven-eighths of an inch in adult females, are directly responsible for the sound called *voice* that is produced by human beings.

The *frequency of vibration* of the vocal bands is determined by their length, thickness, and degree of tension when they begin to vibrate. We think of pitch as being high, medium, or low, or we use such terms as *soprano*, *alto*, *tenor*, *baritone*, or *bass* to designate ranges of vocal pitch.

Although the term *vibration* is used to designate the action of the vocal bands, a more accurate term might be *flutter*. When the column of breath is forced through the narrowed opening between the approximated vocal bands, they are literally blown apart and then come together in a flutterlike manner. If the breath stream is steady and controlled, the result is a sequence of rhythmical flutters that produce in turn a rhythmical sequence of air puffs. The vocal tone is a product of the number of flutters, or "vibrations," per unit of time and the vigor with which the bands are blown apart. The greater the number of flutters, or vibrations, the higher the pitch. The greater the vigor with which the vocal bands are blown apart, the louder the tone. When the vocal bands flutter or vibrate with evenness and regularity, "smooth" or "clear" tone is produced. Irregularity of vibration, caused either by inadequate control of the breath stream (poor motive control) or by an unfavorable condition of the vocal bands, results in the production of uneven or "noisy" vocal tones.

The frequency of vibration varies directly (increases) according to the tension, and varies inversely (decreases) according to the mass and length of the vibrating bodies. Because most men have longer and thicker vocal bands than most women, male voices are on the average lower in pitch than female voices. The average fundamental frequency for male voices is 128 cycles (waves) per second; it is between 200 and 256 cycles per second[1] for adult female voices. Vocal tones are actually a complex of frequencies. Zemlin (1981, p. 253) explained that "the laryngeal tone is complex, composed of a *fundamental frequency* which is determined by the vibratory rate of the vocal folds, and a number of *overtones* that are *integral* multiples of the fundamental frequency." Thus, when the vocal folds vibrate at 100 times per second — the fundamental frequency — the complex tone we hear includes overtones at 200, 300, 400 . . . cps. Hollien, Dew, and Phillips (1971, pp. 755–760) found that the mean frequency (pitch) range for adults exceeded three octaves, with individual ranges varying from one and a half to four and a half octaves: "Further it appears that many normal adults exhibit ranges comparable to those of singers."

Variation from our fundamental frequencies is, for the most part, a result of the changes in tension of our vocal bands. We have considerable control over their state of tension. Such control becomes evident each time we sing the musical scale or a song or raise or lower the pitch level of a sound or a word when talking. Variation also occurs as a result of involuntary changes in the vocal bands associated with overall states of bodily tension. The tensions of the vocal bands vary as other muscles voluntarily or involuntarily become tense or relaxed. If you are habitually a tense individual, you are

---

[1] The letters Hz (Hertz) are now commonly used instead of cycles (waves) in referring to frequency. Hz = cycles per second (cps).

likely to vocalize at a higher pitch level than if you are habitually a relaxed person. Immediate responses to situations produce overall changes in bodily tension that are likely to be associated with tension changes in the vocal bands and therefore in their frequency of vibration. These changes become apparent in situations conducive to excitement and elation at one extreme, and to sadness or depression at the other. (This topic is considered in some detail in Chapter 7, "Pitch and Effective Vocalization.")

The Motive Force

The second requisite for sound production, the force that vibrates the vocal bands, is the column of air or expired breath stream. In ordinary breathing, the vocal bands are open in a wide-shaped **V** so that the stream of breath meets no resistance as it is exhaled. For purposes of vocalization, we recall, the vocal bands are brought together so that there is a narrow, relatively straight opening rather than a **V**-shaped one. The result is that the exhaled air meets resistance. In order for the air to be expired, the air column must be more energetically exhaled than it is in ordinary breathing. The energetic exhalation "vibrates" the vocal bands and voice is produced.

As indicated, vocalization for speech requires control. Control, which normally takes place without conscious effort on our part, is usually achieved by the action of the muscles of the abdominal wall and the muscles of the chest cavity.

The *chest* (thoracic) *cavity* consists of a framework of bones and cartilages that include the collarbone, the shoulder blades, the ribs, the breastbone, and the backbone. At the floor of the chest cavity, and separating it from the abdominal cavity immediately below, is the *diaphragm*. We can locate the large, double-dome–shaped muscle called the *diaphragm* by placing our fingers just below the *sternum*, or breastplate, and moving them around the front, sides, and back of the thoracic cavity to the spinal column. In breathing, the diaphragm rises toward the chest cavity during exhalation and descends toward the abdominal cavity during inhalation. In breathing for purposes of speech, both the normal respiratory rhythm and the extent of the upward and downward excursions may be modified according to the speaker's immediate needs.

The *lungs*, which function as air reservoirs, contain much elastic tissue and consist of a mass of tiny air sacs supplied by a multiple of air tubes and blood vessels. Because the lungs contain no muscle tissue, they can neither expand nor contract directly. They play a passive role in respiration, expanding or contracting because of differences in pressure brought about by the activity of the abdominal and rib muscles that serve to expand and control the thoracic cavity. Air is drawn into the lungs as a result of outside air pressure when the chest cavity, expanded through muscle action, provides increased space for the air. Air is forced out of the lungs when the chest cavity decreases in size and the pressure of the enclosed air is increased. This sequence is normally accomplished through action in which the diaphragm is passively but importantly involved.

Diaphragmatic Action.   When the volume of the chest cavity is increased, air is inhaled into the lungs by way of either the mouth or the nose and the trachea. An increase in the volume of the chest cavity may be effected through a downward, contracting movement of the diaphragm; through an upward, outward movement of the lower ribs; or through a combination of both. During inhalation, the diaphragm is active in contracting, thereby lowering the floor of the thoracic cavity. When inhalation is completed, the diaphragm becomes passive and relaxes. The abdominal organs then exert an upward pressure, and so the diaphragm is returned to its former position. When it becomes necessary to control exhalation for purposes of vocalization and speech, the muscles of the front and sides of the abdominal wall contract and press inward on the liver, the stomach, and the intestines. These abdominal organs exert an upward pressure on the undersurface of the diaphragm. This pressure, combined with the downward and inward movement of the ribs, increases the pressure within the thorax, causing the air to be expelled from the lungs. Throughout the breathing cycle, the diaphragm is roughly dome-shaped. The height of the dome is greater after exhalation than after inhalation. (See Figures 2–3 and 2–4.)

It is important to understand that the diaphragm, though passive in exhalation, does not relax all at once. If it did, breath would be expelled suddenly and in a manner that would make sustained vocalization impossible. Fortunately, the diaphragm maintains some degree of muscle tension at all times. When the diaphragm relaxes because of the pressure of the abdominal organs, it does so slowly and gradually as the air is expired. Thus, a steady stream rather than a sudden rush of breath is provided for the purposes of speech.

In regard to thoracic and diaphragmatic action, what has just been described is in effect an application of the principle of air motion to breathing. Air, regardless of its source, flows from areas of relatively high pressure to areas of relatively low pressure. The pressure of contained air may be decreased by an expansion of the container and increased by compression of the container. As applied to breathing, air (breath) is moved (breathing takes place) as a result of the muscular changes of the thoracic cavity.

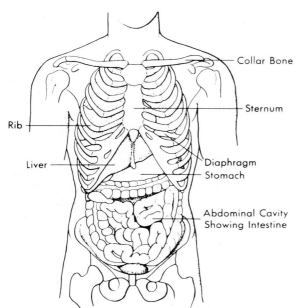

Figure 2–3 The chest (thoracic) and abdominal cavities.

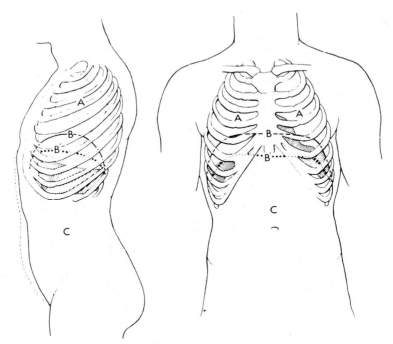

Figure 2–4   Diaphragmatic and abdominal activity in breathing.
   A.   The thorax or chest cavity.
   B.   The diaphragm passive and "relaxed" as at the completion of
        exhalation.
   B'. The diaphragm contracted as in deep inhalation.
   C.   The abdominal cavity. Note the forward movement of the abdomi-
        nal wall that accompanies the downward movement of the dia-
        phragm during inhalation.
(The crosshatched portion of the lung represents the additional volume of
the expanded lung as in deep inhalation.)

Specifically, when the chest cavity is enlarged (pressure is reduced), air flows in; when
the chest cavity is reduced in size (pressure is increased), air flows out.

Breathing for Speech.   In breathing for ordinary life processes, the periods of inhalation and exhalation are approximately equal. Breathing for speech, however, usually
requires that this regular rhythmic respiratory cycle be modified so that the period of
exhalation exceeds that of inhalation. Normally, for speech, we inhale quickly between
units of utterance and exhale slowly while speaking. This modification necessitates a
degree of voluntary control not required for automatic breathing. Such control is usually
achieved by abdominal activity.[2] This point is considered in greater detail in our discussion on voice improvement.

---

[2] See Lieberman (1977, pp. 3–9) for detailed consideration of the physiology of breathing for speech
production.

In normal nonspeech breathing, an average of about a pint of air (500 cc) is interchanged in each respiratory cycle. Conversational speech may require little or no more air; vigorous speaking may require more air. Seldom, however, do we use more than 10–20 percent of the total amount of air that our lungs are capable of holding.

For adequate voice production, voluntary control of breath and the appropriate use of the resonators for the reinforcement of vocal tones are essential.

Figure 2–5 presents a "view from above" of the diaphragm and the organs within the chest cavity. It shows the domelike structure of the diaphragm more clearly than Figure 2–4.

REINFORCEMENT OF SOUND THROUGH RESONANCE

The requisites of sound production are satisfied when a force is applied to a body capable of vibration and is transmitted or conducted through a medium to a receiver. From a strictly physical point of view, a receiver is not necessary. Psychologically, however, there can be no report or corroboration of the occurrence of a sound unless the

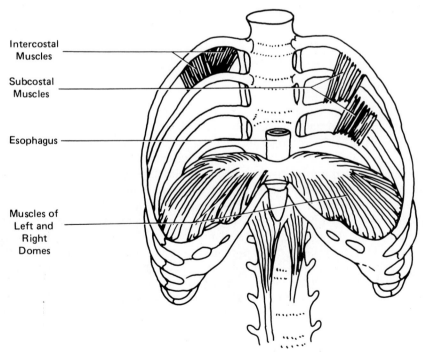

Figure 2–5 The thoracic (chest) cavity showing the domelike structure of the diaphragm and its attachments to the rib cage and the vertebral column.

sound is received. The receiver must be capable of auditory sensitivity within the pitch range of the vibrating body. Furthermore, the receiver's auditory sensitivity or threshold for hearing must be low enough for the intensity level of the sound. If a receiver is far away from the source of a sound (the initiating vibration body), considerable energy has to be used to create vibrations of enough amplitude to be heard. At least, this would be the situation if a body were to be set in vibration in an "open field," by which we mean under conditions in which the sound is not reinforced through resonating bodies. We are assuming, also, that the sound is not amplified through mechanical devices, such as an electrical sound system. Fortunately, the human voice does have the immediate benefit of reinforcement through resonating bodies. Later, we shall consider how reinforcement through resonance is accomplished in the human voice mechanism. For the present, we shall discuss as briefly and as simply as possible two kinds of resonance reinforcement that may be used for any sound.

Forced Resonance

Forced resonance or forced vibration occurs when a body that is set in vibration has a contact with another body that is capable of the same frequency of vibration. The result of this contact is to set the second body in vibration. In effect, a sound has been transmitted directly from one body to a second, and so the sound is reinforced. This is partly what happens when the sounding body of a piano vibrates and when a vibrating string of a violin transmits sound by way of the bridge to the body of the violin. It is also partly what happens when a tuning fork is set on a box or a board or a tabletop. The effect is the production of a sound that we perceive as louder than would be the case if there were no forced vibration or forced resonance.

Cavity Resonance

A second form of reinforcement that is common for musical instruments, and for sound enhancement in general, takes place as a result of cavity resonance. By *cavity*, we mean a partially enclosed body. Examples include the shell or the conventional stage used by an orchestra; the tubular arrangement of a wind instrument; a tumbler or drinking glass; and the "cavities" of the mouth, nose, pharynx, and larynx of the human body. Each cavity, depending on its size, shape, texture of tissue, and opening, has a natural frequency range for the sounds that it will reinforce with *optimum efficiency*, that is, for the sound range with which *the cavity is in tune*. Even a limited knowledge of musical instruments should lead us to generalize that the larger the cavity body, the lower will be its natural frequency range (that is, the more efficiently the resonating cavity will reinforce low-pitched sounds). Conversely, the smaller the cavity body, the higher will be its natural frequency range. Thus, a bass viol, with its large cavity, is tuned for the reinforcement of low-pitched ranges of sound, and a violin (fiddle), which has a smaller body, is tuned for the reinforcement of high-pitched ranges of sound. These ranges, of course, are relative to the family of string instruments. Comparable correlations between the size and the pitch range hold true for wind instruments. Thus, we can account for the differences in the range of sound for musical instruments that are similar in shape but different in size.

═══ REINFORCEMENT AND "COLORING" ═══ OF VOCAL TONES

If we depended only on the energetic use of controlled breathing to make ourselves heard, we would have little "broadcast" ability without the help of mechanical (electrical) amplification. Fortunately, our vocal mechanisms are constructed so that a building up of laryngeal tones takes place through the reinforcement capacities of the resonators of our vocal apparatus. Before considering the contribution of each of our principal resonators—the cavities of the larynx, throat (pharynx), and nose, and the mouth (the oral cavity)—we shall briefly discuss the overall reinforcement of laryngeal tones.

The tones that are initiated in the larynx are modified and reinforced or "built up" in the structures beneath and above the vocal bands. The result of what takes place in these subglottal and supraglottal structures (see Figure 2–6) is production of the voice that emphasizes or brings out the potentialities of some vocal characteristics and minimizes or damps out others.

The chest, or thoracic structure, reinforces and modifies the laryngeal tone through a combination of forced (bone) and cavity resonance. When the vocal bands are set into action, with a resultant vocal tone, the tone is transmitted to the bones of the chest. You can feel this effect by placing a hand on the upper part of the chest while vocalizing an *ah*. You should also be able to note that there is considerably more bone vibration felt with the vocalization of an *ah* than with an *ee*. We may then appropriately conclude that our lower laryngeal tones are given considerably more reinforcement through the forced (bone) resonance than are the higher-pitched laryngeal tones. Except for avoiding cramped postures, there is nothing you can do to enhance this type of vocal reinforcement. There is, however, much that you can do in regard to cavity reinforcement, which we now consider.

As already indicated, the principal human vocal resonators are the cavities of the larynx, pharynx, and mouth, and the nasal passages. To a significant degree, the tracheal area just below the larynx and, to a lesser degree, the bronchi also reinforce laryngeal tones.

Each of the principal respirators, by virtue of its size, shape, and tissue texture, has special properties that enable it to make a unique contribution to the modification and reinforcement of the initial laryngeal tone and the production of the final or "finished" voice that the listener hears. You should be mindful, however, that at all times the vocal tones that emerge are the products of the contributions resulting from combined characteristics of all the resonators as well as the bony structures of the chest and head. Though some tones may have primary or predominant coloring resulting from the properties of one of the principal resonators, the others contribute to the finished voice. The discussion that follows considers the features of each of the principal resonators and the contribution that each makes to voice production.

The Larynx As a Resonator

Vocal tones, as soon as they are initiated, are reinforced in the larynx. If the larynx is free of organic pathology and not under strain, and if the speaker initiates and maintains vocalization without abnormal tension, there is little he or she can or need consciously

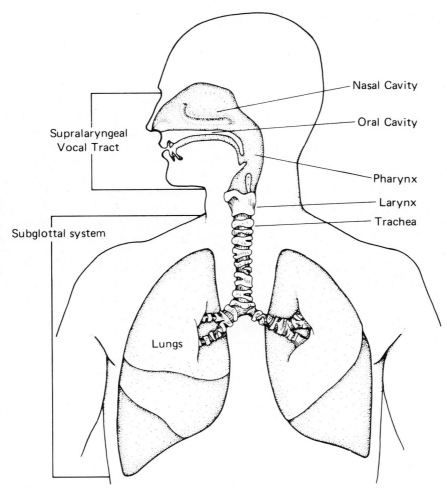

Figure 2–6 The three physiological components of human speech production. [After P. Lieberman, *Speech Physiology and Acoustic Phonetics* (New York: Macmillan Publishing Company, 1977) p. 4.]

do about obtaining good laryngeal resonance. If the speaker has laryngitis, however, normal laryngeal reinforcement is not possible. If you suffer from laryngitis, it is best to reduce your talking to a minimum and, if possible, do no talking. If the condition is recurrent, or persistent, a visit to a physician is in order.

The extrinsic muscles of the larynx are those that connect it to the jaw and other bones and cartilages so that it will maintain its normal position when at rest and be lifted upward and forward for swallowing. Tension of the extrinsic muscles of the larynx, as indicated, interferes with the reinforcing function of the larynx. Such tension is also likely to interfere with the free action of the vocal bands for good tone production. Tension is necessary in the act of swallowing. You can feel the tension of the extrinsic muscles by placing your hand on your throat as you swallow. Such muscular tension should, however, be avoided in most speech efforts. We approximate such tension for the vowels of *see* and *sue* and, to a lesser degree, for the vowels of *hate* and *hat*.

The Pharynx

The pharynx, or throat cavity, has the necessary attributes for optimum sound reinforcement. How a cavity resonates (reinforces) a given tone or range of tones is determined by several factors. These include the size, shape, and nature (material, texture, tension, and the like) of the cavity walls and the size of its opening as related to the source of the sound (the vibrating body) and/or other connecting cavities. The pharynx, because of its size and the control we can exercise over it to modify its shape and tension, is much more important as a vocal reinforcer than is the larynx. We modify the length of the cavity each time we swallow or each time the soft palate is raised or relaxed. We change the quality of vocal tones through changes in the tension of the pharyngeal walls. Growths, such as enlarged adenoids or tonsils, may damp vocal tones and modify loudness as well as sound quality. When, because of infection or emotional tension, the pharynx is abnormally tense, the voice quality tends to become strident and metallic. Higher-pitched tones are reinforced at the expense of low tones. The result sometimes is an unpleasant voice that lacks adequate loudness and carrying power. When the pharyngeal tensions are normal, the voice is likely to be rich and mellow—at least as rich and mellow as the individual throat permits.

Our understanding of the action of the pharynx as a resonator can be enhanced by a brief review of its structure. Figure 2–7 shows us that the pharynx begins just above the larynx and extends up to the entrance of the nasal cavity. The portion near the larynx—the *laryngopharynx*—is capable of considerable modification. The diameter can be changed for the reinforcement of the fundamental tones and overtones produced in the larynx. The tones we identify as the vowels of our language are produced in part as a result of action of the laryngopharynx.

The *oropharynx* is the area just above the laryngopharynx. The oropharynx can pair either with the area below (the laryngopharynx) or above (the nasopharynx), or with the oral cavity (the mouth), or with all three to modify vocal tones. As a result, the oropharynx can act subtly or grossly to reinforce tones and to produce sounds of different qualities.

The *nasopharynx* is the uppermost part of the pharyngeal cavity. This area can in effect be separated from the mouth cavity and connected (coupled) with the nasal cavity through the act of elevating the soft palate (the velum). When the velum is lowered, the nasopharynx can be paired or coupled with the lower part of the pharynx or with the oral cavity. The nasopharynx is directly involved in the reinforcement of the nasal consonants *n*, *m*, and *ng*.

The Oral Cavity

The mouth, or oral cavity, is the most modifiable of all the resonators of importance for speech. Except for that part of the roof of the mouth that constitutes the hard palate, all the parts that together form or are included in the oral cavity are capable of considerable

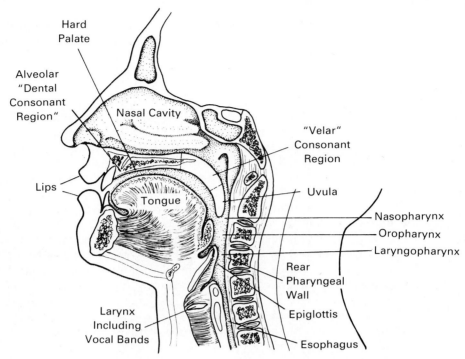

Figure 2–7 Section of head showing principal resonators and organs of articulation. [Adapted from P. Lieberman, *Speech Physiology and Acoustic Phonetics* (New York: Macmillan Publishing Company, 1977), p. 40.]

movement. The lower jaw can move to create an oral cavity limited only by the extent of the jaw's action. The tongue, though attached to the floor of the mouth, can be elevated, flattened, extended out of the mouth, or drawn up and curled within the mouth, or it can almost fill the closed mouth. The lips can close tight along a straight line, open centrally or laterally to apertures of various sizes, or open wide as the lower jaw drops to permit a view of the back of the throat. The velum and the uvula can be elevated to increase the size of the back of the mouth or relaxed to make the back of the mouth continuous with the throat. Through these many modifications, the oral cavity and the organs within it not only produce the various sounds of our language but reinforce them as well.

The Nasal Cavity

Except when the nasopharynx is coupled with the nasal cavity, we have little direct control over the latter. Unfortunately, the linings of the nasal cavity and the cavity itself are considerably affected not only by physical illnesses involving the upper respiratory tract but by emotional disturbances as well. The condition of the nose, it appears, is often an excellent indicator of what is happening to us physically and emotionally. It fills up when we have a cold, when we are allergic, when we are very happy, and when we are acutely sad. When, for any one of numerous reasons, the nasal cavity is not free, adequate reinforcement of nasal sounds in particular and nonnasal sounds in general is difficult, if not impossible.

The Sinuses

The role of the sinuses as resonators has not been clearly established. We have four pairs of sinuses that drain into the nasal cavity. Most of us become aware of our sinuses when they are infected and drain the products of their infection into our respiratory tract. Short of trying to keep well so that we can avoid the unpleasant condition called *sinusitis*, there is little we can do about the sinuses to influence voice. The sinuses are unlike most of the other cavities associated with the respiratory tract in that we cannot control or modify their size, shape, or surface tension to affect the reinforcement of vocal tones.

═══ FLEXIBILITY OF THE VOCAL MECHANISM ═══

Earlier in the chapter we compared the voice mechanism with that of a wind instrument. In our comparison, the point was made that the vocal mechanism was considerably more flexible and therefore superior to any wind instrument as a producer of sound. The reeds of a wind instrument are fixed in size and degree of tension. Human vocal bands, however, can be changed in length and tension so that a comparatively wide range of pitch is possible. Through muscular contraction, our resonating cavities can be modified so that the sound produced by the vocal bands can be variably reinforced. Normally, we can direct our voice through a combination of resonators so that sound emerges either orally or nasally. The manner in which we open and shape our mouths permits us to produce a variety of sounds, which are most readily exemplified in the vowels of our language. When the lips, the tongue, and the palate become more actively involved in the modification of sound, articulation, an aspect of sound production peculiar to human beings, becomes possible. This aspect of sound is considered after our discussion of the attributes of the voice and some factors that are related to vocal changes.

═══ CHARACTERISTICS OF SOUND ═══ AND OF VOICE

All sounds, including those that are vocal, have four fundamental characteristics or attributes. These are *loudness, pitch, duration,* and *quality*. When we respond to a given sound, whether it be the barely audible sound of a dropped pin or a clap of thunder, we are responding to a combination of attributes. The results of our experiences enable us to recognize certain sounds as belonging to the things that make them. So, also we are usually able to associate voices with the persons who produce them.

Susan's voice is a complex of her particular attributes, as are the voices of her friends Mary and Eileen, or of Tom, Dick, and Bill. If you know these persons well enough to consider them friends and have a fair sensitivity to vocal differences, you are usually able to recognize each by voice even over a telephone. If you lack sensitivity to voice, or perhaps have a cold, you may on occasion be mistaken in your identification. Normally, however, one attribute of voice is likely to be different enough from the others so that the sum produces a voice that is sufficiently individualized to permit you to make a correct identification.

The human voice as a sound producer is not limited to one given pitch, loudness, duration, or even quality. The human mechanism, with its subtle and complex neuro-muscular controls, is capable of a range of variation for each of the sound attributes. A baritone vocalizer may produce sounds that overlap the upper range of the bass and the lower range of the tenor. A female contralto may be able to overlap the high tenor and much of the soprano ranges. No speaker produces tones at a single loudness level. As we speak, we vary the intensity of our sounds from syllable to syllable, word to word, sentence to sentence, and, of course, from occasion to occasion. We vary the duration or time given to utterance as well as the pitch and the loudness. We are usually able to speak rapidly, slowly, or at a moderate rate, according to need as well as habit. Although our vocal qualities are relatively limited by the size and the shape of our resonating cavities, these attributes can be modified. Some of us are even able to control vocal attributes well enough to imitate other speakers. Most of us who do not habitually speak nasally or harshly can do so at will. All things considered, the normal human being can do considerably more with her or his sound-making apparatus than expert musicians can do with their musical instruments.

The Individuality of the Human Voice

Although some vocal mimics can simulate the vocal production of popular or well-known personages, each of us has a voice with individual features that are almost as distinctive as our fingerprints. Our ability to hear these distinctive features may not be as keen as our ability to see differences in fingerprints, but vocal differences can be discerned when they are transformed from audible into visible forms. A device that transforms the features of the voice into visible patterns has been developed by the Bell Telephone Laboratories. Voiceprints (such as those in Figures 2–8, 2–9, and 2–10) bring out differences that reveal the individuality of the voice. The recording technique, developed by Lawrence Kersta of Bell Laboratories, indicates loudness, resonance, and pitch. In combination, these features are presumably never the same for any two persons (see Figures 2–9 and 2–10).

Correlates of Vocal Changes

Unless we consciously try to conceal our feelings as we talk, we are likely to reveal them by the way we sound. The voice, when not intentionally controlled, is a barometer of our feelings and our moods. This is so essentially because the voice is a product of

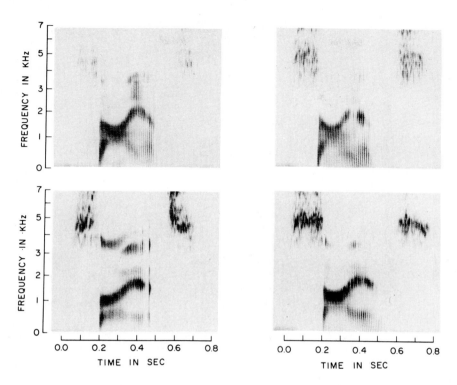

Figure 2–8 Four spectrograms of the spoken word *science*. The vertical scale represents frequency, the horizontal dimension is time, and the darkness represents intensity on a compressed scale. Three of the spectrograms are from three different speakers, and the remaining spectrogram is a repetition of the word by one of the speakers. The spectrograms were made on a Voiceprint Laboratories Sound Spectrograph. [From R. H. Bolt et al., "Identification of a Speaker by Speech Spectrograms," *Science,* 166 (1969): 339.]

The authors of this article were of the opinion that despite the admitted individuality of the human voice, the available results of studies of speech spectrograms are not adequate to establish the reliability of voice identification by this technique. Despite this opinion, several court rulings have admitted voiceprint identification as legal evidence for identification—for example, *United States of America* v. *Albert Raymond and Roland Addison*, United States District Court, Crim. No. 800–71, February 2, 1972, and *State of Minnesota* ex. ref. *Constance L. Trimble,* Supreme Court of Minnesota, No. 43049, November 26, 1971. However, a more recent opinion was provided by the *Maryland Law Review,* 5: 39 (Summer 1980) 629–645. After a case review, the report indicates that testimony on voice identification based on spectrographic analysis is inadmissible because the technique has not gained general acceptance in the scientific community.

The identification of voice through spectrograms continues to be a subject of debate in legal as well as scientific circles. However, both in the United States and abroad, spectographic voice identification continues to be used in litigation. It is likely that in the near future, "computerized analysing will be capable of identifying voices more reliably than a human ear" [Hammerstrom (1987)].

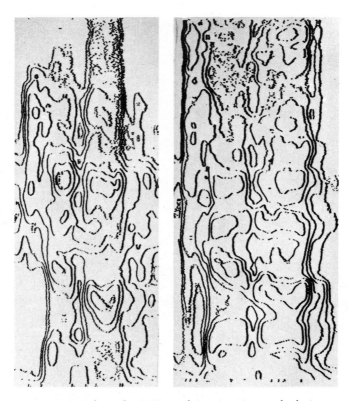

Figure 2–9 *(Left)* John F. Kennedy's voiceprint, made during a talk he gave in the White House, shows Bostonian delivery in the compressed dark lines at the top. [LIFE Magazine© 1963 Time Inc. All Rights Reserved.]

Figure 2–10 *(Right)* Elliott Reid used the same text and intonation as President Kennedy, but the graph that his voice made was radically different. [LIFE Magazine© 1963 Time Inc. All Rights Reserved.]

muscular activity that in turn is intimately related to the emotional state of the organism. In a state of heightened emotion, as in anger or fear, we experience muscular tension. The muscles involved in voice production share in the increased total body tension. Thus, when vocalization takes place, it is on a higher pitch level than normal. Another involuntary change that accompanies heightened emotion is the addition of sugar to the bloodstream. This enables us to engage in the energetic activity that is sometimes an aspect of heightened emotion. The effect on a voice is to increase its loudness. The usual overall effect of heightened feeling on utterance is that the voice becomes high-pitched, loud, and rapid.

In contrast, depressed states are associated with vocal tones that are low in pitch level and relatively weak in loudness. This is so because the muscles of the body as a whole, and the vocal bands in particular, become overrelaxed or hypotonic, and energetic activity is reduced. The likely overall effect on utterance is to make it relatively low in pitch and volume, and slow in rate.

A voice that is dominated by intellect rather than emotion tends to be moderate in pitch as well as in loudness. This does not imply that intellectual efforts are devoid of feeling. It does imply that intellectual efforts accompanied by vocalization are normally not characterized by the exaggerated range and intensity of feeling that is associated with emotional behavior. Under intellectual control, we are able to simulate emotion, to suggest how we would sound if angry, afraid, ecstatically happy, or depressed. When these pretenses are not necessary, we are ourselves. If we are our normal selves, we are usually moderate not only in our behavior in general, but also in the intensity of our feelings and in the manner in which our voices reveal (or sometimes betray) how we feel and think.

Sometimes our voices express our attitudes toward and feelings about our listeners or of the person or persons about whom we are talking. Part of the message we convey may be in what we say, but much more may be in the manner of saying it. Children may sense notes of impatience and irritation in the voices of their parents and may give expression to their own feelings in the way they respond. It does not take long to learn what comes naturally. Our voices, if not controlled, and sometimes when we intentionally pretend that they are not controlled, reflect our evaluation of the listener or a personality. Occasionally, the doubt our voices express is the doubt that we anticipate the listener will entertain if, indeed, he or she has been listening to us.

ARTICULATION: THE SOUNDS OF A LANGUAGE SYSTEM

Articulated Sound

When breath that is set in vibration by the action of the vocal bands reaches the mouth as part of a speech effort, the breath stream is further modified by the action of the tongue, lips, velum, and/or cheeks to produce voiced articulate sound. If the breath stream is not set in vibration, then voiceless articulated sound may be produced. The organs or articulation serve essentially as interrupters, "filters," or modifiers of the breath stream. Some sounds—vowels and diphthongs—are produced only by an adjustment of the size and shape of the oral and adjacent cavities. These adjustments modify but do not impede or interrupt the laryngeal or vocal tone. Other sounds are produced by a stoppage or diversion of the breath or the vocal tone. Thus, we have consonants resulting from sudden interruptions, little explosions, or hissings because air is forced through narrow openings. The manner and place of interruption result in the production of articulate speech sounds. Each sound has its own characteristics or phonetic features. Oral speech consists of combinations of articulated sounds. When these sounds, produced according to the rules and conventions of our language, are appropriately grouped and readily audible, we speak intelligibly.

The Articulators

Most of the articulated sounds of American-English speech are produced as a result of the activity of the lips and parts of the tongue. These mobile articulators assume positions or make contact with fixed or relatively fixed parts of the upper jaw and the roof of the mouth.

The lips and the teeth enclose the oral cavity. The tongue lies within and almost completely fills the oral cavity. From the point of view of articulatory action, the tongue may be divided into the following parts: the anterior portion, or tongue tip; the blade; the midtongue; and the back. The roof of the mouth may be divided into the gum ridge, or alveolar process (directly behind the upper teeth); the hard palate; the velum; and the uvula (see Figure 2–11).

The larynx also serves an articulatory function because the presence or absence of vocalization distinguishes many pairs of sounds, such as *b* and *p* or *z* and *s*. The sound *h* is produced by a contraction within the larynx sufficient to produce audible friction.

Details of the manner in which the articulators function to produce the different sounds of our language are considered in Chapter 12. At the present time, let us consider briefly the controlling mechanism through which we are enabled to make vocal

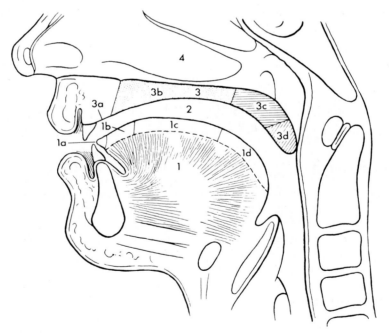

Figure 2–11   The oral cavity and its articulators.
1. Tongue. *1a.* Tongue tip. *1b.* Blade of tongue. *1c.* Front and mid area of tongue. *1d.* Back of tongue.
2. Mouth (oral) cavity.
3. Palate. *3a.* Bum, or alveolar, ridge. *3b.* Hard palate. *3c.* Soft palate (velum). *3d.* Uvula.
4. Nasal cavity.

noises, to modify these noises into distinguishable sounds and intelligible words, to arrange these words into phrases and sentences in order to express our feelings, our wishes, and our needs, and to become members of a symbol-producing and symbol-responding culture. In brief, let us see how we are able to understand and produce spoken language.

THE NEUROLOGICAL MECHANISM FOR SPEECH

The achievement of speech is neurologically related to the development of the cerebrum in humans. Except for the cerebrum of the brain, the nervous system of the human being is surprisingly like that of a dog and almost completely like that of an ape. The cerebrum is significantly different in humans. It is larger in proportion to the nervous system as a whole than it is in other animals, including subhuman primates, and it includes a bulgelike frontal area of greater size than that found in animals with otherwise comparable nervous systems. The brain is a coordinator and integrator of activity. In the brain, impulses set up by sounds and movements that are received by the ear, the eye, and other sense organs are translated into images or into words that have significance and meaning.

The Cerebral Cortex

The gray outer covering of the brain is especially involved in the function of speech. The cortex contains ten to twelve billion or more nerve cells. Parts of the cortex have specialized functions that are involved in the peculiarly human ability to produce and understand oral (speech) or written symbols. These areas are indicated in Figure 2–12. The marked areas include those for *hearing, seeing,* and *speech movement.* These areas are significant because of their evident capacity to evaluate specialized experiences *for the brain as a whole.* For example, the auditory area in the lower middle part of the brain evaluates sounds, so that noises may be interpreted as *barks, wind in the trees,* or *words.* Similarly, the area in the back part of the brain (the occipital lobe) interprets impulses coming from the eye. Through this area, we are able to recognize and identify the objects that we see and to read, and so to make sense of, markings called letters and words.

Recently reported evidence (Eisenson, 1984, Chap. 2; Geschwind, 1979; Springer and Deutsch, 1981; Ornstein and Thompson, 1984) highlights differences as well as similarities in the functions of the left and the right hemispheres, with particular reference to speech and language. Specifically, these are differences in the nature of the auditory events that are perceived and interpreted (processed) by the two temporal lobes. The perception of speech events is normally a function of the left temporal lobe, and the perception of auditory nonspeech events (e.g., environmental noises, musical melody, and animal noises) is usually perceived and processed in the right temporal lobe. Figure 2–12 features the specialized areas of the left cerebral cortex that are related to the processing of spoken and written symbols.

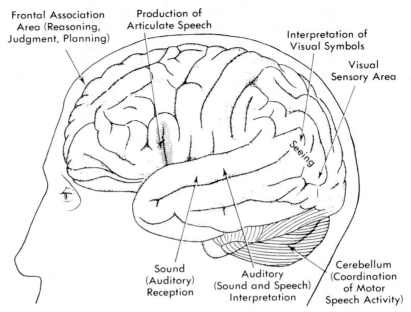

Figure 2–12 The cerebral cortex, the cerebellum, and some "specialized" areas related to speech.

Similarly, the production of spoken language is normally controlled in the left cerebral hemisphere (Figure 2–12). This generalization holds for almost all right-handed persons and for a bare majority of those who are left-handed.

The Neural Network

The basic unit of the cerebral cortex for internal and external communication is the nerve cell or neuron. "Most neurons in the brain are very, very tiny, some no larger than a few millionths of a meter in diameter, but their numbers are legion" (Ornstein and Thompson, 1984, p. 61). The estimated number of "the legion" is as high as 60 billion!

Although the brain is often compared to a computer, and the neurons its elements, the analogy is somewhat misleading. Your brain is alive, both when you are awake and when you are asleep. "Indeed, each nerve cell in the brain functions like an entire computer all by itself" (Ornstein and Thompson, p. 61). Unlike a computer that is on or off, a neuron is always processing the information it receives from thousands of other cells and from chemical messengers in the bloodstream and is always in communication with many other nerve cells" (pp. 61–62). The number of possible connections is as close to infinity as we are ever likely to estimate.

Other Parts of the Central Nervous System and Their Functions in Speech

In addition to the cerebrum, other parts of the central nervous system are essentially involved in the production of speech. These parts, which are represented in Figure 2–13, serve the following functions in the integrated speech act.

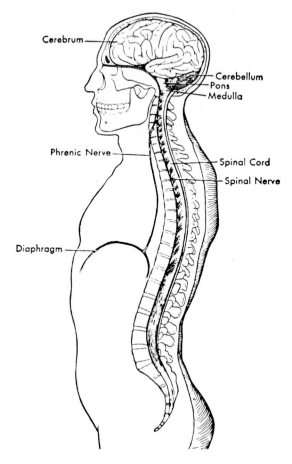

Figure 2–13 The central nervous system in relation to speech.

The *cerebrum* performs the integrative activity on which normal, meaningful speech is dependent.

The *cerebellum* "sorts and arranges" the muscular impulses that come to it from higher brain centers. Impulses are here correlated to make possible the precise muscular activity needed for speech.

The *pons* are a bridge of nerve fibers between the cerebral cortex and the medulla.

The *spinal cord* and its nerves control the respiratory muscles.

The *phrenic nerve* emerges from the spinal cord in the neck region and extends to the diaphragm. It supplies the impulses that cause the diaphragm to contract in breathing.

The *cerebellum*, or little brain, receives impulses from higher brain centers. The impulses are sorted, arranged, and correlated so that the coordinated and precise muscular activity needed for speech becomes possible. Damage to the cerebellum may seriously impair the flow and the control of coordinated speech activity. Damage of this sort is found in many cases of cerebral palsy.

The *medulla* contains the center essential for respiration, and damage to it may impair normal breathing. Bulbar polio involves such damage and requires the use of a mechanical respirator.

The *bulb*, the *spinal cord*, and the nerves emanating from them control the muscles involved in the coordinated act of speaking. The *phrenic* nerve, which emerges from the spinal cord in the region of the neck, extends to the diaphragm. The phrenic nerve supplies the impulse that causes the diaphragm to contract and so brings about inhalation in breathing.

Other nerves that initiate movements involved in speech are the trigeminal (face and jaw muscles), the glossopharyngeal (tongue and pharynx), the recurrent laryngeal (larynx), and the glossal (tongue).

In the absence of pathology, the central nervous system, dominated by the cerebral cortex, controls the impulses involved in the act of speaking. Through this system, we are able to be articulate about our impressions and to reveal what we think and how we feel. Sometimes, if it suits our purpose, we conceal rather than reveal either our feelings or our thoughts, or both. The degree of expertness with which the speech apparatus is used varies considerably from person to person. However, all of us who have unimpaired physical mechanisms and normal personalities should be capable of speaking adequately. How to make the most of our mechanisms so that we fully utilize our capabilities to vocalize and articulate with ease and intelligibility is considered in the chapters that follow.

≡ REFERENCES AND SUGGESTED READINGS ≡

Boone, D.R. (1983). *The voice and voice therapy* (3rd ed.). Englewood Cliffs, N.J.: Prentice-Hall. (A clearly written and practical clinical approach to the understanding and treatment of the most common voice problems.)

Eisenson, J., & Ogilivie, M. (1983). *Communicative disorders in children*. New York: Macmillan. (An introductory text on speech and language disorders. Chapter 5 provides a basic consideration of the mechanism for voice, language, and speech production; Chapter 12 deals with the most frequently occurring voice disturbances).

Eisenson, J. (1984). *Adult aphasia* (2nd ed.) Englewood Cliffs, N.J.: Prentice-Hall. (Chapter 2 considers the neurological correlates of language and speech disorders and the roles of the two cerebral hemispheres in the processing of language functions.)

Geschwind, N. (1979). *Specializations of the human brain* (A Scientific American Book). San Francisco: Freeman. (An illustrated discussion of the specialized processing areas of the human brain, with emphasis on speech and language.)

Hammerstrom, C. (1987). Voice identification. *Australian Journal of Forensic Sciences*, 3, 95–99.

Hollien, H., Dew, D., & Philips, P. (1971). Phonational frequency range of adults. *Journal of Speech and Hearing Research*, 14(4) 755–760.

Lieberman, P. (1977). *Speech physiology and acoustic phonetics*. New York: Macmillan. (A high-level, scientific treatment of the mechanisms controlling speech and how speech is perceived. Includes excellent surveys of relevant literature.)

Moore, P. (1982). Voice disorders. In G. H. Shames & E. H. Wiig (Eds.). *Human communication disorders*. Columbus, Ohio: C.E. Merrill, Chap. 6, p. 152.

Ornstein, R., & Thompson, R. F. (1984). *The amazing brain*. Boston: Houghton Mifflin. (Chapters 6 and 7 are concerned with the brain and its functions, with special consideration for the different functions of the two cerebral hemispheres. The book as a whole is creative, imaginative, and well illustrated.)

Springer, S. P., & Deutsch, G. (1981). *Left brain, right brain*. San Francisco: Freeman. (The book, as the title indicates, considers in detail the different functions of the human cerebral hemispheres.).

Zemlin, W. R. (1981). *Speech and hearing sciences* (2nd ed.). Englewood Cliffs, N.J.: Prentice-Hall, pp. 220–225. (This book is technical, detailed, and authoritative.)

CHAPTER 3

OUR CHANGING SPEECH PATTERNS

≡≡≡

AMERICAN ENGLISH AND THE VOICE OF AMERICA

When did American English achieve dominance over British English to become *lingua franca*, the form of language used throughout most of the world by persons who have another native language? The authors of *The Story of English*, McCrum, Cran, and Mac-Neil (1986, p. 31) set the date as May 8, 1945. On that day Hitler's Third Reich surrendered to the Allied armies. Winston Churchill, then prime minister of Great Britain, announced this momentous event to the world over the British Broadcasting Corporation (BBC). A few hours later, Churchill appeared on the balcony of Buckingham Palace with the king and queen to announce the event in person and to acknowledge the cheers of those who were present and share the acknowledgment with listeners of the BBC. Among those personally present was the respected and distinguished American commentator, Edward R. Murrow. In speech that was characteristically American English but nevertheless also readily recognized as his own, Murrow reported the event for his American audience. "After 1945 the dominant voice of the English-speaking world was no longer British but American." (McCrum, et al.) Further, these authors project:

> For the next generation and more, the enormous strategic, economic and cultural interests of the United States — expressed through international English-speaking institutions like UNESCO and NATO, and corporations like Exxon, Ford and IBM — ensured that the English language would survive and flourish long after its parent culture could no longer sustain it. (p. 31)

During and after the end of World War II, Americans who were stationed at British bases, and later at NATO stations, enriched the English language with such terms as *black market*, the neologism *snafu* for "situation normal, all fouled up," and, however unfortunate, such words as *fireball, fallout, fusion, fission,* and *countdown.*

With the close of military hostilities with Germany and its allies, the superpowers — the United States and the Soviet Union — entered into the Cold War. This was, at least initially, a conflict of interests between democracy and communism as practiced in the Soviet Union and countries behind the iron curtain. In this conflict, The Voice of America and American English became "the language of democracy."

A still-incalculable influence of American English throughout the world comes from American movies, television programs, and cassette tapes of movies, as well as from advertising that promotes the sale of American products. We now have almost universal Americanisms coined by "Madison Avenue"—a term for advertising agencies not necessarily located in New York City—that include *kleenex* for facial tissues, xerox (pronounced zerox) for photocopy, and the entreaty, *try it, you'll like it.* The products, including personal computers (PCs), all presumably promote the American way and the "good life" and, as a by-product, American English as the dominant form of English language. Dillard (1985, p. 249), a sociolinguist, argues emphatically that "more and more, American power and influence are felt throughout the world, and it is American English that now provides the initiatory power for the world's lingua franca."

═══ BRITISH ENGLISH AND ITS VARIANTS ═══

Webster's Third New International Dictionary of the English Language defines American English as "the native language of most American inhabitants of the United States—used especially with the implication that it is a variety of English clearly distinguishable from that used in Great Britain and not deriving its standards of usage from it, yet not so divergent as to be a separate language."

A parallel definition is provided for *British English* as "the native language of most inhabitants of England; especially a variety of English characteristic of England and clearly distinguishable from the varieties used in the U.S., Australia, and elsewhere."

The variants of British English may well include the differences in words and word usages of the same word-forms throughout the nations that were once part of the British Empire. For instance, we may compare *petrol* with *gasoline* (abbreviated to *gas*) and *boot* with *trunk* (for the rear storage compartment of an automobile). A British mechanic uses a *spanner* rather than a *monkey wrench* and is more likely to eat *biscuits* rather than *cookies.* Tools are carried in a *lorry* rather than a *truck.* For the most part variants of English do not carry over to basic grammar. There are, however, differences in pronunciation, vocabulary, and speech melody. In regard to common words within a variant of a language—any language—there is this observation from the *Oxford English Dictionary,* (2nd ed., 1989, p. xxiv):

> The domain of "common words" widens out in the direction of one's own reading, research, business, provincial or foreign residence, and contracts in the direction with which one has no practical connection . . . no one's English is *all* English.

Later in our review of American English and its historical background we will note how our language became enriched by borrowing and adaptation of words of Native Americans and of new Americans who came as emigrants from other countries. All living languages are in a process of change and growth. Computers—we speak of the "Computer Age"—are giving us a large and growing vocabulary and an international terminology. Not only do we use computer language but we also use *computer analysis* to study our language. For example, McCrum and associates note, "Computer analysis of the language has shown that the one hundred most common words in English are all of Anglo-Saxon origin" (p. 61).

VARIANTS WITHIN BRITISH AND AMERICAN ENGLISH

How far can a variant (variety or dialect) depart from a parent language and still not be a new language? Within the British Isles, there are probably more varieties of spoken English than there are throughout the United States and Canada. As an example, McCrum and associates observe: "A conversation between a Dorset shepherd and an Aberdonian farmworker can still be a dialogue of the deaf" (p. 21). (Dorset is in southern England; Aberdeen is in northwest Scotland. The distance between them in miles is much less than that between New York and Minnesota.) Nevertheless, despite differences in dialect, for a large majority of speakers within Great Britain lack of intention is probably a greater barrier to understanding than the variants of word usage and pronunciation that depart from standard BBC English.

Beyond the British Isles, visitors and native speakers of English in Australia, New Zealand, India, Pakistan, the Bahamas, Bermuda, and South Africa almost all find British as well as American English mutually intelligible. The differences in vocabulary, word usage, pronunciation, and speech melody usually do not seriously interfere with mutual intelligibility. To be sure, one has to tune in and be tolerant of the speech of the other, and sometimes it does help to have a small glossary of "native" words and phrases. However, if one is of good intention, the variants are not too large or numerous to surmount. To help them bridge the gap, Qantas, the Australian National Airline, provides a booklet for its passengers, *Understanding "Down Under"—The Australian "Language."* Readers are informed that "visitors to Australia who may consider that they speak perfect English can often experience difficulty in talking to the natives." Further, the traveler is informed that "Australian slang is always growing and changing. Terms once frequently used are constantly falling into disuse and others are being created, or given different meanings."

Following is an example of an extreme Australian variant, rich in slang, produced by an irate speaker in Sydney who, on getting to his car, found a police officer (brown bomber) writing a parking ticket. The irate citizen informed the officer thus: "Some of you cacky-handed galahs would dob in your cheese and kisses—deadset!" Freely translated into American-English idiom, this becomes "Some of you left-handed fools would inform on (betray, tell on) your wives—I'm absolutely certain."

How well would most non-Australian speakers of English understand the meaning of "The Swagman," perhaps better known as "Waltzing Matilda"? This song has almost the status of a national anthem. The words, again rich in slang, follow:

Once a jolly swagman camped by a billabong
  Under the shade of a coolibah tree,
And he sang as he watched and waited till his billy boiled
  "Who'll come a-waltzing Matilda with me?"
    Waltzing Matilda,
    Waltzing Matilda,
Who'll come a-waltzing Matilda with me?"

Down came a jumbuck to drink at the billabong:
  Up jumped the swagman and grabbed him with glee.
And he sang as he shoved the jumbuck in his tucker-bag,
  "You'll come a-waltzing Matilda with me.
    Waltzing Matilda,
    Waltzing Matilda,
You'll come a-waltzing Matilda with me."

Although making sense of the words of a song is not a requisite for its enjoyment, following is a glossary of some of the words for those who think otherwise:

billabong — a stream; a branch of a river

billy — a pot or kettle or a container of any sort in which water may be boiled

jumbuck — a sheep

swagman — a tramp, hobo, or a vagabond or anyone who carries his possessions in a swag (bag) or bundle

tucker-bag — a bag for carrying food

Waltzing Matilda — swag. "To walk or waltz Matilda is to carry one's swag; to travel the road; a Matilda waltzer is a tramp (or a traveller)" (Oxford English Dictionary, 1989)

Waltz (to waltz) — to move lightly, trippingly, or nimbly. Also, unconcernedly or boldly; to walk into, off, up, to (away)

With this glossary in hand, translation into American idiom should be "just a piece of cake." So, try it and enjoy the exercise.

With or without benefit of melody, we may ask whether an Australian would be any better informed than most Americans when exposed to this Washingtonese: "At this point in time we haven't finalized studying the parameters of our thrust in that area."

These examples show just how "far out" a variant of a language may stray from British English. However, for most speakers of English, mutual intelligibility may be expected. Sometimes a listener's puzzled look may elicit a restatement and a clarification of meaning.

Shakespeare's English and Contemporary English

Most of us who have read the plays or poetry of William Shakespeare (1564–1616) probably read them in contemporary language rather than in the language of his time. Stuart Flexner, the senior editor of the *Random House Dictionary* (1987, introduction), speculated that "if Shakespeare were to materialize today in London or in New York, he would be able to understand only five out of every nine words in our vocabulary." Whether this is an exaggeration for the sake of making a point might be tested by a comparison of two versions of Shakespeare's Sonnet 33:

> Full many a glorious morning have I seen
> Flatter the mountain tops with sovereign eye,
> Kissing with golden face the meadows green,
> Gilding pale streams with heavenly alchemy;
> Anon permit the basest clouds to ride
> With ugly rack on his celestial face,
> And from the forlorn world his visage hide,
> Stealing unseen to west with this disgrace.
> Even so my sun one early morn did shine
> With all triumphant splendor on my brow;
> But out alack, he was but one hour mine,
> The region cloud hath masked him from me now.
>   Yet him for this my love no whit disdainedth;
>   Suns of the world may stain when heaven's sun staineth.

William Burto, the editor of *William Shakespeare: The Sonnets* (1965), provides the following footnotes to help us understand Sonnet 33: *Anon,* soon; *basest,* darkest; *rack,* vapory clouds; *forlorn,* forsaken; *out alack,* alas; *region clouds,* clouds of the upper air; *stain,* grow dim. We might also add *whit,* meaning a particle, a bit.

With courage that exceeds humility, I have "rewritten" Sonnet 33 using contemporary English for some of the Shakespearean terms.

Sonnet 33: Shakespeare Revisited

Full many a glorious morning have I seen
The monarch's eye flatter what it rests upon,
Kissing with golden face the meadows green,
Gliding pale streams with heavenly alchemy;
And soon permit the darkest clouds to ride
With angry vapors on his celestial face,
And from the forlorn world his visage hide,
Stealing unseen to west with this disgrace.
Even so my sun one early morn did shine,
With all triumphant splendor on my brow;
But out, alas, he was but one hour mine,
The higher clouds have masked him from me now.
  Yet him for this my love nothing will disdain;
  Suns of the world grow dim when heaven's sun does stain.

A flavor of Shakespearian English is still sensed in some Appalachian mountain areas of the United States. The language there is not, however, Elizabethan (Shakespearean) English. Stewart notes, "By the time the settlement of Appalachia had begun, England had changed considerably from what it had been in Elizabethan times, a century and a half before" (1972a, p. 111).

In the remainder of this chapter, I will provide a brief review of English historical background and the emergence of American English as the dominant, although changing, variant of British English.

AMERICAN ENGLISH: THE AMERICAN LANGUAGE

Long before Americans began to use their own terms for objects, rather than those used by the British, and ate *candies* rather than *sweets*, and those who lived in cities were more likely to occupy *apartments* rather than *flats*, American English was beginning to differ from British English. Considerably before Americans began to play *soccer* (Latin derivative) rather than *football* (German derivative), they were also developing a vocabulary that expressed their new environment, their new activities, their new culture in all of its manifestations. Before the Colonies became the United States, a necessary amount of independence was reflected in the language. Nevertheless, much of what constitutes British English continues to be part of the American heritage and is inherent in the American language. We will review some of the inheritances.

We will also consider some of the historical influences and factors that resulted in the emergence of American English rather than, for instance, Dutch English (Pennsylvania Deutch) as the major and now dominating variant of British English.[1] We will highlight the features that characterize American English and its own dialectal variations and consider some forces, psychological and sociological, that are currently and dynamically influencing the choice of words, the pronunciations, the melody (intonation), and, albeit to a lesser degree, the syntax of the American language. Our concern is with spoken language; differences in spelling will not be considered.

BRITISH HISTORICAL BACKGROUNDS: A BRIEF REVIEW

From the time of the ancient Romans until the eleventh century, the land masses known as the British Isles were successively conquered and for varying times occupied by people of many nationalities. Each of the conquering peoples left traces of influence on

---

[1] Hendrickson (1986, p. 154) argues that the word *Dutch* in Pennsylvania Dutch has nothing to do with Holland and that it is a corruption or Americanization of *Deutsch* (German). The language that came to be known as Pennsylvania Dutch developed as influences of persons who spoke German and who lived along the Rhine Valley, from Switzerland to Germany. They came to southern Pennsylvania in the early 1700s. Many of their descendants continue to live in the "Pennsylvania Dutch" area in southern Pennsylvania.

a language whose basic forms and structures were not to be firmly determined until the sixteenth century.

The Romans under Julius Caesar came to Britain in 55 B.C. They did not leave until about A.D. 400. The inhabitants who remained behind, other than the Romans, spoke a Celtic dialect but retained the use of Roman names for roads and many geographic locations (place names).

In the middle of the fifth century, Angles, Saxons, and Jutes began to invade Britain and drove the Celts westward into Wales and Cornwall and northward toward what is now Scotland. The term *English* is used for the Germanic speech of these groups of invaders and their descendants. It is important to appreciate, however, that the earlier inhabitants of Britain did not suddenly change their speech habits. Those who stayed behind and were not pushed to the west or to the north continued to speak a language much as they had spoken, except that new linguistic forms — those of their conquerors — were incorporated and modified into their previous linguistic habits. Essentially, despite military conquests, the language of the conquered assimilated that of the conquerors.

Christianity came to Saxon England during the first half of the seventh century. With Christianity, Latin was introduced as the spoken and written language for religious and learned purposes. This influence on the common person — on the vast majority of the population — however, was not significantly reflected in everyday speech.

Between the eighth and eleventh centuries, increasing numbers of Scandinavians came to Britain, and with them came Scandinavian influences on what was to become English. The Scandinavians — for the most part, Danes — also invaded and conquered the northeastern parts of France and ultimately became the ruling aristocracy of Normandy. During this period of achievement, the Scandinavians assumed Gallic ways, including French as a language, and their own Germanic speech was lost. Again, the language of the conquerors gave way to the language of the conquered.

In the historically critical year 1066, the descendants of the Scandinavians, who now were Normans and who had become essentially French in culture and in their linguistic habits, invaded England under William the Conqueror and became the established power in England. Although French then became the language of the ruling class in England, the masses continued to speak a Germanic language. In time the language of the Norman conquerors was reduced in influence and all but disappeared, at least as far as the speech of the "common" man and woman was concerned.

The English that most people in England speak today and the American English that most Americans speak are both derived from the speech of the inhabitants of the London area from the time of William the Conqueror through the Elizabethan period. But England throughout its history has never been free of divergent dialects. The Germanic groups — the Angles, Saxons, and Jutes — came from different parts of the continental lowlands. These groups spoke different dialects, settled in different parts of England, and left their linguistic influences where they settled. One important result is that the dialect differences among the inhabitants of England today are greater and more divergent than are the regional dialect differences in the United States.

It does not require an expert ear to discern differences between American English and British speech, even assuming that the comparison is made between an educated Londoner and an educated Bostonian who may be a Radcliffe or Harvard graduate.

These representative speakers are selected because, although the differences between American English and upper-class London English are comparatively few, differences do exist. They exist, as earlier indicated, in idiom and in specific words to denote situations and events as well as in word pronunciation and stress and in manner of articulation. Differences are also found in speech melody. The Londoner and the Bostonian are not likely to express their enthusiasms or their irritations with the same choice of words or in the same vocal melody. A *bloody American mess* has different connotations from a *bloody English mess*. The Bostonian gets about in *streetcars* or *subway* trains, whereas the Londoner gets about in *trams* and by way of the *underground*. The Bostonian may live in an *apartment*; the Londoner lives in a *flat*. The Bostonian leaves his or her car in a *garage* rather than in a *garage* and watches *TV* rather than *telly*. The Bostonian law enforcer is a *police officer* or a *cop*, rather than a *bobby*; the Bostonian is entertained at the *movies* rather than at the *cinema*. The melody pattern of the Londoner, whether his or her utterance is intellectual or emotional, is likely to be characterized by wider inflectional changes than that of the Bostonian. Articulatory differences may also be heard. The sound *t* in an unstressed syllable, as in *pity*, is likely to be more clearly and more lightly articulated by our English representative than it is by the American. Neither speaker is likely to pronounce an *r* when it is in a final position in a word, as in *dear* or *hear*, but the *r* would be articulated differently in words such as *very*. Our English representative pronounces the word *very* in a manner that phoneticians describe as a *single flapped sound*. Americans[2] may think of it as approximating the pronunciation *veddy*, which, of course, it does not, except possibly to the prejudiced ear of an American comic-strip artist trying to get across a notion of English pronunciation to an American comic-strip reader.

═══ STANDARD ENGLISH SPEECH? ═══

Americans living in the first quarter of this century who judged English speech by what they heard from Britishers who were visiting in the United States might well have concluded that all of them spoke pretty much alike. Americans who read Shaw's *Pygmalion* may have been puzzled by Professor Higgins's complaints. Yet both the Americans' and Professor Higgins's observations were correct. It is likely that the Americans, unless they happened to have traveled widely in England, would have been exposed only to the speech of British stage personalities, British political personages, members of the royal family, and well-to-do and well-educated English people with public (really private) secondary-school and Oxford or Cambridge backgrounds. Their speech is almost standard.

The speech of these groups is characterized by English phoneticians as *received pronunciation;* by *received* is meant "accepted in approved circles." This speech is described by the English phonetician Daniel Jones in his *Outline of English Phonetics* (1950). Indi-

---

[2] We refer here to the standard dialects of British English and American English. *American* refers to North Americans who speak English. Much of what is said here also refers to Canadian speakers of English.

vidual recommended pronunciations may be found in Jones's *Pronunciation of English* (1956). "Standard" pronunciations are given in the *Oxford English Dictionary* (OED).

Although "received speech" was the one that Professor Higgins spoke as a matter of course and that Eliza Doolittle learned to speak after much rigorous training (although she still broke down under emotional stress), it is not the standard for the speech of all persons who are natives or long-term residents of England—not even for those with moderate amounts of education who live in or near London. Members of the British Parliament, including those who represent the Conservatives, are today more likely to speak with the accents and pronunciations of the British Broadcasting Corporation than with those identified with Eton and Oxford. Labor members of Parliament are likely to assume Tory accents, or even Tory vocabularies, when they are aware that they may be on the air and that their words may be heard by constituents in the evening news broadcast. In brief, the forces of democracy in England, as well as the forces of the mass media of communicating, have worked in directions away from received pronunciation. Despite Professor Higgins, the Brits will go on being themselves and listening, so that they can appreciate British Broadcasting Company diction, American movies, and American television programs.

There are, of course, variances within the London area that are wide enough to require "translation" for many British as well as American citizens. Charles McCabe, an American journalist, presented the following as an example of the Cockney dialect: "A lorry pranged the banger in the boot and I hadn't the readies to get it out of the ricky, so do you fancy taking the tube to the cinema or slipping around to the pub for a pint?" This translates into "A truck smashed into the trunk of my car and I didn't have the money to fix it, so do you want to take the subway to the movies or go to the neighborhood bar for a beer?"

Despite variations in dialects "within cultures," we may conjecture with the popular linguist Mario Pei, who in 1949 predicted:

> Granted a continuation of present historical conditions, the English language of two hundred years hence will be likely to represent a merger of British and American phonetic habits, with comparatively little in the way of morphological or syntactical innovations, but with a turn-over in vocabulary and semantics that would make it difficult, not to say incomprehensible, to the English speaker of today. (p. 303)

If Mario Pei's prediction is to be realized, changes in English would be greater between our time and the mid-twenty-third century than they were between Shakespeare's time and late into the twentieth century.

=== AMERICAN BEGINNINGS ===

When may we say that American speech became sufficiently different from that of the English to give us the beginning of American English? What were the influences that produced and nurtured these differences? In what ways were they peculiarly the result of a new culture and the new forces related to this culture? What forces, regardless of culture, continue to exert their effects on our ever-changing speech patterns?

At the opening of the nineteenth century, the United States had its critics and deplorers, who raised the hue and cry, "What is happening to our language?" They were referring to English and were warning Americans about the need to keep their language pure and free from new vulgarisms. John Witherspoon, a Scottish clergyman who came to the United States to become the president of Princeton, suffered considerable anguish at the thought of the development of an American language. Mencken, in *The American Language* (1946), cited Witherspoon as being pained by what he heard in "public and solemn discourses." Said Witherspoon:

> I have heard in this country, in the senate, at the bar, and from the pulpit, and see daily in dissertations from the press, errors in grammar, improprieties and vulgarisms which hardly any person of the same class in point of rank and literature would have fallen into in Great Britain. (p. 5)

But persons such as Witherspoon, however great their prestige, were opposed by such Americans as John Adams and Thomas Jefferson. Perhaps more realistically, Jefferson declared:

> The new circumstances under which we are placed call for new words, new phrases, and for the transfer of old words to new objects. An American dialect will therefore be formed. (Mencken, 1946, p. 5)

While the dispute between Americans for English English and those for American English was going on, Noah Webster was busily at work on his *Grammatical Institute of the English Language*. Certainly, with the publication of the latter in 1828, American English achieved status and recognition and became established as a major variant of the English language.

Even a cursory review of the forces that established American English would reveal the following: The American geography and physiography presented new features, new creatures, and new ways of working for a livelihood, and with them, the need for new words. Many of the words came from the Indians and had no competition from the mother tongue. Thus, words such as *coyote, skunk, hickory, moose, opossum, persimmon, powwow, moccasin*, and *squash* came into our language. Place names, Mencken (1946, p. 105) pointed out, also came from the Indians. So did such names for articles of clothing and frequently used objects as *tomahawk, wigwam, toboggan*, and *mackinaw*.

It would, however, be erroneous to conclude that the spirit of rebellion and the influence of the Indians were the only forces that shaped American English. The early colonists, from the very outset, had linguistic influences from the languages of other colonizations. From the French came words such as *cache, portage*, and *voyageur*, as well as *prairie, bureau*, and *gopher*. From the Dutch in New Amsterdam, Mencken (1946, p. 108) tells us, came such words as *cruller, coleslaw, cookey, scow,* and *patroon*, as well as *boss* and *Santa Claus*. Many place names in the Hudson area containing *dorp, kill*, and *hook* are also directly from the Dutch. *Harlem* was originally *Haarlem*. the word *Yankee*, according to Mencken (p. 110), is possibly the most notable of all contributions of the Knickerbocker Dutch to the American language. Our own choice would be the word *dollar*.

Another source of Dutch influence on the speech of the colonists came by way of the Pilgrims. In their migration from England to the colonies, many Pilgrims first went to live in Holland, mostly in Leyden and Amsterdam (1607–1609). Dillard (1976) noted that by the time the Pilgrims arrived in Plymouth on the *Mayflower*, the ship "carried passengers who did not represent the 'regional' dialects of England at all — much less in pure form" (p. 47).

Spanish influences came later, at a time when American English had become well established as a variant of British English. Texas, the Southwest, and California had been colonized by the Spanish and were developed by Mexico when it won its independence from Spain. Spanish and Mexican contributions to American English are readily recognizable in place names, architecture, agriculture, and animal husbandry. Some of the characteristic geographical features of the Southwest and California are known by Mexican-Spanish names such as *mesa, canyon,* and *arroyo*. The American — for the most part of Anglo-Saxon origin — who took over the Southwest not only learned how to construct buildings of mud and straw bricks but also learned to call them *adobes*.

Many of the words that we now associate with cattle raising are also of Spanish origin. These include *ranch, lasso,* and *riata. Chaps*, pant covers worn by cowboys to protect their legs, is an abbreviation of *chaparajos*. The word *rodeo* has as its English translation "roundup." It is now used as well to refer to an exhibition and competition in the skills that cowboys were and to some degree still are expected to perform in cattle raising. The word *ranch* has been extended to refer as a noun to an agricultural establishment and as a verb to farming activities. *Wrangler* comes from *caballarengo*, and *hoosegow* from *juzgado*.

Spanish, as we have indicated, has also given us a large number of place names. These include the names of six of our United States, more than two thousand names for our cities and towns, and thousands of names for our rivers, streams, mountains, valleys, and plains. Flexner (1976) provided the following sampling:

> *Alhambra, Eldorado, El Paso* (the full original name of the city was *El Paso del Norte*, the crossing of the river of the north . . .), *Hermosa Beach* (beautiful beach), *Key West, Los Angeles* (a shortening of the name the Spanish gave it in 1769, *El Pueblo de Nuestra Senora la Reina de Los Angeles de la Porciuncula*, which was a Franciscan shrine near Assisi), *Las Vegas* (originally built by the Mormons in 1855, using the Spanish word vega, meadow, in its name), *Monterey, . . . Palo Alto, Pueblo* (Spanish for town, literally "the town," when it was first established in 1842 it was the only trading post in the area), *Raton Pass, the Rio Grande, Sacramento, St. Augustine* (founded 1565), *San Antonio, San Bernardino, San Diego, San Francisco, San José* (named after San José de Guadaloupe), *San Luis Obispo. . . .* (p. 323)

The American colonists and the early citizens of the United States were ready borrowers of words from other languages, but they were also ready creators of words and phrases that were "coined in English metal" (Mencken, 1946, p. 113). Some of these words were a product of the new circumstances and conditions in which the new Americans found themselves, but others reveal an underlying way that people — any uninhibited and resourceful people — have with words. For a variety of reasons, words were invented. One of the reasons is that inventing words is fun. It is a kind of pleasure in which we indulged ourselves as very young children and again as adolescents. Word inventing can be a sheer delight, and our American colonists needed to be delighted. Mencken (1946) reminded us that "the American, even in the seventeenth century, already showed many of the characteristics that were to set him off from the Englishman later on — his bold and somewhat grotesque imagination, his contempt for dignified authority, his lack of aesthetic sensitiveness, his extravagant humor" (pp. 113–114). Not restrained by grammatical awareness or a knowledge of the structure of their language, and largely illiterate, our uncouth and headstrong early colonists added words as the occasion demanded. So nouns such as *cowhide* and *logroll*, and adjectives and adverbs such as *no-account, nohow*, and *lickitty-split*, became terms to reckon with in the utterances of our seventeenth-century Americans. These speakers also introduced such compound words as *bullfrog, hogwallow*, and *hoecake*. All of these are useful terms for persons who are busy working with or against the creatures and forces of nature in a new environment.

A living language shows the effects of a busy people. Early in our history, the word *cent*, a verbal invention of Gouveneur Morris, was substituted for the two-syllable *Penny*. *Dime* was a Jeffersonian invention derived from the French word *dixième*.

With the movement of colonists and later-arriving Americans from the Eastern seaboard toward the West, terms such as *sky-pilot* (Protestant minister), *prairie schooner* (wagon), and *caboose* (place or construction for food preparation, first on ships and considerably later for the cook wagon and finally for the last unit of a train), were useful additions to the vocabulary of particular people.

As already observed, a living language is in a continuing process of change. A language that remains fixed shows the symptoms of cultural as well as linguistic rigor mortis. A proverb of the South Carolina mountain people is relevant to language: "We ain't what we wants to be, and we ain't what we're going to be, but we ain't what we wuz."

Flexner (1976) summed up the status of the English language in America at the end of the eighteenth century that made American English an established linguistic achievement:

When this new nation took its first census in 1790 there were four million Americans, 90% of them descendants of English colonists. Thus there was no question that English was the mother tongue and native language of the United States. By 1720, however, some English colonists in America had already begun to notice that their language differed seriously from that spoken back home in England. Almost without being aware of it, they had:

(1)   coined some new words for themselves;

(2)   borrowed other words from the Indians, Dutch, French, and Spanish;

(3)   been using English dialect words in their general speech;

(4)   continued to use some English words that had now become obsolete in England;

(5)   evolved some peculiar uses, pronunciations, grammar and syntax.

Doing these things was very natural. Many of the coinages and borrowing were for plants, animals, landscapes, living conditions, institutions, and attitudes which were seldom if ever encountered in England, so the English had no words for them. The widespread use of English dialect words was also natural: most of the Puritans came from England's southern and southeastern counties and spoke the East Anglia dialect, most of the Quakers spoke the midland dialect, and after 1720, many new colonists were Scots-Irish, speaking the Ulster dialect. The continuing use of words that had become obsolete in England, and of unusual usage, pronunciations, grammar, and syntax, was also natural for colonists isolated from the niceties of current English speech and English education. Thus, naturally, a hundred years after the Pilgrims landed, English as spoken in America differed from that spoken in England. (p. 7)

ONGOING FORCES FOR CHANGE

Thus far, we have traced the influences that created an American English and some of the differences in linguistic forms between British English and American English. Now we consider some of the forces that make any living language a changing language, constantly though slowly yielding to human inclinations and to changing verbal habits. To begin with, we should appreciate the effects of our contemporary ability for speed of movement and our general mobility as a nation of people on wheels or on wings. Washington and Julius Caesar traveled on state occasions in much the same kind of vehicles. Except for slight differences in styling and the addition of springs, similar vehicles were used by United States presidents up to McKinley, although out of choice rather than of necessity, to ride to their inaugurations. Recent presidents are no longer earthbound. They may now move about with supersonic speed. (Whether in due time presidents and other high officials will move about with rocket speed is still another projection.) What influence future presidents or future English-speaking citizens, American or British or from other parts of the English-speaking world, will have on American speech or English speech is a matter of conjecture.

Despite the efforts of some of our nineteenth- and early-twentieth-century teachers of elocution and diction who considered British English a more genteel standard than the emerging American differences, the people of the United States do not observe or aspire to a single standard of what constitutes *good American speech*. Differences, however, at least among educated speakers, are relatively small. The members of Congress, regardless of the states they represent, have no difficulty in understanding one another because of differences in pronunciation or idiom. Nevertheless, as McDavid (1958) pointed out, "every speaker of American English knows that other varieties exist, different from the one he speaks, empirically he has learned to distinguish several of these varieties, sometimes with amazing precision and accuracy" (p. 482).

Most of us are aware that there are differences in spoken language features in details of pronunciation, vocabulary, or grammar—that we may as individuals consider substandard and therefore undesirable. Certainly we should exercise our judgment and prerogatives and avoid such forms in our own speech. However, it is also important to appreciate that speakers may show marked differences in the pronunciation of words, word usage, and other details of *dialect* and yet may be speaking a socially accepted variant of English. McDavid (1975) reminds us that "no geographic region is without its local subtypes, and in the United States there is nothing that qualifies as a mythically uniform General American Speech" (p. xxi).

Dialect is a term used for a variety of a language with features of pronunciation, grammar, or vocabulary that distinguish it from other varieties (dialects) of the same language. Most dialects are related to an identified area, that is, a geographic region. However, with a mobile population, dialects may not be restricted to a given region.

Figure 3–1 is a map of the regions of American English and presents five major dialects. (Adapted from Charles A. Ferguson and Shirley B. Heath in *Language in the USA*, 1981.)

Regional Differences

In the continental United States, differences in pronunciation are most striking along the Atlantic Coast. As we move inland and westward, the differences become blurred. Differences are so slight that casual listeners rarely notice them at all. Although the differences are greatest along the Atlantic Coast, merchants from Maine have no anxiety that they will not be readily understood if they speak by telephone to merchants from New York, Maryland, or Florida.

Differences in the pronunciation of words are more likely to be marked by vowel variations than by consonants. For American English speakers, the pronunciation of *Harry* and *hairy* may or may not be different, depending on region and social class. Similarly, there may or may not be differences in the vowel choice for *Mary, merry*, and *marry*. The words *class, not, hot, orange, creek, candy, nurse*, and *first* have vowel variation according to region. In regard to consonants, the major variation for "standard" dialects is in the pronunciation of words ending in *ng*, such as *being, going*, and *talking*. Speakers in some regions of the United States pronounce these words with a final *n* sound; others with an *ng*. Many speakers vary in their pronunciations according to whether they are speaking formally or informally. Others vary according to circumstances, such as speaking to impress or to identify with a particular social class according to the occasion. We will discuss differences in pronunciation (phonology) in the chapters that follow.

Probably the greatest variation in consonant pronunciation is in words that include the letter *r* in a medial or a final position. Most students of American dialects agree with Thomas (1958) that "the most striking differences between the various regional pronunciations, and the difference around which the most likely, though inconclusive, arguments have revolved, is the nature of the sounds which correspond to the letter *r* (p. 195).

Table 3–1 indicates differences in word usage in some parts of the northern, midland, and southern dialect areas within the United States. Readers may compare their own usage of the identified items with those of their friends or associates.

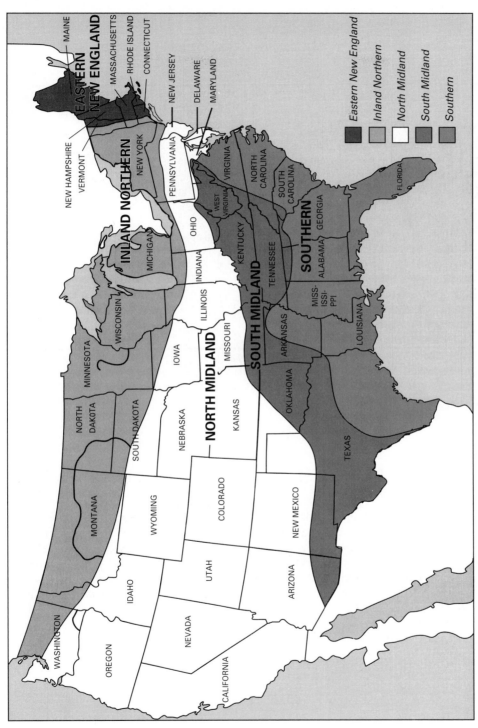

Figure 3–1 This map presents "The Regions of American English." A vast country more than thirty-five times the size of the United Kingdom, the United States has far fewer regional varieties of English. As the first Americans headed westward, their speech merged into the accents of "General American," the flat-voweled speech of the Midwest, the voice most of the world knows as American. General American is the basic dialect of most Americans who are distributed over 80 percent of the land area of the United States.

Legend:
- Eastern New England
- Inland Northern
- North Midland
- South Midland
- Southern

Table 3–1　Word Usage in Major Regional Dialects[1]

Object or Action	Northeastern	General American	Southern
Paper or plastic container for dry contents	bag	sack	sack
Container for fluid contents	pail	bucket	bucket
Hard inner seed of a fruit	pit	seed (stone)	seed (stone)
Flat or battered dough prepared on a griddle or pan	pancake	flapjack	hotcake
Device for releasing fluid from a sink or side of a barrel	faucet, tap	faucet, tap	spigot
Outer covering of corn (maize)	husk	husk	shuck
Small, striped, bushy-tailed animal	skunk	skunk	polecat, skunk
Small stream	brook	brook, creek	branch, creek
Pick up and move	carry	carry	tote
Turn off (extinguish the light)	shut off	shut off	cut off

Major sources for the examples of word usage: F. G. Cassidy (1985); S. B. Flexner (1976); R. Hendrickson (1986); W. McCrum, W. Cran, and R. MacNeil (1986) and R. W. Shuy (1967).
[1]In my own research I did not always find unanimity for the items, but I believe the terms represent a consensus.

═══ DIALECTS AND SOCIOCULTURAL CLASS ═══

Dialect differences are not limited to geographic areas. Within regions there may be variations that are related to socioeconomic status and to social class. Where they are to be found, differences in dialect are usually most evident in word selection and word usage and in "correct" syntax (grammar). In the Southern states and in some parts of Texas, differences in pronunciation are also apparent. In the Southern states, but by no means exclusively in this large geographic area, residents may be dialectal for both economic and social reasons, and some for political purposes. Senators Sam Nunn and Lloyd Bentsen, and perhaps to a lesser degree, President Jimmy Carter may be cited as examples of persons who have been able to accommodate their dialects to those of their constituents as well as to the standards ordinarily observed in Congress and the White House and yet maintain the Southern "flavor" of their speech. John F. Kennedy, in a manner much his own, managed to combine Harvard University speech with Boston Irish. For instance, Kennedy would drop the final *r* in words such as *power* and *never*, but intrude an *r* into *idea(r)* and *extra(r)*. Ronald Reagan, who began his professional career as a sports announcer and was a movie actor before going into politics, first as governor of California and then as a two-term president, spoke "Network Standard." An interesting contrast, is found in the speech of North Carolina's Senator Jesse Helms. Wherever he may be, his dialect is that of the deep Southeast.

McCrum and associates (1986, p. 36) speculate that at sometime in the not-too-distant future, "it is possible that people will express at least two speech loyalties, a local one (Texas, Florida, Brooklyn, Chicago, Wyoming) and a socio-national one, either 'Network Standard' (or something close to it) or mid-American English."

Stuart Flexner (1976, p. 120) argues that "depending on how precise one need be, one can say that America has from three to a dozen dialects." The major dialects are the "New England, the Southern, and the General American." However, Flexner realizes that speakers from Maine and Boston do speak differently; as do those from the Southern states of Virginia and Georgia. Although residents of Illinois and Oregon are identified as speaking General American, there are some differences in word usage and pronunciations that would be readily detectable to a student of dialects. Beyond these rather infrequent dialect differences, there are "scattered pockets of unique dialects and local speech patterns in various valleys, counties, and city neighborhoods all over the country" (p. 120). In many city neighborhoods that have large recent immigrations from Cuba, Porto Rico (Puerto Rico), and Russia, among others, we may have true regional dialects or "dialects of American English spoken with a foreign accent (a different kind of 'dialect' and some are merely local variations."

Two rather strikingly different dialects are Cajan, in the bayou area of Louisiana,[3] and Gullah, spoken by inhabitants of the Sea Islands off the coast of South Carolina. These dialects are not readily intelligible to most American speakers of the major dialects.

Is it possible that we will soon need to entertain a third dialect, or possibly a third "language"—Computerese of Siliconese? The impact of computers on everyday speech is considerable as of this writing and is likely to increase, both in the English-speaking world and beyond, wherever computers become commonplace instruments. This influence will be considered later in our discussion of *argot*. In the meantime, we can try to decode this bit of Silicon Valley verbiage: "He doesn't have both drives on line, but he is high res and an integrated kind of guy." Broadly translated with a generous use of slang, this decodes to "He isn't quite coordinated, but he is on the ball and he does have his act together."

Does this excerpt from an article written in San Francisco by Peter H. Lewis (*New York Times*, April 22, 1990) require translation?

> Tens of thousands of Apple Macintosh users visited the Macworld trade exposition here earlier this month, examining the hardware and software on offer. But unlike the Macworld shows of a couple of years ago, when people in blue jeans and polo shirts came to look at Apple's small and relatively underpowered computer family, this year's show attracted what appeared to be an unusually high percentage of corporate users. "Look at all the suits and ties," one visitor marveled, intrigued more by the changing Apple culture than by the technological wonderland around him.

---

[3] The term *Cajan* is a corruption of Acadian. Acadia (now Nova Scotia) was French until 1716. In 1755 the citizens of Acadia who refused to pledge allegiance to the British were deported to Louisiana.

Indeed as sartorial preferences showed, this Macworld was clearly aimed at the business user. Conferences and seminars addressed such topics as "Hot Mac-to-Vax issues," the Vax being the Digital Equipment Corporation's minicomputer, and "CL/1: the key to Macs and the Corporate Database," CL/1 being a computer language that allows the Mac to work with mainframes made by the International Business Machines Corporation as well as with Vax computers.

As an exercise, the reader may compare her or his term for the entries in Table 3–1. In addition, she or he may check on whether the article is a *sofa*, a *davenport*, a *divan*, a *settee*, or possibly a *cot*.

Black English[4]

A dialect, we recall, is a variety of a language that is spoken in a particular area or by a particular social group. The variants of the language are found in the lexicon (vocabulary), pronunciation, and syntax (grammar). Despite the variations that create identifiable dialects within a language system, mature speakers and listeners of different dialects have little or no difficulty in understanding one another. Speaker-listeners may need some experience to "tune in" so that they can "figure out" what is said, so that their dialects are *mutually intelligible*. As Wardaugh (1972), pointed out, "Cantonese and Mandarin, both of which are called Chinese, are different languages rather than different dialects of one language because they are not mutually intelligible in their spoken forms. However, Danish and Norwegian, sometimes called two different languages, are really dialects of one language in that they *have a high degree of mutual intelligibility*" (p. 191).

Black English is a sociocultural variant (dialect) of English that has no geographic boundaries within the United States. It is spoken, but not as the exclusive dialect, by a majority of black persons, especially by those who live in the "inner cities" of the major cities of the United States. According to Dillard (1972), 80 percent of American blacks speak black English. Labov, a student of dialects, prefers to use the term *black English vernacular* rather than black English. By black English vernacular, Labov (1972, p. xiii) means "the relatively uniform dialect spoken by the majority of black youth in most parts of the United States today, especially in the inner city areas of New York, Boston, Detroit, Philadelphia, Washington, Cleveland, Chicago, St. Louis, San Francisco, Los Angeles, and other urban centers." Moreover, "It is also spoken in most rural areas and used in 'the casual,' intimate conversation of many adults." If we consider black English, or black English vernacular, a dialect, it follows that many black persons are bidialectal. That is, as adults, and probably also as youths, they may on some occasions speak in black English or black English vernacular and on other occasions speak a "standard" dialect of American English.

In Chapter 12, we present some of the phonemic, morphemic, and syntactical fea-

---

[4] The many successful black radio and television personalities as well as actors, actresses, and political figures attest to the use of standard dialects by these speakers who are by no means the exceptions. My own impressions are that black English was a linguistic phenomenon of the post-World War II era, reaching its highest incidence of usage in the 1960s and 1970s, and becoming a matter of historical interest by the 1980s. However, the influence of black English on contemporary slang is undeniable.

tures that have established black English as a variant or dialect of "Standard" American English. Our concern in this chapter is to highlight some of the contributions of black English to post-World War II American English as well as some of the dynamics behind these contributions.

In recent years, much American slang has been taken directly from black English. The phrase *right on* may have achieved respectability beyond its usage as slang. It is heard in political speeches and in radio and television commercials. *Rip off* is a phrase with multiple meanings. When a friend has been *ripped off*, she or he may have been robbed, cheated, overcharged, arrested, or murdered. *To rap* is to talk or to argue or discuss. So, many of us have held *rap sessions*. *Cool* is used to indicate appropriate detachment, to be able to evaluate a situation before taking action. *Bread* is for money and possibly other worthwhile commodities. *Bad*, especially when pronounced with a "stretched-out" vowel, means good. *Uptight* usually means tense and inflexible, but in black English it may also have a positive and desirable implication as "ready for action." These are a few examples of borrowings from black English by American slang. However, there is a rich lexicon that is still used by speakers of black English, blacks and nonblacks included. This lexicon has not become part of the American slang. For a brief summary of the history and influence of black Americans on English and the nature of black English see Dillard (1976, Chap. 7) and Stewart (1972a, Chaps. 6 and 7).

There is considerable poetry in the vocabulary of black English, in that words carry values and associations beyond their immediate meanings. For example, the substitution of *fox* for *woman* implies either an evaluation of women or a description of behavior. *Stone* is a *heavy* adjective, and a *stone fox* is *something else*. A *dude* is the successor of the *hip cat* of the 1950s. However, *dude* may refer to any adult male. *Soul* refers to attitude and feelings that are assumed to be unique to black persons.

Readers who are interested in the features and rules of black English (vernacular) that make it distinctly different from other American English dialects may consult Dillard (1972) and Flexner (1976), who provide historical background for many of the terms of black English.

Hendrickson (1986, pp. 150–151) makes the point that although black English dialect depends on a particular syntax "the city-based dialect definitely has its own distinctive vocabulary of slang expressions. Among the latest slang (which will not be the latest slang when this book [Hendrickson's or mine] is published) is *chill out* for stop acting foolishly, *crib* (instead of *pad*) for apartment, *tude* for attitude . . . and *serious* for something of the highest merit."

Labov's *Language of the Inner City* (1972) is a *must* for readers who wish to understand the social significance of black English in the United States.

Spanish

The influence of Spanish on contemporary American English is ongoing. Puerto Rican, Cuban, Mexican, and other variants of Spanish associated with migrations from Spanish-speaking nations in the Western Hemisphere are adding new terms and linguistic structures to American English. Terms such as *canyon, mañana, mesa*, and *pronto* are among those used with little change in pronunciation. Americans enjoy *chili con carne* and *enchiladas* and *tortillas* in areas of the country quite remote from where these foods were first prepared. In California and the Southwest, American speakers may part company with "Hasta la vista" or use the term *vista* without being aware of its origin.

Because of our shared history, American English has "borrowed" a large lexicon of Spanish-origin words which are yet in common usage. Flexner (1976, p. 118) offers a selected list of such words and asks, "Are the words Spanish or American?" They are, of course, both. Flexner provides dates for the first time each of the words was recorded as an Americanism.

aficionado, 1940s	hacienda, 1808	playa, 1854
bodega, 1849	hombre, 1836	presidio, 1808
cabana, 1890	macho, 1960s	señorita, 1823
embarcadero, 1846	mañana, 1885	siesta, 17th century
fiesta, 1844	padre, 1792	tequila, 1849
frijole, 1759	peon, 1826	tortilla, 1831

Children and adults whose first language is Spanish may have some difficulty in learning the diction, intonation, and grammatical constructions of American English. Davis (1972) reviews the major problems. We shall address some of these difficulties in later chapters.

DICTIONARIES AND STANDARDS OF USAGE

Having briefly sketched some of the forces and influences that have given us American English speech and its dialect variations, both historical and contemporary, we return to Standard American English. Who determines when new words and new usages of older words become acceptable? Who determines what are "proper" pronunciations? When does a slang term cease to be slang and become a "respectable" term? One answer is "When the educated and/or respected members of a culture use the terms." But terms and pronunciations must be recorded, and decisions must be made about what is to be recorded. Because we have no equivalent of a French Academy whose members have stated meetings to make decisions and "fix the language," the responsibility inevitably falls on the editors of dictionaries. Fortunately, even Samuel Johnson noted in the preface to his famous dictionary, published in 1755, that "words are the daughters of earth." Johnson opposed the notion of an academy with the authority to determine what is correct and acceptable. Nevertheless, Johnson admitted personal bias in his lexical selection. For example, he included words that he recognized as obsolete "when they are found in authors not obsolete, or when they have any force or beauty that may deserve revival." Johnson's authorities were the English writers he respected. He recognized that "no dictionary of a living tongue ever can be perfect, since while it is hastening to publication, some words are budding, and some falling away."

Samuel Johnson had six copyists to assist him in the production of *his* dictionary. He did have the benefit of colleagues in the sciences, agriculture, and the arts, but he made the final decisions as to word selection and their definitions. Some of his definitions reveal a highly personal bias. For example: *oats* is defined as "a grain which in England is generally given to horses, but in Scotland supports the people." *Pension* is defined as "an allowance made to any one without an equivalent. In England it is generally understood to mean pay given to a state hireling for treason to his country" (McCadam and Milne 1963, p. xi).

The publishers of large (unabridged) dictionaries today employ hundreds of editorial experts and scholars to determine the principles for the selection of entries and to arrive at acceptable definitions.

The *American Heritage Dictionary* (1969) employed a panel of more than one hundred "educated adults" to determine entries and usage. In the introduction by William Morris, the "educated adult" is described:

> The vocabulary recorded here, ranging from the language of Shakespeare to the idiom of the present day, is that of the "educated adult." The "educated adult" referred to is, of course, a kind of ideal person, for he has at his fingertips a most comprehensive lexicon for the conduct and discussion of everyday affairs, but also for all of the arts and all of the sciences. (p. vi)

The second edition (1982) had a panel of more than two hundred "usage determiners" and forty-plus consultants to arrive at entries and definitions. As for the first edition, the vocabulary entries ranged from those of Shakespeare's time to current idiom.

Noah Webster published his *Compendious Dictionary of the English Language* in 1806. It acknowledged that current usage rather than prescription should determine lexical entries and their definitions and pronunciations. The title page of his *Compendious Dictionary* indicates that five thousand words were added "to the number found in the Best English Compends," and that definitions of many words were "amended and improved."

Contemporary dictionary editors usually insist on recording what is established and current. Harrison Platt, Jr. (1964), presented what we consider a fair view of the degree of responsibility and authority the editors of a respected dictionary cannot avoid. In an appendix to *The American College Dictionary*, Platt said:

> What . . . is the rôle of a dictionary in settling questions of pronunciation or meaning or grammar? It is not a legislating authority on good English. It attempts to record what usage at any time actually is. Insofar as possible, it points out divided usage. It indicates regional variations of pronunciation or meaning wherever practical. It points out meanings and uses peculiar to a trade, profession, or special activity. It suggests the levels on which certain words or usages are appropriate. A dictionary . . . based on a realistic sampling of usage, furnishes the information necessary for a sound judgment of what is good English in a given situation. To this extent the dictionary is an authority, and beyond this authority should not go. (p. 1485)

In the light of this excerpt, we may reassess the significance of the entry on *ain't* in *Webster's Third New International Dictionary*. *Ain't*, according to the entry on page 45, is

In the light of this excerpt, we may reassess the significance of the entry on *ain't* in *Webster's Third New International Dictionary*. *Ain't*, according to the entry on page 45, is a contraction of *are not, is not, am not*, or *have not*. Further, we are told, *ain't* "though disapproved by many, and more common in less educated speech, [is] used orally in most parts of the U.S. by many cultivated speakers esp. In the phrase *ain't I*." Some critics of this dictionary have pointedly asked what is meant by "less educated speech" and imply that somewhere and somehow a comparison seems to be missing. On page 209, we learn that the word *between* is no longer limited to an implication of two but may be used to suggest division or participation by two or more. The entry cites such usage by *Time* magazine and by eminent scholars, including a linguist from Harvard University.

The Increasing Respectability of Ain't

The second edition of the *Random House Dictionary of the English Language* (1987) informs us that *ain't* is nonstandard in some dialects for *am not, are not, have not, has not, do not, does not,* and *did not*. In addition we learn that:

> *Ain't* is more common in uneducated speech than in the educated, but it occurs with some frequency in the informal speech of the educated, especially in the southern and south central states. This is especially true of the interrogative use of *ain't I* for the formal and—to some—stilted *am I not*.

In the Preface of the revised *Random House Dictionary*, attitudes and cultural forces that have influenced recent language changes are noted:

> During the past two decades significant and influential social and cultural movements have taken place, reverberating through our language not only as new words and meanings but in our attitudes toward language and its use. Thus recent influences that have expanded and reshaped our vocabulary and its use come not only from such obvious fields as science and technology and new forms and styles in the arts, fashion, and leisure activities, but also from history itself and from such social and cultural movements as concern with the environment, the women's movement, and a new awareness of and respect for ethnic diversity.

MERRIAM WEBSTER III AND WHO DETERMINES USAGE

In an article in which Sumner Ives (1961) reviewed and in many respects anticipated the strong negative response to the philosophy that resulted in the "liberal" selection of entries to *Webster's Third New International Dictionary*, he made several points that continue to be relevant about word selection and grammatical usage. Ives' article may also be considered a prospective of changes to come. Following is a summary of these points:

1. English has changed more during the past fifty years than during any similar period in the past.

2. Language, any language, is a system of human conventions rather than a system of natural laws.

3. A dictionary is reliable only insofar as it comprehensively and accurately describes current practices in a language, including community opinion, as to the social and regional associations of each practice described.

4. ". . . 'good' English is that which most effectively accomplishes the purpose of the author (or speaker) without drawing irrelevant attention from the purpose to the words or constructions by which this purpose is accomplished. Thus, for ordinary purposes, 'good' English is that which is customary and familiar in a given context and in the pursuit of a given objective."

5. Words may have more than one pronunciation. "Standards" of pronunciation must make allowances for regional variations and for differences related to specific contexts. *Webster's Third New International Dictionary* represents "the normal pronunciation of English as it is spoken by cultured persons in each major section of the country—the 'language of well-bred ease,' culturally determined."

WHICH IS TO BE MASTER — THAT'S ALL

When, in *Through the Looking Glass*, Alice argues with Humpty Dumpty about the meaning of the word *glory*, the following conversation takes place:

"But *glory* does not mean 'a nice knockdown argument,' " Alice objected.

"When I use a word," Humpty Dumpty said, in a rather scornful tone, "it means just what I choose it to mean—neither more nor less."

"The question is," said Alice, "whether you *can* make words mean so many different things."

"The question is," said Humpty Dumpty, "which is to be master—that's all."

The debate over who determines word usage is likely to go on for some time in regard to "which is to be master." The front material of the *American Heritage Dictionary, II* (1982, pp. 30–34) includes two essays in the form of a debate on the matter of responsibility of the editors and publishers of dictionaries for the selection of entries and exclusion of some entries as dictionaries are revised. The participants in the debate are Dwight Bolinger, Professor Emeritus of Literature and Romance Languages (Harvard University) and William F. Buckley, Jr., publisher and media personality and avowed political conservative. Bolinger argues that correct usage is essentially and democratically determined by how persons we respect for their language and knowledge employ linguistic terms. Buckley does not deny that usage determines correctness, but, as an elitist, challenges, "Usage by whom?" He also offers himself as an arbiter of what constitutes *acceptable usage*. (For an expanded and objective evaluation of this debate, I recommend Chapter 12 of Wilson's *Van Winkle's Return* (1987).)

Slang and Argot

Argot is the special vocabulary and idiom of a particular vocation, profession, or social group that serves as an "in" language. Historically, argot has been identified with the vocabulary of underworld characters, devised for private or in-group identification and communication. John Gay's *Beggars' Opera*, written in 1728, was rich in the argot of thieves.

Slang employs highly informal vocabulary and expressions (idioms) that are, at best, metaphorical, playful, vivid, and elliptical. At worst, slang may be abusive and vulgar in that its terms are still considered to be socially taboo. In common with nonvocational or professional argot, slang terms have a short linguistic life.

McDavid (1975) observed of slang and argot:

> The fate of slang and argot terms is unpredictable. Most of them disappear rapidly, some win their way into standard use, and still others remain what they were to begin with. *Mob*, deplored by Swift and other purists of 1700, would never be questioned today, but *moll*, meaning "a prostitute" or "the mistress of a gangster," has been in use since the early 1600's, and is still slang.
>
> Technical terms arise because it is necessary for those who share a scientific or technical interest to have a basis for discussion. The difference between scientific and popular usage may be seen most strikingly in the biological sciences. A Latin term like *Panthera leo* (lion) has a specific reference, while *cougar* may refer to any large wild American feline predator, or *partridge* may designate the bob-white quail, a kind of grouse, or some other game bird, according to local usage. Common words may be used with specific reference in a given field: *fusion* denotes one thing in politics, another in nuclear physics. As a field of inquiry becomes a matter of general interest, its technical terms will be picked up and used with less precision. Because of popular interest in Freudian psychology, such terms as *complex, fixation*, and *transference* are bandied about in senses Freud would never have sanctioned. (p. xxii)

Valley speech (Valspeak), possibly so named because of its supposed origin and wide use among adolescents in the San Fernando Valley of California, is an example of slang and argot. According to one reporter (Demarest, *Time*, September 27, 1982), Valley speech is a combination of slang with the hippie lingo of the 1960s and black street jargon. The characteristics of Valley speech include etymological reversals such as *bad* to mean *good, groovy* to mean *out of fashion*, and many invented terms (neologisms) that may not be readily traced to their origin. *Rolf* is used for *vomit, scarf-out* for *overeat; zod, spaz, goober,* and *geek* may all mean *weird. Rad* implies *excellent* and *shanky* means the opposite. The ultimate in rejection is to be told, "I'm shurr." Demarest provided this sample of discourse: "Shopping is the funnest thing to do cause O.K. clothes. They're important. Like for your image and stuff. Like I'm sure, everything has to match. Like *everything.* And you don't want to wear stuff that people don't wear. Peopl'd look at you and just go 'Ew, she's a zod'; like get away."

We doubt that Valley speech will have a lasting effect on American English speech patterns. It is just too *far-out,* and we use the term in a negative sense. Nevertheless, there is little question that whether or not we are aware of it, most of us employ slang and argot in both informal and formal speaking situations without knowledge of the origin of the terms or the semantic intentions of their originators.

Argot may also come from scientists and educators. From operant learning theorists, we have such terms as *behavior shaping, conditioning, reinforcement,* and *discriminative responses.* The term *gestalt* is used for learning theory and a form — to be sure, rather nebulous — of psychotherapy. A *shrink* is almost an accepted word for a psychiatrist.

In our discussion of black English and Valley speech, we cited terms that are used by persons identified with the *counterculture* as well as by blacks. Some words and terms have a short life. One approach of dictionary editors avoids the labeling of words as either argot or slang; instead, words and phrases are listed as ones that have been in frequent usage for a stated period of time. For example, *The Barnhart Dictionary of New English Since 1963* (Barnhart et al., 1973) lists entries for the period 1963–1973. From this source we get the meanings of terms such as *alpha-helix, bad-mouth, cassette,* and *learning-curve.* A new edition may be expected to include terms of the space age as well as a few from Valley speech.

Terms that started their linguistic life as argot to meet the needs of Silicon Valley (Siliconese) and for our ventures in outer space are, we hope, likely to have a long life. Recently published dictionaries include terms such as *data processing, hardware* and *software, interface, chip* (not related to card playing or gambling), *on-line, hacker, input,* and whatever other terms need to be adapted or invented to reflect the needs of our computerized society.

PSYCHOLOGICAL DETERMINANTS

To conclude our discussion of changing speech patterns, some psychological factors that determine the choice of words, and the effects of such choice on our patterns of verbal behavior, are reviewed. The words we use are generally selected according to our needs as speakers. The words we select to be impressive depend on the situation and the person or persons we wish to impress. Not infrequently, we may want to impress ourselves, rather than the listener. As speakers, we may have occasional need for a large mouthful of sounds, and so we speak polysyllabically and at length in a manner that would make Freudian listeners click their tongues and nod their heads with weighty surmises. More frequently, however, other factors determine the words we select. One such factor is *ease of pronunciation.* With few exceptions, short words are easier to pronounce than long words, and so, other things being equal, if they can be used effectively in communicating our thoughts and feelings, short words are likely to be chosen over long ones. It is no accident that the most frequently used words in our language are shorter than the words that are less frequently used. George K. Zipf (1949) demonstrated that frequency of word usage is related to the length (shortness) of words, and that *words become shorter as spoken words* with increased frequency of usage. Zipf wrote, "There are copious examples of a decrease in magnitude of a word which results so far as one can judge solely from an increase in the relative frequency of its occurrence, as estimated either from the speech of an individual, in which the shortening may occur, or in the language of a minor group. or of the major speech group."

We shorten words by *assimilation*, by *truncation*, and by *abbreviatory substitution*. All three processes, incidentally, also result in ease of pronunciation. As examples of assimilation, we have dropped the *p* from *cupboard*, and most of us drop the *d* from *handkerchief*. Even short phrases are made shorter. For example, the modification of *goodbye* to *gdby*, or just *gby*.

Truncation is exemplified by the change from *amperes* to *amps*, *elevator* to *el*, *telephone* to *phone* as either a verb or a noun, *professor* to *prof* and *automobile* to *auto*. In California, the Bay Area Transportation System is briefly referred to as the *Bart*. *TV* for *television* is an example of truncation by abbreviation, as is *TD* for *touchdown*.

Abbreviatory substitutions are exemplified by *car* for *automobile, pop* for *soda (charged water), GI (Government Issue)* for *soldier* and *spuds* for *potatoes*. The term *cop*, meaning *police officer*, is an example of truncation and is an abbreviation of *copper*. The processes of word shortening by either truncation or substitution are instances of Zipf's "principle of least effort." According to Zipf, the changes associated with word-frequency usage are expressions of an underlying principle of human behavior that, over a period of time, human beings tend to minimize or reduce their average rate of expenditure of energy to accomplish a given objective. In other words, most of us do whatever we need to do in the easiest way we can.

Those of us who work with computers are likely to know that *Fortran* stands for *formula translation* and that *Basic* is an acronym for *Beginners' Symbolic Instruction Code*; but others, who may not yet be so privileged, may need some help in decoding these terms. In the *Grab Bag* column of the *San Francisco Chronicle*, a reader asks: "Why is a telephone 'modem' called that?" The writer is informed: "To send and receive messages, the device converts binary data to analog signals. That's known as MOdulation. And analog signals to binary data. That's DEModulation. Put the capped letters together."[5] The result, obviously, is *modem*.

In one morning's issue of *The New York Times* both the news columnists and the feature writers assumed that the acronyms and abbreviations they used were in such common usage that only rarely were the letters spelled out. The abbreviations and acronyms included AIDS, ATT, IBM, CIA, CPR, HMO, FEMA, GE, GM, NBC, LILCO, UN, UNESCO, UNICEF, and XEROX.

We have come a long way from needing to know only such abbreviations as AWOL, COD, SOP, and, to demonstrate our sophistication, GI and SNAFU. Whether our language is enriched or confused by these contributions is a matter for each reader to decide. With the rapid changes in the computer industry, many of the acronyms may be short-lived. But while they have life, they do represent "the principle of least effort" if not for most of us, at least for those who frequently use the terms.

---

[5] L. M. Boyd, "The Grab Bag," *San Francisco Chronicle*, May 13, 1990.

SQUID is a recent tongue-defiant entry to the linguistic contributions of abbreviatory neologisms. SQUID stands for a Superconducting Interference Device. This is an application of a MEG (Magnetic Encephalography). "This technology works by measuring the faint magnetic field produced when nerve cells fire electrical signals to communicate with one another. Magnetic fields are generated any time electricity flows, whether it's through a television set, a personal computer, or your brain" (Jon Van, "Untangling the Brain," *San Francisco Examiner*, May 17, 1990).

How long SQUID will be a viable entry in the argot of the computer world is presently anyone's guess. Its life will depend on its usefulness among persons to whom SQUID is not just "one of a variety of ten-armed cephalopods with a long, slender body, ink sac, and broad caudal fins."

═══ COUNTERFORCES ═══

There are a variety of counterforces that exert influence, that prevent the high-frequency use of the same word or term, and with it, the process of word shortening. The most potent, and from our point of view, the most acceptable of the counterforces is the human drive for variety of experience, including our experience with the words readily at our command. To avoid monotony, we use synonyms that may be less precise in meaning rather than reiterations of the same word. Early in our school careers, our teachers encouraged us to avoid the repeated use of a word, merely because repetition is considered undesirable. Partly because of the authority of our teachers and partly because of our drive for variety, we go out of our way to use several different words to communicate an idea that might well have been semantically more precise had a previously used word been used (employed) again.

Until recently, verbal taboos and superstitions were cultural forces that worked against the use of some words, mostly of Anglo-Saxon origin, as expletives, adjectives, and verbs. Of late, our daily metropolitan newspapers and our magazines have spelled out rather than abbreviated "four-letter" words, which, incidentally, are not always limited to four letters. For most of us, these words have lost their shock value. We also find there is less difference today in the productive vocabularies of adolescent boys and girls as well as in those of young and older adults in social situations than a generation ago. However, the grandparents, if not the parents, of the emancipated generation may continue to employ circumlocutions and euphemisms to suggest rather than say forcibly what they mean or intend. Thus there are still some children who are *born out of wedlock* and so are *illegitimate*, but there are many more who are *children of single (unmarried) parents*. People still *pass away* or *pass on* because we do not like to have them *die*. *Undertakers* are *morticians*, whose establishments are *mortuaries*. Bodies are *interred* in *memorial parks* or *Gardens of Remembrance* rather than in cemeteries. Verbal habits and defensive attitudes persist in a considerable part of our population and thus maintain or even increase the use of terms that another part of the population may aggressively avoid.

═══ GUARDIANS OF OUR LANGUAGE ═══

John Witherspoon, an American of Scottish ancestry and a signer of the Declaration of Independence and a president of the College of New Jersey (now Princeton), warned Americans about the urgent need to "keep their language pure." Witherspoon referred to British English and not to the changing American English. We have had guardians of our language throughout the years, some who have wanted us to return to British English as our model of purity and others whose hopes were that we would not abandon the old and useful for the new that may be useful for only a brief time. In recent years the neologistic locutions, and all too often the obscure circumlocutions of elected and appointed government officials, politicians, and their representatives, have come in for considerable and justified criticism.

Certainly, many persons in government employment, and especially those who are highly paid as spokespeople, speak a strained, if not strange, form of English. Though the pattern is by no means clear, a common element is to use many words to avoid saying anything that suggests a specific message.

We are not at all sure of the underlying dynamics of the language of politicians, government officials, and their representatives. Newman opened his book *Strictly Speaking* (1974) with a quotation from a White House press secretary. In answer to a reporter's question about the need for a four-day extension of a subpoena, the secretary "explained" that the additional time was needed so that an attorney could "evaluate and make a judgement in terms of a response." Newman suggested that a simpler answer might have been, "The attorney wanted more time to think about it." Perhaps Newman, in his crusade to save the English language from the impact of American speech, may have missed the point. The press secretary may not have wanted to make his meaning clear by direct and simple speech. Perhaps the secretary wanted to keep in practice to avoid being clear and direct, while seeming to respond to intruding and inquisitive reporters.

Newman objected to persons who prefer to say *impacted on* rather than *hit*; he does not like *at that point in time* or *in point of fact*. In essence, Newman was pleading, "I speak . . . for a world from which the stilted and pompous phrase, the slogan and cliché, have not been banished — that would be too much to hope for — but which they do not dominate" (p. 32).

In response to a question about the results of a negotiating session on the reduction of armed forces in Eastern Europe, our secretary of state "explained," "Our counterparts apparently weren't able to respond meaningfully at this time." A more direct reply might have been, "We did not come out even, much less ahead, on this part of our negotiations." However, though the explanation was evasive, we do need to appreciate that inquiring reporters may press too hard and too early for firm answers or explanations. An important purpose of the "language of diplomacy" is to maintain flexibility and thus allow for continued negotiations with a prospect of more satisfactory conclusions.

Politicians and government officials are not the only targets of "gobbledegeze" and "babble" of all sorts, including "psycho-babble" — terms generated by psychotherapists and shared with their clients. These forms of in-group argot are viewed as items of self-expression and intended more for identification than for communication of thinking.

Newman does not like terms such as *our space, self-actualization,* and *owning my power.* He is in no haste to have events *finalized,* though he has no objection to having ideas or objects take form and so *materialize.*

Neither Newman nor his contemporary guardians of our language, including William Saffire and William F. Buckley, Jr., are opposed to changes in language usage or the introduction of new terminology to meet our needs for precise communication. What they share is a desire for precision of language, for the precise word instead of "and such things" that reflect a lack of precision in thinking. They are concerned that high-level government officials, including those we elect as presidents and those who presumably speak for them do not respect the language they use. Because millions of us are exposed to these officials they have obligations to be role models, if not of all of us, then perhaps for the younger members of society who are still idealistic enough to identify with them.

These, briefly, are some of the forces and counterforces that have molded our language, that have influenced our verbal habits, and that continue to modify our slow but ever-changing speech patterns. A living language is a growing language and one that changes forms, adds words and drops others, and modifies pronunciations. Some of the forces are global; others are peculiarly American.

To keep its readers up-to-date, on January 20, 1991, the *San Francisco Examiner* provided a list of military terms, code names, and slang words being used in reports from the Persian Gulf. The following lists a few of those terms. I hope that most of these will not need to be long remembered.

- DUMB BOMBS: Bombs drawn to the ground by gravity.
- SMART BOMBS OR SMART MISSILES: Weapons that have a directional mechanism, such as a heat sensor or radar, that helps them find their targets after they've been fired.
- FUR BALL: Military pilot slang for the hectic tangle of air-to-air dogfights.
- HEADS UP: Code for "enemy got through."
- LIT UP: Identified by radar.
- MORT THEMSELVES OUT: Jet fighter pilot slang for planes shooting one another accidentally. The term fratricide is also used.
- SCUD: Soviet-made surface-to-surface ballistic missile. There are three Iraqi versions that can carry explosive or chemical warheads to targets 360 to 1,200 miles away. They have a reputation for inaccuracy.
- SEBKHA: An Arab word for underground river. Sebkhas that turn the ground into quagmires impossible to cross with tanks lie near the Saudi border and south of Kuwait City.
- STEALTH: Term applied to planes designed to remain nearly invisible to enemy radar. The F-117A, a single seat, stealth-equipped jet was used in the first raid on Baghdad. Its range and armaments are classified.
- TOW: Acronym for tube-launched, optically-tracked, wire-guided missile.
- ZULU: Greenwich Mean Time or GMT. When it's 0000 Zulu (or midnight GMT) it's 4 P.M. in California and 3 A.M. in Iraq, Kuwait and Saudi Arabia. The military uses zulu as its time reference worldwide.

══ REFERENCES ══

American Heritage Dictionary, II, 2nd ed. (1969, 1982). Boston: Houghton Mifflin.

Barnhart, C. L., Steinmetz, S., & Barnhart, R. K. (1973). *Barnhart dictionary of new English since 1963.* New York: Harper and Row.

Burto, W. (1965). *William Shakespeare: The Sonnets.* New York: New American Library.

Cassidy, F. G. (1985). *Dictionary of American Regional English* (DARE), vol. 1 (A–C). Cambridge: Harvard Bellenap Press.

Davis, A. L. (1972). English problems of Spanish speakers. In D.L. Shores (Ed.), *Contemporary English.* Philadelphia: J.B. Lippincott, Chap. 9.

Demarest, M. (1982, September). Living. *Time, 5*(120) 3.

Dillard, J. L. (1972, 1976). *American talk.* New York: Random House.

_____. (1985). *Toward a social history of America.* New York and Amsterdam: Mouton.

Ferguson, C. A., & Heath, S. B. (1981). *Language in the U.S.A.* Cambridge, Mass.: Harvard University Press.

Flexner, S. B. (1976). *I hear America talking.* New York: Van Nostrand.

_____. (1982). *Listening to America..* New York: Simon and Schuster.

Hendrickson, R. (1986). *American talk.* New York: Viking-Penguin Press.

Ives, S. (1961, December). A review of *Webster's third new international dictionary. Word Study.*

Jones, D. (1956). *The Pronunciation of English* (3rd ed.). Cambridge, England: W. Hefner & Sons.

Jones, D. (1950). *An outline of English phonetics* (8th ed.). Cambridge, England: W. Hefner & Sons.

Labov, W. (1972). *Language in the inner city.* Philadelphia: University of Pennsylvania Press.

McCadam, E. L., & Milne, G. (1963). *Johnson's dictionary.* New York: Random House.

McCrum, W., Cran, W., & MacNeil, R. (1986). *The story of English.* New York: Viking Press.

McDavid, R. I. (1975). Usage, dialects, and functional varieties. *The Random House college dictionary,* rev. ed. New York: Random House.

McDavid, R. I., & Francis, W. (1958). *The dialects of American-English.* New York: The Ronald Press.

Mencken, H. L. (1946). *The American language.* New York: Alfred A. Knopf.

Newman, E. (1974). *Strictly speaking.* New York: Alfred A. Knopf.

Nist, J. (1971). American regionalisms. In Kerr, E. M. (Ed.), *Aspects of American English* (2nd ed.). New York: Harcourt, Brace Jovanovich, p. 170.

Oxford English Dictionary, 2nd ed. (1989). Oxford, England: Clarendon Press.

Pei, M. (1949). *The story of language.* Philadelphia: J.B. Lippincott.

Platt, H., Jr. (1964). *The American college dictionary.* New York: Random House.

Random House Dictionary of the English Language, (1987). New York: Random House.

Shuy, R. W. (1967). *Dicovering American dialects.* Urbana, Ill.: National Council of Teachers of English.

Stewart, W. A. (1972a). Language and communication problems in southern Appalachia. In D. L. Shores (Ed.), *Contemporary English.* Philadelphia: J.B. Lippincott.

_____. (1972b). "Sociolinguistic factors in the history of Negro dialects *and* Continuity and change in American Negro dialects," in D. L. Shores (Ed.), *Contemporary English,* Philadelphia: J.B. Lippincott.

Thomas, C. K. (1958). *An introduction to the phonetics of American English* (2nd ed.). New York: Ronald Press.

Wardaugh, R. (1972). *Introduction to linguistics.* New York: McGraw-Hill.

Wilson, K. G. (1987). *Van Winkle's return.* Hanover and London: Universal Press of New England.

Zipf, G. (1949). *Human behavior and the principle of least effort.* Reading, Mass.: Addison Wesley.

CHAPTER 4

AMERICAN-ENGLISH PRONUNCIATION

In the play within a play, Hamlet, Prince of Denmark, exhorts the players, "Speak the speech I pray you, as I pronounced it to you, trippingly on the tongue: but if you mouth it, as many of your players do, I had as lief the town-crier spoke my lines." Further, Hamlet advised the actors, "Suit the action to the word, the word to the action; with this special observance, that you o'erstep not the modesty of nature."

Shakespeare, through Hamlet, was talking primarily about pronunciation with a standard of speech in mind—the standard of his own (Hamlet's) speech ("as I pronounced it to you"). The words were not to be obviously "mouthed" (no exaggerated articulatory activity) and the accompanying action neither unrelated to the spoken words nor flagrant in gesture. On the whole, the words and the actions were not to exceed the "modesty of nature."

PRONUNCIATION: STYLES AND THE OCCASIONS

The term *pronunciation* will mean for us the production of contextual speech—sounds, stress patterns of words, and intonation or speech "melody." These aspects of spoken language are together produced in keeping with the accepted standard(s) as exemplified by respected, educated speakers in a given community. Note the parenthetic plural form for standard(s). This is intended to indicate that a standard of what is appropriate (correct or acceptable) varies with the speaker and the occasion. Even when we allow for regional variations, we can have a variety and range of styles. These may be identified as informal and formal at the extremes, and in between may include: informal-conversational, as when we talk with and among friends; more formal-colloquial, as in participation in a classroom recitation or in a situation when a speaker is responding to a presumed superior or authority; person to group, as in public speaking. However, present practices tend to make little or no distinction in style between the informal-colloquial and the more formal-colloquial. There is, we may conclude, no single "right" style or standard of correctness or acceptability. The ultimate determinants are the situation and the speaker, the relationship of the speaker to the listener or listeners. Professor John Kenyon, a respected authority on American pronunciation, suggested in 1935 that "the most important of all styles is the familiar, cultivated, colloquial." He characterized this style as "the speech of well-bred ease." This style may be identified as a cultivated "standard," a form or forms that may be found in all regional dialects. It is, as Kenyon pointed out, the speech of the well-bred at ease. So let us be at ease as we continue.

There was a time when the use of contractions such as *can't, I'm, he'll, we'll, doesn't, don't, won't,* and *it's* was reserved for informal colloquial situations. Today, except for somewhat wider ranges in pitch and loudness, they are evident in relatively formal situations and may be heard in interviews not only with our politicians but with acknowledged leaders of state.

===== SPECIAL FEATURES OF ENGLISH: ===== STRESS, "WEAK VOWELS," AND INTONATION

Every spoken language has its own way of generating meanings (semantics) by one or a combination of such features as syllable stress, changes in vowels, and intonation or speech-melody pattern. An adult who aspires to speak a second language like a native speaker needs to become aware and practice these features or, despite proficiency in articulation, he or she will still sound "foreign." This may be so even when the person has mastered the production of the individual sounds (phonemes) of a language. However, except for the letters *a, e, i,* and *o* of our alphabet, all letters are pronounced (articulated) with two sounds, as in *bee* for the letter *b, see* for *c,* and *dee* for *d; f* is pronounced *eff,* and so on through the alphabet. It takes two sounds to produce the name of the letter.

Stress and Vowel "Weakening"

A common and frequent feature of English is the change in vowel when a syllable is not in a stressed position within a multisyllable word, or is a single-syllable word in an unstressed position within a phrase. The words *adjust* and *away* are examples of the use of a weak vowel (the schwa [ə]) in the first syllable. In *sofa* we have the same vowel in the second syllable. Prepositions, articles, and conjunctions all show the same vowel weakening, or "obscuration." *At* is usually pronounced as [ət]. *And,* except for semantic emphasis, is usually pronounced as [ənd] or just [n] as in *He'n I are going.* The auxiliary verb *have,* unless intentionally stressed, is likely to be pronounced as [həv] or [əv] or reduced to [v] as in I've. Incidentally, the schwa is the most frequently used vowel in American English. Why?

We will return to discussing the weak vowel in our later consideration of syllable stress.

Intonation

There are three thousand or more spoken languages. Each has a melodic pattern different and distinctive from the others. Bronstein (1987) notes that even within a given language, "major dialects have their own melodies, exhibiting slight variations within the overall intonational patterns of the language."

American-English intonation patterns will be considered in some detail in Chapter 7, "Pitch and Effective Vocalization." For the present, Figure 4–1 provides generalized representative contours of American-English intonation patterns. It is important to appreciate that in normal conversation or, for that matter, in any normal speech, we speak in a flow of utterance rather than in single-word bursts. The latter — single-word productions — may be used in terse "Yes" or "No" responses, in one-word commands, or to indicate doubt or scorn, as in "He?" or "She?" spoken with a rising inflection. In multiword utterances a verbal flow normally incorporates some degree of continuous pitch change within a phrase or sentence (Figure 4–2). Major pitch changes are likely to occur on the most significant words within the speech unit. Major changes also occur at the conclusion of a phrase or sentence.

Note that a rising inflection is *not* used for all questions but is reserved for ones that logically call for either a "Yes" or "No" response. A rising inflection (change of pitch or intensity on a word within a phrase) is also used to indicate doubt or irony, to suggest a dependent thought, or to indicate uncertainty.

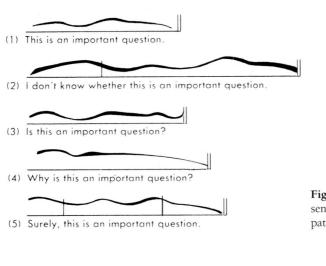

(1) This is an important question.

(2) I don't know whether this is an important question.

(3) Is this an important question?

(4) Why is this an important question?

(5) Surely, this is an important question.

Figure 4–1 Generalized, representative contours (intonation) patterns of American English.

Not one but many men will suffer the results of this action

Figure 4–2 A graphic representation of a relatively complex American-English intonation contour.

DICTION AND PRONUNCIATION
PROBLEMS OF HISPANIC SPEAKERS

Children under age eight or nine are usually and readily able to learn a second language through exposure. They will, of course, acquire the diction (pronunciation) and the intonation of the key speakers to whom they are exposed. If the key speaker or speakers speak an acceptable "standard" of the language, this is what they will learn and, in turn, produce. Adults, however, unless they are especially gifted in language learning, are likely to carry over the speech habits — articulation, pronunciation, and speech melody (intonation) — of their first language to the second which, presumably, they wish to acquire. Some adults can and do, with great effort, acquire a second language through exposure. To achieve this goal, however, does require a total immersion in the new language. It usually takes a period of several months during which a person listens to and responds as best as he or she can to the selected second language. This is the essential procedure for students of the United States military language schools and the commercial schools such as Berlitz.

For those who cannot or do not wish to take time for the language immersion experience, a brief overview of likely carryover errors should help. We will take as an example the tendencies of Hispanic–Chicano speakers. This choice is made because Hispanic speakers particularly those from Mexico and first-generation Americans who live in California and other Southwestern states, constitute the largest minority of persons for whom American English is not a first language. Chicano English is also spoken by many Americans of Hispanic origin, children and adults whose speech patterns represent a special minority dialect of American English (Gonzalez, 1988, p. 71).

Sources of Errors in Chicano Pronunciation

Chicano speakers, in common with other adults for whom English is not a first language, are likely to make the following errors in their approach to learning American English.

For sounds that occur in English but not in their dialect of Spanish, there is a tendency to substitute the nearest equivalent sound from their own speech. Thus *match* is pronounced as *mash*, *chair* as *share*, and *rich* as *rish*. The same tendency occurs for the final sound in *bridge* and *badge*, which are produced as *britch* and *batch*.

The sound *t* is likely to be substituted for the *th* so that *thin* becomes *tin*, and *think* becomes *tink; both* approximates *boat*.

Speakers of Hispanic background have difficulty in distinguishing between the English *b* and *v* in appropriate contexts. (The reasons for the difficulty are complicated. For an explanation, see Gonzalez, 1988, p. 74.)

Consonant clusters are a prominent feature of English speech. Except when they are young children, American speakers have no difficulty with combinations such as *sm, sn, sp, sl,* and *tr* in words such as *small, snow, spin, slow,* and *tree* or in final positions as in *past, snakes, pest, bats, asked,* and *maps.* We even manage triple clusters as in *masked, fists, lapsed,* and *thirst.* These sound combinations do not occur in Spanish. To bring them in line with what a speaker of Spanish produces and may well perceive, the person is likely to intrude the vowel *e* as in *bet* at the beginning of the word and so produce something close to *espin* for *spin* and *estick* for *stick*. "Doing so breaks up the unacceptable clusters into patterns found in Spanish" (Gonzalez, 1988, p. 75). Because triple clusters do not occur in Spanish, the speaker is likely to reduce the first to a single sound or completely eliminate the cluster so that *grasps* becomes *grass*, and *banks* becomes *bank* or, more simply, *back*.

SPELLING AND UNRELIABLE LETTER-TO-SOUND CORRESPONDENCE

English spelling requires that we represent the fifteen vowels, twenty-five consonants, and three distinctive diphthongs by the twenty-six letters of our alphabet. The result is that, unlike Spanish and Italian which have a consistent letter-to-sound relationship within the dialects of the language, English has both a low and unreliable letter-to-sound (grapheme-to-phoneme) correspondence. There are rules—about a hundred or more—that may inform a curious scholar of the whys and vagaries of our spelling. English spelling is, in general, more likely to tell us about the history of a word, its ancestral derivation, than to provide a guide to pronunciation. My own investigation of American-English letter-to-sound correspondence (Eisenson and Solomon, 1970) indicates an incidence of 60 percent at most. The incidence of correspondence is close to 50 percent for the most frequently used words, and higher for those used less frequently.

As examples of inconsistency of correspondence, the letter *c* has a different sound responsibility in the words *ice, cello,* and *click*. The *c* represents still different sounds in *chick, Chicago,* and *coach*. The letter *s* is articulated differently in *seen, sure, bus,* and *was*. It goes silent in *island* but takes on voice in *presume*. The combination of letters *ough* are a challenge because they supposedly represent different single vowels as well as vowel-plus-consonant in words such as *although, through, bough,* and *enough*.

To go from sound to letter, consider that the sound most frequently represented by the letters *sh,* as in *she,* is also represented differently in *sure, nation, machine, patient,* and *mission*. If you have a substantial knowledge of orthography and the ways of the word, you should be able to decode and pronounce the words of the verses that follow:

> In his conscious fashion
> Cautiously Sean rationed
> His unburnished passion
>
> "Pshaw," thought Lucretia,
> Who had her own notion
> Of how Sean should fashion
> His expressions of devotion.

Silent letters such as those in *comb, debt, know,* and *island* present their own problems in spelling and in letter-to-sound representation.

Table 4–1   Vowels of American-English Speech

Front Vowels			Central Vowels			Back Vowels		
	Phonetic Symbol	Dictionary Symbol		Phonetic Symbol	Dictionary Symbol		Phonetic Symbol	Dictionary Symbol
meet	i	ē				boon	u	o͞o
milk	ɪ	ĭ	mirth	ɜ or ɝ	ûr	book	ʊ	o͝o
may	e	ā				boat	o	ō
men	ɛ	ĕ	about	ə	ə			
						ball	ɔ	ô
mat	æ	ă	upper	ɚ	ər	bog	ɒ	ŏ
ask[1]	a	ȧ	mud	ʌ	ŭ	balm	ɑ	ä

[1] When the speaker compromises between the vowels of *mat* and of *balm*. This vowel is intermediate in placement as well as in sound.

The fifteen vowels of American English (see Table 4–1) have only five letters — six if we include the *y* of *hymn, Byzantine,* and *why, bye* (it is actually a diphthong in the last two words) — to represent them. It is generally observed that the relationship between print — spelling — and sound in English is so complex and so unreliable that memory rather than a sounding-out approach is needed to guide us in pronunciation. This, though necessary, does pose a special challenge for speakers of a language whose letter-to-sound correspondence is consistent and reliable as it is for Hispanic and Italian speakers.

═══ **REFERENCES** ═══

Bronstein, A. J. (1987). The pronunciation of American English. In *The Random House dictionary of the English language* (2nd ed.). New York: Random House.

Eisenson, J., & Solomon, H. (1970). Phonemic-graphemic correspondence. Unpublished study. Stanford, Calif.: Stanford University.

Gonzalez, G. (1988). Chicano English. In D. J. Bixler-Marquez & J. Ornstein-Galicia (Eds.), *Chicano speech in the bilingual classroom.* New York: Peter Lang.

Kenyon J. (1935). *American pronunciation.* Ann Arbor: George Wahr.

PART TWO

≡

VOICE
IMPROVEMENT

≡

When the voices of children are heard on the green
And laughing is heard on the hill,
My heart is at rest within my breast
And everything else is still.

—William Blake, *Nurse's Song*

The voice of the intellect is a soft one, but it does
not rest until it has gained a hearing.

—Sigmund Freud, *Future of an Illusion*

Don't look at me, sir, with—ah—in that tone
of voice.

—*Punch*, XCVII, 38, (1884)

CHAPTER 5

BREATHING FOR EFFECTIVE VOCALIZATION

＝＝＝

Stentor, in Homer's Iliad, is described as "The Great-Hearted one, who, with brazen voice, could shout as loud as fifty men." I assume that a brazen voice is a trumpetlike blaring, both bold and shameless. The qualities that Homer (about 700 B.C.E.) considered desirable and positive, especially in a great-hearted herald, are the antithesis of the attributes of an effective voice today. If a person were to emulate Stentor and produce a stentorian voice, he or she (much more likely a he) would probably soon require the help of a voice specialist—a physician such as Dr. Friedrich Brodnitz (1988)—to overcome the physical effects of vocal abuse. We would almost surely discover a person who was using excessive force at an inappropriate pitch range and breathing for shouting rather than for communicative speaking.

Although our experience does not reveal that most speakers breathe incorrectly, or use force inappropriately, or pitch their voices at wrong levels, knowledge of what can be done to improve voice production should be helpful to all of us. Certainly, if you are one who aspires to a better-than-ordinary voice, or who needs to use voice more than most persons do in your vocation or profession, you have an obligation to yourself as well as to your listeners to learn what students in the field of voice recommend about the use of force, pitch, and breathing.[1]

Earlier in our discussion of the mechanism of speech, we learned that breathing for speech calls for a modification of the normal respiratory cycle so that (1) the inspiration–expiration ratio is changed to provide a much longer period of exhalation than of inspiration, and (2) a steady stream of air is initiated and controlled by the speaker to ensure good tone. These modifications, we have found, are usually achieved most easily by the type of breathing that emphasizes abdominal activity.

At the outset, we would like to point out that good breathing for speech production is by no means synonymous with exaggerated, deep breathing. Many good speakers use no more breath for vigorous speaking, or public speaking, than they do for conversa-

---

[1] Lieberman (1977, Chaps. 2 and 6) considers the basic physiology of respiration for speech. Lieberman stresses the point that during respiration the elastic recoil of the lungs is normally sufficient to push the inspired air out of the lungs.

Boone (1983, Chap. 1) reviews some of the physical causes of voice defects (vocal abuse and misuse).

tional speech. Seldom is it necessary for any person to employ more than one fifth of his breath capacity for any ordinary vocal effort.

This is not to suggest that we have any objection to the practice of deep breathing. Most of us breathe (inspire and exhale) between twelve and fourteen times per minute. Some persons who practice deep breathing as part of meditation or voluntary relaxation can reduce the breath cycles by deep inhalations and controlled, slow exhalations to as few as four or five per minute. Though this cycle of breathing may be excellent for biogenics and for physical health in general, it is not a necessary procedure for breathing as far as most vocal needs are concerned. In keeping with this position, our emphasis is on control of the supply of breath rather than on deep breathing.

Breathing for speech should meet the following objectives:

1. It should afford the speaker an adequate and comfortable supply of breath with the least awareness and expenditure of effort.
2. The respiratory cycle — inhalation and exhalation — should be accomplished easily, quickly, and without interference with the flow of utterance.
3. The second objective implies ease of control over the outgoing breath so that breathing and phrasing — the grouping of ideas — can be correlated functions.

If these objectives are not established and are not habitual accomplishments, they can be most readily achieved through establishing abdominal control of breathing.

═══ ABDOMINAL BREATHING ═══

If we observe the breathing of a person or an animal that is sleeping on its back or side, we should be able to note that during inhalation the abdominal area moves upward or forward, whereas during exhalation the abdominal area recedes. Figure 2–4 (p. 24) visualizes what we can see in the way of abdominal activity, as well as what we cannot see in the way of diaphragmatic activity, for breathing that emphasizes abdominal control.

The essential point for us to appreciate is that in breathing characterized by the action of the abdominal muscles, the muscles of the abdomen relax in inhalation and contract in exhalation. When we learn how to contract or pull in the abdominal walls consciously, and how much and how fast to control such contraction, breathing for speech becomes *voluntary if needed*. If you are now exercising such control unconsciously, the suggested exercises that follow are not particularly important. For persons who cannot easily sustain a hum or a gentle whisper for from twenty to thirty seconds, these exercises should be followed. The exercises are designed to create awareness and conscious control of abdominal action in breathing.

Exercises for Awareness and Control of Abdominal Activity in Breathing

1. Lie on a couch or on a bed with a firm mattress. Spread your hands on the abdominal area immediately below the ribs so that your thumbs point away from it (toward the ribs) and your fingers point downward. Inhale as you would for normal, nonspeaking breathing. Your hands should rise during inhalation and fall with the abdomen during exhalation. If the action is reversed, then your breathing is incorrect and should be changed to bring about the suggested activity. Repeat until the suggested action is accomplished easily. Be sure that you are not wearing a tight belt or a confining article of clothing while doing this and the following exercises.

2. Sit in a relaxed position in a comfortable chair with a firm seat. Your feet should be flat on the floor. Place your hands as in Exercise 1. Now the abdominal walls should push forward during inhalation and pull in during exhalation.

3. Repeat Exercise 2. Then inhale gently for about five seconds and exhale slowly, sustaining the exhalation for ten seconds. If you find yourself out of breath before the end of the ten-second period, then you have probably exhaled too quickly. Try the exercise again, intentionally slowing down the exhalation.

4. Inhale fully and then breathe out slowly and completely. Your hands should still be following the movement of the abdominal walls. Repeat, but this time press gently but firmly with your hands to force the expulsion of air from your lungs. Repeat, counting to yourself while exhaling. At this point you should be able to count for about thirty seconds before becoming uncomfortable.

5. Repeat, but this time vocalize a clear *ah* sound while exhaling. *Start your vocalization the moment you begin to exhale.* Stop before becoming uncomfortable. Repeat, vocalizing a sustained *hum* while exhaling. The *ah* and *hum* should be sustained longer than a nonvocalized exhalation.

6. Inhale deeply and then count out evenly and slowly until you feel the need for a second breath. *Maintain even pitch and loudness levels.* Repeat, but this time keep your hands at your sides and concentrate on a gradual pulling in of the abdominal wall during the counting. You should be able to count to at least twenty on a sustained exhalation. In any event, continue to practice until a count of at least fifteen is attained. With continued practice, a count of twenty to thirty (at the rate of two numbers per second) should become possible after a normal inhalation, and a full thirty-second count after a deep inhalation.

7. With hands at your sides, repeat this exercise on two successive breaths. Be certain that you do not exhale to a point of discomfort. Nor should you inhale so deeply that some air has to be exhaled for the sake of comfort.

8. Repeat, reciting the alphabet instead of counting. Avoid wasting breath between utterance of the letters. Note how far you are able to go on a single normal breath and on a single deep breath.

9. Repeat, whispering the alphabet. Note the letter you reach before requiring a second breath. Depending on the degree of whisper, this might be only a third or a half of the number of letters of your vocalized effort. This is normal. A whisper is wasteful of breath.

10. Count, with vocalization, in groups of three. Avoid exhalation during pauses. Did you come close to the number you reached in counting without groupings? If you did not, then you probably exhaled between groups of numbers. Try it again until the two counts are about even.

11. Repeat Exercise 10, using the alphabet instead of counting.

12. Recite the months of the year with pauses after March, June, and September. You should have no difficulty reciting all twelve months even with "seasonal" pauses.

13. Try to say each of the following sentences on a single breath.
    a. Stephen's voice expressed his humility.
    b. Spain is in the southwest corner of Europe.
    c. The night was cooled by a gentle breeze.
    d. Those who learn nothing have nothing to forget.
    e. When we persuade others, we often convince ourselves.
    f. There is little that is new except that which is forgotten.

14. If you had no difficulty with the single sentences, then try to produce these longer sentences and couplets, each on a single, sustained breath. Do not, however, force the expulsion of breath beyond a point of comfort.
    a. Adlai Stevenson advised that a wise man does not try to hurry history.
    b. Plato held that rhetoric was the art of ruling the minds of men.
    c. An Englishman thinks he is moral when he is only uncomfortable.
                                          —George Bernard Shaw, *Man and Superman*
    d. In *The Devil's Disciple*, Shaw observed that indifference rather than hate was the essence of inhumanity.
    e. For he who fights and runs away
       May live to fight another day;
                                          —Oliver Goldsmith, *The Art of Poetry*
    f. Upon what meat doth this our Caesar feed,
       That he is grown so great?
                                          —William Shakespeare, *Julius Caesar*, Act I
    g. Party is the madness of the many for the gain of the few.
                                          —Alexander Pope, *Thoughts on Various Subjects*

    The following are more demanding, but you should be equal to them.

    h. We can secure other people's approval, if we do right and try hard; but our own is worth a hundred of it, and no way has been found of securing that.
                                          —Mark Twain, *Pudd'nhead Wilson's New Calendar*,
                                          Chapter 2

i. I often think it's comical
How nature always does contrive
That every boy and every gal,
That's born into the world alive,
Is either a little Liberal,
Or else a little Conservative!

— Sir William S. Gilbert, *Iolanthe*, Act I

The following exercises involve the use of speech sounds that have an aspirate quality. They are normally more wasteful of breath than most of the previous exercises. They are, however, important in establishing breath control because much of what we say includes nonvocalized (voiceless) sounds as well as those that have a definite whispered, or fricative, quality.

EXERCISES FOR ESTABLISHING BREATH CONTROL

1. Inhale normally and then release the breath while producing the sound *s*. Be sure the sound is evenly maintained. Try to sustain the *s* for ten seconds. Repeat with the sound *sh*, then *th* as in *think*, and *f* as in *fall*.
2. Inhale deeply, but avoid discomfort. Repeat Exercise 1. Compare these efforts with the length of time for a sustained *m* or *ah*. You are not likely to sustain any of these breathy sounds as long as *m* or *ah*, but you should come fairly close.
3. Try saying each of the following sentences on a single breath. If you do not succeed the first time, try a deeper inhalation on successive trials. Do not intentionally whisper.
   a. An ancient Arab proverb informs us that no person is likely to complain of fatigue on a day marked by victory.
   b. A Chinese proverb reminds us that a single picture is worth more than ten thousand words.
   c. Is it true that you can always tell a Harvard or a Stanford University student, but you can't tell her or him very much?
   d. The sun sank slowly and was followed by darkness and an enveloping, foggy chill.
   e. Caspar Smith had a reputation as an excellent conversationalist because he practiced listening in respectful silence.
   f. Some cynical literary critics profess that several of Shakespeare's plays were written by another author with the same name.
4. If you have been successful with all of the sentences, then try these couplets, each on a single breath. If you pause at the end of the line, try not to exhale at the pause.
   a. "Home is the place where, when you have to go there,
   They have to take you in."

   — Robert Frost, *The Death of the Hired Man*

   b. A moral, sensible, and well-bred man
      Will not affront me,—and no other can.

                                — William Cowper, *Conversation*

   c. My life is like a stroll upon the beach,
      As near the ocean's edge as I can go.

                          — Henry David Thoreau, *The Fisher's Boy*

   d. Golden lads and girls all must,
      As chimney-sweepers, come to dust.

                      — William Shakespeare, *Cymbeline,* Act IV, ii

   e. Thunder is good, thunder is impressive; but it is lightning that does the work.

                        — Mark Twain, *Letter to an Unidentified Person*

   f. Can I see another's woe
      And not be in sorrow too?
      Can I see another's grief,
      And not seek for kind relief?

                     — William Blake, *On Another's Sorrow*

5. Try uttering the following longer sentences and triplets, if possible, on a single breath. However, if you do not succeed, be sure you pause for breath between phrases (breath groups).

   a. He who would distinguish the true from the false must have an adequate idea of what is true and false.

                             — Benedict Spinoza, *Ethics*

   b. We must think of our whole economics in terms of a preventive pathology instead of a curative pathology. Don't oppose forces; use them.

                           — Buckminster Fuller,
                           No More Secondhand God

   c. Grow old along with me!
      The best is yet to be,
      The last of life, for which
         the first was made.

                      — Robert Browning, *Rabbi Ben Ezra*

   d. Music resembles poetry; in each
      Are nameless graces which no methods teach,
      And which a master-hand alone can reach.

                      — Alexander Pope, *Essay on Criticism*

   e. Education is what you have left over after you have forgotten everything you have learned.

                                 — Anonymous

   f. Every succeeding scientific discovery makes greater nonsense of old-time conceptions of sovereignty.

                             — Sir Anthony Eden,
               Speech in the House of Commons, 1945

══ CLAVICULAR BREATHING ══

As a basic principle, it is not the amount of breath but evenness and control of the breath stream that is important for speaking. Therefore, any technique that emphasizes increasing the quantity of air for its own sake should not be held in high regard. This, of course, is not to suggest that deep breathing as an exercise to fill and empty your lungs does not have its virtues. However, even if the quantity of air were important, as it might be for public speaking, it is usually best achieved through deep breathing with abdominal and lower rib-cage activity and control than through clavicular breathing which, at best, does no more than elevate the chest as a whole. In fact, clavicular breathing tends to be shallow rather than deep and requires more frequent inhalations than does breathing with abdominal control. Clavicular breathing is inefficient in that it demands too much effort for too little usable breath. Furthermore, it has the disadvantage of producing a tendency for the muscles of the larynx and throat to become too tense for proper vocalization and comfortable reinforcement of tone.

To check on whether you have any tendency toward clavicular breathing, stand before a full-length mirror and breathe deeply. Relax, then exhale fully. Repeat twice or more until you "get the picture." Note, and correct, any inclination of your shoulders to be appreciably elevated, or of your chest as a whole to be raised. Abdominal breathing calls for little or no movement of the shoulders or the upper chest. If any movement is observed, it should be of the lower-chest and abdominal areas. Usually this procedure requires a profile rather than a full-front view.

As an added check, as well as an exercise to correct a tendency toward clavicular breathing, try the following: Place your hands on your chest with your fingers spread and the thumbs pointing toward the collarbone. Take a deep breath, then say the days of the week. Observe — and, if necessary, use the pressure of your hands to prevent — any appreciable upward movement of the upper chest and shoulders. For variety, the exercise might be done with counting from one through ten or reciting the alphabet in sequences from *a* through *l* and *m* through *z*. If upper-chest movement is inhibited, the normal compensatory action will bring about the desired movement of the abdominal and the lower-chest muscles. Be certain that the movement is forward during inhalation and inward during exhalation.

══ BREATHING AND PHRASING ══

In the exercises to establish abdominal breathing and an awareness of breath control, our emphasis was on sustaining a sound, a series of words, or a sentence on a single breath. For ordinary conversational speech, and for most public speaking purposes, the length of uninterrupted utterance is not as important as the interruption of a unit of thought because of the need for additional breath. The occasions are infrequent when a speaker needs to utter more than twelve to fifteen syllables on a single breath. You must learn to anticipate inhalation, and to stop at an appropriate point to inhale. Speakers who learn this will avoid having to stop at an inappropriate point because they cannot continue speaking without another breath. The appropriate or natural stopping places are at the ends of units of thought, *between phrases or sentences*. Unless the speaker is reading or reciting verse with regular meter, the units of thought are likely to be of varying lengths. Breathing must therefore be adjusted to anticipated needs. For example, if you cannot comfortably quote Emerson on a single breath to the effect that "His heart was as great as the world, but there was no room in it to hold the memory of a wrong," you have a choice of at least two stopping places. Without doing violence to the thought, stop at the places indicated by the vertical lines: "His heart was as great as the world || but there was no room in it || to hold the memory of a wrong." Similarly, the sentence "Christopher Morley held that the three ingredients in the good life are learning, earning, and yearning" can be spoken with pauses for phrasing as "Christopher Morley held || that the three ingredients in the good life || are learning, earning, and yearning." Incidentally, we may note that some, but not all of the units of thought (breath-phrase units) are marked off for us by punctuation. Some units of thought have no punctuation marks. As a reader you must, on the basis of meaning, decide where and whether to phrase. The good vocal phraser uses punctuation as a guide but is not a slave to it.

A speaker with a fair breath capacity and good breath control might easily go as far as the second vertical line before stopping for a breath. Unless you feel equal to the entire sentence, however, you should not try to go beyond the second vertical line because to do so would mean interrupting a unit of thought in order to inhale.

In Exercises 1–5 that immediately follow, possible stops for inhalation are indicated by vertical lines. In terms of your own breath capacity, mark off the places at which you plan to inhale. Inhale briefly at these places so that there is no suggestion of awkward pausing. Try to inhale as infrequently as possible so that the reading does not become jerky. Maintain abdominal control of breathing. If necessary, place your hands on the abdominal wall to feel the pushing away at the inhalations and the pulling in at the exhalations while reading aloud.

EXERCISES FOR ABDOMINAL BREATHING AND PHRASING

1. Breathe in as you would for inhalation during casual conversation; then count at the rate of two numbers per second, pausing — and if necessary, inhaling — at the marked places.

    1-2-3-4-5-6-7-8-9-10-11 || 12-13-14-15-16-17-18-19-20-21

    The first grouping should have been produced easily on a single breath; the second would be somewhat more difficult because of the additional syllables.

2. Repeat Exercise 1, but this time pause and renew your breath supply after fourteen; then count from fifteen through twenty-one.

3. Count as long as you can on a single deep breath, but avoid becoming uncomfortable either because of too deep an inhalation or too exhaustive an exhalation. Note the point at which you pause for breath. Then count again, but this time intentionally pause and inhale two numbers earlier in the sequence than where you needed to pause the first time. Count again to the same number.

4. Recite the alphabet, pausing — and inhaling, if necessary — only at the marked places. Be sure to pause even though you do not need to inhale.

    a-b-c-d-e-f-g-h ‖ i-j-k-l-m-n-o-p-q ‖ r-s-t-u-v-w-x-y-z

    Were you able to go beyond the first group? With practice, the entire alphabet should be recited easily after a single moderate inhalation.

5. Read the following sentences aloud, pausing — and breathing, if necessary — at the marked places. In addition to the initial breath, it should not be necessary to inhale more than once for each sentence.
    a. Sheridan advised that conscience ‖ has no more to do with gallantry ‖ than it has to do with politics.
    b. A classic is something that everybody wants to have read ‖ and nobody wants to read.
    — Mark Twain, *The Disappearance of Literature*
    c. The more things a man is ashamed of ‖ the more respectable he is.
    d. Violence does not and cannot exist by itself; ‖ it is invariably intertwined with *the lie*.
    — Alexander Solzhenitsyn, Nobel Lecture, 1972
    e. Coughing in the theater ‖ is not a respiratory ailment. ‖ It is a criticism.
    — Alan Jay Lerner, *My Fair Lady*

6. In the following exercises, read the material aloud to determine where you need to stop for breath. Pause to indicate phrasing, but inhale only when you cannot go on comfortably to the next phrase on the remaining breath.
    a. The philosopher-poet Kahlil Gibran advised us to allow for space in our togetherness.
    b. The realistic cynic Aldo Selfridge observed that things are not as good as they used to be and probably never were.
    c. I am in the habit of looking not so much to the nature of a gift as to the spirit in which it is offered.
    — Robert Louis Stevenson, *New Arabian Nights*
    d. Democracy is the recurrent suspicion that more than half of the people are right more than half of the time.
    — E. B. White, *World Government and Peace*
    e. As citizens of this democracy, you are the rulers and the ruled, the lawgivers and the law-abiding, the beginning and the end.
    — Adlai Stevenson, Speech, Chicago, 1952

f. Adam was but human — this explains it all. He did not want the apple for the apple's sake, he wanted it only because it was forbidden.
— Mark Twain, *Pudd'nhead Wilson*

g. One will rarely err if extreme actions be ascribed to vanity, ordinary actions to habit, and mean actions to fear.
— Friedrich Nietzsche, *Human, All Too Human*

h. An anonymous saying informs us:
   Fools' names, like fools' faces
   Are often seen in public places.

i. Hippocrates advised: "There are in fact two things, science and opinion; the former begets knowledge, the latter ignorance."

Avoiding Waste of Breath

If while executing the exercises earlier in the chapter you had difficulty in counting up to fifteen on a single breath, you may have wasted too much breath in the vocal effort. The most likely cause of wasted breath is a failure to bring the vocal bands close enough together to prevent leakage of air during vocalized speech efforts. Whispered or semi-whispered speech is necessarily wasteful of breath because the vocal bands are kept fully or partially open. This effect may be noted in Figure 5–1, which shows the positions of the voice bands in quiet breathing, whispering, and vocalized speaking. In order to overcome breathiness, it will help first to become aware of a speech effort, which, by the nature of the sounds employed, is necessarily breathy.

PRACTICE EXERCISES

The sentences that follow include a number of voiceless fricative and breath-stop sounds that are normally and appropriately produced with a breathy quality. Hold your hand, palm turned toward your face, about six inches in front of your mouth as you say:

a. The ship set sail in the chill of the morning fog.
b. Paula and Fred liked to watch football.
c. Few of us can resist listening to short and simple scandals.
d. Francine insisted that she had less privacy than a fish in a glass bowl.
e. Except for sophisticated hikers, the terrain was too steep and hazardous for crossing without a guide.

In contrast with these sentences, those that follow contain only voiced sounds and few that have a plosive quality. Say the following, again holding your hand in front of your mouth to feel the difference in breathiness.

a. Lou will do all a man may do.
b. Belle was never ill.

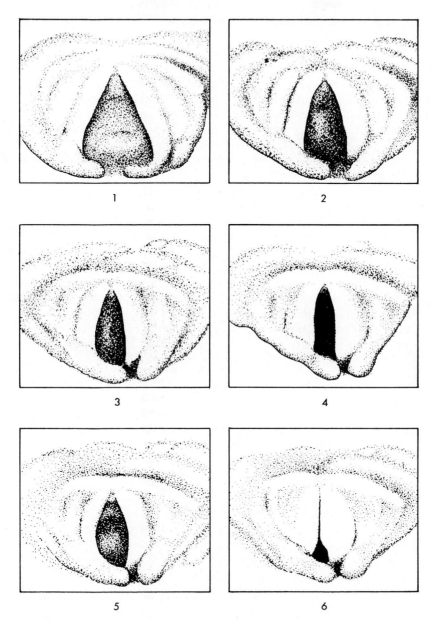

Figure 5–1   Diagrams based on high-speed photos showing changes in positions of vocal bands from quiet breathing *(1, 2)* to whispering *(3, 4, 5)* to vocalization *(6)*.

    c. The boys and girls ran around the bend.

    d. None knew the old woman.

    e. We were all willing, able, and ready.

The following sentences contain a few sounds that are normally breathy. Try to say them with as little waste of breath as possible. Shorten all *f, v, th, s, z,* and *sh* sounds to reduce the length of these normally breathy consonants. With good breath control, each sentence should require only a single inhalation.

    a. Henry Thoreau had three chairs in his house; one was for solitude; two were for friendship; three were for society.

    b. Sometimes the spin-offs of inventions are worth more than the initially invented products.

    c. The siren warned us that a house was on fire.

    d. Despite the fierce storm, the ship set out to sea.

    e. In his essay "The Square Egg," H. H. Munro advised, "In baiting a mouse-trap with cheese, always leave room for the mouse."

Excessive breathiness may be a result of carrying over the aspirate quality of a sound to the succeeding vowel. You may avoid this effect, or reduce it, by taking care not to prolong the aspirate sounds and to emphasize the full vocalization of the vowels and diphthongs. Special caution is necessary when the initial sound is an *h*, as it is a particularly breath-consuming sound. With these thoughts in mind, try to say the following pairs of words so that there is no more aspiration on the vowel or diphthong of the second word of the pair than there is on those of the first. There should, of course, be no aspirate quality in the first word of each pair.

bye	high	arm	charm
ale	pale	own	shown
oar	core	arc	park
air	fair	eel	feel
ear	tear	mold	hold
add	fad	end	send
am	ham	will	dill
awe	saw	aid	spade

In each of the following sentences, emphasize the production of the vowel or diphthong sounds. Despite the temptation provided by initial aspirate sounds, avoid an excessive carry-over of breathiness to the succeeding sounds.

    a. Harry wished his friends health and happiness.

    b. Hoping against hope is hoping still.

    c. Paul hiked four miles through the forest.

    d. People need not be poets to be impressed by the coming of spring.

    e. George Eliot wrote that because a woman's hopes are woven of sunbeams, a shadow can quickly disperse them.

    f. Goldsmith pointed out that people seldom improve when they simulate themselves.

    g. In one of his campaign speeches, Adlai Stevenson asserted, "A hungry man is not a free man."

    h. You do not have to shout. But if you whisper . . . the whisper had better
       be good.   —Robert K. Leavitt, *Voyages and Discovery*
    i. The test of a first-rate intelligence is the ability to hold two opposed ideas
       in the mind at the same time, and still retain the ability to function.
                        —F. Scott Fitzgerald, *The Crack-up*
    j. In *The Course of Empire*, Bernard De Voto observed: "History abhors deter-
       minism but cannot tolerate chance."

AFFECTED OR IMITATIVE BREATHINESS

Many persons vocalize with a breathy quality out of habit; few by choice. The choice is
not always a conscious one. It may have had its beginning in an imitation born of
admiration of a popular figure. For adolescents and young adults, the figure is often a
performer, a star of radio, screen, or television. So-called "sultry-voiced" singers influence the vocal efforts of many high school and college adolescents who want to be
sultry-voiced whether or not they can sing. Many young children have husky and·
breathy voices because of unconscious imitation of their mothers, and a few, perhaps,
of their fathers. Unfortunately, excessive breathiness frequently has an adverse effect on
the laryngeal mechanism as well as on the ability of the speaker to maintain as long a
series of phrases or sentences as the nonbreathy speaker. The overall result is a vocal
habit that loses its attractiveness in the postadolescent period. Breathy vocalizers then
find themselves fatigued speakers and occasionally ones with thickened vocal bands. If
this becomes the case, then considerable vocal reeducation is in order. Good voice
production is achieved with good breath control in an appropriate pitch range. With
such control, a clear rather than a breathy quality should be established throughout the
normal pitch range. Clear tones are then produced with a minimum use of air for an
efficient and maximum vocal effort.

    The following exercises are intended as a general review opportunity for the practice
of breath control. In doing them, make certain (1) that there is no evidence of clavicular
breathing; (2) that abdominal activity and lower-chest activity characterize the breathing
for vocalizations; (3) that inhalations are correlated with units of meaning; and (4) that
there is no waste of breath at pauses for phrasing when there is no need for inhalation,
or because of excessive aspiration on specific speech sounds, or as a characteristic of the
vocal effort as a whole.

EXERCISES FOR PRACTICE OF BREATH CONTROL

    a. The most beautiful thing we can experience is the mysterious. It is the
       source of all true art and science.
                      —Albert Einstein, *What I Believe*

b. Man consists of body, mind, and imagination. His body is faulty, his mind untrustworthy, but his imagination has made him remarkable.
—John Masefield, *Shakespeare and Spiritual Life*

c. Speech is civilization itself. The word, even the most contradictory word, preserves contact — it is silence which isolates.
—Thomas Mann, *The Magic Mountain*

d. Training is everything. The peach was once a bitter almond; cauliflower is nothing but cabbage with a college education.
—Mark Twain, *Pudd'nhead Wilson*

e. Laughter is not at all a bad beginning for a friendship, and it is far the best ending for one.
—Oscar Wilde, *The Picture of Dorian Gray*

f. Horace Mann considered the telling of truth a serious responsibility. He advised, "You need not tell all the truth, unless to those who have a right to know it all. But let all you tell be truth."

g. The time which we have at our disposal every day is elastic; the passions that we feel every day expand it; those that we inspire contract it; and habit fills up what remains.
—Marcel Proust, *Within a Budding Grove*

h. Strange, when you come to think of it, that of all the countless folk who have lived before our time on this planet not one is known in history or in legend as having died of laughter.
—Max Beerbohm, *Laughter*

i. A good society is a means to a good life for those who compose it; not something having a kind of excellence on its own account.
—Bertrand Russell, *Authority and the Individual*

j. Future shock . . . the shattering stress and disorientation that we induce in individuals by subjecting them to too much change in too short a time.
—Alvin Toffler, *Future Shock*, Chapter 1

REFERENCES AND SUGGESTED READINGS

Andrews, M. L., & Summers, A. (1988). *Voice therapy for adolescents.* San Diego, Calif.: College-Hill Press. (The authors describe the major physical and psychological causes of voice problems. They recommend making explicit contracts for establishing goals, expectations, and procedures for dealing with individual voice problems.)

Aronson, A. E. (1985). *Clinical voice disorders.* New York: Thieme, 1985. (This work is an interdisciplinary approach — by physicians and speech clinicians — for the treatment of voice disorders.)

Boone, D. R. (1983). *The voice and voice therapy.* Englewood Cliffs, N.J.: Prentice-Hall. (The author reviews some of the physical causes of voice disorders. Chapter 1 considers appropriate breathing for voice production.)

Brodnitz, F. S. (1988). *Keep your voice healthy* (2nd ed.). San Diego, Calif.: College-Hill Press. (The author, a physician with a special interest in voice, offers advice on vocal hygiene.)

Colton, R. H. (1990). *Understanding voice problems*. Baltimore: Williams & Wilkins. (This is a relatively technical consideration that provides a physiological perspective for the understanding of voice problems.)

Greene, M. C. (1980). *The voice and its disorders* (4th ed.). Baltimore: Williams & Wilkins. (This is a precise, nontechnical, and clearly written book on voice production and voice disorders.)

Laver, J. (1980). *The phonetic description of voice quality*. Cambridge, England: Cambridge University Press. (The author applies phonetic principles in his description of vocal qualities. The treatment is detailed, technical, and generously illustrated.)

Lieberman, P. (1977). *Speech perception and acoustic phonetics*. New York: Macmillan. (The author believes that the reader will understand his exposition even though he or she may lack any knowledge of mathematics or physics beyond the high school level. His book "provides a step-by-step introduction that starts with simple examples that put the subject into perspective.")

Perkins, W. H. (1986). *Functional anatomy of speech, language, and hearing*. San Diego, Calif.: College-Hill Press. (This monograph is a primer that includes a consideration of the vocal mechanism.)

Wilson, D. K. (1979). *Voice problems of children* (2nd ed.). Baltimore: Williams & Wilkins. (Although this book is primarily about the voice problems of children, the causes of these problems and the author's advice holds as well for adolescents and adults.)

CHAPTER 6

PRODUCTION OF CLEAR TONES

In this chapter we will consider how to produce clear vocal tones and to avoid such negative qualities as hoarseness and click-like sounds (glottal fry) in speaking. Hoarseness is often associated with excessive breathiness, glottal fry with tension in the larynx and pharynx. We will build on what we have learned about breathing for effective vocalization as we expand our discussion.

Voice, we now realize, is a product of integrated muscular activity. The combination of tendinous tissue and muscles that constitute the vocal bands is set in vibration as a result of integrated activity of the muscles of respiration and those controlling laryngeal action. When the integration is right and the vocal bands are brought together (approximated) closely enough so that there is sufficient resistance to the column of air being forced up from the lungs, voice is produced. If the vocal bands are not sufficiently approximated to create adequate resistance to the column of air, the result is either a semivocalized effort or unvocalized breathing, depending on the degree of approximation (see Figure 5–1). Our immediate concern is to establish the concept and technique for the initiation of good, clear tones.

Tone, or *vocal tone,* as we will use these terms, is the vocal product considered with reference to its attributes: quality, pitch, loudness, and duration.

Good tones are free from the effects of tension or strain. Good tones are initiated with ease, appropriately reinforced by the resonating cavities, and sustained with ease. Tonal (vocal) impurities result most frequently from tensions of the muscles of the throat and neck that interfere with the free action of the muscles of the larynx, and so of the vocal bands. Tonal impurities may arise indirectly from incorrect breathing habits that may be associated with laryngeal tension. They may also be caused by inappropriate resonance.

In the absence of any structural defect of the voice-producing mechanism, of a defect of hearing that makes vocal monitoring difficult, or of any emotional disturbance associated with either excessive or inadequate muscular tonicity, reasonably good vocal tones should be possible for all speakers. Some speakers, we realize, have mechanisms whose parts are so well combined that they have excellent voices without effort or training. Others may not be so fortunate in the structure of their vocal mechanisms. For them, effort and training are necessary to make the most of their vocal instruments. Our concern is to consider how you can use your voice mechanism so that, without too much effort, you will be able to initiate and sustain good vocal tones.

═══ INITIATION OF TONE ═══

To initiate and maintain good tone, the vocal mechanism must be *ready for vocalization*. Readiness implies anticipation and preparation. For voice production, this means that the vocal bands must be aligned (approximated) a moment before the column of air is forced up from the lungs to set them into action. If the column of air precedes the approximation of the vocal bands, then the vocal product will begin with a whisper or an unvocalized breath. The vocal bands must be tense enough to set up resistance to the column of air, but not so tense as to be fully successful in their resistance. With excessive tension (hypertension), the vocal bands may not be able to vibrate. With a lack of sufficient tension (hypotension), vibration may take place, but with an accompanying air leakage or breathiness. What is needed is sufficient tension to require a forceful, sustained column of air to set and maintain the vocal bands in action. In brief, the tension should be just enough to permit the sustained column of air to produce an even fluttering of the vocal bands (see the discussion in Chapter 2). Although the voice can be produced even though the laryngeal tensions become excessive, the vocal tones become strained and generally unpleasant.

The exercises that follow will help to establish awareness of *proper laryngeal tension* as well as *readiness for vocalization*.

Before undertaking these exercises, review the discussion on the avoidance of breathiness in Chapter 5.

═══

EXERCISES FOR ESTABLISHING
READINESS TO VOCALIZE

1. Contract the throat muscles as you would to swallow some food or water. Note the sensation of the contracted muscles. Now open your mouth as if to produce a gentle *ah* sound. Do your throat muscles feel more or less tense than they did when you pretended to swallow? Unless they are more relaxed than for swallowing, they are likely to be too tense for the initiation of a good tone. Note the sensation of the contracted muscles so that you will know what to avoid. Be sure that your *ah* production is gentle and sustained.
2. *Yawn gently* with your mouth half open. Breathe in and out through your mouth. Note the feeling of air in the back of the throat. Now swallow, and contrast the easy breathing sensations with those in swallowing. If the yawning is gentle and the breathing easy, your throat muscles should be relaxed. This is the state of muscle tonus needed for vocalization.
3. Sit comfortably in a chair with your feet flat on the floor. Permit your head to drop to your chest as if your head were a dead weight. Yawn gently and then breathe in and out three or four times through your mouth. Note the sensation. Now swallow, and again contrast the tonus of the throat muscles in swallowing with that in gentle yawning. Repeat the gentle yawning and the

easy mouth breathing until the sensation of relaxed throat muscles is fixed in your mind.

4. Stand erect but at ease. Repeat Exercise 3 in a standing position.

5. In a standing position, with the throat muscles relaxed, say the *vowels* only of the following words, each to a slow count of from one to three: *alms, all, Alps, ooze, eel.* Now vocalize from one vowel to the next without interruption. You should be able to note somewhat increased throat and laryngeal tension for the vowels of *ooze* and *eel* as compared with those of *alms, all,* and *Alps.* This change in tension is proper if the different vowel values are to be produced. Try, however, to avoid excessive tension.

6. Open your mouth as though for a gentle yawn, but instead of yawning say *ha, how, ho, ha, haw, ho.* Next try the sentence *Who am I?* These efforts should begin with some breathiness on the words that begin with an *h* sound, but the breath should not be noticeably carried over to the vowel that follows. Be sure that you maintain a relaxed throat throughout the exercise.

7. With a relaxed throat, count from one to ten, emphasizing the activity of the lips and the tongue. Try to become aware of oral activity in the *front of your mouth.* Now, count from one to twenty. Do not force your exhalation beyond a point of comfort. If you note any tendency to tighten the throat muscles, it may be because you are attempting too much speech on a single exhalation. Pause to inhale before excessive tension sets in.

8. Say the alphabet while emphasizing activity in the front of the mouth. Do not attempt to go beyond the letter *k* on your first attempt. On successive attempts, go as far as you can in the alphabet up to the point of laryngeal or throat tension. You may note a feeling of lip fatigue. If so, it is likely that you do not habitually articulate with sufficient activity at the front of the mouth. With practice, the feeling of fatigue should disappear.

9. Read the following materials aloud, always maintaining a relaxed throat. Make certain that you are *set for vocalization* before you begin to speak. If at any time your throat muscles become tense, or you become aware of laryngeal tension, return to Exercises 1–7.

    a. In his *Institute of Oratory,* Quintilian observed, "The voice of a person is as easily distinguished by the ear as the face by the eye."

    b. James Abbott McNeill Whistler, an American etcher and painter, spent much of his active life as an artist in England.

    c. All progress is based upon a universal innate desire on the part of every organism to live beyond its income.

    — Samuel Butler, *What Is Man?*

    d. A handful of sand is an anthology of the universe.

    — David McCord, *Once and for All*

    e. Andrew was unfortunately not inclined to let facts get in the way of his opinions.

    f.   But what am I?
    An infant crying in the night:
    An infant crying for the light:
    And with no language but a cry

    — Alfred, Lord Tennyson, *In Memoriam*

g. Aristotle held that liberty and equality will be best attained when all persons alike share in the government to the utmost.

h. Emerson asked, "Can anybody remember when the times were not hard and money not scarce?"

i. James Thurber argued that often emotional chaos is remembered in tranquility.

j. Albright admitted that, though it was not unique, his idea of an agreeable person is one who is apt to agree with him.

k. Ah, but a man's reach should exceed his grasp,
   Or what's a heaven for?
   — Robert Browning, *Andrea del Sarto*

l. Our revels now are ended. These our actors
   As I foretold you, were all spirits, and
   Are melted into air, into thin air,
   And like the baseless fabric of this vision
   The cloudcapped towers, the gorgeous palaces,
   The solemn temples, the great globe itself,
   Yea, all which it inherit, shall dissolve,
   And like this insubstantial pageant faded
   Leave not a wrack behind. We are such stuff
   As dreams are made on; and our little life
   Is rounded with a sleep.
   — William Shakespeare, *The Tempest*, Act IV, i

m. In his essay on *Civil Disobedience*, the individualist Henry Thoreau advised, "Any man more right than his neighbor constitutes a majority of one."

n. The new electronic interdependence recreates the world in the image of a global village.
   — Marshall McLuhan, *The Medium Is the Message*

Glottal Attack or Glottal Catch

The *glottis* is the opening in the larynx between the vocal bands. *Glottal* refers to sounds that are produced as a result of tension that stops the air flow and is followed by a sudden release of tension. This results in a "pop" or "click" sound. When this action is unconscious and unintentional, after the initial glottal attack voice production may continue with a strained and strident quality. We will soon consider how to avoid glottal attack and the associated undesirable voice quality.

Vocal Fry

In contrast to the high-pitch register associated with glottal initiation is a voice quality identified as *vocal fry*. This negative quality usually occurs at the lower part of a speaker's pitch range and is often characteristically associated with hoarseness. Subjectively, the vocal output sounds like rapid-fire corn popping during ongoing articulation. One of my students who listened to a taping of vocal fry said that the speaker's voice sounded to her as though he were engaged in rapid gargling while talking. Usually if the speaker can follow the direction to "stay out of the lower depths" of his or her pitch range, vocal fry is reduced. How to initiate vocalization at the optimum pitch within an appropriate pitch range is considered in the next chapter.

How to Avoid Glottal Initiation

In the first page of this chapter, we noted that human voice is a product of integrated muscular activity. Integration implies synchronization — timing — necessary to produce the desired vocal result. The glottal attack or glottal catch, unless intentionally produced, is an expression of faulty synchronization. Basically, phonation that is characterized by glottal catch results from excessive tension of the laryngeal muscles. This, in turn, demands more than the normal amount of energy to provide the breath pressure to set the vocal bands in motion. The consequence of this combination of factors is that the vocal bands are violently blown apart, producing a "catch" or "click" instead of the even and controlled phonation required for "flutter" action. Terms such as "pop," "click," and "crackle" are used to identify glottal initiation.

Glottal-attack sounds most often occur on the first word of a phrase that begins with a vowel, especially for the higher-pitched (tense) vowels in such words as *each, it, ease, aim,* and *use.* In some languages, such as those of the Zulu (Bantu) and the African Bush People, click sounds have phonemic (consonant) value. This is also so in Turkish and in the Scottish dialect of English. Although considered substandard, such sounds are characteristic of Cockney English.

If you are still uncertain about a tendency to initiate phonation with a glottal attack, the following added explanation illustrates what you should generally avoid. A glottal catch sound is normally and appropriately produced when you clear your throat with an unvocalized cough. You can feel this stroke, click, or flap sounds of the vocal bands by gently holding your thumb and index finger just below the Adam's apple. If you add voice to the cough, the product is likely to be an "ugh" sound.

The exercises in the first part of this chapter to establish proper tension and readiness for vocalization should be reviewed before undertaking the following:

EXERCISES FOR OVERCOMING GLOTTAL PHONATION

1. Produce the sound *aw* as in *awful* with intentional breathiness (in a semi-whisper). Repeat, prolonging the *aw* for the equivalent of a count of six. Decrease the breathiness so that on the final two counts the *aw* is fully vocalized. Maintain a relaxed throat so that there is neither glottal initiation nor tension as vocalization increases.
2. Repeat Exercise 1, using the vowels of *alms, ooze, ohms, any,* and *ease.* Be especially careful that on the last vowel there is no excessive strain or glottal "explosion."

3. Try to say each of the following words without initial glottalization. If you note a glottal attack, prefix a lengthened *h* before each of the words, and move from the *h* to the word without increasing the laryngeal tension and without glottalization.

eel	eager	I'll	even	eke	eon
inch	arm	ohm	ale	eat	easy
instant	ant	own	at	am	east
only	all	ill	ace	amp	Alfred

4. Repeat Exercise 3, prefixing the sound *m* if there is any tendency to a glottal attack. Repeat with an initial *n*.

5. Try each of the following sentences, being especially careful to avoid glottalization on the initial vowels. Words that begin with vowels *within a phrase* should be pronounced as though they were actually linked, or blended, to the last sound of the preceding word. The sounds that are most likely to be glottalized are in italics.
   a. *A*ndrew and *E*ve *e*njoy *all a*ctive sports.
   b. *All* of us must *at o*ne time *i*nhabit *our own i*sland.
   c. *E*dward *e*njoyed cakes *a*nd *a*le.
   d. *An o*hm *is a* unit *of e*lectrical resistance.
   e. *It is e*asy to grow *a*sters *in* the *e*ast.

6. The following phrases may be somewhat more difficult because they contain many normally tense vowels in initial positions and so provide opportunities for glottal initiation. If you initiate the vocalization with just enough tension for the proper articulation of the vowel, but with no more than that much tension, the glottal shock should be avoided.

eerie images	eat an eel
easy access	apt and alert
up and over	apprehensive attitudes
every opportunity	insistent inclination
each event	esoteric antics
in every instance	anxious acts
any avenue	alien enemy
ancient egress	alternate actions
inner insights	euphonic eulogy
evil eye	evident eviction

7. The following selections offer opportunity for additional practice.
   a. There is a feeling of Eternity in youth, which makes us amends for everything. To be young is to be as one of the Immortal Gods.
      —William Hazlitt, *The Feeling of Eternity in Youth*
   b. Inconsistencies of opinion, arising from changes of circumstances, are often justifiable.
      —Daniel Webster, Speech, July 25, 1846
   c. History is the essence of innumerable biographies.
      —Thomas Carlyle, *On History*

d. I am in earnest. I will not equivocate; I will not excuse; I will not retreat a single inch; and I will be heard.

— William Lloyd Garrison, Speech, January 1831

e. A hen is only an egg's way of making another egg.

— Samuel Butler, *The Way of All Flesh*

f. The actual enemy is the unknown.

— Thomas Mann, *The Magic Mountain*

g. Samuel Johnson, essayist and ardent critic, argued in his romantic endeavor, *Rasselas*, that an appropriate example is more efficacious than precept.

h. Plato held that time is the image of eternity.

i. In her essay "Our Inner Conflicts," Karen Horney observed, "Life itself still remains a very effective therapist."

j. In the *Declaration on Atomic Energy*, Harry Truman, the American president, and Clement Atlee were neither ambiguous nor equivocal in arguing that effective, reciprocal, and always enforceable safeguards must be available to all nations.

k. Everything passes — Robust art
Alone is eternal.

— Theophile Gautier, *L'Art*

l. Art attempts to find in the universe, in matters as well as in facts of life, what is fundamental, enduring, essential.

— Saul Bellow, Speech upon receiving the
Nobel Prize for Literature, 1976

m. Art should be independent of all claptrap — should stand alone, and appeal to the artistic sense of eye and ear, without confounding this with emotions entirely foreign to it.

— James McNeill Whistler,
The Gentle Art of Making Enemies

EUGENE AND EMIL AND THE WORLD OF ART

Eugene Eagleton was eager to augment his impressive assortment of ancient objets d'art. Unhappily for Eugene, he was often inhibited at art auctions and did not indicate his bids at the immediate and appropriate instant. In contrast, Emil Ambrose Ashton, Eugene's earnest associate, was equally eager but not at all inhibited. In fact, Emil often initiated the bidding and was often so impatient to obtain the art that he was inclined to bid excessively high. However, it was fortunate for Eugene and Emil that there were others at the auctions who had more urge than acumen and also overbid. So it is, as the awesome Bard of Avon once informed his audience, "All's well that ends well." Eugene and his associate Emil organized an impressive array of objets d'art without excess assault on their exchequer.

The Glottal Stop As an Articulatory Fault

Although many persons initiate voice without a glottal attack, they may have a glottal quality in their speech because of an articulatory habit. The habit or fault is one of substituting a glottal grunt or click for a *t* or a *d* in words in which either of these sounds is followed by an *l* or an *n*. This sound substitution is considered in somewhat greater detail in our discussion of specific sound improvement. For the present, test yourself on the list of words and materials that follow. If you can feel or hear yourself produce a glottal explosive for the *t* or *d* on more than one or two of the words, make a special effort to articulate a clear but light and not exaggerated *t* or *d* and so to avoid giving your speech an overall glottal quality.

PRACTICE EXERCISES

bottle	fettle	button	ladle
kettle	rattle	mutton	paddle
settle	written	patent	saddle
metal	bitten	mountain	hidden
little	subtle	kitten	nettle

a. Tender-handed stroke a nettle
    And it stings you for your pains:
  Grasp it like a man of mettle,
    And it soft as silk remains.
                        —Aaron Hill, *Verses Written on a Window in Scotland*
b. Benton was in fine fettle because he was awarded a little metal button to place on his saddle.
c. However little the applause, Fenton was ready for a curtain call.
d. Preston held a patent for brewing his favorite concoction in either a kettle or a metal bottle.
e. Brenton enjoyed mutton after a paddle on the mountain river.

SUGGESTED READINGS

Boone, D. R. (1983). *The voice and voice therapy*. (3rd ed.). Englewood Cliffs, N.J.: Prentice-Hall. (See note in Chapter 2; vocal catch and glottal fry are described on pp. 102–104.)
Fisher, H. (1975). *Improving voice and articulation* (2nd ed.). Boston: Houghton Mifflin. (Vocal fry and glottal attack are described on pp. 73–75; includes exercises for dealing with these vocal features.)

Lieberman, P. (1977). *Speech physiology and vocal phonetics*. New York: Macmillan. (Vocal fry is described on page 82.)

Perkins, W. H. (1977). *Speech pathology*. (2nd ed.), St. Louis: Mosby. (Chapter 3 is concerned with the processes of speech and includes a discussion of voice production. Chapter 13 is on disorders of voice production.)

Van Riper, C., & Emerick, L. (1984). *Speech correction*. (7th ed.). Englewood Cliffs, N.J.: Prentice-Hall. (Chapter 7 is devoted to disorders of voice. Psychological causes and "associates" of voice disorders, including vocal "fry" are included on pp. 227–228.)

CHAPTER 7

PITCH AND EFFECTIVE VOCALIZATION

═══

In Chapter 6 we considered two undesirable vocal qualities identified as vocal catch (click) and vocal fry. These qualities were discussed as faults in the initiation of phonation and/or in maintaining phonation at inappropriate pitch levels. This chapter will emphasize the importance of pitch for normal, effective voice production.

In our discussion of the mechanism for voice production (Chapter 2), we learned that vocal pitch, both the initiating pitch and pitch range, should be related to the properties inherent in one's vocal mechanism. Accordingly, it is not advisable to choose a habitual pitch level or pitch range on the basis of emulation or identification with another speaker. Nor is it advisable to decide on a habitual pitch range according to changing tastes, attitudes, or whims, or according to mood or fashion. We would view with suspicion a musician who chose to play a violin like a cello and expected it to produce the cello's range and quality of sound. The properties built into the structure and the composition of these related but still different instruments determine the pitch range and the essential quality of the sound. The proficiency of the musician then determines what can be produced with the instrument. Comparably, your task as a speaker is to make the best use of your vocal equipment. The best use begins with first determining the pitch level and pitch range most appropriate for you to maintain a healthy and effective voice.

Fortunately, most speakers normally vocalize at pitch levels and within pitch ranges that are appropriate for them. Under abnormal conditions, with or without a conscious awareness of the pitch level and range that we consider optimum, vocalization may suffer because control is impaired. A professor may vocalize quite well, except when annoyed by her students, at which time her pitch may rise beyond the range of easy vocalization. If the occasions for annoyance are frequent, so are the opportunities for inappropriate vocalization. A salesman may have no cause for thinking about his voice until he becomes anxiously concerned while talking to a sales prospect. On such occasions, he may phonate within an elevated pitch range, with accompanying strain and excessive effort. The resulting effects may be both displeasing and potentially harmful to his laryngeal mechanism. A few persons, however, may habitually vocalize at pitches that are not natural or optimum, and so their voices are less effective, less pleasant, and frequently much less comfortable than they could be. Before discussing how to arrive at

optimal initiating pitch and the most suitable pitch range, a few working definitions are
in order.

Optimum (optimal) or *natural pitch* is the level within a speaker's pitch range at which
he or she can initiate vocalization with ease and effectiveness in a *given set of circumstances.* This pitch level is basically determined by the specific physical characteristics
of each person's vocal mechanism. However, optimum pitch level is not fixed. It may
vary, but probably not more than a level or two, according to the speaker's state of
fatigue, the amount of speaking the speaker has done during a time period, the speaker's
physical environment (the size and the acoustic features of the place of speaking), the
number of listeners, the availability of mechanical amplification, and the degree of emotion associated with the speech content and the overall situation. Optimum pitch also
varies with the amount of airflow, which is in turn associated with the loudness of the
vocalization. With all the factors and circumstances considered, optimum pitch is still
the level at which the individual's vocal mechanism functions with the greatest ease and
efficiency. Because optimum pitch is related to the structure of the vocal apparatus, it is
sometimes referred to as *structural pitch.* Moreover, because optimum pitch is usually the
product of "doing what comes naturally," providing there are no negating physical,
emotional, or cultural pressures, the term *natural pitch* is also used. However, nothing
we have said about optimum pitch should suggest that it would be natural or desirable
for a speaker to maintain a monotone vocalization even at her or his optimum level.
This level is the desirable one, "other things being equal," at which to initiate vocalization, and so determines the base for the optimum range for effective voice production.

For most speakers, optimum pitch is likely to be the level that is one fourth to one
third above the lowest level within the entire pitch range. If, for example, the speaker
has a twelve-level pitch range (analogous to musical tones according to the scale), her
or his optimum pitch would probably be the third or fourth level above the lowest. If
her or his pitch range were wider and were to include fifteen levels, the optimum pitch
would most likely be at about level five. For a speaker with a twenty-one-level pitch
range, the optimum pitch would be at about level six.

Several approaches and techniques may be used to arrive at optimum pitch. Ultimately, the best technique is the one that works successfully for the individual; it should
not be limited by any voice or speech teacher's personal prejudices. We consider here
the techniques that we personally have found useful and easily demonstrable without
any pretense of having a monopoly on all the workable ones. For most cases, the first
of these techniques is usually sufficient to establish awareness of optimal pitch.

You should not interpret our explanations of optimum (natural) pitch and habitual
pitch and pitch range as a suggestion that, regardless of the situation and the responses
of the speaker to the circumstances, vocalization should be initiated at a given pitch
level or confined to a predetermined pitch range. Vocal behavior is a natural expression
of a speaker's inner responses to situations. In an imaginary interview, Eric Sander
(1982) "argued" that there is no single pitch that is best for all situations. (We assume
that Sander meant *pitch range* rather than *pitch.*) Sander "admitted" the possibility that
singers may develop vocal calluses from singing at too high a pitch, but nevertheless he
took the position that no one pitch (range) is better than another. Sander suggested that
the best pitch (again, we assume that he meant *range of pitch*) is the one that may be

most pleasant, or the one that permits the speaker to communicate most effectively, or the one that is least tiring to the vocalizer's larynx. Sander also made a positive suggestion that the best pitch (range) is determined by testing "how well the voice holds up when it is pitched in different ways." With due recognition that Sander was engaging in irony if not in satire, we have no reason to take issue with him. The danger in Sander's position is that one may decide that anything goes. What may in effect happen is that, in some instances, *the voice will go!*

We suggest that for speakers who do suffer from vocal fatigue, or who do have difficulty with easy and effective vocalization, there is considerable value in determining initial optimum pitch and, even more important, optimum pitch range. Deviations according to circumstances—vocalizing beyond (above or below) the range—are natural and so are not to be avoided unless such vocal behavior produces strain or discomfort and/or interferes with communication. The discussion that follows is intended to help to prevent vocal difficulties or to correct inappropriate vocal behavior in those who may experience difficulty in vocalization.

DETERMINING OPTIMUM PITCH AND PITCH RANGE

As implied in our review of Sander's critical position, the concept of optimum pitch as a strict scientific phenomenon is subject to challenge. However, it is a useful clinical notion. Boone (1983) pointed out that the concept of an "easy, natural pitch level is useful in voice therapy. . . . If the patient can produce good voice easily, such a voice can become an immediate therapy goal" (p. 98). Our goal is to prevent the speaker from becoming a patient by providing techniques for recognizing and producing a voice that is both easy and effective in communication. We begin with the previously stated assumption that each person does have a pitch level that, as Boone emphasized, can be produced "with an economy of physical effort and energy. This relatively effortless voice production is known as *optimum pitch*" (p. 97).

We recommend that optimum pitch range should be "built" around an individual's optimum pitch.

Pitch range may be defined as the "distance" between the lowest pitch, including low falsetto (vocal fry), and the highest pitch, including falsetto or vocal fry.

Habitual pitch is the pitch level at which an individual most often initiates vocalization. *Habitual range* refers to the pitch levels that are most frequently employed in speaking. *Range* itself refers to the pitch levels that a speaker is capable of producing below and above habitual pitch level. It is obviously desirable that the speaker's optimum pitch and optimum range be the ones that are habitually used. If this is not the case, then changes need to be directed toward (1) becoming aware of optimum pitch and learning to produce this pitch level at will; (2) establishing the optimum pitch as a habit; and (3) developing a pitch range with optimum pitch as the basic level for initiating vocalization.

TECHNIQUES FOR ACHIEVING OPTIMUM PITCH

1. Relax the throat muscles. Take a moderately deep breath and vocalize an evenly sustained *ah* at whatever pitch comes out naturally. Do not think of the pitch until after you hear yourself produce it. Do not attempt to modify the tone once it has been initiated.
2. Relax, and vocalize, but this time intentionally do so at a level lower than in Exercise 1.
3. Continue, going down the scale, until you have produced the lowest-pitched tone you are capable of vocalizing. It may help to think of a descending musical scale in going from your initial pitch level to your lowest. Do not strain for an abnormally low pitch. Stop at the level at which your voice becomes a low-pitched whisper.
4. Return to the initial pitch you produced in Exercise 1. Now produce tones on an upward scale until you reach the highest-pitched falsetto. If you started vocalization at your natural pitch, you should be able to go up in pitch about twice the number of tones you were able to descend below your initial level. If this is the situation, then you are probably initiating vocalization at or very close to your optimum or natural pitch.

An alternate technique for determining optimum pitch is through the matching of vocal and piano tones throughout the pitch range, including the first low and the first high falsetto tones.

1. Sing or chant from your lowest to your highest tone, matching each tone with a corresponding one on a well-tuned piano. If your own sense of pitch discrimination is not reliable, obtain the help of a friend with a reliable ear to establish your vocal range.
2. Repeat the singing or chanting several times so that you are certain that you have established your entire range. Your optimum or natural pitch is likely to be between one fourth and one third above the lowest tone you can produce.
3. Reproduce this tone until it is firmly fixed in your mind and you can initiate it without the help of the piano.

This approach should be repeated at different times during a day and on several different days. Pitch range may vary somewhat under conditions of fatigue or tension, but unless the variation is great, the optimum pitch level should not deviate by more than a single level.

Another easy to administer approach is to produce a relaxed yawn followed by a long sigh. If you are really relaxed, the follow-up sigh should be at or close to your optimal pitch.

Still another technique recommended by Boone (1983, p. 98) is to pretend that you are indicating agreement with what someone is saying to you by uttering "uh-huh." If you are also feeling relaxed as well as agreeable, the "uh-huh" is likely to be at or close to your optimal pitch.

HABITUAL PITCH

To learn whether you have any need to make a conscious effort to initiate vocalization at optimal pitch level, it is necessary to compare your habitual pitch with your optimum pitch. If the two pitch levels are the same, or no more than a single pitch level (a half or a full tone) apart, then you do not need to be concerned about your initial habitual pitch. For most of us who have not had or are not suffering from a physical or emotional ailment, the great likelihood is that habitual and optimal pitch are sufficiently close that there is no cause for concern. However, just to be certain that you are initiating voice at or close to your optimal level, observe the suggestions that follow for determining and comparing optimal with habitual pitch.

Look over several easy-to-read prose passages and select one that is neutral in emotional content and not particularly intellectually challenging. A "How to Do Something Around the House" book is a likely source for bland material. Three candidates for your selection are provided under "Reading Selections to Determine Habitual Pitch" which follow. Make sure that the selection does not include words you cannot readily pronounce. Then: (1) Read the selection aloud in as natural and conversational manner as possible. Record the reading, using an electrically powered instrument. (A battery-powered recorder is not as reliable as one powered by electricity.) Read the passage a second and a third time. When the thought content is reduced to insignificance because of the effect of repetition, level off to a monotonous pitch. You can achieve this by intentionally avoiding inflectional changes. (2) Read the material a fourth and fifth time. Permit your voice to sound like a chant. When this happens, you have probably arrived at a single level, or at least a narrow pitch range, at or close to your habitual pitch. At the conclusion of the chanted passage, vocalize a sustained *ah* at the same pitch level.

(3) Locate this last level on a piano. Then say a series of *ah's*, matching your voice with the piano note. Count from one to ten at this level. Then say the alphabet at this level. If possible, have a companion listen to you to help you locate the pitch.

Compare your optimum pitch with your habitual pitch. Are the two nearly the same or no more than a tone or two apart? If they are, then you need not be further concerned about the matter of initial pitch. If not, then work to bring your habitual pitch closer to your optimum pitch. This accomplishment will pay large dividends if you are interested in good voice production. The most generous permissible margin of error between habitual and optimum pitch should not exceed two levels for persons with a narrow pitch range. This may be extended to one third of an octave for individuals with a wide pitch range (two or more octaves). In general, the closer habitual pitch is to optimum pitch, the better your voice is likely to be.

READING SELECTIONS TO DETERMINE HABITUAL PITCH

The following selections are essentially of an intellectual nature and so would normally be read aloud with relatively "neutral" feeling. The pitch range is likely to be fairly narrow.

a. Statistics is the branch of mathematics that describes how things are on the average. The idea of statistics is that a single observation may not be reliable, and that if the observation is repeated many times the result may not always be the same. In such cases it is necessary to talk about the likelihood rather than the certainty that some particular event will occur.

— George Miller, *Language and Communication*

b. Physiology is the science that deals with the function of biological systems. An anatomist . . . could describe the bones and muscles of the human foot without considering how these elements work together in activities like bipedal locomotion. A physiologist would have to consider these same bones and muscles in terms of their functional value in locomotion and other activities.

c. The Canadian National Railway is a government-owned transportation system that provides coast-to-coast service in Canada. It has branches that extend to all of the Canadian provinces and to the northern parts of the United States. The present system incorporates what were originally five separate services. The incorporation took place in 1922. The Canadian National Railway also operates airlines, ships, and a telegraph service.

WIDENING THE PITCH RANGE

How wide a pitch range should we have? Practically, the answer is *wide enough to be effective as a speaker*, but not at the expense of strain or discomfort. Some persons with a demonstrably wide pitch range tend to speak habitually only at the lower end of their range. Others, especially when they are under emotional stress, may confine their vocalizations to the higher end of their range. The result for both types of speakers may be inefficient vocalization. For the listeners, the result may be unpleasant exposure to monotonous or strained vocal efforts. Although the experimental evidence is not consistent, some studies have shown that effective speakers, and those who are regarded as having good voices, tend to use both greater variability and a wider range of pitch than do less effective speakers. Better speakers, by and large, make greater use of the upper part of their pitch ranges, and their pitch ranges generally cover at least an octave and a half. Poor speakers, in contrast, tend to have pitch ranges limited to about half an octave.

Extending Pitch Range Upward

As one's optimum pitch level is at the lower end of the pitch range, it follows that the direction for extending the pitch range for most persons is likely to be up rather than down. With this in mind, undertake the following exercises.

EXERCISES FOR EXTENDING PITCH RANGE UPWARD

1. Review the discussion of optimum pitch. Check your optimum pitch and your total pitch range.
2. Count from one through ten at your optimum pitch level. Now count to ten in a monotone three tones above your optimum pitch. Raise the pitch level three more tones above your optimum pitch. Raise the pitch level three more tones and repeat the count. Finally, count to ten at the very top of your normal pitch range. Repeat with the letters of the alphabet, *a* through *j*.
3. Say the sentence "We're going for a walk" at your optimum pitch. Practice the same sentence, initiating the first word on successively lower levels until you reach the lowest comfortable pitch level. Start again from your optimum pitch, and now initiate the first word of the sentence at successively higher pitch levels until you have reached the top of your range.
4. First, read the following sentences and paragraphs in a manner that is natural or habitual for you, and then intentionally extend your pitch range upward.
    a. As the traveler who has once been from home is wiser than he who has never left his doorstep, so a knowledge of one other culture should sharpen our ability to scrutinize more steadily, to appreciate more lovingly, our own.
       —Margaret Mead, *Coming of Age in Samoa*
    b. Nature is neutral. Man has wrested from nature the power to make the world a desert or to make the desert bloom. There is no evil in the atom; only in men's souls.
       —Adlai Stevenson, Speech, Hartford,
       Connecticut, September 18, 1952
    c. Ennui, felt on the proper occasions, is a sign of intelligence.
       —Clifton Fadiman, *Reading I've Liked*
    d. Among animals, *one* has a sense of humor. Humor saves a few steps, it saves years.
       —Marianne Moore, *The Pangolin*
    e. Benjamin Franklin held that "there are two ways of being happy: we may either diminish our wants or augment our means. Either will do, the result is the same. And it is for each man to decide for himself and do that which happens to be the easiest."
    f. Young men are fitter to invent than to judge; fitter for execution than for counsel; and fitter for new projects than for settled business.
       —Francis Bacon, *Of Youth and Age*

g. In his *Proverbs of Hell* the mystic poet William Blake wrote, "No bird soars too high if he soars with his own wings."

h. In his poem *Miracles* Walt Whitman shared his appreciation for being alive with the lines:
   "To me every hour of the light and dark is a miracle,
   Every cubic inch of space is a miracle."

======

EXTENDING PITCH RANGE DOWNWARD

Unless you have an unusually narrow pitch range, you are likely to have more levels available to you at the upper part of your pitch range than toward the lower end. However, there is "room" (pitch range) toward the bottom level that can be used effectively for expressing feeling and communicating meaning through vocal variety that is appropriate to the speech content. Thus, if after determining your optimum pitch and your habitual pitch range, it becomes apparent that you are making little use of your lower pitch levels, some practice is in order. Do not, however, go so low in your range that your voice becomes throaty, excessively breathy, or barely audible. Avoid strain or any low tone that seems to be lacking in substance or that is difficult to sustain or that results in the production of a low-pitched falsetto (vocal fry). In general, try to incorporate tones into your pitch range that are one or two levels above your lowest tone within your pitch range. The following exercises, which present material on sober matters, should provide you with the opportunity to emphasize tones at the lower end of your pitch range.

EXERCISES FOR EXTENDING PITCH RANGE DOWNWARD

1. Sorrow and sadness and how human beings experience these emotions are a recurring theme of philosophers and poets. Following are some versions of sorrow through the ages.
   a. In every adversity of fortune, to have been happy is the most unhappy kind of misfortune.
      —Boethius, *De Consolatione Philosphiae*
   b. The deeper the sorrow, the less tongue it hath.
      —*The Talmud*
   c. Weep no more, nor sigh, nor groan,
      Sorrow calls no time that's gone—
      —John Fletcher, *The Honest Man's Fortune*

d. I have had playmates, I have had companions,
   In my days of childhood, in my joyful school days —
   All, all are gone, the old familiar faces.

   —Charles Lamb, *Old Familiar Faces*

e. My heart hath followed all my days
   Something I cannot name.

   —Donald P. Marquis, *The Name*

f. Remember me when I am gone away,
   Gone far away into the silent land.

   —Christina Rossetti, *Remember*

g. This is truth the poet sings,
   That a sorrow's crown of sorrows is remembering happier things.

   —Alfred, Lord Tennyson, *Locksley Hall*

2. Loneliness and lonesomeness are two related themes of poets and philosophers. However, the choice of being alone, often expressed in the writings of Henry David Thoreau, should not be confused with either loneliness or lonesomeness. Following are some observations on these states.
   a. James Russell Lowell advised, "The nurse of full-grown souls is solitude."
   b. Mark Twain warned, "Be good and you will be lonesome."
   c. Edwin Markham wrote that Lincoln's death left "a lonesome place against the sky."
   d. Robert Nathan, in *A Cedar Box*, philosophically observed, "Joy has its friends, but grief its loneliness."
   e. On a happier note, Rudyard Kipling believed that "He travels the fastest who travels alone."
   f. Thoreau, a lone man if not a lonely one, seemed to enjoy solitude. He wrote, in *Solitude*, "I never found the companion that was so companionable as solitude. . . . A man thinking or writing is always alone, let him be where he will."
   g. Whenever you make a conscious choice to be alone, you give up your claim to loneliness.
   h. In his novel *Look Homeward, Angel*, Thomas Wolfe asks, "Which of us has known his brother? Which of us has looked into his father's heart? Which of us has not remained forever prison-pent? Which of us is not forever a stranger and alone?"
   i. Edwin Markham wrote that when Abraham Lincoln died he left "a lonesome place against the sky."
   j. In his poem *The Creation* James Weldon Johnson wrote
        And God stepped out on space
        And He looked around and said,
        "I'm lonely —
        I'll make me a world."
   k. In *The Autumn Garden* Lillian Hellman observed that "lonely people talking to each other can make each other lonelier."

══ INTONATION: THE MELODY OF SPEECH ══

Speaking and Singing

All of us, including those who are resigned to being classed among the nonsingers because of the violence we are accused of doing to the melody of a song, nevertheless use melody in our speech. The music of speech, however, is usually subtle, and the changes seldom as discrete and distinct as they are in singing. In speaking, our voices glide from sound to sound within a phrase or a sentence unless we take a momentary pause at the end of a phrase. More often than not, we mark the end of a phrase by some change in pitch rather than by an identifiable pause. In contrast, when we sing, changes in pitch are usually more clear-cut and are likely to occur in discrete steps equivalent to musical tones. There are exceptions. Some singers depart from the musical score and do produce glides and vibrato effects as their individual expressions in the rendition of a song. Some of us, without intention, somehow manage to sing between the musical tones, and our voices fall "flat" into the cracks between the notes of the piano. Interestingly, a few singers have earned their reputation by doing intentionally and with control what seems to come naturally, accidentally, and inconsistently for others.

Intonation

Intonation, or patterned vocal variation, is an inherent feature of spoken utterance. Interestingly, despite phonological (speech sound system) and morphemic[1] variations in natural languages, intonation contours, especially in declarative sentences, are essentially alike. On the basis of data provided by Lieberman (1968, chap. 4), we may generalize that short declarative sentences are likely to end with a falling pitch contour.

In some languages, the changes in vocal tones are relatively slight, whereas in others, such as Chinese, the changes are marked. Languages such as Norwegian, Swedish, and Lithuanian have relatively fixed patterns of pitch changes. English pitch variation is relatively free. The melody of English speech is determined in part by conventions of sentence formation and in part by the mood and the subjective responses of the speaker to the content of her or his speech and the overall speech situation. Despite this highly individual determinant of American-English speech melody, there are several features that characterize the direction of inflectional changes (pitch changes that occur without interruption of phonation) for sounds of words. There are also characteristic pitch changes within word groups that constitute recognizable intonation patterns in our language.

Figures 7–1 and 7–2 (adapted from Lieberman, 1968) present spectrograms for a short declarative sentence. The variations in contour according to the word stressed should be noted.

---

[1] A morpheme is a word or a minimal part of a word that carries meaning. The words *the, to,* and *for* are single-syllable word morphemes, as are *jump* and *like*. Adding *ed* to the word *jump* (*jumped*) or *s* to *like* (*likes*) provides tense ending changes of meaning. The morpheme *s* in *likes* could also signify a plural, as in *cakes.* Root-word syllables, prefixes, and suffixes are morphemes. In general, a morpheme is the minimal grammatical unit of a language that carries meaning.

Figure 7–1 Spectrogram of a speaker reading the declarative sentence *"Joe* ate his soup." [Adapted from P. Lieberman, *Intonation, Perception, and Language.* M.I.T. Research Mongraph, No. 38 (Cambridge, Mass.: M.I.T. Press, 1968), p. 69.]

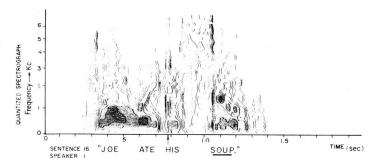

Figure 7–2 Spectrogram of a speaker reading the declarative sentence "Joe ate his *soup."* [Adapted from P. Lieberman, *Intonation, Perception, and Language.* M.I.T. Research Mongraph, No. 38 (Cambridge, Mass.: M.I.T. Press, 1968), p. 70.]

Figure 7–3 shows several other "representative" simplified and generalized intonation contour patterns of American English. These patterns illustrate the basic downward inflection of the simple declarative sentence and the pitch elevation of the stressed word within the sentence or within the breath group (phrase) in multiple-phrase sentences. In contrast, note the difference in contour of the question sentence. So-called *wh* questions end with falling inflections, whereas questions that ordinarily may be answered by a "yes" or "no" end with rising inflections.

Figure 7–4 is a graphic representation of a somewhat more complex sentence than most of the others.

Types of Pitch Changes

Two categories of pitch changes together constitute the overall pitch variation, or *intonation*, of American-English speech. These are inflections and shifts, or steps. *Inflections* are modulations of pitch that occur during phonation. *Shifts* are changes of pitch that occur

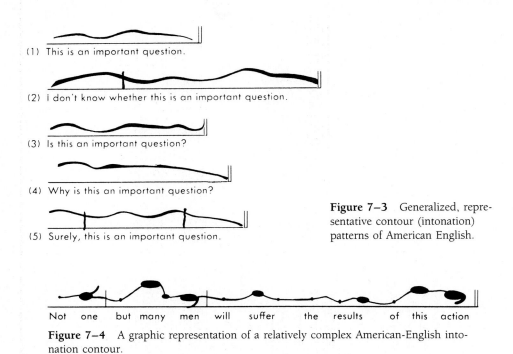

(1) This is an important question.

(2) I don't know whether this is an important question.

(3) Is this an important question?

(4) Why is this an important question?

(5) Surely, this is an important question.

Figure 7–3 Generalized, representative contour (intonation) patterns of American English.

Not   one   but   many   men   will   suffer   the   results   of   this   action

Figure 7–4 A graphic representation of a relatively complex American-English intonation contour.

between phonations. Inflections may be subclassified according to contour, or "direction" of change, as downward, upward, or circumflex. For any but very short, uninterrupted phonatory efforts or flows of utterance we are likely to have several inflectional changes. Because shifts properly occur only between subunits of utterances when the speaker takes a moment to pause to indicate a unit of thought or a "phrase," inflectional changes almost always outnumber shifts. The uses and implications of pitch changes are considered in the discussions that follow.

Shifts

Shifts, steps, or "intervals" in pitch, indicate the importance we give to a unit of thought within an utterance or a phonatory effort. If we regard a phonatory effort as a sentence, even a two-word sentence may have two related subunits of thought, each appropriately uttered at a different pitch level. Thus, sentences such as "Go now" or "Come here" may be uttered for effect with a momentary pause at the end of the first word and a shift in level of pitch from the first to the second word. In both of the examples given, the "normal" shift in level of pitch would be upward, so that we might represent the sentences as:

Go ‖ now

Come ‖ here

======

EXERCISES FOR CHANGE IN PITCH LEVEL

1. Practice the following short sentences using a higher pitch level on the second word than on the first. However, end the second word on a downward inflection.

Mom's here.	Please, stop.
Don't laugh.	Hurry, fly.
That's enough.	We're late.
We're in!	It's sad.
You're out.	Mary grinned.
Sam sneered.	Bob smiled.
Now, go!	Bill winced.
Jill jumped.	Nobody slept.

2. What would be the effect on the meaning of the statement if the second words were produced on a lower pitch level than the first?

3. Practice these longer sentences, changing the level of pitch as indicated by the direction of the arrow.
   a. Winter came —| ↑ | wind, freeze, and snow.
   b. He stopped suddenly, | ↑ | then turned to the right.
   c. Why Tom did it, | ↓ | he could not tell.
   d. Our team lost, | ↓ | but the game was close.
   e. Will you | ↓ | or won't you?
   f. No matter how much you beg, | ↑ | it won't be done.
   g. I've had it, | ↓ | that's just enough.
   h. Come now, | ↑ | that will do.

4. How would you be inclined to shift the pitch for the following sentences after the indicated places for pause? What changes in meaning would you imply by reversing the direction of the pitch change? By using the same general level on the second part of the sentence as on the first?
   a. It's late, ‖ perhaps too late.
   b. Come early, ‖ come often.
   c. Did you care ‖ or just pretend?
   d. It can be done ‖ if you really try.
   e. Waste not, ‖ want not.
   f. He spoke quietly ‖ but with certainty.
   g. He stopped ‖ just in time.
   h. Don't write, ‖ phone him.
   i. He sped away ‖ out of sight.
   j. Look out, ‖ look out!

5. *Downward or falling inflections* (↘) are generally used to indicate the completion of a thought, and to give emphasis to an idea. The sample sentences that follow would end with falling inflections. The second sentence would probably have falling inflections on both italicized words. In the examples that

immediately follow, the italicized words are those on which inflectional changes are "normally" anticipated. A change in the emphasis of a key word within the sentence would, however, alter the pitch contour.

   a. This is your *pen*.

   b. *Certainly*, this is your *pen*.

       Command statements also end with falling inflections.

   c. Stop *now!*

6. A question that begins with an interrogative word — *when, where, who, why, how,* or *whom* — for which an answer other than the single word "yes" or "no" is anticipated, also ends with a falling inflection.

   d. When will Jane *go?*

   e. Why did he do *it?*

   f. Where is my *hat?*

   g. Who is *going?*

   h. How did Sue do *it?*

7. *Upward or rising inflections* (↗) are generally used to suggest doubt, uncertainty, or incompleteness. They are also used for questions that call for a simple "yes" or "no" answer. And we are likely to use rising inflections in statements that enumerate a series of items, until the last item is stated. The last item is spoken with a falling inflection.

   i. It apparently didn't occur to *us* that this was your *book*.

   j. Is this your *book?*

   k. We bought *groceries, meat,* and *fruit* at the supermarket.

   l. Few persons are heroes to their *families, friends,* or *close neighbors*.

CIRCUMFLEX INFLECTIONS

We would be inviting difficulty if we dogmatically illustrated how irony, innuendo, sarcasm, cynicism, skepticism, or surprise combined with disbelief or incredulity are expressed in pitch. These "intellectual" states and attitudes that are laden with feeling are a challenge. Most American speakers would probably employ some form or forms of circumflex inflection (down-up, or up-down, or down-up-and-down) to express what they think or how they feel about something at a given moment. For example, if a speaker entertains not only surprise but disbelief (*It can't possibly be so!*) at the choice of a candidate for a political office, the use of the single word *Him!* inflected as *Him!* ↗ might do.

   A longer statement, such as "Of all persons, to choose — him!" — in which a related sentiment is expressed relative to the same person — might employ a series of circumflex inflections. The specific form of inflection is likely to be even more individualized than in the illustrations previously presented.

Generalizations Relative to Intonation and Inflectional Changes

The examples presented and the generalizations about to be made should serve as guides for a speaker who has somehow not been able to get the melody of American-English speech. Once the basic melody is learned, the speaker should feel free to indulge in variations from the fundamental melodic theme or pattern.

1. Some degree of pitch change is almost continuous in normal conversational speech.

2. Major pitch changes occur at the ends of phrases and sentences and on the most significant words within the phrase or sentence.

3. Falling or downward inflections are used when we make definite or positive assertions and when we wish to indicate the completion of a thought (Examples a, b, and c on page 116). A falling inflection is also used on the final word of a question that begins with an interrogative word (Examples d–h on page 116).

4. A rising inflection is used to suggest incomplete or dependent thoughts and to express doubt or uncertainty. The rising inflection is also used in questions that may logically be answered by the words "yes" or "no" (Examples i–l on page 116).

5. The pitch level of the most important word within a phrase or a unit of thought is likely to be at a level different from that of the other words of the unit. Most frequently, it is higher in level, but occasionally the emphasized word is uttered at a distinctively lower level than the other words of the unit.

6. The stressed syllable of a word is usually spoken on a higher pitch level than the unstressed syllable or syllables of the word.

The exercises that follow afford an opportunity for the application of the generalizations relative to inflectional changes and intonation patterns of American-English speech.

The first group of sentences would ordinarily end with falling inflections unless special meanings are read into them. For the present, avoid special meanings and read the sentences "straight" to indicate assertions and completed thoughts. Avoid any inclination for your voice to fade out at the end of the sentence so that you cannot be easily heard.

EXERCISES FOR FALLING INFLECTIONS

a. Pam is always prompt.
b. Clouds hid the sun.
c. Irene is a dedicated swimmer.
d. The Northern California coast is often foggy.
e. Bill will eat any given amount of almost anything.
f. Susan enjoys historical novels.
g. It's good to be through.
h. A good lawn requires considerable care.
i. Presently, we have no cure for the common cold.
j. That's the only way to go.

k. Take your time to do it right.
l. It's high time for tea.
m. Sorry, but that's not so!
n. Sara writes scripts for the movies.
o. Not all roses are either red or redolent.
p. Wendy Perkins ran for mayor of the city.
q. Ted is a speed reader.
r. Francine is a professional golfer.
s. Coffee and cake will be served at the break.
t. Dan enjoys solving jigsaw puzzles.

Many of the items in the next group, if read straight, would normally employ falling inflections on the last words. If they are read to suggest doubt or uncertainty or to express an incomplete thought, rising inflections are employed. The questions ordinarily answered by a "yes" or "no" also end with rising inflections.

EXERCISES FOR RISING INFLECTIONS

a. I'm just not sure.
b. Well, perhaps.
c. You're going to ski?
d. I guess that's right.
e. Well, we'll see.
f. Is Tom going?
g. Do you meditate?
h. Shall we start?
i. Is this a rose?
j. Do you enjoy football?
k. Does Frances speak Spanish?
l. Is Bill on time?

All questions, as we recall, do not end with rising inflections. Those that begin with interrogative words usually end with falling inflections when the questions are intended to elicit information. When a rising inflection is used for questions beginning with interrogative words, some special implication or meaning is intended other than a request for information. Read the following sentences first with an expected falling inflection and then with a final rising inflection and note the change in implied meaning.

a. Is today Friday?
b. Do you know your name?
c. Who came late?
d. Where are we going?
e. When shall we leave?
f. Why should we go?
g. Who knows his lines?

    h. What does this cost?
    i. How long is the road?
    j. What is the right time?
    k. How did Sue find out?
    l. What makes this correct?

EXERCISES FOR PRACTICE OF INFLECTIONAL CHANGES

1. Say the word *yes* to indicate (a) certainty, (b) doubt, (c) indecision, and (d) sarcasm.
2. Say the word *no* and, by changes of inflection, indicate the following.
    a. "Definitely not."
    b. "Well, maybe."
    c. "I'm surprised to learn that."
    d. "I'm annoyed to learn that."
    e. "I'm pleased and surprised to learn that."
3. Say the sentence "I shall go" so that the following attitudes are implied.
    a. Determination.
    b. Pleasant agreement.
    c. Surprise.
    d. Annoyance.
4. Say the sentence "He's really somebody" to bring out the following meanings.
    a. You admire the person about whom you're talking.
    b. You dislike the person.
    c. You can't decide whether you like or dislike the person.
    d. You have a begrudging admiration for the person.
    e. You are surprised at the newly discovered qualities of the person.
5. Speak the sentence "I like Bill" to bring out the following.
    a. A direct statement of fact. (You mean literally what the words say.)
    b. A contradiction of the literal meaning of the words. (You definitely do not like Bill.)
    c. Irritation and surprise that anyone could conceivably accuse you of liking Bill.
    d. Indecision as to your feelings about Bill.
    e. A specific indication that your liking is for Bill and not for anyone else who may be present.
    f. Your answer to the question, "Who likes Bill?"
    g. An aggressive, emphatic answer to the question, "Who could possibly care for a fellow like Bill?"
    h. No matter what, he's still my Bill.

Avoidance of Monotony

In discussing the differences in pitch variation between singing and speaking, we pointed out that most pitch changes in song melody are discrete and take place in distinct steps. Each song syllable is likely to be maintained on a recognizable pitch level (note) longer than is likely to be the case in either conversational or public speech. Variation in speaking is almost continuous. Distinctive changes, however, should be noted when pitch is used for purposes of emphasis. For emphasis, pitch change is likely to be on a higher rather than on a lower level than the preceding or following words. When the pitch change is to a lower level, the speaker must maintain or increase voice volume to give the word or phrase the desired emphasis.

Repetition of pattern in singing constitutes melody. This is considered a desirable characteristic of classical song. In speaking, where verbal content rather than pitch pattern is usually important, the repetition of pitch pattern should be avoided. In American and English speech, subtleties of ideational content are expressed through pitch change. If pitch changes become patterned and repeated, shades of meaning cannot readily be communicated. In addition, pitch changes, if they can be anticipated, no longer command attention and tend to work against rather than for the maintenance of interest. For these reasons, for you to be an effective speaker you should not only use as wide a range of pitch as you can within your normal pitch range but also be careful to avoid pitch patterning and its consequent monotony.

Although our present discussion is concerned with pitch changes, the unmodified production of voice quality, loudness, or rate can all be monotonous. We have all heard radio or television commercials, usually presented by nonprofessionals — the owners of a business who somehow think that they can do a better job of announcing than the studio announcer — literally shout their messages "at the tops of their voices." The effect is that nothing in the announcement comes across as important. At the extreme other end are the ministerial voices, by no means limited to the clergy, who vocalize every syllable in orotund if not in profound tones. In effect, such vocalization minimizes the possible effect of most of the message. In a critique of the voices of public figures, one of my students observed of his senator, "His voice reserves nothing for God."

Pitch Variation in Content Characterized by Strong Feeling

Speech content that is characterized by strong and heightened feelings such as anger, rage, and fear — feelings that are more significant for their emotional rather than for their intellectual messages — tends to use more pitch variation than most conversational speech. These states are usually expressed with wide pitch changes at the upper end of the speaker's range. In contrast, grief and sorrow are usually expressed with few pitch changes and variations, at the low end of the individual's range. Sometimes, when we wish to establish a dominant mood, or to share a strong feeling with a listener, we begin to approximate the melody of song or the relatively sustained pitch of lyrical poetry. A passage from the Bible should not be read as one reads an item from the day's news. Neither should it be read with an unvarying cadence and stereotyped intonations.

In general the pitch changes in an effective reading of poetry or emotional prose are individually more extensive but collectively less varied and longer sustained than in an effective reading of intellectual material. The exception is content of heightened feeling

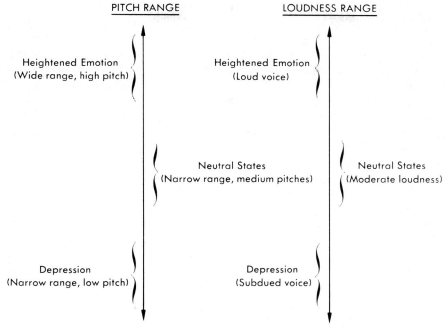

Figure 7–5 The relationship between changes in pitch and loudness and the states of feeling.

when lightness rather than loftiness is to be expressed. Then, the changes in pitch are likely to be more sweeping and to occur as often as or more often than they do in predominantly intellectual material. Anger is also likely to be expressed with relatively wide pitch changes and in the upper pitch range. With these points in mind, read the following passages. Use pitch variation to emphasize changes in thought and feeling. Sober and solemn moods are probably best expressed through the use of relatively low, sustained pitch levels. Figure 7–5 summarizes the changes in pitch and in loudness associated with states of feeling and emotion.

EXERCISES FOR PRACTICING PITCH VARIATION

In the following exercises try to emphasize changes in pitch rather than loudness to bring out what you consider to be the writer's underlying meaning of the content. However, do not completely suppress your inclination to speak just a bit louder to communicate your interpretation. First, read the material silently to determine the writer's underlying mood.

    a. The optimist proclaims that we live in the best of all possible worlds, and the pessimist fears that it is true.

            —James Branch Cabell, *The Silver Stallion*

b. And the earth was without form, and voice, and darkness was on the face of the deep.

—Genesis 1

c. During the whole of a dull, dark, and resoundless day in the autumn of the year, when the clouds hung oppressively low in the heavens, I had been passing alone, on horseback, through a singularly dreary tract of country, and at length found myself, as the shades of evening drew on, within view of the melancholy House of Usher. I know not how it was— but with the first glimpse of the building, a sense of insufferable gloom pervaded my spirit.

—Edgar Allan Poe,
The Fall of the House of Usher

d. Jenny kissed me when we met
      Jumping from the chair she sat in;
Time, you thief, who loves to get
      Sweet into your list, put that in:

Say I'm weary, say I'm sad,
      Say that health and wealth have missed me,
Say I'm growing old, but add
      Jenny kissed me.

—Leigh Hunt, *Rondeau*

e. If you forgive people enough you belong to them, and they to you, whether either person likes it or not—squatter's rights of the heart.

—James Hilton, *Time and Time Again*

f. Time goes, you say? Ah no!
   Alas, Time stays, *we* go.

—Henry Austin Dobson, *The Paradox of Time*

g. You have not converted a man because you have silenced him.

—John, Viscount Morley, *On Compromise*

In your reading of Psalm 23, level, sustained tones will help to establish the solemnity and reverence of your thought. Do not, however, fall into a patterned, unchanging reading.

h. The Lord is my shepherd, I shall not want. He maketh me to lie down in green pastures: he leadeth me beside the still waters. He restoreth my soul; he leadeth me in the paths of righteousness for his name's sake. Yea, though I walk through the valley of the shadow of death, I will fear no evil: for thou art with me; thy rod and thy staff they comfort me.

—Psalm 23

i. Golden lads and girls all must
   As chimney sweepers, come to dust.

—William Shakespeare, *Cymbeline*

j. I was angry with my friend:
   I told my wrath, my wrath did end.
   I was angry with my foe:
   I told it not, my wrath did grow.

—William Blake, *A Poison Tree*

k. Modesty and unselfishness — these are virtues which men praise — and pass by.

—André Maurois, *Ariel*

l. The perversion of the mind is only possible when those who should be heard in its defense are silent.

—Archibald Macleish, *The Irresponsibles*

m. In a real dark night of the soul it is always three o'clock in the morning.

—F. Scott Fitzgerald, *The Crack-up*

n. Man must evolve for all human conflict a method which rejects revenge, aggression and retaliation. The foundation of such a method is love.

—Martin Luther King Jr.,
Speech accepting the Nobel Prize, 1964

o. In his essay *Design Science* Buckminster Fuller advised: "Change the environment; do not try to change man."

p. Many sensible things banished from high life find an asylum among the mob.

—Herman Melville, *White Jacket*

Additional exercises for practicing pitch changes are provided in the Chapter 11, "Vocal Variety in Speaking and Reading."

REFERENCES

Boone, D. R. (1983). *The voice and voice therapy.* (3rd ed.). Englewood Cliffs, N.J.: Prentice-Hall. (Chapter 7 deals with voice therapy for special problems.)

Lieberman, P. (1968). *Intonation, perception, and language.* M.I.T. research monograph, no. 38. Cambridge, Mass.: M.I.T. Press. (Chapter 7 deals with intonation and questions; syntactic and semantic aspects are considered on pages 141–142. The discussion, though quite informative, is also highly technical.)

Sander, E. K. (1982). *Optimal vocal behavior. ASHA, 24:* 1, 35. (Sander is somewhat cynical about how to determine optimal pitch level for voice. He suggests that "doing what comes naturally" is as good an approach as any. This is not the approach of the author of this book.)

CHAPTER 8

REINFORCEMENT OF VOICE THROUGH RESONANCE

As children most of us learned that a string with ends tied to paper cups or cereal boxes permitted us to talk with little more than conversational loudness and still be heard at distances considerably beyond our normal vocal range. What we were accomplishing with this rudimentary telephone system was reinforcement of the voice through additional cavity resonance — provided by the cup or box. Later, with some sophistication, we learned that a plucked string or rubber band produces a noise that can just barely be heard if the listener is close to it. We discovered that the same plucked string or band is more easily heard if it is attached to or close to a cavity opening, even an open mouth. With increasing sophistication we also learned that most musical instruments depend upon resonation. Resonators build up or reinforce the sounds that are initially produced by applying energy to a body capable of being set in vibration. Common ways of applying energy include plucking strings; rubbing strings against strings; striking a skin or a metallic, wooden, or other stringlike substance; or blowing air (breath) across a vibrator into tubes of varying lengths, widths, shapes, and materials.

Another form of reinforcement for musical instruments is the forced vibration of sounding-board resonance. This is exemplified by the sounding board of a piano as well as the bridge of a violin or other string instruments.

IMPROVING REINFORCEMENT THROUGH RESONANCE

The manner in which the combination of our resonators reinforces our vocal tones also produces the attributes by which the quality or timbre of the individual voice is identified. Unless we are good at vocal deception and try to sound like someone else, our voices can usually be recognized even when speaking over the low-fidelity telephone. A master of vocal deception is the entertainer Rich Little.

Our present concern is to create awareness of resonance as one of the objectives for an effective voice. As we continue our discussion of resonance, we must bear in mind that none of our resonating cavities acts independently of the others. Changes in the oral cavity are likely to affect the pharynx, and changes in the pharynx are likely to affect the oral cavity, the larynx, and/or the nasal cavity. Despite this interdependence (coupling), specific modifications in one of the reasonating cavities can result in vocal qualities that may be described by such terms as *oral, guttural,* and *nasal.*

The chief resonators, we recall, are the cavities of the larynx, the pharynx (throat), the mouth, and the nose. If these cavities are not temporarily irritated or inflamed by a respiratory ailment or obstructed by an organic growth such as enlarged tonsils or adenoids, good reinforcement of tone should be possible. Muscular tension may also impair the effective production of vocal tones, but unless such tension is chronic or regularly associated with some speech efforts, the effect of tension is likely to be transitory. For the sake of convenience, we are repeating a diagram (Figure 8–1) that originally appeared in Chapter 2.

Pharyngeal Resonance

In Chapter 2, we considered the pharynx and its characteristics as a cavity resonator. We pointed out that this large resonating structure may enable the voice to sound full and rich if it is open and relaxed, or strident and metallic when the walls of the pharynx are tense. The implications of abnormal tissue growth or of infection relative to the damping of tone were also suggested. We now expand on this discussion.

Because the pharynx is a large resonator, it is best suited to the reinforcement of vocal tones in the lower pitch range. Normally, also, the relatively "soft" or relaxed tissue of the pharynx damps out the higher-pitched tones and reinforces the lower, or fundamental, vocal tones. If, therefore, the pharynx is relaxed and "open," the full potentialities of the pharynx are exercised for the reinforcement and coloring of the low vocal tones. If, however, as a result of tension or pathology the pharyngeal walls are tense, the potentialities of the pharynx as a resonator are not realized. The tense or "hardened" surface reinforces the higher pitches and the vocal overtones.

A "tight" pharynx, often resulting from a speaker's wish to talk "deep down in the throat," is likely to produce an unpleasant, "throaty" voice. (Review the earlier discussion of glottal fry.) A "throaty" voice quality sometimes follows an episode of sore throat (laryngitis and/or pharyngitis), and the speaker's voice continues to be characteristically "heavy" and narrow in pitch range. Often, however, the vocal quality we respond to as "heavy" and "throaty" is associated with a habit on the part of the speaker of keeping the tongue in a retracted and humped position while speaking. Such a tongue position modifies the shape of the oral cavity and produces an effect that suggests a muffled, "thick and heavy" voice—a vocal quality that is frequently accompanied by indistinct articulation, which is a likely result of the restricted mobility of the tongue.

Unless there is a medical basis for throatiness—a condition that should be evaluated by a physician and, it at all possible, by a laryngologist—the exercises that follow should help to improve this undesirable vocal quality.

Because of the relationship between the continuous and coupled oral and pharyngeal cavities, suggestions and exercises for optimal pharyngeal resonance are presented following the discussion of oral resonance.

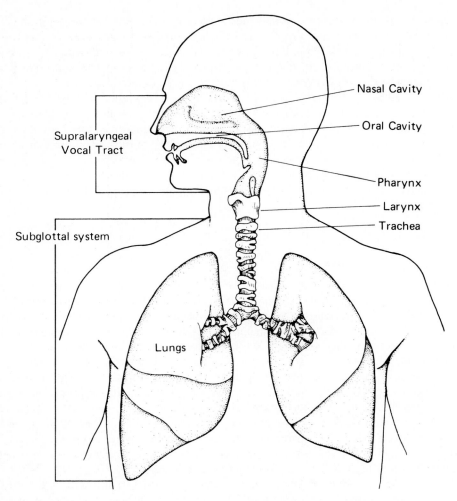

Supralaryngeal
Vocal Tract

Subglottal system

Nasal Cavity

Oral Cavity

Pharynx

Larynx

Trachea

Lungs

Figure 8–1 Diagrammatic representation of the human speech production mechanism featuring the principal resonating cavities. [After P. Lieberman, *Speech Physiology and Acoustic Phonetics* (New York: Macmillan Publishing Company, 1977), p. 4.]

Oral Resonance

Oral resonance is likely to be improved if the speaker makes a conscious effort to emphasize lip and tongue activity while speaking. Such activity helps to accomplish the objective of the singing teacher who directs students to "place their tones forward in the mouth." In our attempt to achieve oral resonance, however, we must not so exaggerate articulatory activity as to make it obvious to our listener-observer, and so to make us self-conscious. Nor should we create a condition of excessive articulatory tension that will carry over to the muscles of the throat.

Optimum oral resonance can be obtained only when the back of the oral cavity is open and relaxed so that we are able to initiate and maintain vocalization with an open throat. The following exercises should be of help for this purpose. In practice, think of your mouth as a megaphone. What is the effect when you extend this "megaphone" with your hands?

EXERCISES FOR ORAL AND PHARYNGEAL RESONANCE

1. The optimal use of the pharynx as a resonator presupposes proper breath control and the avoidance of any tension that might result from forced breathing or vocalization with residual air. The first step, therefore, is a review of the exposition and the exercises for breathing in effective vocalization (see Chapter 5).

2. Establish a feeling of overall bodily relaxation, as follows: (a) Slowly clench your hands to make tight fists. Note the related tension in the arms as well as in the fingers. Note also the associated tension of the jaw as your fingers are clenched into fists. (b) Relax slowly and gently until your fingers are extended. Do not, however, extend your fingers so that they become tense. Now note the associated relaxation of your arms and the muscles that control the jaw. Note also the easing of the muscles of the throat.

3. Establish your overall relaxation. Now, intentionally tense the biceps of your arms while you make tight fists. Relax slowly as you undo your fists and note the associated relaxation of your throat.

4. Breathe in gently and then exhale with a "soft" sigh. Note the relaxed feeling in your throat. If your throat is not relaxed, it is likely that either your inhalation or your exhalation was not sufficiently gentle. Try again until you achieve a gentle, sustained, vocalized sigh. Your tongue should lie almost completely flat at the bottom of the mouth, with a minimum of back-of-the-tongue elevation.

5. Inhale deeply, but not to a point of discomfort, and then yawn as if you were sleepy. Open your mouth wide, but avoid any feeling of tension in the muscles of your face or jaw. Your throat should feel relaxed if the yawn was convincingly but not energetically produced.

6. Optimum pharyngeal resonance is inconsistent with excessive back-of-the-tongue tension. Were you aware of an inclination toward such tension in any of the preceding exercises? Recall that the mouth and the throat are continuous, coupled resonating cavities. If the back of the tongue is buckled or humped, the result is a narrowing of the coupling passage. The effect is a narrowed resonator, constriction, and a loss of reinforcement of the low-pitched tones. So, produce a free, open, and sustained *ah*. Note the state and feeling of the back of the tongue. The back of the tongue should be elevated

slightly, but not enough to block the view of the pharynx. Use a mirror, preferably a hand mirror, so that you can see the position and the feeling of an almost flattened tongue and an open, easy-to-view throat.

7. Drop your head to your chest, and vocalize an easy, sustained *aw*. Now roll your head gently and smoothly from shoulder to shoulder while sustaining the *aw*. Repeat with a long *ah*.

8. Begin as in Exercise 6, but this time add an *m* to the *ah* so that the result is *ahm*. Repeat five times.

9. With an open throat and a relaxed lower jaw, say each of the following three times. Say each slowly, and stop for a breath between vocalizations.

      lah, mah, bah, dah, nah, hah, pah, fah, thah, shah, yah

In the immediately succeeding exercises, it will not be possible to keep your throat as relaxed as for Exercises 1–5. Make certain, however, that your throat and mouth muscles are as relaxed as they can be while you are producing the indicated sounds. The exercises will emphasize oral activity and articulation in the front of the mouth.

10. Observe your mouth in a mirror as you say the following words in pairs. Note the changes in lip and jaw positions.

heal	who'll	elf	off	eat	ought
hit	hook	am	ohm	yen	yawn
hale	whole	alp	alm	ate	oat
high	hoe	eager	auger	heed	hod
him	home	heap	hop	ace	ice

11. Observe your lip and tongue activity as you say each of the following.

eternal tomes	teapot tempest
entertaining trips	ship to shore
tiny tidbits	precious prize
twisted and turned	balmy breeze
do or die	petty person
tense times	polished pewter
twice-told tales	pretty polly
tip to toe	winsome wiles

12. Say the following with proper regard for tongue and lip activity.
    a. The need to seek an answer to the question "Who and what am I?" is not unique to persons who are identified as philosophers.
    b. Twice-told tales may still be well told; three times told, they begin to sound stale and old.
    c. Dan was persistent in his request for a game of tiddlywinks.
    d. Jeanie tiptoed up the hill.
    e. The wind whistled a tune in the trees.
    f. The silvery moon shed its light on the lake.

    g. A wag once defined an American college as a football stadium with a few associated academic buildings.

    h. Is basketball replacing baseball as the most popular American sport?

    i. In a message to Congress, President Truman warned, "The release of atomic energy constitutes a new force too revolutionary to consider in the framework of old ideas."

13. The following selections should be read with emphasis on articulatory action in the front of the mouth.

    a. According to a Chinese proverb, two barrels of tears do not heal a bruise.

    b. In *The Magic Mountain*, Thomas Mann observed, "Order and simplification are the first steps toward the mastery of a subject—the actual enemy is the unknown."

    c. The essayist and critic George Hazlitt held that the only persons who truly deserve a monument are those who do not need one.

    d. Robert Louis Stevenson advised that to travel hopefully may be a better thing than to arrive.

    e. Stevenson also said that, in the last resort, every person is her or his own doctor of divinity.

    f. I speak severely to my boy,
      I beat him when he sneezes,
      For he can thoroughly enjoy
      The pepper when he pleases.
               —Lewis Carroll, *Alice's Adventures in Wonderland*

    g. In his poem *Don Juan* the rather cynical Lord Byron insisted that a lie is the truth in masquerade.

Nasal Resonance

Can you recall your last head cold or an allergy that involved the nasal passages? These conditions not only deprive you of the ability to produce proper nasal sounds but more generally and adversely affect all vocal efforts. We become especially aware of the need for nasal cavity reinforcement when we try to produce the nasal consonants *n*, *m*, and *ng* /ŋ/. These sounds are articulated orally, but they are reinforced in the nasal cavities and emitted through the nose. For the sound to enter the nasal cavities, the soft palate must be relaxed and lowered. Lowering the soft palate creates a large opening at the posterior entrance of the nasal cavities (the nares) and a narrow avenue through the nares for the sound to be reinforced (resonated) before it emerges from the nostrils. The characteristic differences in the three nasal consonants result from the modifications within the oral cavity.

For the sound *m*, the entire cavity is used because the tongue lies comparatively flat at the floor of the mouth; for *n*, the tongue is raised so that a smaller part of the mouth is used; for the *ng*, only a narrow area at the back of the mouth behind the raised tongue is used as a supplemental reinforcer.

Although there are only three English sounds that are characteristically (predominantly) nasal, there is little doubt that, in connected speech, sounds in close proximity to the nasals are also partly reinforced, nasally. It is virtually impossible to avoid some degree of nasality in the vowels of words such as *nine, mine,* and *ring.* How to avoid inappropriate and excessive nasalization of vowels is considered later. At the present time, we prefer to make a case for proper nasal reinforcement, rather than to create anxiety about excessive nasality as a defect of vocal production.

Appropriate nasal reinforcement provides both roundness and carrying power to the voice. It permits us to be heard with relatively little expenditure of energy. We can become aware of these effects by sustained, easy humming. To hum easily, make certain that the throat muscles, the tongue, and the soft palate are relaxed. The jaws should be almost but not quite together. The lips should barely touch so that a slight tickling sensation is experienced when humming. An easy, properly produced hum should be felt as well as heard. You should be able to feel it not only on the lips, but also at the sides of the nostrils if your thumb and index finger are placed gently at these areas.

The fullness of tone and vibrating effects associated with proper nasal reinforcement can be appreciated when we contrast a phrase or sentence with many nasal sounds with another containing no nasals, such as the following:

1. Mary meanders. Sue walks briskly.
2. Malcolm murmured enticingly. Babs appeared to be heartless.
3. Newington enjoyed strolling in the moonlight. Peters preferred daylight jogs.
4. Norman, enough of complaining and self-pitying mournful moping. While you're at it, erase those surly looks.
5. Donald MacDonald was the canniest member of an enormous clan. Jock Trusdale, a close relative, was reputed to be the brightest.
6. Milton won fame and fortune as an economist. Bob, his brother, had little use for worldly wealth.

The exercises that follow should help increase your awareness of nasal resonance as well as give you an appreciation of the fullness of tone and carrying power that you can achieve through the careful production of nasal sounds. At first, exaggerate the length of each nasal sound, but avoid any intentional increase of effort in vocalization. Also, be certain that each exercise is performed with a relaxed throat and jaw. Sustain your tones evenly through controlled, gradual abdominal contraction on exhalation.

EXERCISES FOR AWARENESS AND IMPROVEMENT OF NASAL RESONANCE

1. Hum up and down the musical scale. Then sing the musical scale with the conventional *do — re — mi. . . .* Compare the two vocal efforts. Request a friend to do the same while you listen to his or her vocal efforts. Which sounds

fuller? Was humming easier than the conventional singing? If your humming was done with your lips barely touching, the result should have been the production of a series of full, or relatively full, easy-to-produce tones.

2. Close your nostrils by pinching them and count from one through ten. Which numbers were not normally produced? Why?

3. Hum gently for the equivalent of a count of four on a sustained breath. Repeat five times.

4. Drop your jaw and bring the tip of the tongue into the position for *n*. Produce *n* for the equivalent of a count of four. Repeat five times. Repeat with the sound *m*.

5. Blend a hum with the sound *ah* (*mah*). Make certain that the soft palate is raised for the *ah*. Repeat five times.

6. Blend a lengthened *n* with *ah*, then do the same for *n* and *aw*. Repeat each five times.

7. Blend a lengthened *m* and *ah* and follow with another *m* (*mahm*). Do the same for *m* and *aw* (*mawm*). Repeat each five times.

8. Repeat Exercise 5 with *n* before and after the sounds *ah* and *aw* (*nahn and nawn*). Repeat each five times.

9. Exaggerate the length, but *not the loudness*, of the nasal sounds in the materials that follow:

aimless movements	nominal amount
meaningful motions	ninety-nine and one
lament for humankind	monumental mansions
means to an end	mournful numbers
human inclination	nameless memories
mundane miscellany	nameless and unknown
fame beyond reason	Neanderthal thinking

a. In Montreal, many Canadians speak both French and English.

b. In the Northern Hemisphere, November is often a rainy month.

c. In the Southern Hemisphere, November is a month of the spring season.

d. Nancy is known for her mathematical acumen.

e. Newman was keen on digging for clams on weekends.

f. A monody is a poem or a song in which one person laments the passing of another.

g. Norma enjoyed meandering through winding lanes.

h. Manganese is a chemical element employed in the making of steel from iron to give it hardness and toughness.

i. Milton wanted to be known as a man-about-town.

j. Nicaragua and Panama are Central American nations.

k. For the common man, the best memorial is some beneficient thing or function that shall bear his name.

— Charles T. Copeland, Speech, 1906

l. In his actions, however various,
Dixon was consistently nefarious.

— J. E., *The Variable Man*

m. Of manners gentle, of affections mild,
   In wit a man; simplicity a child.

   —Alexander Pope, *Epitaph on Gay*

n. To many Elizabethans, punning was considered a manifestation of intellectual acumen. A pun demands that the person must entertain two lines of thinking at the same moment. Why so many contemporary men and women respond to punning as a low form of humor is something of a mystery.

o. All too many physicians have an inordinate capacity to endure their patients' pains.

p. The Ming Dynasty is considered by some historians the last one of true Chinese origin. This dynasty is now renowned for its numerous contributions to scholarship and art, perhaps most notably for the making of luminous porcelain.

q. Martin, who had a well-earned reputation as a string saver, claimed that if you keep anything for a minimum of from seven to nine years, you are bound to find a need for it.

INAPPROPRIATE NASALITY

Our orientation in this book is to emphasize the positive. We prefer, for example, to explain how vocal tones can be produced clearly, with adequate loudness and proper breath control, rather than to discuss how to overcome hoarseness, breathiness, or any other vocal inadequacy or defect. This was also our approach in considering resonance and the reinforcement of tone by the nasal cavities. As a precautionary measure, however, we believe it advisable at this point to discuss separately the prevalent fault of excessive (inappropriate) nasality. Fortunately, when you learn either to avoid or to overcome excessive nasality, you will also attain the positive goal of appropriate nasal cavity reinforcement.

Causes of Excessive Nasality

The most common cause of excessive nasality is failure of the soft palate to rise when necessary to block off the stream of breath (sound) as it enters the oral pharynx. If the soft palate is elevated, the sound is directed forward and emitted orally. A relaxed soft palate permits the sound to enter the nasal cavities, where it is reinforced to become qualitatively nasal.

If failure to elevate the soft palate has a physical basis, medical attention is in order. If the failure is caused by a general indifference to speech efforts, to listener reactions, and superficially at least to the world in general, psychotherapy may be indicated. Excessive nasality is frequently associated with articulatory sluggishness. Often the jaw, lips, and tongue as well as the soft palate move without precision and alertness. The overall result is speech that sounds slovenly and a voice that sounds tired, monotonous, and nasal.

For the most part, excessive nasality is a manner of speech that has been learned unconsciously. Even if this manner of speaking reflected at one time an attitude of thinking or of behavior, change for the better can take place if the will to change is present.

The following exercises are based on the assumption that there is no organic basis for the excessive (inappropriate) nasality and no psychological need for its persistence.

EXERCISES FOR AWARENESS OF PALATAL ACTION

1. Stand before a mirror and yawn with a wide-open mouth. Note the upward movement of the soft palate and the uvula while the yawn is maintained. Stop the yawn and relax. Repeat and note the feeling as well as the action of the elevated palate.

2. Hum gently; then think but do not vocalize a lengthy *ah*. Be certain that your mouth is open and your tongue almost flat. Observe the action of the soft palate as it is elevated and maintained for the *ah*. Now by way of contrast, permit the soft palate to relax and produce a nasalized *ah*. Again, raise the soft palate for an appropriately vocalized *nonnasal ah*. Capture the feeling of the elevated soft palate when the *ah* is properly vocalized and orally reinforced. Repeat for the vowels of *all, ooze,* and *ease*.

3. Close your nostrils by pinching them. Say *ah*. Repeat with open nostrils. Whether your nostrils are pinched or free, there should be no identifiable nasality for the sound. Repeat with the vowels of *whose, hull, host, haw, hot, harsh*.

4. Say *n* while noting (feeling) the action and position of a relaxed soft palate. Then say *ah*, and again note the action and position of the elevated palate. Alternate between the two sounds until you have an immediate awareness of the difference in palatal position.

5. Place a clean, cold hand mirror under your nostrils and produce a lengthy *ah*. If the soft palate is elevated, there should be no clouding of the mirror. Practice until there is no clouding, then repeat with all the vowels of Exercise 3.

6. Repeat Exercise 5 with the vowels of *eel, if, ail, elf, hat,* and *ask*. Check with a mirror for nasalization. Be especially careful about the vowels of *elf, hat,* and *ask*.

7. Pinch your nostrils closed as you say each of the following sentences. (If you note a feeling of stuffiness in your nose, or a feeling of pressure in your ears, then you are being excessively nasal. Lift your soft palate to block off the entrance of air to the nasal cavity.)
   a. The beagle chased the fox through the fields.
   b. Bob walked his horse up the hill.
   c. The heavy fog rested atop the tall trees.
   d. What is it you wish to see?

    e. Peter helped Pat pick the flowers.

    f. Shakespeare held that brevity was the soul of wit.

    g. Paula preferred tea to coffee for supper.

    h. Ted liked to tell droll stories.

    i. All causes have effects; all effects have causes.

    j. Rita played the flute with great skill.

8. Say the following pairs of words with your attention focused on the avoidance of nasality in the second member of each pair. Make certain that your palate is elevated immediately after the nasal consonant is produced in the first member of each pair and through the production of the second member. It may also help to lessen any tendency toward nasality if you exaggerate the articulatory activity of the lips and the front part of the tongue.

neat	feat	moat	coat	nerve	verve
me	be	new	do	nest	lest
knit	lit	nook	book	knife	life
nail	dale	note	dote	meat	beat
met	wet	nought	bought	more	bore
mat	bat	not	dot	may	bay

mask	bask	man	ban	my	bye
need	bead	mare	bare	meal	keel
mud	bud	near	dear	male	bale
mile	bile	maze	daze	mike	bike
nice	dice	new	due	mob	bob
Nile	file	knob	sob	nice	dice
Nick	Dick	mace	race	mop	fop

Associated or Assimilated Nasality

Earlier, we learned that three sounds in American and English speech appropriately require nasal reinforcement for their production. These sounds are *m, n,* and *ng* /ŋ/. In connected speech, unless there is almost anxious care taken to avoid the effect, sounds in close proximity to nasal consonants are likely to be slightly nasalized. The nasalization is a "contamination by association" resulting from the manner of the articulation of the nasal sounds. Specifically, one of the following may happen:

1. The lowered soft palate may not be raised in time to prevent the following sound from being somewhat nasalized. Delay in raising the soft palate after the production of a nasal consonant probably accounts for the nasalization of the vowels that succeed the nasals in words such as *my, may, mate, new,* and *note.*

2. The soft palate may be lowered while the sound preceding the nasal is articulated, as in words such as *aim, and, whom, only, sing,* and *young.* Here the

nasalization is in *anticipation* of required articulatory movement (the lowering of the soft palate for the appropriate reinforcement of a succeeding nasal sound).

3. The soft palate may not be sufficiently elevated because of the influence of *preceding* as well as *succeeding* nasal consonants, as in *name, man, among, number, singing, ringing,* and *longing*.

There is no reasonable objection to some traces of nasalization resulting from the assimilative influence of nasal consonants. *What you need to avoid is an overall effect of dominant nasality* merely because some nasal sounds are present.

The exercises recommended earlier for gaining awareness and control of the soft palate are, of course, applicable to overcoming the effects of excessive nasalization resulting from the influence of nasal consonants. Here also, emphasis on front-of-the-mouth (tongue and lip) activity is important. The following additional exercises should also be helpful.

EXERCISES FOR AVOIDANCE OR REDUCTION OF ASSIMILATIVE NASALITY

When the nasal consonant precedes the vowel, lengthen the nasal consonant. Lengthening the consonant will afford you the extra moment of time needed to elevate the soft palate. This action should reduce the "contaminating" assimilative effect of associated nasality and permit you to give appropriate reinforcement to the nasal sound in the given context.

1. Practice on the following sound combinations. At the outset, exaggerate the length of the nasals to a marked degree. Then reduce the degree of exaggeration, but maintain the actual duration of the nasal sound for a time you consider about twice as long as normal. Finally, reduce the length of the nasals so that they are of normal duration, or as close to normal as possible, without nasalizing the succeeding sounds.

m	ee	n	ee
m	oo	n	oo
m	ay	n	ay
m	ah	n	ah
m	aw	n	aw
m	ice	n	ice
m	ap	n	ap

2. Practice saying the following words, at first exaggerating the length of the nasal sounds. Then practice with the same words, this time with as little exaggeration as possible consistent with the avoidance of assimilated nasality.

meet	mock	need	nick	mice
meal	mood	neat	noose	mole

mill	mull	nil	nook	moss
melt	mode	nail	note	moist
mate	maul	never	nought	moat
mat	mob	knave	not	must
mask	moth	nap	nock	mule
mud	mirth	nut	nerve	might

3. Practice with the following phrases, being careful at first to lengthen the nasal sounds and to avoid excessive nasality on the sounds that follow. Go over the same phrases, this time lengthening the nasals only as much as necessary to avoid assimilated nasality.

inquiring scientist	Sunday and Monday	many mice
a man of moods	not my meat	normal noise
more and more	now or never	nine miles
new to me	native of Norway	mighty mites
no news	many a moon	neither nor
move the map	next-door neighbor	mimics manners

4. Practice with the following sentences, observing the same precautions as in the preceding exercise.
   a. Martha enjoyed her work as a postmistress.
   b. Noah Webster believed that language as well as speech are immediate gifts of God.
   c. Ben Franklin observed that laws that are too gentle are seldom obeyed and those that are too severe are seldom enforced.
   d. Seneca advised that one learns best when one teaches.
   e. Is the primary business of the scientist to determine truths or to uncover beguiling untruths?
5. Emphasize oral activity for the sounds that precede the nasal consonants in the following words.

am	rant	lounge	turned	chance
aim	town	lunch	joined	game
end	any	round	found	want
own	only	yearn	haunt	find
on	anger	hunger	penny	sign

6. Incorporate the words of the preceding exercise into short sentences such as the following.
   a. There is nothing without an end.
   b. Big Jim owned the town.
   c. Jim, a noted gambler, won the town in a questionable game of chance.
   d. Neanderthal man no doubt had his own haunts and entertained hunger of the mind.

The following exercises emphasize combinations in which the nasal consonants both precede and follow vowels or diphthongs. They therefore provide an opportunity for careful control to avoid temptation and inclination to excessive assimilative nasality. Nasality of the nonnasal sounds can be minimized if you lengthen the first nasal consonant and emphasize oral activity for the succeeding vowel or diphthong. Your objective should be only as much lengthening of the nasals as is necessary to avoid assimilated nasality. Add a column of your own "pitfall" words to the list.

7. Practice on words such as the following.

mine	noon	innumerable	murmuring
mean	nine	rumbling	Neanderthal
nimble	meander	underneath	known
main	numerous	crowning	mentor
meant	numb	ambition	mince
moan	mournful	grinding	minnow
moon	meaningful	reminding	muttering

8. Avoid excessive assimilative nasality in these phrases.

inquiring mind	attending physician
mournful ruminations	beneficent donation
immense and imaginative	nine miles from the Nile
understanding response	management decision
magnificent mansions	unconscious manners

9. In sentence contexts, the tendency toward assimilative nasality is increased. Practice careful enunciation of the following.
   a. A living language is dynamic and undergoes constant change.
   b. Martin, in common with most persons, was more mindful of his own misfortunes than those of his next-door neighbors.
   c. The winter snows were followed by spring rains.
   d. If Benson had any inclination toward genius, it was in his ability to ignore any suggestion that he might resist temptation.
   e. Antonia was against any position initially taken by another. This inclination earned her the nickname of Contrary Toni.
   f. Samuel Johnson's famous dictionary included a number of personalized definitions. One example is for the term *pension*, which Johnson defined as "an allowance made to anyone without an equivalent. In England it is generally understood to mean pay given to a state hireling for treason to his country."
   g. "And all the days of Methuselah were nine hundred sixty and nine years," says Genesis IV:27.
   h. "One precedent creates another. They soon accumulate and constitute law"; this is a principle in *The Letters of Junius*.
   i. The island was in mournful fog in the winter; but with the coming of spring, life was dynamically renewed.

10. The following provide additional combinations in which the nasal consonants both precede and follow vowels or diphthongs.

    a. American football teams consist of eleven men.

    b. Dreams furnish opportunities for persons who are meek to become strong and to crown their unconscious ambitions and strivings with neither qualms nor anxieties about consequences.

    c. Mournful sounds are often made by nonmournful, gainfully employed minstrels.

    d. According to a Persian maxim, a person endowed with a long tongue may have a shortened life.

    e. Morton's farm background did not prepare him for employment on Madison Avenue.

    f. Anne preferred a short plane trip to a long one by train.

    g. The human being is a subject of thought, of scorn, of controversy, and of near divinity. Poets and thinkers through ancient times to the present have expressed their views. Here are two of them.

    —Carlyle maintained that humankind is the miracle beyond all miracles, "the great inscrutable mystery of God."

    —Mark Twain, not entirely in humor, once proclaimed: "There are times when one would like to hang the whole human race, and finish the farce."

11. As a test of your ability to resist the temptation of assimilated nasality, use the materials of Exercises 1, 2, and 4, intentionally exaggerating the overall nasality of your speech. Then, to demonstrate your control, go over the exercise materials without yielding to the temptation of assimilated nasality. By way of variety, try the same techniques for the following.

    a. Thomas Henry Huxley insisted that Nature never overlooks a mistake or makes even the smallest allowance for ignorance.

    b. In *Thunder on the Left*, Christopher Morley noted, "If you have to keep reminding yourself of a thing, perhaps it isn't so."

    c. As it is an ancient truth that freedom cannot be legislated into existence, so it is no less obvious that freedom cannot be censored into existence.
    —Dwight D. Eisenhower, President's Letter to American
    Library Association, June 1953

    d. Somewhere, behind Space and Time,
    Is wetter water, slimier slime!

    —Rupert Brooke, *Heaven*

    e. The morns are meeker than they were,
    The nuts are getting brown;
    The berry's cheek is plumper,
    The rose is out of town.

    —Emily Dickinson, *Nature*, Part II

    f. What a man needs in gardening is a cast-iron back, with a hinge in it.
    —Charles D. Warner, *My Summer in a Garden*

    g. In a letter to a friend, John Keats wrote: "The imagination may be compared to a dream—He awoke, and found it truth."

PRACTICE DIALOGUE FOR NASAL REINFORCEMENT

A MODEST INSPIRATION

Norman: Pam, have you any interesting plans for our outing tonight?

Pam: Not at the moment, Norman, but I've been hoping for an inspiration. Darling, I'm ready to have you inspire me.

Norman: Would you consider a hand-in-hand meander through Mason Meadow? Then we can go on to the Museum of Modern Masterpieces.

Pam: Let's keep that in mind for another evening. I have controlled enthusiasm for modern art. Tonight, let's be mundane and consider taking in a new movie. I learned this morning that a romantic yet not maudlin movie is packing them in.

Norman: Consider me inspired. The cinema it is. If we make an early start we can walk the twenty-nine blocks to the Cinema on the Town Mall.

Pam: Now, that's really an inspiration. I'll help with the cleanup and we'll be on our way. But don't forget, it's hand-in-hand.

SUGGESTED READINGS

Virtually all contemporary textbooks on speech pathology, speech disorders, or human communication disorders include discussions of resonance and nasality. The following references are tokens of what is available.

Bloodstein, O. (1979). *Speech pathology: An introduction.* Boston: Houghton Mifflin. (Disorders of resonation and specifically problems of nasality, are considered on pages 206–215.)

Boone, D. R. (1983). *The voice and voice therapy.* (3rd ed.). Englewood Cliffs, N.J.: Prentice-Hall. (Chapter 7 deals with disorders of resonance and includes specific suggestions for problems of faulty nasal resonance.)

Eisenson, J., & Ogilvie, M. (1977). *Communication disorders in children.* New York: Macmillan. (Although the problems of communication in this text are those primarily of children, the discussion on nasality in Chapter 12 is relevant for adults.)

Van Riper, C., & Emerick, L. (1984). *Speech correction* (7th ed.). Englewood Cliffs, N.J.: Prentice-Hall. (Chapter 7 deals with voice disorders and includes a discussion of excessive nasality, denasality, and assimilation nasality.)

CHAPTER 9

MAKING YOURSELF HEARD

Do your listeners have any difficulty in hearing you? Can you be readily heard without straining your voice? Are you easily able to adjust the loudness level of your voice to meet the needs of your listeners in specific and not always ideal circumstances? Are you sometimes accused of yelling when an ordinary conversational voice level is sufficient for the situation? On the other hand, are you occasionally accused of talking as if you were sharing a secret with the person closest to you in a conversational group while ignoring other members who are farther away?

Adequate loudness, as was previously pointed out, is an essential attribute of an effective voice. For most of us, adequate loudness usually means being easily heard in conversational situations. Sometimes it means competing with environmental noises, both human and mechanical. Occasionally, however, we must speak to a group in a physical setting that demands a louder-than-normal conversational voice. Sometimes we must speak under conditions that demand more loudness than is ordinarily needed. We may, for example, have to yell a warning, issue a command, or address a large group without the assistance of electronic amplification, or we may suddenly have to rise to the demands of the occasion when electronic amplification fails.

CONTROL OF LOUDNESS

Loudness is best regulated through control of breathing. One way to speak loudly is to increase the amount of energy used to set the vocal bands in vibration. (Actually, it is to increase the amplitude of the flutter action of the vocal bands, which in turn set the column of air [breath] in vibration.) The greater the amplitude, the louder the vocal tone will be. In addition, loudness is related to the way resonating cavities reinforce vocal tones. (This was discussed at some length in Chapter 8.) When we vocalize, the fundamental frequency — the tone produced as a result of vocal-band action — is amplified throughout the vocal tract. The tones we identify as vowels or diphthongs are products of the particular cavity or coupling of cavities that are most actively involved in the speech effort. (See the discussion of vowel sounds in Chapter 13 for an expansion of this point.) Because of the phenomenon of the reinforcement of vocal tones through resonance, vocalizing loudly enough to be readily heard usually demands less energy than might otherwise be required.

If we recognize that the vocal attribute we think of as loudness is a result of the amplitude or swing of the vocal bands and the amount of reinforcement afforded the initiated tone by the resonating cavities acting as reinforcers, we will not overstress the amount of force or energy it takes to speak as loudly as the occasion requires. The danger in using added energetic action to produce loud tones is that pharyngeal and laryngeal strain may result. The effect of such strain is to reduce the efficiency of the cavities of the pharynx and the larynx as reinforcing cavities. As a result, the vocal tones are less loud than they might otherwise be. In carrying out the suggestions for increasing loudness, avoid increasing tension of the larynx or of the throat. In addition to the physical feeling of strain, be aware of any elevation of pitch. If your vocal tones are higher in pitch than normal, the muscles (walls) of your resonating cavities are probably excessively tense.

To understand the change in action of the abdominal wall in loud vocalization, place your hands on the abdomen and shout aloud, "Ready, go!" You will (or should be able to) note that there is a sudden pulling in of the abdominal muscles and that the pulling in is greater than for normal conversation. If this does not occur, and you are not readily able to speak as loudly as you would like to and should reasonably expect to, then the following exercise should be of help in establishing adequate loudness, that is, a voice that can project easily and effectively.

For the exercises that follow, as well as for all vocal exercises, the use of an area such as a music practice room where you can vocalize freely and without undue self-consciousness is of considerable help.

EXERCISES FOR DEVELOPING ADEQUATE LOUDNESS

1. Review the exercises for proper breath control (see Chapter 5). This review should create or increase your awareness of the abdominal action established for conversation voice needs.
2. Place your hands on your abdomen and say *ah* as you might for a throat examination. Then take a moderately deep but comfortable breath and again begin to say *ah*. This time apply pressure suddenly with your hands. The tone should increase in loudness. If you have not caught yourself by surprise, and exhaled without vocalization, the *ah* should have become appreciably louder. Whether or not you have caught yourself by surprise, repeat the exercise and produce a loud *ah*.
3. Repeat Exercise 2, producing three loud *ah's* without straining. Breathe in if necessary after each *ah*. Loud voice production requires more breath than normal conversation, so that more frequent inhalation becomes necessary to maintain a loud voice without strain. Try again, this time with *aw*.
4. Repeat, except this time exert direct control over the abdominal muscles as you produce your loud *ah's* and *aw's*.

5. Say the following short commands, each on a single breath, without strain and without an elevation of pitch level toward the end of the phrase.
    a. Let's go!
    b. Do it now!
    c. We're ready!
    d. Stop him!
    e. Look lively!
    f. Give him a hand.
    g. Lower away!
    h. Throw them out.
    i. Turn around.
    j. Silence, please!
    k. Not that!
    l. I've had it with you!
    m. None of that nonsense!
    n. Hello out there.
    o. I'm going, and that's that.
    p. I won't listen even if you shout!
    q. You may leave, but not with me.
    r. Jump, before it's too late.

6. Try the following sentences on a single breath, if possible. Speak as if there were a need to use a loud voice to assert yourself.
    a. No, this will not do.
    b. Let's waste no more time.
    c. Certainly, I meant what I said.
    d. Old fellow, just pack up and go.
    e. We'll talk about this matter later.
    f. I want my full share.
    g. Yes, I do like him.
    h. Consider me gone but not forgotten.

The following exercises are intended to help in the building up and control of degrees of loudness rather than in the sudden production of a loud voice. Such practice is closer to the normal use of loudness for emphasis and vocal variety in speaking.

EXERCISES FOR CONTROLLING LOUDNESS

1. Initiate an *ah* in a tone that is barely audible; gradually increase the loudness of the *ah* until it is louder than your usual conversational voice, and then reduce the loudness until the tone is again barely audible. Do not change the pitch or force the length of exhalation beyond a point of comfort.

2. Count from one to five, increasing the loudness on each number. Begin with a barely audible *one* and end with a *five* that can be easily heard across a forty-foot room.

3. Count to seven, increasing the loudness up to *four* and then decreasing in loudness from *five* through *seven*. Maintain the same pitch level throughout the count.

4. Say each of the following phrases or sentences three times, increasing in loudness from a normal conversational level to one that can be easily heard across a forty-foot room.
   a. He's gone.
   b. Come back!
   c. Please!
   d. No! Not now.
   e. I will not.
   f. Enough is enough.
   g. Who's there?
   h. Why won't you?
   i. Tomorrow will be time enough.

5. Lengthen the vowel in each of the following words and maintain uniform loudness throughout the lengthened production of the vowel. Do not, however, distort the vowel by excessive lengthening.

fawn	brawn	mourned
alms	gnaw	rover
bomb	thaw	garnish
father	walk	normal
pause	tall	dawned
awe	mall	roster

6. Lengthen and maintain the force of the vowels or diphthongs of the stressed syllables in the following phrases. Again, avoid distorting the vowel or diphthong to the point where a listener would not be certain of the words you are saying.

High mountain	Stand aside
Do go now	Raving madness
Loud laughing	Welcome applause
Come real early	Large mansion
Almost ready	Ardent and awesome
Bounce the ball	Gone, long gone
Worthwhile	Honest to the core

7. Read the sentences that follow, first at your conversational voice level, and then as if you were trying to address a person in the last row of a crowded room.
   a. Dorothy, when will you arrive?
   b. I'll be ready in a few minutes.
   c. The time for action is now!

d. I am saying this for the last time.
e. If you really wish to understand, listen!
f. Why are you always late?

STRENGTHENING THE VOICE

Thus far, our discussion of loudness has been based on the assumption that you can make yourself heard under normal conditions, but might need assistance in making yourself heard under more difficult conditions. Occasionally, however, we find persons whose habitual loudness levels are too weak for easy listening in relatively good speaking situations. A few such persons may need help in being heard even in quiet conversations.

In some instances, the cause of a weak voice is physical and may be attributed to a structural disturbance or an anomaly of the vocal mechanism. Such instances are comparatively rare and require specialized treatment rather than self-help to improve the voice as much as possible. Sometimes, a weak voice may be a carryover from a physical state that had its beginnings during a period of illness or a subsequent period of convalescence. Some persons, when ill, may not have the energy to make themselves heard. In the early stages of recovery, they may not care whether they are heard.

When well enough to care, some persons may decide that making others strain to listen is not without advantage. So, a habit of weak vocalization may persist. There is also a possibility that a speaker was brought up as a child in a home with an ill relative, or one who believes that children should be seen, if necessary, but were not ordinarily worthy of being heard. The barely audible voice may then have become the safer one, the one that did not bring isolation or a scolding.

Occasionally, the weak or barely audible voice characterizes the individual who feels that what he or she has to say is unworthy of a listener or that as a speaker he or she lacks value. Weak vocalization may be interpreted as apologetic noises or noises that are produced because one has a social need to say something and, at the same time, fears that, if heard, he or she may be held responsible for what is said. We associate these traits with shyness.

Such physical and mental conditions, however, are not the usual causes of a weak voice. Much more frequently, a weak voice is the result of poor vocal habits, such as poor breath control, habitual breathiness, excessive tension of the vocal mechanism, inappropriate pitch, or improper use of the resonating cavities to reinforce vocal tones.

If you have no reason to believe that there is anything physically wrong with your vocal apparatus, if you are not pining for the supposed advantages and immunities of the ill or the attentions associated with convalescence, and if you are a reasonably well-adjusted person, then readily audible voice should be no problem.

The earlier discussions on how to control loudness through control of breathing obviously holds for a person with a weak voice. In addition, the exercises that follow should help.

EXERCISES FOR STRENGTHENING A WEAK VOICE

1. Drop your jaw for a gentle but open-mouthed yawn. Inhale with your mouth open, and then pull in slowly but firmly on the abdominal muscles. Now permit a yawn to escape as you exhale as a "by-product" of the position of your mouth and of your controlled breathing.

2. Repeat Exercise 1 five times, making the yawn louder each time but maintaining the same pitch.

3. Now, instead of yawning, prepare to say *aw* as in *awful*. Maintain an even pitch. Repeat five times.

4. Repeat Exercise 3, but this time with the sound *oh*.

5. Say *oh* as follows: (a) as if surprised; (b) as if horrified; (c) as if pleased; and (d) as if you are shouting a warning.

6. Pretend you are imitating a siren on a fire truck, increasing and decreasing the loudness of your voice on the sound *oh*. Repeat, using the sound *aw*. Avoid any feeling of tension of the throat or larynx, and do not extend the length of vocalization to a point of discomfort.

7. Imagine that you are speaking to an audience of five hundred people. Suddenly you discover that the amplifying system has failed. You wish to accomplish the following:

   a. Notify the audience that you and they will have to get along without the benefit of mechanical amplification.

   b. Get the members in the rear rows and the side sections to fill in the empty seats in the front and center sections.

   c. Determine whether you are speaking loudly enough by asking, "How many of you are right-handed?"

   d. Instruct your listeners to raise the right hand whenever they cannot hear you.

8. Count from one through five, increasing the loudness on each count but maintaining the same pitch level. Repeat three times.

9. Practice each of the following in a voice loud enough to be readily heard across the length of your living room.

   a. A great nose indicates a great man—
      Genial, courteous, intellectual,
      Virile, courageous.

      —Edmond Rostand, *Cyrano de Bergerac*

   b. The greatest task before civilization at present is to make machines what they ought to be, the slaves instead of the masters of men.

      —Havelock Ellis, *Little Essays of Love and Virtue*

   c. Let's talk sense to the American people. Let's tell them the truth, that there are no gains without pains.

      —Adlai Stevenson, Speech, Chicago, 1952

   d. The policy of repression of ideas cannot work and never has worked.

      —Robert Hutchins, Testimony before a congressional committee

e. And we are here as on a darkling plain
      Swept with confused alarms of struggle and flight,
        Where ignorant armies clash by night.
                                              —Matthew Arnold, *Dover Beach*

f. Ah, Faustus
      Now hast thou but one bare hour to live,
      And then thou must be damn'd perpetually!
                                          —Christopher Marlowe, *Faustus*

g. Are you through? Are you finally and completely through?

h. Let the great world spin forever down the ringing grooves of change.
                                      —Alfred, Lord Tennyson, *Locksley Hall*

i. He flung himself from the room, flung himself upon his horse and rode
   madly off in all directions.
                                  —Stephen Leacock, *Gertrude the Governess*

j. Shrill and high, newsboys cry
      The worst of the city's infamy.
                                      —William Vaughn Moody, *In New York*

k. Lay on, Macduff
   And damn'd be him, that first cries,
   "Hold, enough!"
                                          —William Shakespeare, *Macbeth*

l. Pour the sweet milk of concord into hell,
      Uproar the universal peace, confound
      All unity on earth.
                                          —William Shakespeare, *Macbeth*

10. If you have no difficulty making yourself heard across your living room, try
    the same selections again, but this time pretend that your room is forty feet
    long and as many feet wide. If you are successful in this exercise, then repeat
    the selections as if you were addressing an audience from the stage of a
    moderate-sized theater.

11. Read the following as if you were addressing four hundred persons waiting
    for your announcements in an auditorium that has no public address system.
    a. The meeting is adjourned until 1:00 P.M.
    b. Lunch is now being served in the dining room.
    c. Walk; do not run to the dining room.
    d. Jan Brown is wanted on the phone.
    e. When the session is over, please leave by the exit nearest to you.

12. Assume that you are in an auditorium and are about to address a large
    audience. You are informed that the amplifying system is not working.
    Nevertheless, you are determined that you will be heard through your own
    vocal efforts. To present your point of view on nuclear energy, you are
    prepared to read the following:
    Since I do not foresee that atomic energy is to be a great boon for a long
    time, I have to say that for the present it is a menace. Perhaps it is well that

it should be. It may intimidate the human race into bringing order into its international affairs, which, without the pressure of fear, it would not do.
—Albert Einstein, on the atomic bomb,
Atlantic Monthly, November, 1945

FORCE, STRESS, AND VOCAL VARIETY

At this point, let us assume you have no problem in controlling loudness so that you can be heard even under less than optimum conditions. You can be heard! Now let us consider how you can employ subtle changes in force to provide color and shades of meaning for what you have to say.

Syllable Stress

Differential syllable stress is a feature of English speech. We use differential stress or accent in the pronunciation of polysyllabic words so that "normally" a word such as *rainy* or *beautiful* would be uttered with the primary stress, or accent, on the first syllable. In the word *beautiful*, a secondary stress may be heard on the final syllable. In a word such as *unkind*, the "normal" syllable stress is on the second syllable. In some contexts, however, a speaker may intentionally stress the first syllable of the word *unkind* to communicate his meaning, for example, "Yes, he certainly is an *un*kind man." Syllable stress in polysyllabic words is characterized by an increased force or loudness associated with relatively longer duration and higher pitch than for the unstressed syllables of the words.

PRACTICE MATERIALS

1. Some words differ in parts of speech, and so in meaning, according to their syllable stress. What are the differences in meaning of the following words when the accent or syllable stress is shifted from the first to the second syllable?

ap*pro*priate	appropri*ate*
*con*duct	con*duct*
*con*vert	con*vert*
*con*vict	con*vict*
*di*gest	di*gest*
*dis*charge	dis*charge*
*ex*tract	ex*tract*
*fre*quent	fre*quent*

object   *object*
permit   *permit*
progress   *progress*
produce   *produce*
rebel   *rebel*
survey   *survey*
suspect   *suspect*

2. Apply the differential stress to the appropriate syllable:
   a. Conduct the convert to the place of discharge.
   b. Joe made rapid progress when his object was a shop that sold his favorite grape extract.
   c. I will not object to your buying this art object.
   d. The farmer produced a bumper crop of produce.
   e. We had reason to suspect that Barton was the prime suspect.
   f. The prosecutor was unable to convict the accused without the testimony of a cooperating convict.

Stress in Compound Words

In general, compound words differ from polysyllabic words in stress. For compounds, the stress is "normally" equal or almost so for each of the components. Compounds are similarly distinguished in stress from the components of the compound by relatively equal stress for the two parts of the former. Thus, we may distinguish the meaning of "Jack is in the green house" from "Jack is in the greenhouse," or "After a half hour of fishing, I hauled in a weak fish" from "After a half hour of fishing, I hauled in a weakfish."

PRACTICE MATERIALS

1. Through the use of differential syllable stress, indicate the differences in meaning of the words in the previous list and the paired words that follow by incorporating them into sentences, such as "Bill made progress in his field" and "Bill was determined to progress in his field." In addition to changes in syllable stress, what other vocal features do you detect in the production of the compound words?

birthday	birth day
blackbird	black bird
blowout	blow out
bluebell	blue bell
breakthrough	break through
campground	camp ground

greenhouse	green house
flatfoot	flat foot
blowpipe	blow pipe
layout	lay out
freeway	free way
turnaround	turn around
briefcase	brief case
hideout	hide out
Irishman	Irish man
lightmeter	light meter
paperback	paper back
sometime	some time

2. How do you determine the meaning of the following pairs of sentences?

   a. Since childhood, she had had her eye on the White House.
   Since childhood, she had had her eye on the white house.

   b. Please, may I have my paper back?
   Please, may I have my paperback?

   c. Hilary was a lighthouse keeper.
   Hilary was a light housekeeper.

   d. Sue spent considerable time in the greenhouse.
   Sue spent considerable time in the green house.

   e. Joe took his handout.
   Joe took his hand out.

   f. Fran talked to the bluebird.
   Fran talked to the blue bird.

===

Change in Syllabic Stress for Polysyllabic Words

Many words that are modified in meaning as they are lengthened by affixes (suffixes) usually are pronounced with a shift in primary stress but maintain a secondary stress as in their shorter root form. For example, *refer* and *referential*, *product* and *production*, *object* (as noun) and *objection*. In these instances, the primary stress shifts from the first part of the word to a later syllable.

===

PRACTICE MATERIALS

1. Determine the primary and secondary stress for the following word pairs:

answer	answerable
anxious	anxiety

banal	banality
bounty	bountiful
concept	conceptualize
converse	conversation
occupy	occupation
person	personality
simple	simplify
stable	stability

2. Note the shift in syllable stress in the following:
   a. Major Domo won a majority of his arguments.
   b. Eileen, herself a beauty, enjoyed beautifying her garden.
   c. Dick was rarely objective about the subjects he espoused.
   d. Doris had no difficulty in conceptualizing theoretic concepts.
   e. Bob was driven to abstraction in trying to appreciate abstract art.

Variety for Emphasis

Except in public speaking situations in which the speaker does not have the help of electronic amplification, large differences in the use of force are rarely necessary. Changes in degree rather than "quantum jumps" provide variety that will permit you, even as a public speaker, to indicate the relative importance of the ideas you are presenting. Not always does importance dictate an increase in loudness. Sometimes a desired effect to give special meaning to an idea is better achieved when the significant words are spoken with deliberate slowness and reduced, rather than increased, loudness. The sentence "Please, my only love, do listen" is an example of this point. If the words "do listen" are spoken so that they are barely audible, the sentence as a whole is given more complete meaning than might otherwise be possible.

A change in loudness may be used to achieve dramatic, as well as subtle, intellectual effects. A deliberate, degree-by-degree increase in loudness from a low to a high level helps to produce a dramatic effect. A reduction from a moderately high to a low level may also be dramatic as well as sophisticated, providing *the content is worthy of the technique.*

EXERCISES FOR SUBTLE CHANGES IN LOUDNESS

1. Read the following lines with both "ascending" and "descending" changes in loudness.
   a. I believe that man will not merely endure: he will prevail.
                                 — William Faulkner, Speech upon
                            receiving the Nobel Prize in Literature, 1950
   b. All animals are equal, but some animals are more equal than others.
                                     — George Orwell, *Animal Farm*
2. Read the following sentences, changing the stress from the first word of the

sentence to each succeeding word. Do not, however, stress articles, conjunctions, or prepositions. How does the meaning of each sentence change with the differences in word stress?

   a. Roberta said that only she and Susan will go.
   b. Richard was poor but honest to the core.
   c. Either you or I must leave.
   d. Janet is quite fond of Jim.
   e. Is she the one you said you like?
   f. Well, what is your answer now?
   g. At last, this is your just reward.
   h. Joe is indeed a brilliant fellow.
   i. We thought he had returned.
   j. He will not be long for this world.
   k. Thursday was the day of reckoning.
   l. She and she alone can do anything.
   m. Fred was almost run down.
   n. Are you sure that this is the whole truth?

3. Read sentences a, b, and c of Exercise 2, stressing the conjunction. What are the changes in meaning?

4. Use controlled and moderate changes in stress to bring out the flavor and meaning of the wit and wisdom of the following items from Benjamin Franklin's *Poor Richard's Almanac.*

   a. The worst wheel of the cart makes the most noise.
   b. Genius without education is like silver in the mine.
   c. He that would live in peace and at ease, must not speak all he knows, nor judge all he sees.
   d. A man in a passion rides a mad horse.
   e. None but the well-bred man knows how to confess a fault, or acknowledge himself in an error.

5. The same approach—the use of controlled and moderate changes in stress—should be used in bringing out the essential meanings of the following passages.

   a. What I must do is all that concerns me, not what the people think. This rule, equally arduous in actual and intellectual life, may serve for the whole distinction between greatness and meanness. It is the harder because you will always find those who think they know what is your duty better than you know it. It is easy in the world to live after the world's opinion; it is easy in solitude to live after our own; but the great man is he who in the midst of the crowd keeps with perfect sweetness the independence of solitude.
   — Ralph Waldo Emerson, *Self-Reliance*

   b. He may as well concern himself with his shadow on the wall. Speak what you think now in hard words and tomorrow speak what tomorrow thinks in hard words again, though it contradict everything you said today—"Ah, so you shall be sure to be misunderstood"—Is it so bad, then, to be misunderstood? Pythagoras was misunderstood, and Socrates, and Jesus, and Luther, and Copernicus, and Galileo, and Newton, and every pure and wise spirit that ever took flesh. To be great is to be misunderstood.
   — Ralph Waldo Emerson, *Essays*

   c. More important than winning the election, is governing the nation. That is the test of a political party — the acid, final test.

        — Adlai Stevenson, Speech accepting
        presidential nomination, July 20, 1952

   d. Man, unlike any other thing organic or inorganic in the universe, grows beyond his work, walks up the stairs of his concepts, emerges ahead of his accomplishments.

        — John Steinbeck, *The Grapes of Wrath*

6. Use more marked changes in stress to communicate the meanings of the following passages.

   a. Four freedoms: The first is freedom of speech and expression — everything in the world. The second is freedom of every person to worship God in his own way — everywhere in the world. The third is freedom from want — everywhere in the world. The fourth is freedom from fear — anywhere in the world.

        — Franklin D. Roosevelt,
        Message to Congress, January 1941

   b. The death of democracy is not likely to be an assassination from ambush. It will be slow extinction from apathy, indifference, and undernourishment.

        — Robert Hutchins, *Great Books*

   c. The fact that man knows right from wrong proves his *intellectual* superiority to the other creatures; but the fact that he can *do* wrong proves his *moral* inferiority to any creature that *cannot*.

        — Mark Twain, *What Is Man?*

   d. John Milton asked, "What is strength without a double share of wisdom? Vast, unwieldy, burdensome, proudly secure, yet liable to fall by weakest subtleties; strength's not made to rule, but to subserve, where wisdom bears command."

   e. Two and two continue to make four, in spite of the whine of the amateur for three, or the cry of the critic for five.

        — James M. Whistler, *Whistler v. Ruskin*

   f. Read the following stanza with increased but controlled force up to the next to the last line; try reading the last line with a marked reduction in force to achieve dramatic contrast.

      O masters, lords and rulers in all lands,
      How will the future reckon with this man?
      How answer his brute question in that hour
      When whirlwinds of rebellion shake all shores?
      How will it be with kingdoms and with kings —
      With those who shaped him to the thing he is —
      When this dumb terror shall rise to judge the world,
      After the silence of the centuries?

        — Edwin Markham, *The Man with the Hoe*

CHAPTER 10

TIMING: RATE, DURATION, AND PAUSE

What things have we seen
Done at the Mermaid? Heard words that have been
So nimble, and so full of subtle flame,
As if that everyone from whence they came,
Had meant to put his whole wit in a jest,
And resolved to live a fool, the rest
Of his dull life.

In a letter to his friend Ben Jonson, Francis Beaumont (1640) expressed the admiration of the writer for the apt use of language, for words that are "so nimble and full of flame." Admittedly, only a few of us have the verbal facility to be as witty as we would like *at the right moment*. But almost all of us can make use of the attributes of voice as well as a considered choice of words, to be effective in day-to-day communication.

In Chapter 9 we discussed the use of changes in force, word and syllable stress, and vocal variety to enhance communication. The present chapter, in essence, is an expansion of the discussion, considering how to convey nuances and subtleties in meaning and feeling. We will not, however, lose sight of the need to convey marked changes when the situation calls for it. The felicitous "subtle flame" may continue to elude you, or it may be a happy rare occurrence. However, it is well within your potential to employ changes in timing, in variations of rate, duration, and pause, to enable you to convey how you feel about what you think when you so choose.

Changes in rate and duration—the time we give to an utterance—and the intentional moments of pause between words and phrases permit us to express our thoughts and related feelings. They also permit us to emphasize some aspects of what we wish to communicate and to subordinate others. There are no hard or inflexible rules about the use of timing, but there are general guides. To express a feeling such as depression, sadness, or solemnity, a discernibly slow rate is usually effective. In contrast, a marked increase in rate is associated with happier states, lightheartedness, and heightened feelings. However, a heightened feeling need not always be pleasant. Anger and rage are usually expressed through an increased rate of utterance.

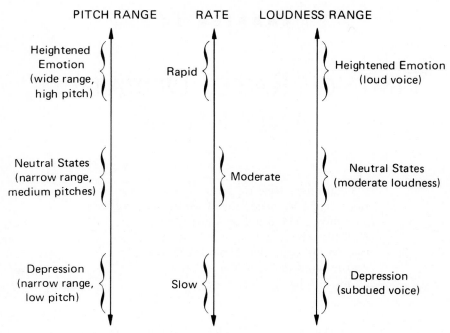

Figure 10–1   The relationship between changes in pitch and loudness and the states of feeling. (This is similar to Figure 7–5, repeated for convenience.)

Variations in pitch and force tend to be associated with changes in the rate of utterance. As pointed out in Chapter 7, heightened feelings are usually accompanied by increases in range and higher levels of pitch and force. Figure 7–5 summarizes these variations. Figure 10–1 includes rates of utterance and articulation associated with various states of feeling.

As indicated earlier, changes in duration are achieved through variation in the rate of articulation or the use of pauses between groups of articulated sounds, or both. In general, content that is articulated slowly is considered more important — intellectually more significant — than rapidly articulated content. If we listen to what is spoken slowly and are able to maintain attention while listening, we assume that what we have heard is more important than more quickly spoken content.

Some speech sounds — vowels and vowel-like consonants — lend themselves to a varied and controlled rate of articulation. Words such as *lonely, awesome, home, gone, away, loom, always,* and *evermore* contain these sounds. They can be uttered quickly or slowly according to your will as a speaker. On the other hand, words such as *pit, tip, bit, stop, quick,* and *put* are usually articulated rapidly. In lyric prose and poetry, dominant moods can be established through language that incorporates "slow" sounds and "rapid" sounds. Compare, for example, Poe's lines.

> Sorrow for the lost Lenore —
> For the rare and radiant maiden whom the angels name Lenore —
> Nameless *here* for evermore.

or Coleridge's

> Alone, alone, all, all alone;
> Alone on a wide, wide sea.

with Gilbert's

> Life's a pudding
>   full of plums;
> Care's a canker
>   that benumbs,
> Wherefore waste our
>   elocution
> On impossible
>   solution?
> Life's a pleasant
>   institution,
> Let us take it as
>   it comes!

or his observation:

> The meaning doesn't matter if it's only idle
>   chatter of a transcendental kind.

The differences in mood become readily apparent in Poe's lines from *The Raven* and Coleridge's *The Ancient Mariner* compared with Gilbert's *The Gondoliers* and *Patience*. Poe's lines lend themselves to a slow rate of articulation, whereas those from Gilbert, even without a reader's trying, are articulated quickly. A competent patter-song actor articulates them even more rapidly to produce the essential nonsense effect.

═══ RATE AND MEANING ═══

We must, of course, appreciate that when the rate of utterance is conspicuously changed to be either relatively rapid or relatively slow, the most significant word within the phrase, or the most significant phrase within the sentence, is usually spoken more slowly than the rest of the phrase or sentence. Any sustained, unvarying rate may become monotonous. Nothing of any considerable content that we say or read aloud should be uttered at the same rate, regardless of the feeling or mood.

The *use of pause* as a technique for varying rate is perhaps the best single indication of control and sophistication in speech. When a speaker pauses at the end of a phrase, the listeners wait. While waiting, they tend to fill in the time gaps with the last bit of content they heard. The inner listener repetition of what the speaker has last said reinforces this content. A pause before and after a word or a phrase sets either off from the rest of the context and so becomes a technique for the vocal underlining of an idea or a unit of thought.

A pause may also be used to indicate transition of thought in a larger context. This is the case when a speaker pauses after the evident completion of a thought. A short pause may separate sentences, a moderate pause may separate paragraphs, and a longer pause may prepare the listeners for a new line of thought.

Dramatic effects may be achieved by the combination of a pause with a rising inflection. If the phrase before the pause ends with an upward inflection, the result is the "suspension" of a thought. The thought is then completed in the content that follows. A similar effect may be achieved with a pause before and after a presented idea. In general, a pause before the beginning of a new phrase tends to create a feeling of suspense to be satisfied by what follows in the speaker's utterance.

When an intentional pause is used, the speaker has an obligation to satisfy the expectations of the listeners. If the content that follows the pause turns out to be of no greater importance or significance than what preceded it, the speaker has failed to meet the implied obligation, and the listeners are likely to become disappointed and distrusting.

We all use pauses as one device to separate or group our phrases. In conversational speech such word groupings come naturally with the flow of thought. When our thoughts do not flow as freely as we might like, when we search for words to communicate our thoughts, we reveal this hesitation in our unintentional pauses. Under the pressure of a large or formal audience, we may become fearful and anxious about pausing, and we may fill in the gaps with *uh-uh's* or their equivalent in nonverbal sounds to avoid moments of silence. Speakers who are poised enough to wait, who pause with intent and without fear, and who do not resort to repetitious fillers to avoid the void of silence will gain the respect of their listeners if what they have to say is worth the waiting and the listening. With these points in mind, you should find the exercises that follow of help in your practice of some of the uses of timing for vocal variety to maintain interest and attention and as a technique for expressing feeling and communicating your thinking.

EXERCISES FOR PRACTICE OF CONTROLLED RATE

1. Read the following sentences so that full value is given to the italicized words. The sentences as a whole are to be spoken slowly, and the italicized words more slowly than the others.
    a. *Innocence* is *inconsistent* with the *acquisition* of *riches*.
    b. The *air* was *still*, the sea was *calm*.
    c. *All* rivers *find* their *way* to the *sea*.
    d. In *solitude* we may be *least alone*.
    e. *Life* is what the *living make it*.
    f. The *snow* fell and *silently* concealed the *earth*.
    g. *Freedom* can *survive only* when it is *shared*.
    h. *Tomorrow* will *come* and pass into *yesterday*.
    i. Man's *inhumanity* to *man* makes *countless* thousands *mourn*.

j. Through *memory* we can *recreate* a *yesterday* and project a *tomorrow*.

k. Are we *now* at a *time* when knowledge has *outrun wisdom*?

l. *Novelists*, whatever else they may be besides, are *also children talking to children — in the dark*.

>   —Bernard De Voto, *The World of Fiction*

m. A *handful* of *sand* is an *anthology* of the *universe*.

>   —David McCord, *Once and for All*

n. *Fanaticism* consists in *redoubling* your *efforts* when you have forgotten *your aim*.

>   —George Santayana, *The Life of Reason*

o. You *can't hold a man down* without *staying down* with him.

>   —Attributed to Booker T. Washington

p. *War* is at best *barbarism*. . . . Its glory is *all moonshine*. It is only *those* who have *neither fired* a *shot* nor *heard* the *shrieks* and *groans* of the *wounded* who *cry aloud* for *blood*, more *vengeance, more desolation. War* is *hell*.

>   —William T. Sherman, Address at Michigan
>   Military Academy, June 19, 1879

2. The next group of sentences should be spoken at a moderate rate; for emphasis, the italicized words should be said more slowly and somewhat more loudly than other parts of the sentences.

a. *Life* does *not* give itself to *one* who tries to *keep all* its advantages *at once*. I have often thought *morality* may perhaps *consist solely* in the *courage* of making a *choice*.

>   —Leon Blum, *On Marriage*

b. I don't know *why* it is we are in such a *hurry* to *get up* when we *fall down*. You might *think* we should *lie there* and *rest a while*.

>   —Max Eastman, *The Enjoyment of Laughter*

c. I had *rather* take my *chance* that *some traitors* will *escape detection* than *spread* abroad a *spirit* of general *suspicion* and *distrust*, which *accepts rumor* and *gossip* in *place* of *undismayed and unintimidated inquiry*.

>   —Learned Hand, Address to Board of Regents, New York, 1952

d. *No* one can *build* his *security* upon the *nobleness* of *another* person.

>   —Willa Cather, *Alexander's Bridge*

e. The *acquisition* of *great wealth* and the *maintenance* of great *innocence* may *mutually exclude each other*.

f. For it to be *safe anywhere, freedom* must *grow everywhere*.

g. As more *oxygen*-producing *forests* are *burned*, more *carbon dioxide* is *produced*, which *traps heat* and prevents it from *radiating* from the *surface* of the *planet*. This results in a *loss* of *vegetation* and an *overall warming* of the *planet Earth*. When *photographed from space*, the *Earth* appears to be *brown*. Ironically, this *browning* is called "the *Greenhouse Effect*."

h. The *optimist proclaims* that we *live* in the *best of all* possible *worlds*, and the *pessimist fears this is true*.

>   —James Branch Cabell, *The Silver Stallion*

i. A *mother* is not a person to *lean on*, but a person to make *leaning unnecessary*.

>   —Dorothy Canfield, *Her Son's Wife*

j. It might be said of *Thoreau* that he *loved not humankind* the *less*, but loved *nature* more.

k. Was it *Mark Twain* who *quipped* that *cauliflower* was *nothing* but *cabbage with* an *education*?

l. I had to *create* an *equivalent* for what I *felt* about what I was *looking* at — *not copy it.*

—Georgia O'Keeffe, *Georgia O'Keeffe*

Rate and Subordination

When a sentence has several clauses, though each clause may carry significant meaning one is likely to be subordinate to the other(s). Sometimes the subordinate clause is almost parenthetic and could be dropped without serious impairment to the message of the sentence as a whole. For example, in the sentence "Joe Smith, a native of Texas, won the mile race," which is rather simple in terms of content, the phrase "a native of Texas" could be omitted without a change in the essential meaning of the sentence, except perhaps to a Texan. Changes in rate (duration) direct attention to what the speaker considers the most important part of a sentence, and within a paragraph, to the sentence and its relatively important part or parts. In general, directing attention for emphasis is achieved by a slower rate for the main clause compared with the rate of utterance for the subordinate phrases and clauses.

3. The following materials provide opportunities for practicing changes in rate to emphasize main ideas and to subordinate the other idea(s) within a sentence or paragraph.

a. Nonviolence, the first article of my faith, is also the last article of my creed.

—Adapted from Mahatma Gandhi,
Defense against charge of sedition, 1922

b. B. F. Skinner, a behavioral psychologist, regards the real problem as not whether machines think but whether people do.

c. Equality and justice, the two great distinguishing characteristics of democracy, follow inevitably from conception of men, all men, as rational and spiritual beings.

—Robert M. Hutchins, *Democracy and Human Nature*

d. Lawyers soon learn that however valuable their opinion may be it becomes even more valuable in proportion to the fees they charge.

e. Heraclitus, a Greek philosopher who lived from about 535 to 475 B.C., held that there was no permanent reality except the reality of change. Thus, Heraclitus argued, one cannot step into the same river twice. Wendell Johnson, a contemporary General Semanticist, enlarged on this contention. Johnson, in keeping with his philosophy, pointed out that "one may not step in the same river twice not only because the river flows and changes, but also because the one who steps into it changes too, and so is never at any two moments identical."

—Adapted from Wendell Johnson, *People in Quandaries*

Rate and Its Correlates Used to Emphasize Meaning

4. A study of Figure 10–1 should properly lead to the conclusion that we are not likely to use a single factor — pitch, loudness, or duration — to highlight meaning within a phrase or a sentence. We are more likely to change all three of these vocal attributes together. However, a subtle and controlled change in rate with pitch and loudness "taking care of themselves" is often a sophisticated way of bringing out a desired meaning.

   Practice the following materials to control the rate according to the meaning or meanings you consider important. Note the "reflective" (associated) changes that occur when any one of the vocal factors is intentionally emphasized.

   a. Is that Pam's? I thought it was mine.
   b. Scrooge was a mean man of considerable means.
   c. Tammy insisted that it was still possible to achieve a natural look without the use of cosmetics.
   d. It was said of Lincoln that he was a homely man, but somehow beautiful in his homeliness.
   e. Individual culture is the residual of learning; culture is expressed in the tastes and attitudes of persons, more than in the specifics of what they may have learned.
   f. Glenda called Tom, but what she called him when she called him, Tom refused to tell.
   g. Silence can be the epitome of either tact, or aggression.
   h. Susan had a warm personality, which never overheated.
   i. When Walt Whitman sang of himself, he also sang of and for all human beings.
   j. Birdsong has been so much analyzed for its content of business communication that there seems little time left for music, but it is there. Behind the glossaries of warning call, alarms, mating messages, pronouncements of territory, calls for recruitment, and demands for dispersal, there is redundant, elegant sound that is unaccountable as part of the working day.

   > — Lewis Thomas,
   > *The Lives of a Cell*

5. Read the following excerpts at appropriate basic rates but with variation to emphasize the key words and so the essential ideas. The more serious or solemn the content, the slower the basic rate should be.

   a. They say my verse is sad: no wonder
      Its narrow measure spans
      Tears of eternity and sorrow,
      Not mine, but man's.

   > — A. E. Housman, *More Poems*

   b. Ah, distinctly I remember it was in the bleak December,
      And each separate dying ember wrought its ghost upon the floor.

   > — Edgar Allan Poe, *The Raven*

    c. The sea is calm tonight,
       The tide is full, the moon lies fair
       Upon the Straits.

> —Matthew Arnold, *Dover Beach*

    d. "All right," said the Cat; and this time it vanished quite slowly, beginning with the end of the tail, and ending with the grin, which remained some time after the rest of it had gone.

> —Lewis Carroll, *Alice's Adventures in Wonderland*

    e. The only secret people keep
       Is Immortality.

> —Emily Dickinson, *Poems*, No. 1748

6. Read the following passages, using intentional pauses to set off the significant thought groups. Punctuation may help, but occasionally it may be misleading. Determine the units of thought, and pause whether or not the material is punctuated. Indicate pauses by inserting the sign ‖ at the end of thought units at which you intend to pause. Underline the words that carry the essential meanings in each selection.

    a. If well enough off to be able to pay for one's travel, a vagabond at heart may be called a tourist. If rich enough, he or she may be thought of as a world traveler.

    b. The secret of being a bore is to tell everything.

> —Voltaire, *L'Enfant Prodigue*

    c. The proper study of mankind is man.

> —Alexander Pope, *Essays on Man*

    d. Cleopatra's nose, had it been shorter, the whole aspect of the world would have been changed.

> —Blaise Pascal, *Pensées*

    e. He was a bold man that first ate an oyster.

> —Jonathan Swift, *Dialogue II*

    f. The sky is low, the clouds are mean,
       A travelling flake of snow
       Across a bar or through a rut
       Debates if it will go.

> —Emily Dickinson, *Nature, Part II*

    g. There is nothing more tragic in life than the utter impossibility of changing what you have done.

> —John Galsworthy, *Justice*

    h. Volumes might be written upon the impiety of the pious.

> —Herbert Spencer, *First Principles*

    i. If a man hasn't discovered something that he will die for, he isn't fit to live.

> —Martin Luther King Jr., Speech, Detroit, 1963

    j. No man who has once heartily and wholly laughed can be altogether irreclaimably bad.

> —Thomas Carlyle, *Sartor Resartus*

     k. Once you have become permanently startled, as I am, by the realization that we are a social species, you tend to keep an eye out for pieces of evidence that this is, by and large, a good thing for us.

                                        —Lewis Thomas, *Lives of a Cell*

7. The passages that follow call for more deliberate pauses to achieve emotional impact or to heighten dramatic meaning. In many instances, these effects may be attained by pauses before as well as after the significant words or phrases.

     a. As I walked out in the streets of Laredo,
       As I walked out in Laredo one day,
       I spied a poor cowboy wrapped up in white linen,
       Wrapped up in white linen as cold as the clay.

                                     —Anonymous, *The Cowboy's Lament*

     b. The deepest thing in our nature is this dumb region of the heart in which we dwell alone with our willingnesses and our unwillingnesses, our faiths and our fears.

                                   —William James, *The Will to Believe*

     c. Tom appeared on the sidewalk with a bucket of whitewash and a long-handled brush. He surveyed the fence, and all gladness left him and a deep melancholy settled down upon his spirit. Thirty yards of board fence nine feet high. Life to him seemed hollow, and existence but a burden.

                               —Mark Twain, *The Adventures of Tom Sawyer*

     d. A little work, a little play,
       To keep us going—and so, good day!
       A little warmth, a little light,
       Of love's bestowing—and so, good night!

                                   —George Du Maurier, *Trilby*

     e. Yes, I do recall what happened; but I was so much older then. Can't you see, I'm much younger now.

     f. Then darkness enveloped the whole American armada. Not a pinpoint of light showed from those hundreds of ships as they surged on through the night toward their destiny, carrying across the ageless and indifferent sea tens of thousands of young men, fighting for . . . for . . . well, at least for each other.

                                    —Ernie Pyle, *Brave Men*

     g. I have learned silence from the talkative, toleration from the intolerant, and kindness from the unkind; yet strange, I am ungrateful to these teachers.

                                    —Kahlil Gibran, *Sand and Foam*

     h. If we open a quarrel between the past and the present, we shall find that we have lost the future.

                        —Winston Churchill, Speech, House of Commons, 1940

     i. That which has always been accepted by everyone, everywhere, is almost certain to be false.

                                     —Paul Valery, *Tel Quel*

The next chapter—"Vocal Variety in Speaking and Reading"—provides opportunity for you to review and apply information and techniques for voice improvement and effective communication. The unique qualities and individuality of the human voice will again be considered. But first, let us pause to appreciate the significance of George Noel Gordon's (Lord Byron's) excerpt from his dramatic poem, *Don Juan*:

> The devil hath not, in all his quiver's choice,
> An arrow for the heart like a sweet voice.
>
> —*Don Juan,* Canto XVI

and the insightful and surprisingly optimistic observation of the psychoanalyst Sigmund Freud:

> The voice of intellect is a soft one, but it does not rest until it has gained a hearing.
>
> —*Future of an Illusion*

CHAPTER 11

VOCAL VARIETY IN SPEAKING AND READING

Although this chapter is specifically concerned with vocal variety, we have been anticipating and considering aspects and implications of this subject in several of the preceding chapters. When we discussed *loudness*, we considered first the fundamental need for the speaker to be heard if his or her intentions to communicate were to be fruitful. Beyond this, we also considered the use of vocal force as related to word meanings, sentence meanings, and overall communicative efforts. *Pitch* was likewise considered a basic attribute of the voice that can be used to enhance vocalization per se. Pitch was also discussed in relationship to linguistic melody, to word and phrase meaning, and to the expression of states of feeling. Similarly, the vocal attribute *duration* (timing) was viewed in relationship to the speaker's physiological state, to feeling, and to semantic implications.

This chapter is in one sense a review and reconsideration of some aspects of vocal variety previously discussed. It also provides us with an opportunity to emphasize some aspects that were briefly touched on in the earlier chapters that deal separately with individual attributes of the voice.

Through the attributes of the voice—pitch, quality, loudness, and duration—we tend as we speak to reveal our thoughts and our feelings or to express those thoughts and feelings that we wish others to believe we entertain. The less inhibited we are, the more the component of feeling is expressed through our voices. When we were very young and had little or no awareness of cultural pressures, our voices faithfully and reflexively indicated our changes in feeling and mood. As we matured, cultural pressures exerted an increasing influence on us, and we learned, almost always without awareness, of *how* we are expected to show our feelings in our overt behavior, including the way we give voice to our utterances. Pitch changes came increasingly under our voluntary control and conformed more and more to the pattern and the linguistic code of our culture. By the time we were of school age, most of us spoke the sounds and the melody (intonation) of the language or languages of our culture. We learned also that American-English speech has syllable stress within a word and word stress within a phrase. So we came to be able to emphasize ideas as we spoke. Our tendency to talk at changing rates according to mood—to talk more rapidly under heightened feelings, more slowly in the absence of heightened feelings, and quite slowly when sad or depressed—also became modified by cultural influences. Although these cultural modifica-

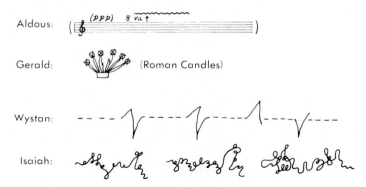

Aldous:

Gerald: (Roman Candles)

Wystan:

Isaiah:

FIGURE 11–1 "Four Friends. Gerald [Herad] is a virtuoso talker, the most brilliant I have ever heard, and he *likes* to talk, just as Arthur Rubinstein *likes* to play the piano. Isaiah Berlin is even faster and funnier—an ironical gaiety underlies everything he says—but Isaiah tends to speak in spurts, like a ticker tape. Wystan Auden, by comparison, fishes, though profoundly, between words, and Aldous [Huxley] is too serenely high in tessitura, and in volume too suavely soft." [From *Dialogues and a Diary* by Igor Stravinsky and Robert Craft. Copyright © 1961, 1962, 1963 by Igor Stravinsky. Reprinted by permission of Doubleday & Company, Inc., and Faber and Faber, Ltd.]

tions direct us toward norms of behavior, most of us still maintain and express ourselves as individuals. Sometimes we kick over the traces, and our voices minimize the influences and effects of environmental training and pressures. But usually we manage to conform to a sufficient degree to behave considerably as do the persons with whom we identify, while still giving expression to our individual selves.

Igor Stravinsky, the noted composer, with considerably more sophistication and a much better than average ear for vocal nuances, listened carefully to how people talked. In one of his books, Stravinsky presented graphic as well as verbal descriptions of the vocal characteristics of several of his friends.[1] Stravinsky described one friend as a "virtuoso talker who *likes* to talk, just as Rubinstein *likes* to play the piano." A second friend is described as "fast and funny." A third "talks in spurts like a ticker tape." Another "fishes . . . profoundly, between words." Still another is "too serenely high in tessitura and in volume too suavely soft." (See Figure 11–1.)

IMPLICATIONS OF VOCAL ATTRIBUTES

With the possible exception of quality, each vocal attribute, as we have noted, is capable of revealing thought as well as feeling. Within a phrase, the important word is likely to be spoken more loudly, more slowly, and at a different pitch from the other words. These changes are paralleled in phrase–sentence relationships, as well as in sentence–paragraph relationships, and so forth.

Through the use of vocal variety we are also able to capture attention and to main-

[1] Igor Stravinsky and Robert Craft, *Dialogues and a Diary* (Garden City, N.Y.: Doubleday & Company. Inc., 1963).

tain listener interest. In brief, through the voice, as well as through the selection of words and the construction of our sentences, we are able to reveal thought and feeling, to emphasize ideas, and to keep listeners attentive to our communicative efforts.

Quality

In our earlier discussions of quality, we considered its relationship to resonance and to the avoidance of undesirable vocal aspects such as excessive nasality and breathiness. At this time, we consider quality as it is related to feelings and moods and as an aspect of vocal variety.

Although modifications in vocal quality take place as a result of the inherent characteristics of our resonating cavities, except for those of us who tend to be either nasal or denasal there is little that we normally should do consciously to bring about these changes. Normal changes in quality are related to feelings and moods, to the emotional rather than the intellectual aspects of our behavior. Except for greatly inhibited persons, feelings are spontaneously reflected and expressed through voice. Usually, we have more difficulty in concealing our feelings than in revealing them. The speaker who does not strive to conceal or inhibit inner feelings, and yet does not make a point of putting them on display, will have no difficulty with quality changes. If you are a normally responsive speaker who initiates vocal tones properly and who uses an appropriate and flexible pitch range, you will do best with the quality that emerges spontaneously and naturally.

Reading Aloud to Interpret and Communicate Another's Thoughts and Feelings

Persons who choose to read aloud to a listener or listeners have the dual responsibilities of translating (decoding) and transmitting thoughts and feelings not of their own origin. The reader-speaker who is about to speak another person's words must first decide as *faithfully as possible* what are or were the thoughts and feelings of the writer. With such an awareness of responsibility, and with such an appreciation of the task, you—the reader-speaker—must now determine the dominant mood and nuances of feeling of each selection to be read aloud, as well as the underlying theme and the specific thoughts to be communicated. Even the most proficient of professional actors—*who are essentially readers because they are dealing with the verbal formulations of others*—accept the need to study their lines carefully before they read them aloud. Such study is, of course, recommended to you as a student-reader.

When, as a reader, you are able to understand the mood, feelings, and thoughts inherent in the selections studied-to-be-read-aloud, you should begin to do your reading aloud. If at all possible, record and play back your efforts. Listen objectively and determine whether what you thought you thought, and felt you felt, is being expressed in your speaking of another person's words. With such preparation and appreciation, the appropriate initial vocal qualities to establish the dominant mood, as well as changes in quality to suggest the particular feelings associated with particular ideas, should take place almost as spontaneously as if the words and feelings were initially your own. But because they are not quite your own (you may not even believe them), you will just have to work a bit harder to be effective in your role as a decoder and a communicator of someone else's words.

EXERCISES FOR VOCAL QUALITY: ESTABLISHING MOOD

a. Somewhere — in desolate wind-swept space —
   In Twilight-land — in no man's land —
   Two hurrying Shapes met face to face,
   And bade each other stand.

   —Thomas B. Aldrich, *Identity*

b. Nothing could have been more obvious to the people of the early twentieth
   century than the rapidity with which war was becoming impossible. And
   as certainly they did not see it. They did not see it until the atomic bombs
   burst in their fumbling hands.

   —H. G. Wells, *The World Set Free*

c. All sorts of things and weather
   Must be taken in together
   To make up a year
   And a Sphere.

   —Ralph Waldo Emerson, *The Mountain and the Squirrel*

d. She left the web, she left the loom,
   She made three paces thro' the room,
   She saw the water lily bloom,
   She saw the helmet and the plume,
     She look'd down to Camelot.

   —Alfred, Lord Tennyson, *The Lady of Shalott*

e. The centipede was happy quite
     Until a toad in fun
   Said, "Pray, which leg goes after which?"
   That worked her mind to such a pitch,
   She lay distracted in a ditch
     Considering how to run.

   —Mrs. Edward Craster, *Pinafore Poems*

f. Shall I, wasting in despair,
   Die because a woman's fair?
   Or make pale my cheeks with care
   'Cause another's rosy are?
   Be she fairer than the day
   Or the flow'ry meads in May,
   If she be not so for me,
   What care I how fair she be?

   —George Wither, *Fair Virtue*

g. A word is dead
   When it is said,
   Some say.
   I say it just

Begins to live
That day.

—Emily Dickinson, No. 1212

h. The sea lies all about us. The commerce of all lands must cross it. The very winds that move over the lands have been cradled on its broad expanse and seek ever to return to it. The continents themselves dissolve and pass to the sea, in grain after grain of eroded land. So the rains that rose from it return again in rivers. In its mysterious past it encompasses all the dim origins of life and receives in the end, after, it may be, many transmutations, the dead husks of that same life. For all at last returns to the sea — to Oceanus, the ocean river, like the ever flowing stream of time, the beginning and the end.

—Rachel L. Carson, The Sea Around Us

i. It is better to lose health like a spendthrift than to waste it like a miser. It is better to live and be done with it, than to die daily in the sickroom. By all means begin your folio; even if the doctor does not give you a year, even if he hesitates about a month, make one brave push and see what can be accomplished in a week. It is not only in finished undertakings that we ought to honour useful labour. A spirit goes out of the man who means execution, which outlives the most untimely ending. All who have meant good work with their whole hearts, have done good work, although they may die before they have the time to sign it. Every heart that has beat strong and cheerfully has left a hopeful impulse behind it in the world, and bettered the tradition of mankind.

—Robert Louis Stevenson, Aes Triplex

j. I learned three things in Zurich during the war. I wrote them down. Firstly, you're either a revolutionary or you're not, and if you're not you might as well be an artist as anything else. Secondly, if you can't be an artist, you might as well be a revolutionary. . . . I forgot the third thing.

—Tom Stoppard, Travesties

PRACTICE MATERIALS

1. The materials that follow will afford opportunities, some in depth, to employ knowledge and skill in the use of vocal variety. Be sure that you first read and understand the entire selection, and note the underlying, fundamental thought and mood as well as the nuances in feeling and thought. Experiment, using different techniques of emphasis (e.g., basic pitch change, force, or duration), and decide which of these is most appropriate to express the dominant meaning of each selection.

    a. The place became full of a watchful intensity now; for when other things sank brooding to sleep, the heath appeared slowly to awake and listen.

—Thomas Hardy, The Return of the Native

b. On his ninetieth birthday, a reporter asked the eminent jurist and Supreme
   Court Justice Oliver Wendell Holmes, Jr., to what did he attribute the
   secret of his success. Justice Holmes replied, "Young man, the secret of my
   success is that at an early age I discovered I was not God."

   > In a radio address on the same day, Justice Holmes told his listeners:
   > The riders in a race do not stop short when they reach the goal. There
   > is a little finishing canter before coming to a standstill. There is time to
   > hear the kind voice of friends and to say to one's self, "The work is
   > done." But just as one says that, the answer comes: "The race is over,
   > but the work never is done while the power to work remains." The
   > canter that brings you to a standstill need not be only coming to rest.
   > It cannot be, while you still live. For to live is to function. That is all
   > there is in living.

c. Wit has truth in it; wisecracking is simply calisthenics with words.

   —Dorothy Parker, *Paris Review*, 1936

d. To return to Associate Justice Holmes, and on a lighter note, his biographer, H. C. Shriver, in *What Gusto*, tells this anecdote:

   > Once, nearly ninety, the Justice went walking with a friend in the
   > Capitol. A pretty girl passed and Holmes, after glancing over his shoul-
   > der, clapped his forehead in mock anguish. "Oh," he cried, "Oh, to be
   > seventy again."

e. I refuse to accept the cynical notion that nation after nation must spiral
   down a militaristic stairway into the hell of nuclear destruction. I believe
   that unarmed truth and unconditional love will have the final word in
   reality.

   —Martin Luther King Jr.,
   Address accepting the Nobel Prize, December 1964

f. Too long did I wallow
   In the cold lap of sorrow,
   Knowing that each day I would mourn
   Hours I feared to scorn—
   Until I learned at last to see
   Sadness I nurtured deep in me.

   —J. E., *Delayed Confrontation*

g. When all the world is young, lad,
     And all the trees are green;
   And every goose a swan, lad,
     And every lass a queen;
   Then hey for boot and horse, lad,
     And round the world away;
   Young blood must have its course, lad,
     And every dog his day.

   When all the world is old, lad,
     And all the trees are brown;
   And all the sport is stale, lad,
     And all the wheels run down:

Creep home, and take your place there,
The spent and maimed among:
God grant you find one face there,
You loved when all was young.

— Charles Kingsley, *Water Babies*

h. Remember me when I am gone away,
Gone far away into the silent land;
When you can no more hold me by the hand,
Nor I half turn to go, yet turning stay.
Remember me when no more, day by day,
You tell me of our future that you planned;
Only remember me; you understand.
It will be late to counsel then or pray.
Yet if you should forget me for a while
And afterwards remember, do not grieve:
For if the darkness and corruption leave
A vestige of the thoughts that once I had,
Better by far you should forget and smile
Than that you should remember and be sad.

— Christina Rossetti, *Remember*

i. To every thing there is a season, and a time to every purpose under the heaven: a time to be born, and a time to die; a time to plant, and a time to pluck up that which is planted; a time to kill, and a time to heal; a time to break down, and a time to build up; a time to weep, and a time to laugh; a time to mourn, and a time to dance; a time to cast away stones, and a time to gather stones together; a time to embrace, and a time to refrain from embracing; a time to seek, and a time to lose; a time to keep, and a time to cast away; a time to rend, and a time to sew; a time to keep silence, and a time to speak; a time to love, and a time to hate; a time for war, and a time for peace.

— Ecclesiastes 3:1–8

2. In the following excerpts from the speeches and writings of John F. Kennedy, essential ideas are brought out by the balancing of phrases and by verbal contrasts resulting from positions of words within phrases. The same words often occur in contexts that are *almost but not quite the same*. Be certain that in your study of the selections you anticipate and prepare to bring out the related yet contrasting thoughts and the subtleties and nuances in feeling as well as in thought by appropriate vocal changes.

a. . . . democracy means much more than popular government and majority rule, much more than a system of political techniques to flatter or deceive powerful blocs of voters . . . the true democracy, living and growing and inspiring, puts its faith in the people — faith that the people will not simply elect men who will represent their views ably and faithfully, but also elect men who will exercise their conscientious judgment — faith that the people will not condone those whose devotion to principle leads them to unpopular causes, but reward courage, respect honor and ultimately recognize right.

— John F. Kennedy, *Profiles in Courage*

b. And thus, in the days ahead, only the very courageous will be able to take the hard and unpopular decisions necessary for our survival in the struggle with a powerful enemy—an enemy with leaders who need give little thought to the popularity of their course, who need pay little tribute to the public opinion they themselves manipulate, and who may force, without fear of retaliation at the polls, their citizens to sacrifice present laughter for future glory. And only the very courageous will be able to keep alive the spirit of individualism and dissent which gave birth to this nation, nourished it as an infant and carried it through its severest tests upon the attainment of its majority.

—John F. Kennedy, *Profiles in Courage*

c. So let us begin anew—remembering on both sides that civility is not a sign of weakness, and sincerity is always subject to proof. Let us never negotiate out of fear. But let us never fear to negotiate.

Let both sides explore what problems unite us instead of belaboring those problems which divide us.

Let both sides, for the first time, formulate serious and precise proposals for the inspection and control of arms—and bring the absolute power to destroy other nations under the absolute control of all nations.

—John F. Kennedy, Inaugural Address, 1961

3. The following short selections and excerpts require careful phrasing for their full import.

a. Nothing in life is so exhilarating as to be shot at without result.

—Winston Churchill, *The Malakand Field Force*

b. Dictators ride to and fro upon tigers which they dare not dismount. And the tigers are getting hungry.

—Winston Churchill, *While England Slept*

c. A truth that's told with bad intent
Beats all the lies you can invent.

—William Blake, *Auguries of Innocence*

d. My only books
Were woman's looks
And folly's all they've taught me.

—Thomas Moore, *The Time I've Lost in Wooing*

EXERCISES FOR ROLE-PLAYING

1. Role-playing provides opportunity for vocal variety. Following are some dialogues to be read silently and then aloud. The dialogues may be read by one person, using a feature or features of voice to indicate a change of character (or speaker). The selections may also be read by two persons, each assuming a role. On a second go-round, the roles may be changed. *Do not resort to falsetto* to indicate your role.

The dialogue between Alice and Humpty Dumpty has been adapted without intended offense to Lewis Carroll or to either of the "actors."

Alice: But *glory* doesn't mean "a nice knockdown argument."

Humpty Dumpty (*scornfully*):   When *I* use a word it means just what I want it to mean — neither more nor less.

Alice: The question is whether you *can* make words mean so many different things.

Humpty Dumpty: The question is which is to be master — that's all.

Alice: Sir, you seem very clear at explaining words. Thank you. But now I must be off. I'll just go on my way.

Humpty Dumpty: You'll do no such thing. Now you had better tell me how you can be getting *off and on at the same time.*

Alice (*perplexed*):   Sir, it never occurred to me that I was about to do two things at once. But remember, it was you who told me that words can mean anything I choose them to mean.

Humpty Dumpty (*arrogantly*):   Of course I did, but what I said was that *I* can make words mean what I choose them to mean. I said nothing *about you.* I also said, which is to be master — that's all.

Alice (*abashed at Humpty Dumpty's explanation, says no more; and when she does not hear any further wisdom from Humpty Dumpty, she tiptoes off on her way. When she is far enough away to be away, she recalls some lines about her companion and says them aloud*):

> Humpty Dumpty sat on a wall,
> Humpty Dumpty had a great fall;
> All the king's horses
> And all the king's men
> Couldn't put Humpty Dumpty together again.

(*To herself*)   What might have happened to Humpty Dumpty and to me if only the horses and not the king's men had tried to put him together again?

2. Read the sentences that follow with an intentional change of rate, inflection, and/or pause to convey either sarcasm, irony, or a meaning contrary to what the words, if read "straight," would imply.
    a. Am I pleased? Of course I'm pleased. Why do you bother to ask?
    b. I'm so excited. Imagine winning that prize!
    c. Of course he's a good listener — especially when he's doing the talking.
    d. To go or not to go; that isn't even a question!
    e. I like spinach, cauliflower, and burnt-to-a-crisp hamburgers, all in that disorder.
    f. Well, let me congratulate you. You did it after all.
    g. Go ahead, go ahead, be my guest.
    h. Though it was a task to find, she fought for his honor.
    i. Experience is the word many persons use for their mistakes.
    j. June said that Tom was quite a piece of work — a little rusty and broken-down.

3. Now try some nursery rhymes to bring out a possible critical, political mean-

ing. (Many so-called nursery rhymes were, in fact, intended as satire and directed at a person running for political office or already in government.)

    a. Little Jack Horner sat in the corner
       Eating a Christmas pie.
       He put in his thumb, and pulled out a plum,
       And said "What a good boy am I!"

    b. A dillar, a dollar,
       A ten o'clock scholar,
       What makes you come so soon?
       You used to come at ten o'clock,
       And now you come at noon.

4. The following is from the concluding act of Henrik Ibsen's play, *A Doll's House*. Nora, wife and mother of three children, rebels against her husband's treating her as if she were a child, as being immature and without a sense of responsibility. She is no longer willing to play this role. Nora is determined to leave her husband.

Helmer: This is outrageous! You are betraying your most sacred duty.

Nora: And what do you consider to be my most sacred duty?

Helmer: Does it take me to tell you that? Isn't it your duty to your husband and your children?

Nora: I have another duty equally sacred.

Helmer: You have not. What duty might *that* be?

Nora: My duty to myself.

Helmer: First and foremost, you are a wife and mother.

Nora: That I don't believe anymore. I believe that first and foremost I am an individual, just as you are — or at least I'm going to try to be. I know most people agree with you, Torvald, and that's also what it says in books. But I'm not content anymore with what most people say, or what it says in books. I have to think things out for myself, and get things clear.

TO WIT — TO WIT

5. James McNeill Whistler, whom most of us know for his portrait *Whistler's Mother*, was also an etcher, a writer, and a self-acknowledged wit. He enjoyed opportunities for brief interchanges in social situations that would permit him to express his often acerbic witticisms.

    On one occasion an enthusiastic admirer said to him, "I only know of two painters in the world, yourself and Velasquez."

    To which Whistler responded in dulcet tones, "Why drag in Velasquez?"

    On another occasion, Oscar Wilde, who was also given to witticisms, evoked this interchange:

Wilde: Oh, Mr. Whistler, I wish I'd said that.

Whistler: You will, Oscar, you will.

                    —Adapted from D. C. Seitz, *Whistler Stories*,
                    and L. C. Ingleby, *Oscar Wilde*

6. The longer selections that follow are intended to offer you an opportunity to choose the way you want to bring out the range of thought and feeling inherent in the content. You may wish to experiment, using one attribute of voice as dominant, but not exclusively so throughout your reading.

   a. These are the times that try men's souls. The Summer soldier and the sunshine patriot will, in this crisis, shrink from the service of their country, but he that stands it *now* deserves the love and thanks of man and woman. Tyranny, like Hell, is not easily conquered; yet we have this consolation with us, that the harder the conflict the more glorious the triumph. What we obtain too cheaply we esteem too lightly; it is dearness only that gives everything its value. Heaven knows how to put a proper price upon its goods; and it would be strange indeed if so celestial an article as *freedom* should not be highly rated.

   —Thomas Paine, *The Crisis*

   b. The greatest thing a human soul ever does in the world is to *see* something, and tell what it *saw* in a plain way. Hundreds of people can talk for one who can think, but thousands can think for one who can see. To see clearly is poetry, prophecy, and religion, all in one.

   —John Ruskin, *Modern Painters*

   c. The future offers very little hope for those who expect that our new mechanical slaves will offer us a world in which we may rest from thinking. Help us they may, but at the cost of supreme demands upon our honesty and our intelligence. The world of the future will be an ever more demanding struggle against limitations of our intelligence, not a comfortable hammock in which we can lie down to be waited upon by our robot slaves.

   —Norbert Wiener, *God and Golem, Inc.*

   d. The codfish lays ten thousand eggs,
   The homely hen lays one.
   The codfish never cackles
   To tell you what she's done.
   And so we scorn the codfish,
   While the humble hen we prize,
   Which only goes to show you
   That it pays to advertise.

   —Anonymous

SUMMARY: VOCAL VARIETY

Vocal variety may be used to express feelings, to communicate intended meanings, to extablish and maintain attention, and to make speaking and listening interesting. Any of the attributes of voice—pitch, quality, loudness, or duration—may be used toward these goals. However, it is rare for a single attribute to be used alone. Changes in pitch and loudness frequently and spontaneously occur together. Usually, words you speak slowly are likely to be produced with accompanying changes in loudness, sometimes with increased force, but on occasion with a marked reduction in force. To be an effective speaker, you achieve your purpose through a combination of vocal factors *under your control*. Of course, the nature of the content as well as the composition of your audience will help you to determine your choices in how you say you feel about what you think. You may have a rhetorical style that to some degree will influence your choice of vocal attributes, but you should not be oblivious to your listeners' tastes in rhetorical style. Beyond this, we should consider Samuel Johnson's reminder in *The Idler*, "The joy of life is variety, the tenderest of love requires to be renewed by intervals of absence."

PART THREE

DICTION

One ought, every day at least, to hear a little song,
read a good poem, see a fine picture, and, if it
were possible, to speak a few reasonable words.

—Johann Wolfgang von Goethe,
Wilhelm Meister's Apprenticeship

CHAPTER 12

INTRODUCTION TO THE STUDY OF AMERICAN-ENGLISH SPEECH SOUNDS

Part Three of this text has two related purposes. The first is to provide some general but fundamental information about the characteristics and production of American-English speech sounds. The second is to offer more specific information about each of the sounds of our language and provide practice materials for the sounds (phonemes). Both purposes are intended to help you toward your objective of increasing your effectiveness as a speaker and a communicator using American English as your language.

IMPROVING DICTION

In this and in subsequent chapters there will be no attempt to be prescriptive or to urge that any one standard of diction (pronunciation) is either more desirable or superior to any other. However, I do make a basic assumption that any manner of speaking in a given community which is so different that it attracts attention to itself and thus detracts from the intended message might benefit from modification. Let us nevertheless be mindful that the listener also has some obligation to take a little time to tune in to the speaker's manner of speaking before coming to a negative judgment. Shakespeare presented by actors who speak British Broadcast English is not exactly the same as Shakespeare presented by actors who speak General American, but if the acting is of high quality, after just a few minutes it is Shakespeare who comes through.

The sounds of speech, occasionally singly but usually in combination, constitute the symbol code for a spoken language. American English employs forty-four different sounds or *phonemes* in its spoken symbol code. Within the United States there are regional variants in this code, as there are in Canada and in virtually all parts of the English-speaking world. Major variants within the United States will be pointed out. For the most part, the variants are relatively few and seldom so great that they prevent ready communication between educated speakers from widely separated geographic areas within the United States. Those few persons who have difficulty in communicating in the areas in which they reside are likely to have increased difficulty in their attempts to make themselves understood when they travel to places distant from their homes. However, in the vast majority of instances, with due allowance for brief "tuning in" periods, the proficient speaker whose home base is New Orleans or Dallas will have little or no difficulty in communicating with a resident of New York or Chicago. The inhabitants of each of these regional areas may for a brief time be aware and perhaps even amused at the differences in pronunciation and even, to a lesser degree, in speech melody; yet with good will, communication should not be impaired. In brief, American English has not been homogenized into a single dialect.

A review of Chapters 3 and 4 should help you to appreciate how American English departed from the dialects of British English and developed its own regional dialects. I also recommend reading at least the first and last chapters of Hendrickson's (1986) *American Talk*. In the preface, the author notes, "Dialects, like languages themselves, are simply different ways people have of speaking, and by better understanding their own American dialects we can better understand our fellow Americans who speak them."

═══ DIALECTS ═══

A *dialect* is a linguistic system within a system that is related to a special cultural group, a community of persons, or an "identifiable" regional (geographic) area. Langacker (1967) indicated that "the basis for distinguishing various dialects of a language is that the linguistic system used by speakers of one dialect differs in certain respects from that used by speakers of others" (p. 47). The differences may be in pronunciation (diction), vocabulary (word usage or meaning for the same word forms), and/or syntactic constructions. For example, American-English speakers differ in the vowels used in words such as *roof, class, burn, after,* and *marry*. We *fetch something* in some parts of the United States that is *carried* in other areas; American-English speakers go *to the hospital* or are *in the hospital*, whereas those in England are more likely just to go *to hospital* or to be *in hospital*.

These dialectal variations are not likely to cause any difficulty in communication. However, there are dialects within the United States as well as within other parts of the English-speaking world in which the differences are so great as to constitute barriers to communication. For example, speakers from the Appalachian region might have great difficulty in communicating with speakers from rural Maine or from southern Louisiana.

Adults who wish to learn a second dialect, to change from one regional dialect to another, or to become bidialectal must be willing to immerse themselves in the effort. To a degree, it is much like learning a second language. It will not be achieved by silent study or even by careful listening, though both will help. Learning a new dialect, or modifying a dialect influence, requires a willingness to hear ourselves as others hear us, and to practice orally as well as aurally whatever needs to be practiced to modify our linguistic habits in the direction of a desired goal. It can be done!

═══ THE SOUNDS OF AMERICAN ENGLISH ═══

Sound Representation

There are two ways of representing the sounds of our language: through spelling (orthographic representation), and through a system in which there is greater consistency between the visible symbol (letter or letters) and the sound. It is obvious that a spoken language that has only twenty-six letter symbols and more than forty different sounds cannot have sufficient consistency between letter and sound to provide a reliable guide to articulation and pronunciation. Most of our dictionaries therefore employ a system of diacritical markings and symbols to help the reader appreciate how a word should be pronounced because of or despite its spelling.[1] Unfortunately, even the use of diacritical markings fails to provide a clear one-to-one relationship between sound and symbol. Still another system, more consistent than either of the others, employs selected symbols of the International Phonetic Alphabet (IPA). In the IPA system, one symbol is used for each distinctively different sound. Our approach emphasizes the use of this system of representation. However, we shall also indicate the dictionary close equivalents of the IPA symbols. Through this approach it should be possible for you (1) to learn the sounds (phonemes) of our language, (2) to make distinctions according to the features or characteristics of the different sounds, and (3) to establish a visual basis for cueing as to the manner of production for the individual sound, or for a sequence of sounds in the normal flow of spoken language.

The different sounds of American-English speech and their phonetic and dictionary symbol representations are shown in Tables 12–1 and 12–2.[2]

═══ THE PHONEME ═══

We approach our study of the sound of American English through a consideration of the basic unit or sound family: the *phoneme*. Phonemes are distinctive phonetic (sound) elements of words. The phonetic elements are distinctive in that they incorporate sound features that enable us to distinguish between spoken words. For example, the word *bad* has three phonemes. If we change the first, we can distinguish between *bad* and *sad*. If we change the second, we can distinguish between *bad* and *bid*; if we change the last, we can distinguish between *bad* and *ban*. These changes of phonemes included ones with several different sound features that made the differences readily apparent. How-

---

[1] The *American Heritage Dictionary*, Second Edition (1982), provides a table (pp. 42–46) "designed to aid the user in locating in the Dictionary words whose pronunciation is known but whose spelling presents difficulties."

[2] With minor exceptions, the dictionary symbols are those used in the *American Heritage Dictionary* (Boston: Houghton Mifflin, 1982). Essentially the same symbols are used by other leading dictionaries, including the *Random House Dictionary of the English Language* (New York: Random House, Inc., 1987), and the *Doubleday Dictionary* (New York: Doubleday and Co., 1975).

Table 12–1.   The Common Phonemes of
American English (Consonants)

Key Word	Most Frequent Dictionary Symbol	IPA Symbol
1. *pat*	p	p
2. *bee*	b	b
3. *tin*	t	t
4. *den*	d	d
5. *cook*, *key*	k	k
6. *get*	g	g
7. *fast*	f	f
8. *van*	v	v
9. *thin*	th	θ
10. *this*	~~th~~, *th*	ð
11. *sea*	s	s
12. *zoo*	z	z
13. *she*	sh	ʃ
14. *treasure*	zh	ʒ
15. *chick*	ch	tʃ
16. *jump*	j	dʒ
17. *me*	m	m
18. *no*	n	n
19. *sing*	ng	ŋ
20. *let*	l	l
21. *run*	r	r
22. *yell*	y	j
23. *hat*	h	h
24. *won*	w	w
25. *what*	hw	ʍ or hw

ever, we can bring the phoneme "closer" by changing the *b* to *p* and so have *bad* and *pad*, or by changing the vowel and so have *bad* and *bed*, or by changing the last sound and so have *bad* and *bat*. In regard to the consonants, our substitutions here are of cognate sounds, ones that differ only by the feature of voicing. In contextual speech, we might well need to depend on the overall meaning of the utterance to perceive the differences in the consonants of the key words.

Allophones

A second aspect of the phoneme concept is variation. Speech sounds vary in production according to context. The /t/ in *tell* is somewhat different from the /t/ in *its* and *plate*. Despite the variations in sound, however, they are essentially more alike than different,

Table 12–2. The Common Phonemes of American English (Vowels)

Key Word	Dictionary Symbol	IPA Symbol
26. fee	ē	i
27. sit	ĭ	ɪ
28. take	ā	e
29. met	ĕ	ɛ
30. cat	ă	æ
31. task	ă or ȧ	æ or a depending on regional or individual variations
32. calm	ä	ɑ
33. hot	ŏ or ä	ɒ or ɑ depending on regional or individual variations
34. saw	ô	ɔ
35. vote	ō	o or ou
36. bull	o͝o	ʊ
37. too	o͞o	u
38. hut	ŭ	ʌ
39. about	ə	ə
40. upper	ər	ɝ by most Americans and ə by many others
41. bird	ûr	ɝ, ɝr by most Americans and ɜ by many others
Phonemic Diphthongs		
42. ice	ī	aɪ
43. now	ou	au or ɑu
44. boy, toys	oi	ɔɪ

and we respond to all of these words as containing a /t/. These sound variations, which do not affect our understanding of what we hear, constitute the members of the phoneme or sound family. The individual variants are called *allophones*.

If our pronunciations and articulatory efforts do not show regard for possible phonemic differences, our listeners may become confused. If the vowel of *bad* begins to approximate the vowel of *bed*, we may be misunderstood if we utter a sentence such as "This will be bad for you." Similarly, if an /s/ is produced so that it begins to suggest an /ʃ/ (**sh**), we may not know whether something is for *sipping* or for *shipping*.

Some of the difficulty that foreign-born persons have in learning to speak English may be attributed to the fact that the phonemes in their native language are not always directly equivalent to ours. For example, we make a significant distinction between the vowels of words such as *heel* and *hill* and *seen* and *sin*. By way of television, radio, or the movies, if not by direct experience, most of us know that many of our Spanish-speaking neighbors pronounce *think* with the vowel of *seen*. Hispanic speakers may also have difficulty with distinctions that almost all Americans for whom American English is a first language make without difficulty, such as the differences between vowels in *hail* and *hell*. We are, of course, not immune from comparable errors when we begin to learn a foreign language. When we speak a second language learned in adulthood we often produce the vowels and consonants that are closest to our own in phonetic features and thus manage to sound like foreigners.

Distinctive Features

Linguists and phoneticians view phonemes as sounds of a spoken language that, by virtue of the ways in which they are produced (articulated), comprise "bundles" of features that serve to distinguish (contrast) one phoneme from another. Thus, breath-stop is a distinctive feature or characteristic of the phonemes /p/, /t/, /k/, /d/, and /g/. In contexts in which these sounds are immediately followed by a vowel in the same syllable, the breath-stop is followed by a puff of breath (an "explosion") so that these phonemes may be identified as *stop-plosives*. This feature distinguishes the sounds from all others in American English. The sounds /b/ and /p/ differ in that the former is accompanied by vocalization and the latter is voiceless; /d/ and /t/, and /g/ and /k/, differ in the same way. Phonemes that differ only in regard to voice are known as *cognate sounds*. The phonemes /m/, /n/, and /ŋ/ (**ng**) are featured by intentional nasality. In this respect these sounds are distinctive; that is, the feature of nasality distinguishes them from all other sounds in spoken English. Tables 12–1 and 12–2 present the common phonemes of American English.

Linguists and phoneticians have devised rather complex, distinctive feature systems that are intended to apply to all natural spoken languages. A few of these are included in the reference section at the end of this chapter. A more modest system will be used for our purposes of describing the sounds of American English and as a guide to pronunciation and the improvement of diction. For a relatively nontechnical discussion of distinctive feature theory and its application to correction of articulatory defects or differences, see Eisenson and Ogilvie (1983), pages 126–132 and 272–275.

══ CLASSIFICATION OF SOUNDS ══

The sounds of our language may be classified into three large groups: consonants, vowels, and diphthongs. All are produced as a result of some modification of the outgoing breath by the organs of articulation.

Consonants are speech sounds that are produced by either a complete or a partial obstruction of modification of the breath channel by the organs of articulation. Aside from voice, the sound characteristics of each consonant result from the manner of vibration of the breath stream. This is determined by the way in which the breath stream is

(1) modified by the closures produced by articulatory activity; (2) released by the activity of the opening of the closure; or (3) modified but not completely obstructed (stopped) by the narrowing of the breath channel.

Vowels are produced by articulatory movements of the speech organs without obstruction or interference of the vibrating breath stream in its passage through the breath channel. We determine the characteristic features of the vowels of our language by modifying the size and shape of the mouth cavity, by changing the position of the tongue within the mouth, and by differing the degree of tension.

Diphthongs are voiced glides that are uttered in a single breath impulse within the limits or confines of one syllable, as in the words *dine* and *out*. Some diphthongs are blends of two vowels. Most, however, represent an instability or "breakdown" of what at one time in the history of our language was one vowel.

A diphthong may be defined as a syllable in which two vowel resonances are clearly identified, but with *a change of resonance as an essential characteristic*. We shall discuss diphthongs in Chapter 14, where we shall also present a less technical, descriptive definition.

Nonphonemic Diphthongs

A diphthong, by definition, is a blend of two vowels that distinguish the product from all other vowels and consonants. The result is that the identification of the word that includes a diphthong has semantic significance. American English has two nonphonemic diphthongs, /ei/ and /ou/ which can do without the second vowel without altering the meaning of the word. Words such as *gate, hate, base, fail, main, blame,* and *chase* can be produced with either the diphthong /ei/ or just the vowel /e/. If for any reason the vowel is lengthened, it will generate into the diphthong. This is less likely to happen in words in which the vowel /e/ is followed by a stop sound rather than a continuant consonant. When any of these words are produced without the second component, the articulation sounds "clipped" and possibly more British than American.

Essentially the same circumstances hold for /o/, as in words such as *boat, coat, rote, rose, pose, toes,* and *chose*. Whether produced with only the vowel /o/ or with the vowel blend /ou/, the meaning of the word is not altered. What do you do in the sentence "I chased Mason, grabbed him by his coattails, and chose not to let him go until we reached the main gate to our home"?

Voice

All vowels and diphthongs, unless intentionally whispered, are produced with vocalization accompanying the articulatory activity. Consonants, however, may be produced with or without accompanying vocalization. Those that are produced with vocalization are known as *voiced* consonants; those produced without vocalization are referred to as *voiceless*.

Manner and Place of Articulation

In the individual descriptions of the consonant sounds that are presented later, the manner and place of articulation are considered for each sound. Some consonants are described as *stops*, others as either *fricatives, glides,* or *nasals.* We anticipate some of the descriptions by defining a few terms here.

Stop sounds are produced by a stopping of the breath stream. The stop sounds are /p/, /b/, /t/, /d/, /k/, and /g/.

Fricatives are produced by a partial closure of the articulators. This action results in the creation of a constricted passage through which the stream of air must be forced. The partial closures may take place as a result of the grooving of the tongue or of having other organs of articulation come close together. The distinctively fricative sounds are /f/, /v/, /θ/ (th), /ð/ (th), /s/, /z/, /ʃ/ (sh), and /ʒ/ (zh). The sound /h/ is produced with laryngeal constriction.

Nasal sounds are reinforced and emitted nasally. The three nasals are /m/, /n/, and /ŋ/ (ng).

Glides are sounds that are produced with a continuous movement of the articulators, rather than with a fixed articulatory position. The glide consonants are /w/, /j/ (y), and most varieties of /r/.

Affricates are blends of two sounds, one a stop and the other a fricative. There are two affricates, /tʃ/ (ch), as in *chum,* and /dʒ/ (j), as in *jam.*

The sound /l/ is a *lateral* consonant. It is produced by the emission of vocalized breath at both sides of the tongue while the tip of the tongue is in contact with the gum ridge. The /l/ is designated as a *liquid* by some phoneticians and linguists.

SOUNDS IN CONTEXT

Although our approach to the study of diction begins with a descriptive analysis of the individual sounds of our language, speech does not consist of a series of individual sounds. Speech is a sequence of sounds. In context, individual sounds are modified and produced differently from the way they would be in isolation. If we were to speak as though our linguistic symbols were a series of sounds, we would be uttering phonetic nonsense. In context, differences in force and duration that emphasize meanings, differences according to the formality or informality of the speech situation, and differences according to the size of the listening group all result in modifications of individual sounds in the flow of speech. Some of these differences are considered here briefly.

ASSIMILATION

If asked for the pronunciation of the words *education, mature,* and *income,* many persons would carefully pronounce these words differently from their pronunciations in contextual speech. The word *education* may regularly be pronounced [ɛdjukeʃən] (ĕdūkāshən) by some persons, but most of us are likely to say [ɛdʒəkeʃən] (ĕjəkāshən) in talking about "the education of our children" or in asserting that "education means. . . ." When we change from the careful but less usual pronunciation of words such as *educate, income,* and *handkerchief* or phrases such as *don't you* and *meet you* to the easier and more usual ones, we are yielding to and demonstrating the effects of *assimilation in connected speech.*

Assimilation refers to the phonetic changes that take place when one sound is modified by a neighboring sound or sounds in connected speech. Some of these changes become relatively fixed and therefore regularly influence the pronunciations of many words.[3] Other assimilations depend on particular verbal contexts and therefore influence the articulation and pronunciation of words only in these contexts. Examples of each are given in our brief discussions of some types of assimilative modifications.

Anticipatory Changes

Most assimilations reflect the influences of anticipatory changes. That is, the organs of articulation, in anticipation of a sound to follow, modify a preceding sound. The change tends to simplify or facilitate articulation. For example, in the word *congress,* the letter *n* is sounded as an /ŋ/ (**ng**) in anticipation of the sound /g/ that follows. It is easier to articulate /ŋg/ than (**n + g**) simply because both the /ŋ/ (**ng**) and the /g/ are produced with the same parts of the tongue and the palate. For the same reason, *income* is pronounced with an /ŋ/ (**ng**) rather than an /n/ followed by a /k/. Similarly, it is easier to say *this shoe* with a lengthened /ʃ/ (**sh**) than with an /s/ followed by an /ʃ/. The pronunciation of *this shoe,* incidentally, is an example of contextual, temporary assimilation.

Voicing

Changes produced in voicing by assimilation are perhaps best exemplified in words that end with a final *s* or *d.* In the words *liked, heaped, rasped,* and *guessed,* and *ropes, takes,* and *plates,* the next-to-the-last produced sound is a voiceless consonant. (The letter *e,* in each case, is silent.) As a result, the final *d* is pronounced as /t/ rather than /d/ and the final *s* as an /s/ rather than /z/.

In words such as *passes, hedges, riches,* and *roses,* the final *s* is produced as /z/ because the next-to-the-last sound is a vowel and is vocalized. Similarly, *grounded, breaded,* and *heeded* are each pronounced with a final /d/. In the words *begs, seems, togs,* and *roams,* the final sound is voiced because of the influence of the preceding voiced consonant.

As a rule, we may generalize that when the next-to-the-last sound in a word is unvoiced, the last sound will also be unvoiced; if the next-to-the-last sound is voiced, the last sound is also voiced.

Other Assimilations

In some cases assimilations may result in the complete loss of one or more sounds, which are replaced by a third sound. This happens in the assimilated pronunciation of *picture, nature,* and *feature,* where the sound /tʃ/ (**ch**) is heard in the second syllable of each of the words.

---

[3] The pronunciation of /ŋ/ (ng) for the letter *n* in words such as *income, congress,* and *bank* are examples of "fixed" assimilative changes.

In both manner and content, speech is appropriate or inappropriate, correct or incorrect, according to the circumstances and the occasion. Despite possible differences in education, profession, and speaking ability, an individual's manner of communicating will or should vary according to the time, the place, and the speaking situation. The minister who feels the need to deliver a sermon to his or her family is likely to do so differently from the way he or she would speak to the congregation in church. The minister should certainly not converse at home — with family members or with visiting members of the congregation — as if talking to them from the pulpit. The lecturer speaking to a large audience on a formal occasion is likely to use more "elevated" language than the same speaker at his or her club, on a picnic, with friends, or at a home social gathering.

Informal speech employs many contractions. We use more *he's*, *don'ts*, *I'ms*, and *gonnas* when speaking informally and intimately than when speaking formally. We do not, however, usually employ contracted forms when emphasis is intended. Public addresses, with the exception of the humorous after-dinner speech, are generally delivered formally unless, for special purposes (usually political), the speaker wants to establish an air of "folksiness" with the listeners.

As an exercise, listen to an interview on your favorite radio or television station or one on the PBR network; note the number of assimilated contracted pronunciations used by the interviewer and interviewee. Did the subject matter make a difference? Compare your observations with what you hear on a "talk back" program.

═══ SPEECH STANDARDS[4] ═══

Pronunciation Variants

In going over the list of consonant and vowel sounds, we may make some observations about minor differences in the pronunciation of the key words among speakers of American English. For example, many of us do not distinguish between the /hw/ in *what* and the /w/ of *watt*; both may be produced as we do the first sound of *will*. Other paired examples are *when* and *wen*, *whale* and *wail*, *whine* and *wine*, *whether* and *weather*.

There is considerable variation in the pronunciation of the vowel of the word *ask*. Most Americans use the same vowel in the words *ask* and *hat*; others broaden the vowel in *ask* to that of the /ɑ/ (ä) of *calm*; a smaller number of Americans use the vowel /a/ (ȧ), which is phonetically between /æ/ (ă) and /ɑ/ (ä).

Most Americans use the same vowel in *hot* as they do in *calm*. A few, however, use a vowel intermediate between the vowel of *call* and the vowel of *calm*. This usage is similar to that of "standard" (London) British English.

There is considerable variation in the production of the vowel of words such as *bird* and *heard*. Some use the vowel /ɝ/, which has an *r* coloring. Others include a clear-cut *r* preceded by a vowel much like the vowel in the word *bud*.

---

[4] In preparation for this part of our discussion, a review of Chapter 4, "American-English Pronunciation," is in order.

Paralleling the variations in the vowel of words such as *bird, heard, surf,* and *mirth* are those in the final sound of words such as *after, supper,* and *thunder.* Most of us use the vowel /ɚ/, which is much like the first sound of the word *above* with the addition of r coloring. Others add a clear-cut /r/ sound after the same vowel, and a smaller number of people make no distinction between the first sound of the word *above* and the last sound of *after* and use /ə/ for both.

To this short list of variants in American pronunciation, we might add another relative to the articulation of the /r/ sound in words in which the spelling includes the letter *r.* We are in common agreement that an /r/ sound is produced whenever a word contains an initial r in its spelling, as in *rug, rice, rain,* and *runs* and in words in which the r is preceded by a consonant and followed by a vowel, as in *tree, grease,* and *prize.* The /r/ is also pronounced in medial positions when it is followed by a vowel, as in *forest* and *touring.* Practice differs, however, in words in which the r is medial in spelling and followed by a consonant, as in *farm, card,* and *sharp,* or final in the spelling, as in *car, far,* and *soar.* These differences are considered again in more detail in Chapter 22.

Assimilations and Speech Standards

Most of the examples of assimilation given earlier are considered acceptable by all except the most pedantic people. Some persons may prefer the unassimilated pronunciations of words such as *congress* and *income* and tax themselves to maintain the /n/ rather than yielding to economy in articulation and produce an /ŋ/ (**ng**). Not all assimilations, however, are acceptable, even to our liberal dictionary editors. For example, the word *open,* despite temptation and frequent mispronunciation by small children, should still be produced with a final /n/ rather than an /m/. The word *gas* is still better pronounced with a final /s/ than with a /z/, although the second pronunciation is frequently given by persons not habitually careless in their speech.

Criteria for Speech Standards

Speech in general and pronunciation in particular are appropriate if they are consistent with the objectives of the speaker in his or her role of a communicator of ideas. The listeners, the occasion, and the speaker as a personality are some of the factors that determine appropriateness. *What is appropriate may be accepted as standard. Speech becomes substandard if the pronunciations are such that they violate the judgments and tastes of the listeners.* We are likely to sense such violations if an official in high government office speaks to us when we are members of a large audience as he or she might to some intimate friends on a fishing trip. We might also sense some violation if a college president talking on the topic "The Need for a Liberal Arts Education" were to do so in the manner of a sports announcer at a football game.

Speech becomes distinctly substandard if it employs pronunciations that are not currently used by any persons whose backgrounds as speakers make their judgments in regard to linguistic usage worthy of respect. Even a liberal attitude toward pronunciation would still not justify pronouncing *asked* as [æst] (ăst) or *something* as [sʌmpɪm] (sŭmpĭm)—except for speakers of a dialect for whom these pronunciations are acceptable.

Pronunciations that reveal foreign-language influence, such as the substitution of a sound that approximates the appropriate one in English, would also constitute substandard speech. The substitution of a /v/ for a /w/ in words such as *wife* and *went* or an /f/ for a /v/ in words such as *give* and *leave* are examples of substandard pronunciations frequently resulting from foreign language influence. Occasionally, they may reflect persistent foreign language influences in dialectal speech within this country.

Speakers who wish to improve their speech, their articulation, and their pronunciation, as well as their word usage, must be good listeners. They must listen with discrimination for what is best and current in the community in which they live. They must listen to the educated and to the respected members of the community and use them as models but should not imitate them slavishly. Above all, they should avoid trying to sound like somebody else, thus seeming to deny individuality and place of origin. This does not mean that you or any other person should maintain what may have been nonstandard in your background. It does mean that the man or woman from New York should not consciously try to sound as though he or she were brought up in Atlanta, Georgia, and that a speaker from Houston, Texas, should not try to sound like a Harvard-educated Bostonian unless the speaker happens to be one. In time, if any of these speakers live long enough in an area, some of the flavor of the area's speech will naturally begin to appear. Careful listening is likely to translate itself into unconscious imitation of the speech of the immediate environment unless the speaker is negatively motivated toward the person to whom he or she is listening.

REFERENCES AND SUGGESTED READINGS

Bronstein, A. J. (1987). "The pronunciation of American-English," *The Random House dictionary of the English language*. (2nd ed.). New York: Random House, Inc.

Chomsky, N., & Halle, M. (1968). *The sound patterns of English*. New York: Harper & Row, Chap. 7.

Dillard, J. L. (1976). *American talk*. New York: Random House.

_____ . (1972). *Black English: Its history and usage in the United States*. New York: Random House.

Eisenson, J., & Ogilvie, M. (1983). *Communicative disorders in children*. New York: Macmillan.

Hendrickson, R. (1986). *American talk: The words and ways of American dialects*. New York: Viking Penguin.

Labov, W. (1972). *Language in the inner city*. Philadelphia: University of Pennsylvania Press.

Langacker, R. W. (1967). *Language and its structure*. New York: Harcourt Brace Jovanovich.

Stewart, W. A. (1972). "Sociolinguistic factors in the history of Negro dialects," in D. L. Shores (Ed.). *Contemporary English*. Philadelphia: J.B. Lippincott Company.

Van Riper, C., & Smith, D. E. (1979). *An introduction to general American phonetics*. New York: Harper & Row.

Winitz, H. (1975). *From syllable to conversation*. Baltimore: University Park Press.

CHAPTER 13

INDIVIDUAL STUDY OF AMERICAN-ENGLISH SOUNDS: THE VOWELS

═══

We will study the sounds (phonemes) of American English on the assumption that interest and knowledge and opportunity for practice of the phonemic system will enhance your improvement of diction. Through experience, we know that some sounds are more troublesome to produce than others. Persons for whom American English is a second language, acquired in late childhood, adolescence, or adulthood, may have particular difficulty with sounds that are not phonemes in their first language. A common tendency for such persons is to carry over the nearest phoneme of their first language to the newly acquired system. These sounds, and others that may be troublesome for persons for whom American English is a first language, will be treated in greater detail than those sounds that seldom present any difficulty.

Although we will study the individual phonemes of American English, it is important to understand that sounds in context—in a flow of speech—do not have all of the characteristics or features of the isolated phonemes. (Review the discussion in Chapter 12 of *sounds in context and assimilation*.) A normal (natural) utterance involves sounds that are coarticulated. In this process, both the acoustic and physiological characteristics of a sound are influenced by the sound that preceded it and the one the speaker is about to produce. Thus, the /s/ and /t/ in *stew* or *stem* are produced somewhat differently from these sounds in *sunset*, or *it's tame*, or *hat's off*, or *at least*.

Although it is neither possible nor practical to consider all possible combinations of sounds that may occur in contextual speech, we will consider a number of the most frequently coarticulated sounds in our discussion of sound blends. Our practice materials include lists of words, usually those used with high frequency, phrases incorporating such words as well as others used frequently, sentences, paragraphs, and wherever the creative impulse took hold, some dialogues. Selections of literary value were chosen on the basis of their use of words that featured the sounds under discussion.

We begin our study of the sounds of American English with the vowels. Although there are variations in choice of vowels for some words in different regional dialects, in context there is seldom any difficulty in understanding the intended meaning of an utterance. Pronunciation habits related to regional practice may result in the persistent use of a particular vowel in words for which most Americans use another. For example, there is considerable variation in pronunciation of the vowel in the words *had, have, bad, candy,* and *sad.* We do not all pronounce *Washington* or *orange* with the same first vowel. There is also a considerable amount of regional variation in the vowel of words such as *word, bird, herd* and *heard, curt, earth, mirth, urge,* and *emerge.* We are by no means unanimous in our choice of vowel sounds for the words *and, bath, path, ask, aunt,* and *chance.* Most of the variants of vowel sounds are considered in the discussions that soon follow. As already indicated, the carry-over influence of a first language on the diction of persons for whom American English is a second language will be given special consideration. Fortunately, because of their intensity and "open-mouthed" production, vowels are easy to imitate.

═══ VOWEL PRODUCTION ═══

All vowels share several characteristics: (1) they are all voiced sounds; (2) all are articulated in essentially the same manner in that they are continuant sounds, without interruption and without restriction of the stream of breath; and (3) although lip activity is involved, the activity of the tongue and the modifications of the resonating cavities make the essential difference in the production of the different vowel sounds.

Vowels become acoustically identifiable to the listener, including the speaker-listener, by virtue of the changes in quality that occur both because of what the articulators do and because of the modifications in the resonating cavities above the larynx — mostly in the structures of the mouth and pharynx. These cavities function as "filters" and so permit different concentrations of energy known as *formant frequencies.*[1]

Vowel Classification

Vowels may be conveniently classified according to the part of the tongue that is most actively involved in the production of the sound. If you concentrate on the vowel sounds of the words *me* and *moo,* you should become aware that the blade of the tongue moves forward toward the hard palate for *me.* For *moo,* the back of the tongue moves toward the soft palate. Similar activity may be noted if you compare the vowels of *pet* and *paw.* For *pet,* the front of the tongue is most active, and for *paw,* the back of the tongue is most active. For neither of these vowels, however, does the tongue move as high as for the vowels of *me* and *moo.* Comparable activity may be observed for all the other *front* vowels (those produced with the front, or blade, of the tongue most active) in contrast with the corresponding *back* vowels (those produced with the back of the tongue most active). Table 13–1 presents the vowels of American English.

The approximate differences in tongue position for the front and the back vowels are illustrated in Figures 13–1 (see page 193) and 13–2 (see page 210).

---

[1] A technical classification for vowels is based on the *formant frequency,* or "regions of energy concentration," for each sound. P. Lieberman provided this definition of *formant frequency:* "The formant frequencies are essentially the center frequencies of the supralaryngeal vocal tract acting as a complex filter that lets maximum sound energy through it several levels of frequency" (P. Lieberman, *Speech Physiology and Acoustic Phonetics,* New York: Macmillan, 1977, p. 34).

Table 13–1. Vowels of American-English Speech

Front Vowels			Central Vowels			Back Vowels		
	Phonetic Symbol	Dictionary Symbol		Phonetic Symbol	Dictionary Symbol		Phonetic Symbol	Dictionary Symbol
meet	i	ē				boon	u	o͞o
milk	ɪ	ĭ	mirth	ɜ or ɝ	ûr	book	ʊ	o͝o
may	e	ā				boat	o	ō
men	ɛ	ĕ	about	ə	ə			
						ball	ɔ	ô
mat	æ	ă	upper	ɚ	ər	bog	ɒ	ŏ
ask¹	a	ȧ	mud	ʌ	ŭ	balm	ɑ	ä

[1]When the speaker compromises between the vowels of *mat* and of *balm*. This vowel is intermediate in placement as well as in sound between æ and a.

Figures 13–3 (see page 223) and 13–4 (see page 229) illustrate the position of the tongue for the central vowels, or midvowels (those produced with the middle of the tongue most active).

You may test these representative tongue positions with your own articulatory behavior relative to these vowels by incorporating them in the following key words.

Front	Central	Back
me		boot
mitt		book
made	mirth	boat
met	above, upper	bought
mat	mud	box
mask		balm

On the basis of the production of the key vowels, a four-fold basis for classification can be made.

First, vowels differ in production according to *place of articulation* — and so may be classified as *front, mid (central),* or *back* vowels according to the part of the tongue that is most actively involved in their production.

Second, vowels differ as to *height-of-tongue* position. The vowel of *me* is a high front vowel; the vowel of *moon* is a high back vowel. The vowel of *mask* is a low front vowel; that of *balm* is a low back vowel.

A *third basis* for the classification of vowels is *muscle tension.* If we compare the vowel of *peek* with that of *pick,* we should feel that the tongue is more tense for the vowel of *peek* than it is for the one in *pick.* Similarly, the vowel of *boat* is produced with the tongue somewhat more tense than in the production of the vowel of *book.* Tension may also be felt in the muscles behind the chin.

A fourth feature that distinguishes some vowels from others is lip-rounding. This is more evident when the vowel /u/ as in *coo* and *two* is produced in isolation than when produced in context. Back vowels, with the exception of /ɑ/, all have some degree of lip-rounding. Front vowels do not. It is possible to produce the vowel /u/ even in isolation without rounding the lips, but it is easier to say *coo* or *moo* with the lips rounded than with the lips spread as for the front vowels.

Before we go into our more detailed discussion of the individual sounds of our language, we might review briefly some features of vowel production. All vowels, unless intentionally whispered, are voiced, continuant sounds. When they are produced as isolated sounds, the tongue tip is usually placed behind the lower gum ridge. The vowel sounds are differentiated as a result of the activity of the blade, the middle, or the back of the tongue elevated to different positions (heights) within the mouth cavity. Some vowels are produced with muscle tension as an additional characteristic. The articulatory aspects that characterize the production of each of the vowels are now considered.

═══ THE FRONT VOWELS ═══

/i/ (ē) As in *See* and /ɪ/ (ĭ) As in *Sit*[2]

The vowel /i/ is a high, front, tense vowel.

If you study the front vowel diagram (Figure 13–1) you should note that /i/ is produced with the blade of the tongue arched high in the front of the mouth. This vowel is produced with a considerable degree of tongue tension and a lesser degree of lip tension. If you produce /i/ as an isolated sound, your lip position approximates a tight-lipped grin. You should also be able to feel tension in the muscle bulge behind your chin. Muscle tension is required to produce a clear /i/ and to distinguish it from the vowel /ɪ/ which is a more relaxed sound.

The sound /i/ has several different spellings in English. These include *e, ee, ea, i*, and *ie*, as in *even* and *be, see* and *bee, each* and *peas, ski, conceit* and *receipt*, and *believe* and *yield*.

The exercises that follow are intended to establish the /i/ sound. Later we will have materials to contrast the /i/ and /ɪ/.

═══ PRACTICE MATERIALS ═══

Yvette	reap	leak	freeze
Enid	eager	eke	ego
either	eel	equate	steel

[2] Hereafter, the phonetic symbol (IPA) and the usual dictionary symbol are presented only at the head of each section for the sound to be studied. Thereafter, only the IPA symbol will be used.

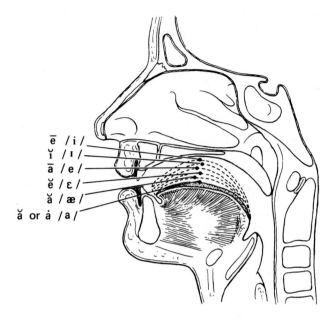

ē /i/
ĭ /ɪ/
ā /e/
ĕ /ɛ/
ă /æ/
ȧ or ȧ /a/

Figure 13–1 Representative tongue positions for front vowels.

east	eerie	cheese	meat
sweep	Sweden	eagle	freedom
beach	breeze	team	please
glee	esprit	quay	sneeze

beech tree	belief to achieve
field and stream	feel equal
sleek fleet	scenic peaks
weird dream	esteemed colleague
cheerless and dreary	piqued by Cleo
decent scheme	appease to please
pleasingly neat	deals and steals
Oakie from Muskogee	secret intrigue
peaches in season	fields and trees
Eve in Eden	Brie cheese

a. A team of Marines beat the Seabees in beach baseball.
b. Yvonne assured Yvette that it would not be sheer caprice if she leaped off the quay into the deep sea to get away from the steamy heat of Miami.
c. Gene was piqued that his esteemed friend Steve did not share his belief that the esprit among his colleagues lacked collegiality.
d. Pete steam cleaned his machine and then took to his easy chair.
e. Snead insisted that a decent dish of green peas and beans has an amount of protein at least the equal of cuts of lean beef.

   f. Pete MacNeil reached for a ball-peen hammer and proceeded to beat the
      sheet of steel.
   g. Anita was displeased with Rita's teasing.
   h. The sneak thief speedily beat his way up the creek.
   i. Speed freaks are exceedingly heedless of their bodies' needs.
   j. Breedon, a weaver, dreamed of using steel beads.

   a. In his *Fables* Jean de la Fontaine preached that "we believe no evil 'til the
      evil's done." He also held that "it is a double pleasure to deceive the
      deceiver."
   b. John Ruskin believed that in a state of grief we may deceive ourselves as
      to our ability to reason.
   c. Even the weariest river
      Winds somewhere safe to sea.

                                                    —Algernon Charles Swinburne,
                                                        The Garden of Proserpine

   d. Speak roughly to your little boy,
          And beat him when he sneezes:
      He only does it to annoy,
          Because he knows it teases.

                                                                  —Lewis Carroll,
                                                    Alice's Adventures in Wonderland

   e. We are the music-makers,
          And we are the dreamers of dreams,
      Wandering by lone sea-breakers,
          And sitting by desolate streams;

      World-losers and world-forsakers,
          On whom the pale moon gleams;
      Yet we are the movers and shakers
          Of the world for ever, it seems.

                                          —Arthur W. O'Shaughnessy, *Ode*, Stanza I

/ɪ/ (ĭ) As in Bit

/ɪ/ is also a high, front vowel. /ɪ/ differs from /i/ in two respects; /ɪ/ is produced with a
tongue position somewhat lower than is /i/ and *without articulatory tension.*

The lip position for /ɪ/ is approximately a relaxed smile in contrast with the tight-
lipped grin for /i/. The difference in tension and lip position may be observed if you
place your hand behind your chin and look in the mirror as you change from the word
heat to *hit.*

The most frequent spelling for /ɪ/ is the letter *i* as in *sit, wit, fit,* and *lit;* other
spellings include *u, ui,* and *e,* as in *busy, build,* and *English.*

Some speakers use the vowel /ɪ/ for the final *y* in words such as *busy, city,* and *petty.*
Other speakers are likely to use a vowel somewhere between /i/ and /ɪ/. Still others may

use a vowel closer to /i/ than to /ɪ/. The shorter /ɪ/ vowel provides the effect of "clipped" British pronunciation. Unless you have other pronunciations that reflect British influence, the use of /ɪ/ may sound pretentious. However, the choice is yours.

Persons who speak Spanish as a first language may have difficulty in distinguishing between /ɪ/ and /i/. The tendency is to produce the /i/ in context. Chinese and persons from East-Asian countries may have the same difficulty. Determine your own practice and, if necessary, correct your usage with the following list of words. The words are to be read across the page. Avoid any suggestion of the vowel /i/ for the words in the third column.

═══

PRACTICE MATERIALS

i and ɪ

heap	hippy	hip
greed	greedy	grid
fleet	flitty	flit
seat	city	sit
peat	pity	pit
key	kitty	kit
meat	meaty	mitt
cheese	cheesy	chit
we	weedy	wit
leak	leaky	lick
reed	reedy	rid
bead	beady	bid
meal	mealy	mill

ibid	idiom	ignite	igloo
ilk	its	ingot	infer
imp	is	Italy	intake
ink	itch	indicate	ignore
Indian	inch	inn	insert
into	imply	ignorant	image
imbue	ingrate	impale	impact
build	quip	pinnacle	children
mist	list	fist	grip
business	tryst	strip	flick
differ	women	shrimp	whisk
fill	wishes	shrill	hymn
quick	drip	grill	quilt
wilt	mince	lick	think

eclipse	instill	bib	admit
addict	crib	simple	spin
insipid	insistent	timidity	willy-nilly
frantic	abyss	aphid	antic
flint	frisk	ticklish	twitch

hit and miss	frantic antics	tryst in the mist	skip the ship
twist and spin	hint of wit	skinny fists	fill the till
lick the lips	flick of the wrist	itch to be rich	Tim is slim
win and grin	grilled shrimp	busy and dizzy	pickled with dill
lift the lid	inch by inch	spilled milk	written with quill
lit pit	tipped lid	kith and kin	kissin' cousin

a. Winter weather along the Mississippi River varies from the misty and semi-tropical in Louisiana to the grim and insistently frigid in Minnesota.
b. Twin British ships drifted into an Atlantic slip in April.
c. Jim Dillon, a detective investigator, discovered that Philip Whipple and his cousin Bill had built an illegal liquor still.
d. Chip Wilson, the village druggist, filled prescriptions with insight and skill.
e. Rick Simmons made a quick trip to River City.
f. Dick Simpson, who lives in Missouri, wished to be convinced of the merits of the big-money spending bill before he voted to increase taxes.
g. "The wit is insipid," insisted Plimpton, a grim and often livid critic.
h. In a writ Martin Nixon, the head of the city's transit system, was positive that the citizen's petition was insipid and, in his opinion, illegal.
i. Whenever Rick felt "in the pink" he whistled "Dixie" while he kept busy.
j. Linda's kitten was sitting pretty on top of the kitchen cabinet.

a. "Dear pig, are you willing to sell for one shilling
   Your ring?" Said the piggy, "I will."
                                      —Edward Lear, *Nonsense Songs*

b. Walt Whitman remembered things for us, impossible but intelligible, and which will become unintelligible at our peril.
                            —Karle Wilson, *Classic Americans: Walt Whitman*

c. In his novel *The Egoist*, George Meredith reiterated that cynicism was uninspired intellectual dandyism. Some of his critics did not spare him from bitter criticism, implying that he, himself, was guilty of dandyism. Perhaps it is possible for you, the reader, to be a critic and exercise your own intellect with a reading of these lines from Meredith's poem *The Lark Ascending*:

> For singing till his heaven fills
> 'Tis love of earth that he instills,
> And ever winging up and up,
> Our valley in his garden cup,
> And he the wine which over flows
> To lift us with him as he goes.

d. The moving finger writes, and having writ,
   Moves on. Nor all your piety nor wit
   Shall lure it back to cancel half a line,
   Nor all your tears wash out a word of it.
   —*The Rubáiyát of Omar Khayyám*
   (Translated by Edward Fitzgerald)

e. As someday it may happen that a victim must be found,
   I've got a little list—I've got a little list,
   Of society's offenders who might well be underground,
   And who never would be missed—who never would be missed.
   —Sir William S. Gilbert, *The Mikado*

/i/ (ē) and /ɪ/ (ĭ)

For persons with Spanish as a first language and others who may have difficulty in distinguishing between the front tense vowel /i/ and relaxed /ɪ/, the following material should be of help.

ADDITIONAL PRACTICE MATERIALS

peal	pin	deep	dip
seat	sit	leak	lick
beat	bit	sheep	ship
meat	mit	sleep	slip
heat	hit	peach	pitch
greet	grit	leap	lip
cheap	chip	green	grin
bean	bin	deal	dill
reap	rip	sleek	slick
peep	pip	heap	hip
fleet	flit	peak	pick
reed	rid	greed	grid
feel	fill	heel	hill
steal	still	neat	knit

In the following sentences, the first italicized word has the tense vowel [i]; the second has the relaxed vowel /ɪ/.

a. They climbed to *reach* the *rich* mine.
b. The *beans* were stored in *bins* in sixteen neat hills.
c. Much *steel* is *still* imported to meet our needs.
d. The *team* counted on *Tim* to win the prize for the fleet.
e. Ten *sheep* were sent by *ship*.

   f. A rod and *reel* were lost in the *rill.*
   g. The *deed* he *did* took courage but it made Phil feel good.
   h. At *least* ten items were on the *list.*
   i. His *feet* were the right size; the shoes didn't *fit.*
   j. *Cheap* paint will *chip.*
   k. Sue broke her *heel* when she climbed up the *hill.*
   l. The *leaking* jar was good for *licking.*

/ɪ/ (ĭ) in Unstressed Syllables

The vowel /ɪ/ occurs rather frequently in the unstressed syllables of many polysyllabic words, as in add*ed*, frett*ed*, tep*id*, *in*ept, *in*stead, and *im*ply. In some instances, the speaker may use the vowel /ə/ rather than /ɪ/ in the unstressed syllable.

PRACTICE MATERIALS

The following word list will provide practice with the /ɪ/ in unstressed positions.

practice	wedded	impart	plosive
merit	sterile	instead	corrosive
encrusted	junket	inept	listed
frosting	rusted	immerse	watches
bursting	tempted	intend	matches

   In the following list, the /ɪ/ may occur in either the stressed or the unstressed syllable or syllables, as well as in both syllables of the compound words. Some of the unstressed syllables may be pronounced with /ə/.

finish	filmstrip	imprinting	hissing
impending	picnic	finicky	statistics
implicit	rivet	instinctive	simplicity
inflict	impinge	misgiving	indicative
intuitive	kindling	consistent	linguistic
limpid	thicket	insipid	trivet

primitive instincts	simplistic insistence
vivid intelligence	implicit statistic
thrilling tidbit	inhibited kinship
consistent winning	missing invalid

/i/ or /ɪ/ As a Final Sound

In polysyllabic words that have *y* as the final letter, we have a choice in pronunciation between a sound close to /i/ or one closer to /ɪ/—in effect, a sound intermediate between the two high front vowels. For example, *daily, Monday, Tuesday,* and so forth provide this choice. So do *pony, lonely, homely,* and *Jenny*. If your choice is the /i/ as in *see,* the final sound may be overstressed. If your choice is /ɪ/ as in *bit,* you may sound a bit British. In words such as *prophecy, heresy, formally, certainly,* the last syllable has a secondary stress and so the pronunciation may be closer to /i/ than to /ɪ/. However, whatever the choice, the meaning of the word in context does not change. Following are some practice materials. You may want to record your pronunciation to determine if the choice is the one you would really like to make.

———

PRACTICE MATERIALS

cheer	cheery
tear	teary
crisp	crispy
keen	keenly
beast	beastly
grim	grimly

logic	logically
pleasant	pleasantly
moral	morally
second	secondary
capable	capably
tearful	tearfully

logically but pleasantly	unseemly density
grimly but eagerly	princely royalty
morally and capably	kindly but justifiably
strangely dreary	grimly but timidly
secondary philosophy	naughtily but effectively

a. Stephen Kingsley bitterly concluded that the morality of Pete, his kissin' cousin, was strangely but indecently effective.
b. Our judiciary has the legal responsibility of protecting a citizen's liberty and property from seizure through chicanery and trickery.
c. Painfully and grimly, Beasley reached the reality that taxes, even ever-increasing taxes, are what we need to pay for living in a civilized society.
d. Ruskin truly believed that "to see clearly is poetry, prophecy, and religion—all in one."

e. On January 14, 1667, Pepys's diary had this entry: "Busy till night, pleasing myself mightily to see what a deal of business goes off a man's hands when he stays by it."

f. Thomas Henry Huxley wrote in his *Coming of Age of the Origin of Species*, "It is the customary fate of new truths to begin as heresies and to end as superstitions."

g. William S. Gilbert insistently reminded us that:
   Things are seldom what they seem,
   Skim milk masquerades as cream.

and

   Stick to your desks and *never go to sea*
   And you all may be Rulers of the Queen's Navee.
                                                    —*H.M.S. Pinafore*, Act 1

h. With relatively little hostility, Hartley agreed that he was individually responsible for the majority of recent less-than-splendid decisions.

/e/ (ā) As in *Mate*

/e/ is a midhigh, front vowel. Most Americans are more likely to produce the vowel /e/ as part of the diphthong /eɪ/ than as a pure vowel. Whether produced as part of a diphthong or as a pure sound, /e/ is a tense, front, midhigh vowel (see the front-vowel diagram, Figure 13-1).

Some speakers use the diphthongal form more or less regularly in a stressed syllable and the pure vowel form in an unstressed syllable. There are, however, no words in our language that would be distinguished in meaning from one another on the basis of the use of a pure vowel /e/ or the diphthongal form /eɪ/. We do not recommend the cultivation of either form for the sake of consistency. We do, however, recommend that you avoid excessive prolongation of the diphthong to a triphthong [eɪə].

The vowel /e/ or the diphthong /eɪ/ is most frequently represented in spelling by the letter *a*, as in *date, mate,* and *hate*; other frequent spellings include *ay, ai, ey,* and *ei,* as in *say, mail, they,* and *vein*.

PRACTICE MATERIALS

dame	gaze	quail	flail
ace	angel	aviary	ate
ail	April	ape	ache
age	aim	aviator	aid
apex	Asia	eighteen	aphid
base	brake	trait	braided
bait	crate	chaotic	fateful
bail	place	grate	station

deign	plate	lace	caged
date	rate	chaste	strafe
sake	flake	awake	failure

away	filet	sleigh	replay
dray	repay	dismay	relay
shay	delay	bay	ray
pay	hay	neigh	portray
day	may	betray	fray
weigh	they	play	display
native	abate	restate	ratio

brain drain	safely tamed
break of day	stately name
daily pay	trace of rain
displayed portrait	safe haven
faithful mate	dismaying tale
pain of failure	vain aching
plaintive wailing	wakeful waif

famous jailhouse tales
hail to Dave Shay
late dated mail
playful, graceful Mabel
native's strange ways
made of stabilized clay
razor-edged scale

Note whether you distinguish between the vowel and the diphthong forms in the following sentences. Careful listening may help you to decide that the sentence context may make a difference.

    a. Peyton draped crepe paper around his place.

    b. Jesse James was outraged by the railroad station's great unbreakable safe.

    c. May has thirty-one days.

    d. Jane was fond of angel food cake or anything else that Nathan would bake for her.

    e. Casco Bay is in the state of Maine.

    f. Dale won the relay race on Saturday.

    g. Amie and Dale saw strange shapes rising from the gray mist.

    h. Rachel gazed in dismay at the pale, stagestruck Raymond who had made claims to being a macho male.

    i. Grace watched the plane fly away into the chaos of space.

    j. Stacey Blake complained to Dr. Chase of a range of aches and pains.

    k. The caged lion was enraged when he was awakened and not fed his share of steak.

    l. Lady Fay, a famous dame, could not be blamed for raising the question, "Is a cake, baked all day with May daisies and twenty-four tamed blackbirds, really a dainty dish?"

m. An old saying states, "The more things change, the more they remain the same."

a.   Nothing that is can pause or stay;
The moon will wax, the moon will wane,
The mist and cloud will turn to rain,
The rain to mist, and cloud again,
Tomorrow be today.
                                        —Henry W. Longfellow, *Keramos*

b. Dale said, "Good day,
And left the fray
And lived to play
Another day.

c. In one of his fables, Aesop stated that it is easy to be brave from a safe and distant place.

d. Let us have faith that right makes might.
                                        —Abraham Lincoln, Address,
                                        Cooper Union, 1860

e. He left the name at which the world grew pale,
To point a moral, or adorn a tale.
                                        —Samuel Johnson, *The Vanity of Human Wishes*

f. A little rule, a little sway,
A sunbeam in a winter's day,
Is all the proud and mighty have
Between the cradle and the grave.
                                        —John Dyer, *Grongar Hill*

Establishing a Distinction Between /e/ and /eɪ/

For Hispanics and others who do not have the /eɪ/ diphthong in their first language, the sound should be established by contrasting it with the close-sounding /e/. In the following list you should note that the vowel form /e/ is in the first and third columns, with words that end in an unvoiced stop sound: /t/, /p/, or /k/. The second and fourth columns have words with either a voiced stop or a continuant rather than a stop sound. (Review the discussion of sound features in Chapter 12.)

PRACTICE MATERIALS

ape	Abe	rate	raid
grate	grade	trace	trade
fate	fade	pate	paid
flake	flayed	race	raise

late	laid	shape	shade
mate	maid	grace	grade
mace	maze	relate	relayed

stay with staples	chaotic fate
stayed in Nepal	relate to the cake
an ace navigator	flakes of tasty pastry

a. Tate Baker tasted the cake and proclaimed, "Take it away and feed it to the whales."
b. Hale Payton prayed that there would be no rain on his parade.
c. Nathan Damon crated the bacon and mailed it by the daily air freight.
d. To navigate Mason Bay was Raymond's aspiration.
e. The air base became safe when the ice flaked away.

/ɛ/ (ĕ) As in *Help*

/ɛ/ (ĕ) is a midfront vowel. The vowel /ɛ/ (ĕ) differs from /e/ (ā) in that the former is produced with a slightly lower front tongue position and *without articulary tension.*

The most frequent spelling for the vowel /ɛ/ is the single letter *e*; other spellings include *a* as in *any, ay* as in *says, ai* as in *said,* and *ea* as in *bread.* The vowel /ɛ/ is also heard in the words *bury, guess,* and *leopard.*

PRACTICE MATERIALS

In the lists of words and phrases for initial and medial /ɛ/, avoid any tendency to prolong the vowel into the diphthong /ɛə/.

edit	enemy	elegant	engineer
effort	emblem	enzyme	enterprise
ebb	empty	enter	engine
end	any	energy	exit
echo	elf	elk	elder
egg	elbow	edge	effort
etch	edible	entry	extra
else	edit	ensign	empire

attend	second	tether	trend
reckon	restless	festive	gender
beckon	said	jest	center
lend	gem	wren	theft
guess	thread	deaf	health

pleasant	meant	check	pensive
self	tent	ready	settler
friend	chest	descent	weather

meant well	bent for hell
guess again	friend in the end
steady trend	desert weather
elfin jests	tense elders
edible eggs	pensive Frenchmen
ready guests	gentle echoes
enter and exit	thefts of gems
pleasant self	beckon the deaf
messy chest	lent the rent
bent head	spent wealth
guest for the quest	stealthy elf

a. Betty sent a letter every day to her best friend, Edna Phelps.
b. Ned, although wealthy, avoided getting into debt.
c. Many men and women are deaf because they will not attend to any but themselves.
d. Jerrie sent her regrets to Heddy because she could not attend the weekend reception.
e. Stella was energetic and often restless, yet seldom ready for steady effort.
f. A leopard spends little effort in meaningless or unintended gestures.
g. Oscar Wilde is not alone in being inept at resisting everything except temptation.
h. A well-trained terrier is adept at picking up a selected scent.
i. The poetic Ben Bellow held that his den was never empty because it held the breath of Beth's perfume.
j. Shelly did not pretend that she felt on edge and expressed her regrets that she was not her pleasant self.

a. In *Iolanthe* Sir William Schwenck held that
      The law is the true embodiment
      Of everything that's excellent.
b. The Soul unto itself
   Is an imperial friend —
   Or the most agonizing spy —
   An enemy could send.

—Emily Dickinson, *No. 683*, Stanza 1

c. In her poem *Despondency* Letitia Landon asked:
      Were it not better to forget
      Than but remember and regret?
d. The rest to some faint meaning make pretense,
   But Shadwell never deviates into sense.

—John Dryden, *Mac Flecknoe*

e. I do not love thee, Doctor Fell.
The reason why I cannot tell;
But this alone I know full well,
I do not love thee, Doctor Fell.

—Thomas Brown,
Verses written as a student at Oxford

Distinction Between /ɛ/ and Other High, Front Vowels /e/, /i/, and /ɪ/

Ken	Kean	red	raid	wreck	rick
wren	ream	bread	braid	peck	pick
ten	teen	Bess	base	sell	sill
set	seat	men	main	self	sylph

Make certain that clear distinctions are made for the vowels in the italicized words in the sentences that follow.

a. The *pen* was placed next to the *pin* on the *rim* of the *desk*.
b. *Ed* called for *aid* to prepare for the *imminent parade*.
c. *Fred* was seldom *afraid*, but this *gesture* was not a *charade*.
d. *Ben*, where have you *been*? It's *today* or *never*!
e. All *seven men* were *mean* and *lean*.
f. The singer was *ready*, but his voice was *reedy* and his formal *dress* was *seedy*.
g. Sue *said* that she found the *seed* that she *desperately needed*.
h. *Fred* fought to be *freed* from *petty questions* and *appeals*.

═══

/æ/ (ă) As in *Bat*

/æ/ (ă) is a low, front vowel. It is almost always produced with a lax tongue; occasionally some contexts call for a slightly tense tongue, but emphatic tension should be avoided. The tongue is lower in position and the mouth wider open for /æ/ than it is for /ɛ/ (see the front-vowel diagram, Figure 13–1).

The letter *a*, as in *mash, pack, rack,* and *sack,* is the most frequent spelling representation for the vowel /æ/.

In some parts of the United States, the vowel blend /ɛə/ tends to be substituted for the vowel /æ/. In much of the United States, a vowel closer to /ɛ/ than to /æ/ is heard in words in which the vowel is followed by the sound /r/, as in *marry, parry, Harry,* and *Mary.*

=====

PRACTICE MATERIALS

Determine your own practice for the following words in which the vowel /æ/ is an acceptable pronunciation. Doubts, if they exist, should be determined by the usage of respected speakers in your community.

bad	parrot	clan	slam
map	match	jam	tank
cap	shall	hack	bag
can	carry	fact	trapped
chance	jackal	began	begat
hag	Sally	lamb	path
gasp	frantic	laugh	cash
black	ant	stand	answer

Atlantic	massive	graft	Agnes
plaid	plank	aster	astral
atrophy	rank	placid	dragon
apple	apt	draft	graft
jaguar	jangle	tangle	lamb
annual	Alps	craft	anvil

happy antics	tank of mash
splash and dash	ham sandwich
basket of jams	planned stand
apple candy	fantastic and grand
wham bam	chatter and laughter
tactful answer	clapping of hands
stranded band	Dandy Jack
pack Dan's bags	mad chap
random passage	cracked crab
clannish family	canceled attack

a. Sally and Mack are crackerjacks at stacking and racking glasses and pans.
b. Dan was in a time jam and had to use Pam's notes to cram for the last exam.
c. The Swiss Alps have many jagged peaks and crags.
d. Into the camp came Hank, carrying a bag of dappled apples strapped to his tan backpack.
e. Ramsey fancied himself as a man of unflagging stamina and action.
f. Ham and pancakes make a snack for a boy, but a handsome meal for a man.
g. To have a good match, we first need an acceptable catch.
h. Alan went to California to enhance his agonizing acting career.
i. Stan apparently did not know that a small hammer rather than an ax should be used for banging a tack on a rack.

j. Though he was hatless and ragged, Brandon's spirits never lagged.

k. The wheels of the taxicab sank deep into the sandy path.

l. Sally wrapped her lap-top computer into a neat pack.

In the following sentences be careful to avoid excessive tension or nasality in the vowels of the italicized words. Keep your lower jaw and tongue relaxed.

a. *Nathaniel* asked, "*Can lanky Hank manage* the task without a *mask?*"

b. Pam was happy that the *canned ham and* apple *jam* passed customs.

c. *Dan and Sam ran* a fast race on the *sandy strand*.

d. Whenever she *catnapped* Alfreda had *random* thoughts with strange *angles*.

e. *Frank and Ann planned* to raise *Angus* cattle on their *land*.

f. *Francine and Andrew* enjoyed active sports *and planned matches*.

g. Sally, who was seldom *angry* but no *namby-pamby*, lived in a well-*planned* house in a *narrow* alley.

h. *Brandon* enjoyed *bran* muffins *and* apple *jam*.

a. As with my hat upon my head
   I walked along the Strand,
   I there did meet another man
   With his hat in his hand.

   — George Stevens, *Anecdotes of Johnson*

b. Close to the sun in lonely lands,
   He clasps the crag with crooked hands;
   Ring'd with azure world he stands.

   — Alfred, Lord Tennyson, *In Memoriam*

c. Oscar Fingal O'Flahertie Wilde wanted us to accept his belief that "the only difference between a caprice and a lifelong passion is that the caprice lasts a little longer." In his *Aphorisms* he wrote, "Anybody can make history. Only a great man can write it."

   If we can accept Wilde as a man, or perhaps as an adolescent who aspired to be a verbal superman, we may begin to understand him. On analysis it would seem that Wilde attempted to disentangle established claptrap from truth. This may have been his passion. But another view is that more than anything else, he needed to attract attention to himself. Wilde traveled in the shadow of Whistler who, perhaps, was even more cynical than his sycophantic, transparent admirer.

d. Daniel wanted a girl to marry:
   He loved Pam and Fran and also Sharrie;
   He asked, then prayed one would not tarry —
   She'd be the girl that he would marry.

   But Dan, because he was not chary,
   Found that his plan would soon miscarry,
   For Pam and Fran as well as Sharrie
   Would not accept Dan as one to marry.

Now Dan, poor Dan,
Had neither Pam
Nor Fran
Nor Sharrie;
Said Dan, "I will not tarry,
The girl for me
Is really Carrie."

—J. E., *Miscarried Aspiration*

e. The time which we have at our disposal every day is elastic; the passions that we feel expand it, those that we inspire contract it; and habit fills up what remains.

—Marcel Proust, *Within a Budding Grove*

f. Jack Tanner asked:
When you get down to brass tacks
What are perceptions, what are the facts?

/a/ (ȧ)

/a/ (ȧ) is a low, front, lax vowel.

We are intentionally excluding a key word for the vowel /a/ because most Americans use this sound not as a pure vowel but only as the first element of the diphthong /aɪ/, as in *I, my,* and *ice*. The pure vowel /a/ is used by a minority of American speakers, most of whom probably reside in the New England area. These speakers would use the vowel in words such as *ask, grass,* and *mask*.

In regard to tongue position, the vowel /a/ is a compromise between the front vowel /æ/ (ă), and the low, back vowel /ɑ/ (ä), as in *calm*.

There is, of course, no objection to cultivating the /a/ vowel whatever your reason may be for doing so. I would suggest, however, if you do cultivate this vowel, that your practice should reflect consistency and you avoid fluctuating between the /a/ in *dance, plants,* and *mask* and /æ/ in *France, laugh,* and *ask*. Further, you should also avoid the vowel sound in *fair, dare,* and *hair*. (Actually, /ɛə/ is a nonphonemic diphthong which we will consider later.)

PRACTICE MATERIALS

Determine your practice in the use of the vowel /æ/ or /a/ for the following materials. Consistency of vowel pronunciation is recommended but not prescribed.

chance	draft	path	aunt
half	class	last	mast
ask	calf	advance	dance
grass	task	craft	demand

mask	laugh	France	bath
pass	staff	laugh	bask

a. A flock of blackbirds stopped their flight to take their bath in the moist grass.
b. Pam and Don attended a dance wearing black masks.
c. On demand, the craft took off for France.
d. Wrangler Bob's task was to rope the calf.
e. Babs and Dan attended a dance before their last class at Harvard.
f. Fran danced along the sandy path after her master of arts degree was granted.
g. Bradley and Cranston, top-line members of the command staff, studied their plans, which were spread on top of a tan cask.
h. Calf branding is fast becoming a vanishing craft.
i. Half of the staff enjoyed the laugh while the other half was baffled.
j. By chance, Randy found the pass through the cragged mountain.
k. The advanced math class was equal to the demanding task of solving what was considered to be an insolvable problem.
l. Laughingly, Frampton took his stance as he clasped his black-banded hat in his hot hand.

We shall continue our study of the vowels, going now to the back vowel /ɑ/ as in *palm* and *calm*, which for most speakers of American English is more regularly used than /a/.

THE BACK VOWELS

/ɑ/ (ä) As in *Calm*

/ɑ/ (ä) is a low, back, lax vowel. The back vowels, we recall, are those that are produced with the back of the tongue most active (see Figure 13–2). In changing from the low, front vowel /æ/ to the back vowel /ɑ/, the tongue arching is moved from the front to the back of the tongue.

The vowel /ɑ/ is produced with the tongue in about as low a position as it is likely to assume without the application of direct external pressure to the flat of the tongue. The mouth is open wide and the lips are unrounded.

In spelling, the /ɑ/ is most frequently represented by the letters *a* and *o*. In words such as *ah*, *alms*, *charm*, *psalm*, and *balm*, the sound /ɑ/ is consistently heard throughout the United States. In the words *hot*, *cot*, *cog*, *ox*, and *stock*, there is less consistency in pronunciation. Many speakers use the /ɑ/ vowel, but others use a variant with lip rounding /ɒ/ (ŏ), which is absent for /ɑ/.

Still others use the vowel /ɔ/ (ô), or one very close to it, in words such as *toss*, *cross*, *orange*, and *wash*.

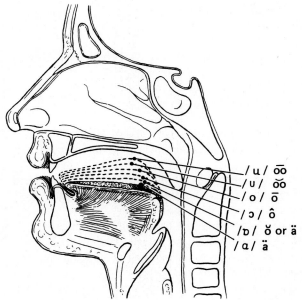

/ u / ōō
/ u / ŏŏ
/ o / ō
/ ɔ / ô
/ ɒ / ŏ or ä
/ ɑ / ä

Figure 13–2 Representative tongue positions for back vowels.

PRACTICE MATERIALS

bah	charm	art	father
harm	alarm	dart	start
barn	farm	arbor	ardent
bond	swab	swan	Charles
John	army	harmed	Arthur
cart	cargo	parked	starve
qualify	hearten	balmy	sergeant
quad	smock	lock	job

guarded cargo	calming psalms
charming Charles	Artic stars
darkened and scarred	smart partner
artful archer	parked car
farm products	ardent farmer

a. Art and Martha enjoyed pasta as did their father.
b. Arnold was an honest and watchful guard.
c. Tom Parker, an ardent farmer, enjoyed problem solving.
d. Rodney Clark was the first to spot the star in the darkening sky.
e. In foggy weather, the Army sergeant wore his many-pocketed dark cloth parka.

   f. Varnish may conceal a large amount of harmful tarnish.

   g. When Charles became a father he had to be on guard to maintain his calm and his charm.

   h. Martha, who is an ardent bargain hunter, does not squabble over the cost of carved-wood art products.

   i. Noah's ark had a well-guarded cargo.

   j. Bart had an armor of calmness that concealed his artful and not always honest propositions.

Most speakers use the vowel /ɑ/ for the following words with *o* spellings. Others modify the sound by some lip rounding and so produce a vowel that is or approximates /ɒ/ (ɔ̌).

Determine your tendency by looking at your mouth in a mirror as you practice with the following materials.

bog	odd	nod	pod	groggy
cod	option	cot	otter	docket
olive	cog	job	fodder	potted
Bob	Robin	knob	farthing	rotted
bomb	job	cobweb	sodden	cognate
robin	rocky	romp	swab	motto
occupy	frog	rob	locket	socket
ox	hot	hod	respond	rocket
got	golf	pocket	stop	topper

spotted the plot	locked box
soggy frock	toss the rock
shock of fodder	hot pot
dogged golfer	frog on a log
mock bomb	rotted bog

socked in by fog
lost her spotted clogs
promptly on the spot

   a. Jock, an old Scot, carried a frog in the pocket of his golf bag.

   b. Stockwell was shocked to learn that a robber stole his stopwatch.

   c. *Lox* is a term for the liquid oxygen used as a fuel for rockets.

   d. Robert sat calmly on the rock despite the cold, foggy, soggy weather.

   e. Alfalfa is a crop used as fodder for stock.

   f. Mollie, the fishmonger, sold cod and haddock.

   g. Botwell was locked up for watering stock.

   h. A frog may frighten an ox.

   i. Olive had to exercise an odd option to sell her locked-up clock.

   j. We were too shocked to respond after we were robbed of our potted cotton plant.

k. Bob Stockton contends that nobody knows who killed Cock Robin.
l. Lucy put her locket in her pocket to hide it from Curly Locks.

a. Hickory dickory dock,
   A frog jumped on the clock;
   The clock struck one,
   This was no fun,
   The frog preferred a log.
b. Camelot, a dot
   Of space in time,
   Begot
   By need of man
   To spot and plot
   A dream
   Of what
   Man hopes of man:
   Of Lancelot
   Tried by Guinevere,
   Of Arthur
   Tried by love and fear
   And knowing
   More than he could know.
   Camelot, a dot
   Of time that was, to be
   A spot to plot
   And prophetically, to see.

—J. E., Suggested by T. H. White's
The Once and Future King

c. "Who killed Cock Robin?"
   "Not I," said Rob.
   "Not I," said Bob.
   So we'll not know
   Who did this job.

/ɒ/ (ŏ)

/ɒ/ is a low, back, lax, rounded vowel.

As noted in the immediately preceding discussion, the vowel /ɒ/ is used by some Americans in words in which the vowel /ɑ/ is used by others. The vowel /ɒ/ is also used as a variant for the vowel /ɔ/ (ô) as in *dog* and *cough*.

In manner of production and in acoustic impression /ɒ/ is somewhere between /ɔ/ and /ɑ/. The vowel /ɑ/ is low and lax and is produced with a slight rounding of the lips.

No list can be given of words for which the vowel /ɒ/ is consistently used throughout the United States, or even in any major area within the United States. Although not confined to eastern New England, the sound /ɒ/ is more likely to be heard there than elsewhere.

The vowel /ɒ/ may be heard in words in which the spelling includes the letter *o* followed by the consonants /f/, /θ/ (*th*), or /s/. It is not, however, limited to these spellings.

PRACTICE MATERIALS

In the practice materials that follow, determine what your pronunciation is for the key words, and compare your pronunciation with that of the respected members of your community. First, however, you may wish to review the previous word lists and sentences for the vowels /ɑ/ or /ɒ/. Do you pronounce any with the vowel /ɔ/ (ô), as in *ball*? Does your choice make a difference in meaning?

boss	froth	across	office
cloth	loft	along	aloft
cost	lost	glossy	choral
florid	song	moral	floral
floss	toss	mossy	wrongly
fog	crotch	Tom	porridge
doff	flock	Don	dodder

costly crossing	frothy broth
flossy moss	odd job
lost officer	immoral choral
tossed aloft	sorry loss
soft morals	hot coffee
lot of bombast	potted hogwash
dotted cloth	crotchety Scot

a. Ross, a cop, objected to the accusation that he was lost in the fog.
b. Socrates and Aristotle were ancient Greek philosophers.
c. Olga was not superstitious, but she was often seen to knock on wood.
d. Roth crossed the office to the hot coffeepot.
e. Bob and Rosalie scoffed at the florid Bostonian officer's morals.
f. Foster tossed glossy paint on the canvas in his loft and admitted that he had botched the job.
g. Roxanne trodded softly on the mossy forest sod.
h. A moth should not seek nor scoff at the flame.
i. Rockford was prompt in offering his objections to what he considered to be a dishonest stock deal.
j. Coffee has become a costly broth.

a. The moonlight is the softest, in Kentucky,
   Summer days come oftest, in Kentucky,
   Friendship is the strongest
   Love's fires glow the longest
   Yet a wrong is always wrongest
   In Kentucky.

—James H. Mulligan, *In Kentucky*

Additional practice material is provided following the discussion of the vowel /ɔ/ (ô).

/ɔ/ (ô) As in *Author*

/ɔ/ (ô) is a low, back vowel produced with definite lip rounding. The tongue is slightly higher for /ɔ/ than it is for /ɑ/ and /ɒ/ (see the back-vowel diagram, Figure 13–2).

The most frequent spellings for /ɔ/ include *a* as in *ball, aw* as in *lawful, au* as in *taught, ou* as in *bought,* and *o* as in *horse.*

In many words, including some of those used as examples in the previous paragraph, the vowel /ɑ/, and less frequently /ɒ/, may by heard instead of /ɔ/. Some of the variations are more-or-less uniform according to geographic regions; others seem to be more individualized, according to the speaker's choice.

PRACTICE MATERIALS

If you are not certain of your own pronunciation habits, practice before a mirror will help to distinguish the /ɔ/ from the /ɑ/ pronunciation. If you wish to establish a clear distinction, make certain that your lips are rounded for /ɔ/; for /ɑ/, the lips are less rounded, and the tongue is lax.

In the list that follows, the words of the first two columns are most likely to be pronounced with the vowel /ɔ/; the words of the other columns are likely to be pronounced with /ɑ/, or /ɒ/. The vowel /ɔ/ may, however, by used for any of these words.

hall	hawk	song	frog
ball	sawing	wrong	torrid
fought	call	soft	orange
taught	chalk	lost	foreign
wall	flawless	off	porridge
August	awesome	cost	forest
auto	claws	coffin	horrible

The words in the following lists are most likely to be pronounced with the vowel /ɔ/ rather than either of the other back vowels we have studied.

author	calked	orphan	stall	appall
awkward	yawn	north	organ	recourse
tall	falter	halt	thorn	ignore
nought	ordeal	shawl	horse	restore
horn	fourth	reform	snort	implore
corn	born	morbid	scorned	rewarm
fortune	mourning	normal	storm	undaunted
maul	haul	salt	drawn	prawn

stalking-horse	morbid author
August storm	law and order
normally warm	orphan of the storm
corn stalk	born to yawn
pause for nought	caulked yawl
warm shawl	fourth brawl
orderly borders	snort in scorn
fawn at dawn	flora and fauna
faulty stall	ward of the court

a. Dawson was taught to be a quarterback.
b. The cautious crew balked at manning the yawl into a squall.
c. Sawyer, a politician, called for law and order though he was appalled at the faults of the laws.
d. Augusta found it an awful ordeal to listen to the author's halting, faltering reading of his paltry lines.
e. Morbid tall stories leave some people yawning.
f. Kansas is proud to be corny in August.
g. Quarter horses don't always cost a fortune.
h. Saul's widow wore a black shawl as a token of her mourning.
i. Paul called to inform us that automobile traffic was stalled on the north-bound lanes, but normal toward the south.
j. Norman, a tall adolescent, was normally awkward.
k. Any safe port is a good port to be sought in a storm.
l. Coventry Patmore held that "love was the sole mortal thing of worth immortal."

a. Small showers last long, but sudden storms are short.

—William Shakespeare, *Richard II*

b. I am the daughter of earth and water,
   And the nursling of the sky:
   I pass through the pores of the ocean and shores,
   I change but I cannot die.

—Percy B. Shelley, *The Cloud,* Stanza 6

c. The law is the true embodiment
   Of everything that's excellent.
   It has no kind of fault or flaw,
   And I, my Lords, embody the law.

—W. S. Gilbert, *Iolanthe*, Act 1

=====

/o/ (ō) As in *Mode*[3]

/o/ (ō) is a midhigh, rounded, back vowel. (See back-vowel diagram, Figure 13–2). The tongue position is higher for /o/ than for the vowel /ɔ/. The vowel /o/ is only infrequently used as a pure sound. In most contexts, this sound is likely to be lengthened into the diphthong [oʊ].

The most frequent spellings of the vowel /o/ or the diphthong /oʊ/ are the letters *o, oe, oa,* and *ow,* as in *no, foe, boat,* and *grow.*

There is no special value in working to maintain a distinction between the vowel /o/ and the diphthong variant /oʊ/. The phonetic context will generally determine whether the vowel or the diphthong will be used. There is value in avoiding an excessive prolongation so that a triphthong ending with a weak vowel /ə/ is produced, and a word such as *hold* becomes [hoʊəld].

=====

PRACTICE MATERIALS FOR /o/ OR /oʊ/

oh	goad	rogue	forego
oak	ogre	Olympic	open
oath	okay	omen	opium
oboe	okra	omit	over
ocher	oleander	opal	owe
clove	stove	sew	story
abode	cone	moat	scone
bloat	float	mowing	sole
bowl	grown	roast	stone
chose	hone	rote	tome
coast	lode	soak	towel
coke	lope	sold	whole
cold	lower	soap	zone
ago	follow	Ohio	sloe
beau	glow	potato	slow
doe	hollow	roe	though
ego	Joe	row	toe
flow	low	show	woe

---

[3] See nonphonemic /oʊ/, Chapter 14, page 247.

Idaho potato	yeoman host	bony ghost
frozen cold	approach the post	Ohio Post
bold fellow	notorious host	Roman oaks
strove for glory	old domain	nose aglow
stoic chauffeur	most thorough	phony clone
bony roast	honing stone	home alone

a. Yellow Hair's soldiers opened the road to the Dakota goldfields.
b. Jones had a toehold on the steep slope but still had to hold on to the rope or else he was beyond hope.
c. Joe's host served a roast that was worthy of his glowing boast.
d. Low clouds drifted over the glorious coast.
e. Some folks make their homes in geodesic domes.
f. The old tug slowly towed the showboat down the Ohio with the river's flow.
g. Smoke from burning coke and coal rose into the ozone.
h. Homer's epic poetry told of hope and sorrow and sad tomorrows.
i. Hogan's goat loped over the frozen slope.
j. O'Neal was broke, but no one would float him a loan or even offer him a scone.

a. Rattle his bones over the stones.
   He's only a pauper whom nobody owns.
   — Thomas Noll, *The Pauper's Drive*

b. Silence is no certain token
      That no secret grief is there;
   Sorrow which is never spoken
      Is the heaviest load to bear.
   — Frances R. Havergal, *Misunderstood*

c. Said Joe to Flo,
   "I saw a ghost beating a pole against a post."

   Said Flo to Joe,
   "Forget your ghost or I'll not have you as my wholesome host."

d. Carl Sandburg, who wrote the notable poem *Chicago*, also wrote the hopeful lines, "Sometime they'll give a war and nobody will come." Along those lines Charlotte Keyes probed, "Suppose they give a war and no one came?"

e. Oh, give me a home where the buffalo roam
   And the deer and the antelope play. . . .
   — Anonymous, *Home on the Range*

=====

/ʊ/ (o͝o) As in *Book* and /u/ (o͞o) As in *Pool*

/ʊ/ (o͝o) is a high, back, lip-rounded vowel. The tongue is lax and in a higher position than for the vowel /o/.

The spellings for /ʊ/ include *u* as in *pull, full,* and *put; oo* as in *book* and *cook; ou* as in *could* and *would;* and *o* as in *wolf.*

In many words of Old English origin, especially those spelled with *oo*, practice varies as to the use of /ʊ/ or the vowel /u/ (o͞o). For comparative purposes, therefore, we need to describe the vowel /u/.

/u/ (o͞o) is characterized by more lip rounding than any of the other vowels in American-English speech. /u/ is the highest of the back vowels (see back-vowel diagram, Figure 13–2, and compare /ʊ/ and /u/). The tongue is tense, in contrast with the lax tongue for /ʊ/. The most frequent spellings for /u/ are *oo* as in *school, fool, ooze,* and *choose; o* as in *do; u* as in *dupe;* and *ou* as in *coup* and *soup.*

The distinction between /ʊ/ and /u/ may be brought out by a comparison of the pronunciation of the following pairs of words.

/ʊ/	/u/	/ʊ/	/u/
book	boon	pull	pool
brook	bruise	roof	rule
crook	croon	shook	shoed
look	Luke	stood	stewed
nook	noon	wood	wooed

Determine your pronunciation of the words in the following lists. If your tongue is tense and your lips rounded, you are using the vowel phoneme /u/; if your tongue feels relaxed and your lips are not so distinctively rounded, then you are probably using the vowel phoneme /ʊ/. Do not be surprised if you are not entirely consistent in your vowel usage for the words that follow. Many Americans vary according to the individual word. Make certain, however, that your pronunciation is distinctly either /u/ or /ʊ/.

pull	pool
roof	hoop
room	hooves
broom	root
group	rule
soot	suit
stood	stoop

PRACTICE MATERIALS

The material that follows is for practice with the vowel /ʊ/. Note its regular occurrence as a medial sound.

cushion	bullet	courier	footwear
would	bully	crooked	tourist

hook	bulwark	cuckoo	woody
boor	bushing	durable	woofer
moor	butcher	rookie	wool
booklet	bouillon	hooded	goodness
Buddhism	boulevard	took	soot
ambush	cookie	bushel	pushed

hooked a cookie	took the books
boorish moor	bushel of soot
good wood	wooden bookcase
rookie courier	Lynbrook Boulevard
durable bulwark	took booklets
sugary pudding	neighborhood bulletin

a. Through the woods the horse's hooves flew over the rotted roots.
b. Woodson, a cook, could not decide whether the butcher was really an unhooded crook.
c. The rookie cook took the cookies from the oven and put in a well-seasoned pullet.
d. Pullman did not believe that because he was good-looking he would be misunderstood.
e. Brooks, a bulwark in her neighborhood, read the bulletin from a wooden platform on the sooty roof.
f. Cardinal Moore read the papal bull from his pulpit.
g. The Buddhist took the bushy path across the moor.
h. Good Mrs. Bull gave Captain Hook a bushel of cookies.
i. To be hoodwinked means to have the wool pulled over your eyes.
j. When "Tootsie" Woodley saw the wolf, she pulled quickly out of the woods.

a. One impulse from a vernal wood
   Can teach you more of man,
   Of moral evil and of good,
   Than all the sages can.
                    — William Wordsworth, *The Tables Turned*
b. Seven centuries earlier, St. Bernard advised in his *Epistles*, "You will find something more in woods than in books."
c. And Shakespeare wrote in *As You Like It*,
     And this our life, exempt from public haunt
     Finds tongues in trees, books in the running brooks,
     Sermons in stones, and good in everything.

/u/ (oo)

The following material is for practice with the vowel /u/.

PRACTICE MATERIALS

hoop	cool	doom	fruit	recluse
jubilee	raccoon	dual	gooey	fluid
junior	cooper	dues	goon	wooing
roost	coulee	duel	glue	construe
womb	coupon	duke	goose	tuna
croup	croon	dune	hoot	cruise
boob	crouton	duty	July	refuse
boon	crude	fluid	loop	whose
boot	clue	fool	loose	noodles
bouffant	crusade	frugal	rumor	stupor

booted fools	June moon
crusading duke	shrewd baboon
gloomy groom	soup spoon
womb to tomb	cool fruit
loose rumors	crude glue
Lou and Sue	too soon to sue
ruined the stew	rude duke

a. During July, at noon, Cooper Luke cools off in the pool.
b. The duke led his troops in the crusade.
c. Ruth gets moody when someone croons "Blue Moon."
d. Lou said he was one who knew the plural of mongoose.
e. Fools in some groups prefer rumors to truth.
f. Newman did not choose the brew; he preferred the stew.
g. The shrew threw a soup spoon at the goose.
h. The overripe fruit oozed a sugary gooey fluid.
i. Cooper rued the day he played the buffoon before Prudy.
j. June proved to be a woman of many moods.
k. Dooley, a crooner, enjoyed songs that had rhymes of *moon* and *soon*.
l. A few doomsday fools still fight their duels in the dunes.

Many /u/ words are preceded by the sound /j/ (y) as in *you, youth, use,* and *hue*. In some of these words, the spelling *y* suggests the sound /j/, but in others the spelling is not a guide to the pronunciation. The following list contains some of the more frequent /ju/ words. Note the frequency of *hu* spellings.

fuse	useful	feud	hew
you	utilize	cue	accuse
youth	mule	mute	huge
usury	hue	imbue	humor
unique	pupil	review	pew
eulogy	amuse	few	humid
humus	humane	Hugh	Hugo

Utah uranium	uniform usage
unique humor	huge pew
humane use	used a few
refused to review	fused the feud
amusing eulogy	mute accusation
accused youth	mute pupil

a. Few youths enjoy humid weather, but Hugh and Hugo did.
b. Our usury laws need review and not rebuke.
c. The mute mule carried a huge load of uranium.
d. Eulogies are not intended to be amusing nor unduly platitudinous.
e. The unique feud began over a ewe and was resumed every Tuesday, though few know whom to accuse.

There is considerable regional and individual variation in the use of /**ju**/ (**yōō**) or /**u**/ (**ōō**) for some words. Tendencies exist on historical bases and may influence local and individual pronunciations. In general, our advice is to follow the pronunciations of persons in your community whose speech is deserving of respect. Do not strain for consistency for groups of words. Instead, work for consistency in the acceptable pronunciation of individual words.

ADDITIONAL PRACTICE MATERIALS

a. There was much ado about loose rumors that Hughes, now a recluse, was once involved in a feud.
b. Lucy had to choose between buying new boots and purchasing two unique books.
c. Only partly in humor, Hubert held that a eulogy at a funeral is really a superfluous review.
d. Although the garden was not huge, one humid corner had a few groupings of ever-blooming roses.
e. Prudence reviewed her clues about her puny store of stolen jewels.
f. The unruly mule was forced to move through the humus-covered woods.
g. Too few students utilize the knowledge they accrue while still youths.

h. Rupert spooned out the raccoon stew and put a few croutons in the soup.
i. Susan and Hugo saw a blue bull in the bushes, but refused to pursue it.
j. Drury was neither crude nor rude, but on cue he did enjoy a chance to brood.
k. The youthful Hooper tootled his flute and played music to suit his usually euphemistic mood.

a. Give me the room whose every nook
   Is dedicated to a book.
                                        —Frank Dempster Sherman, *The Library*
b. Every new movement or manifestation of human activity, when unfamiliar to people's minds, is sure to be misrepresented and misunderstood.
                                        —Edward Carpenter, *The Drama of Love and Death*
c. Lewis was mute about an issue he considered to be moot. Rufus wanted to pursue the issue and viewed Lewis as being snooty for his mutism. When Lewis finally did choose to speak, all that he said was, "Rufus, you may choose to argue, but I don't give a hoot."
d. In his review of *Aikin's Life of Addison*, Macaulay, an astute critic, wrote, "The highest proof of virtue is to possess boundless power without abusing it."
e. W. S. Gilbert, who wrote spoofy lines to Arthur Sullivan's tunes, with good humor asked:
      Wherefore waste our elocution
      On impossible solution?
   Surely, and astutely, he advised:
      Life's a pleasant institution,
      Let us take it as it comes.
                                        —Adapted from *The Gondoliers*

f. Was Hubert humane
   Or uniquely astute
   When he eschewed comment
   On how his pupil Drew
   Played the flute?

CENTRAL VOWELS

The *central vowels* are those that are made with the middle of the tongue arched toward the palate. The central vowels include /ɝ/ (ûr), /ɜ/ (ûr), /ɚ/ (ər), /ə/ (ə), and /ʌ/ (ŭ) (see central-vowel diagram, Figure 13–3).

Syllable stress is often the determining factor that differentiates one central vowel from another. A second feature is the presence or absence of *r* coloring. For example, the vowels of *further* may be either /ɝ/ (ûr), or /ʌr/ (ûr) in the stressed syllable and /ɚ/

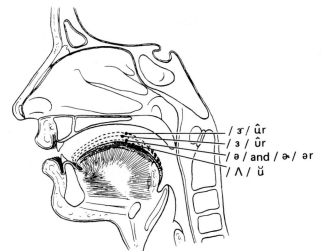

/ ɝ / ûr
/ ɜ / ûr
/ ə / and / ɚ / ər
/ ʌ / ŭ

Figure 13–3 Representative tongue positions for the central vowels, or midvowels.

or /ə/ in the unstressed syllable, depending on regional usage. Similar vowel differences are found in the words *curler, hurler,* and *purser.* In our descriptions of the central vowels we will note that syllable stress and *r* coloring are significant features and vary somewhat according to regional pronunciations.

/ɝ/ (ûr) or /ɜ/ As in *Bird, Curl,* and *World*

Most Americans use the vowel /ɝ/ in the previously indicated key words and in the accented syllable of words such as *avert, guerdon, journal,* and *unfurl.* We may think of the sound /ɝ/ as a vowel blended with the vowelized consonant /r/. The lips are unrounded for the production of /ɝ/.

Speakers who generally do not use the /r/ sound except when the letter *r* is immediately followed by a vowel are likely also to use /ɜ/ rather than /ɝ/ in the key words given in the preceding paragraph. The sound /ɜ/ is produced with a slightly lower tongue position, with the lips unrounded, and without the /r/ coloring of /ɝ/.

The use of /ɝ/ or /ɜ/ is largely a matter of regional practice. In the list of words that follows, most Americans would use /ɝ/. Many speakers in New England, in New York City, and in the Southern coastal states, however, use /ɜ/. Individual speakers who have been influenced by British speech or who were trained for the stage with Eastern or British "standard" diction might also use /ɜ/ regardless of where they live.

We may note that the spelling of words in which /ɝ/ or /ɜ/ is used usually includes the letters, *ur, or, ir,* or *ear.* The word *colonel* is one of the few exceptions in which the spelling does not include the letter *r.*

Some speakers substitute the diphthongal blend /ɜɪ/ for the vowel /ɜ/. The word *bird* may then become [bɜɪd] and *girl* may become [gɜɪl]. This diphthongal variant seems acceptable to many speakers in the South.

=====

PRACTICE MATERIALS

earl	ergot	irk	urbane
early	ermine	Irma	urchin
earn	err	Irwin	urgent
erg	erstwhile	urban	urn
birch	germ	lurk	term
birth	gird	mirth	terse
curb	gurgle	nerve	turban
curt	herb	pearl	turf
dirge	herd	purse	turn
dirt	hurt	spurn	verse
fern	jerk	surge	virtue
flirt	learn	swerve	work
aver	deter	inter	sir
blur	err	occur	spur
burr	fur	purr	stir
burden	furnish	attorney	current
version	burnish	sunburn	curtail
Berlin	rehearse	curdle	curry
Herbert	Myrtle	Ernest	revert

surly hermit	burgeoning purse
assert firmly	disturbed purser
curved surface	certain person
tense sermon	earnest urging
affirm and aver	unfurl with a swirl
irksome urchin	avert being hurt
determined person	swerving skirts
shirk the burden	certain purpose
worried personnel	worthy circles
burrow in the furrow	rehearse the verse

a. Birds work to find worms lurking in turf.
b. The crew worked in earnest to avert collision with the iceberg.
c. Sir Bertram Burbank preferred to adjourn rather than demur.
d. Colonel Burton took his furlough in Berkeley.
e. Erwin was stirred by the fervent urge of the sermon.
f. The whirring turbine produced the urgently needed current.
g. It took courage for Curt to spur his pony into the whirling herd.
h. The customers were terse but the merchant far from taciturn.
i. A bird in the hand is worth a good deal on earth.

j. Shirley did not bestir herself to avert the falling urn but murmured a terse apology.

k. Turner spurned any purse he did not earn.

l. Gilbert's captain of the *Pinafore* served a term in an attorney's firm and seldom yearned for the turbulent ocean.

---

a. Werther had a love for Charlotte
   Such as words could never utter;
Would you know how first he met her?
   She was cutting bread and butter.

Charlotte was a married lady,
   And a moral man was Werther,
And for all the wealth of Indies,
   Would do nothing for to hurt her.
                                   —William Makepeace Thackeray, *Sorrows of Werther*

b. The flowers appear on the earth; the time of the singing of birds is come, and the voice of the turtle is heard in our land.
                                   —The Song of Solomon 2:10–12

c. In his essay *The World*, the Earl of Chesterton wrote: "I assisted at the birth of that most significant word 'flirtation' which dropped from the most beautiful mouth in the world."

d. There once was a girl named Myrtle
Whose mind was earnest and fertile;
She trained Burton, her purple pet turtle
A thirty foot fence to hurtle.
   Poor Myrtle,
   Poor turtle!
Had Myrtle trained Burton to skirtle
Or spurn what he could not hurtle
Myrtle would still have her turtle
As well as a mind that was earnest and fertile.
                                   —J. E., *Dirge for a Purple Turtle*

e. The poet Schiller, who wrote with concern about his burning pen, asserted that "world history is the world's court."

/ɝ/ /ər/ (ər) and /ə/ (ə) As in Unstressed Syllables of *Ever* and *Other; About* and *Sofa*

The vowel /ɚ/ is the unstressed "equivalent" of /ɝ/. In words such as *earner* and *murmur*, the first syllable vowels are stressed and so are pronounced as /ɝ/ by most American speakers. The second, unstressed, syllable is pronounced /ɚ/ by the same speakers—the majority of Americans who habitually pronounce medial or final *r*'s whenever the letter occurs in the spelling of the word.

/ɚ/ is a lax, unrounded midvowel. It has a lower tongue position than /ɝ/. Because of its occurrence in the unstressed position /ɚ/ is less intense and shorter in duration than its stressed counterpart.

/ə/ is a midvowel produced with a lax tongue and unrounded lips in a position slightly lower than /ɜ/.

/ə/, the vowel *schwa* (a weak or neutral vowel), is probably the most frequently used vowel in our language for the following reasons:

1. It is the most frequently used vowel in unstressed syllables regardless of the spelling of the vowel. Some examples of the varied spellings are indicated in the italicized letters of *a*lone, sof*a*, foc*u*s, lab*e*l, and preci*ou*s.

2. In addition to its occurrence in unstressed syllables of polysyllabic words, /ə/ is also the most frequently used vowel when prepositions, articles, conjunctions, and auxiliary verbs are unstressed in sentence context. For example, in the sentence, "I of*ten* find it difficult *to* believe *the* man," each italicized word or syllable may appropriately be pronounced with the vowel /ə/.

3. The vowel /ə/ also replaces /r/ in words such as *hear, dare,* and *cure* for those of us who do not pronounce final *r*'s or *r*'s in general unless they are immediately followed by vowels. These, of course, are the same speakers from New England, New York City, and parts of the South who use /ɜ/ rather than /ɝ/ in stressed syllables.

═══

PRACTICE MATERIALS

Check the pronunciation in your community and decide whether you prefer /ɚ/ or /ə/ for the unstressed syllables of the following words and phrases.

amber	cluster	hatter	otter
after	collar	hunter	other
alter	dollar	junior	ponder
answer	drummer	learner	rather
baker	either	leisure	settler
center	further	matter	tether
cleaner	greater	nadir	whether

a. Selma Merton's speech pattern reflects a General American dialect influence.
b. When played as a solo, a tuba is too ponderous for pleasurable listening.
c. Victoria is the third largest island of Canada.
d. Canberra is the capital of Australia.
e. Sir Walter Raleigh, man of letters, adventurer, and sometime Queen Elizabeth's lover, literally lost his head for having fallen out with the queen.

f. Mervin pondered the news at leisure while eating his breakfast cereal.

g. Not until the baritone was assured that he would be accompanied by the famous Minnesota Opera Orchestra did he agree to sing his favorite and unaltered arias.

h. Eva, a psychotherapist, advised Robert on how to avoid annoying gorillas who appeared to pursue him when he was about to come awake from his troubled sleep.

i. Ella Hurlahy was appointed as a professor at the Junior College of Northern Idaho.

j. Hershey planted azaleas and petunias in the early fall.

around and about	miracle potato
another bother	Roberta Sheila
agreeably alone	wonderful blunder
under the weather	roller coaster
under and above	eager beaver
kinder and gentler	genial editor
tender murmurs	clever brother

a. Dina's letter to her older brother deserved a longer and better answer.

b. The official solution was arrived at by consensus.

c. Peter's neighbors sent him azaleas and their hope that he would soon recover from his indisposition.

d. After they squandered their purse, the brothers returned to honest labor.

e. Benson, a reporter and editor, affirmed that a newspaper must forever be responsible to its readers.

f. Herman Diller Junior could not decide whether he enjoyed more seeing himself in a mirror or reflected in the accomplishments of his children.

In the materials that immediately follow, note the occurrence of the "weak" central vowel *schwa* /ə/ in the unstressed syllable.

above	annoy	tuba	American
about	agree	soda	urban
grammar	coma	parade	murmur
oppose	offense	opinion	parade
allow	anoint	data	surgeon
appoint	Texas	Canada	precious
avoid	assist	circus	stirrup
amiss	asunder	opera	typical

around and about	alone in Texas
azaleas and petunias	Alberta in Canada
agree and disagree	Emma and Stella

Pearl and Earl and Friend Gertrude

Gertrude: I've been hearing murmurs that you and Earl are no longer certain about preserving your unswerving relationship.

Pearl: Dear Gertrude, for the moment I will not demur nor will I accept the burden of what is disturbing you. Tell me in earnest, what have you heard?

Gertrude: I know that your Earl was never overtalkative, yet of late he has become not only terse, but taciturn. If I didn't know better, I would consider him sternly reserved. But knowing better, my perception is that he is worried and hurt, perhaps even unnerved.

Pearl: Thanks, Gertrude, for your concern. Earl is somewhat subject to moods, but they are not irksome. If my Earl seems to be excessively reserved, it's because of our secret engagement. His feet hardly touch the earth when we wander down our flower-clustered land. No, neither Earl nor I rides an emotional roller coaster.

Gertrude: Then what is amiss? Why the murmurs and rumors?

Pearl: Nothing's amiss. All's right with our world! Our secret will soon be public property. We've just told my parents and Mother and Father Burton. They are delighted beyond measure. We plan to live in the suburbs — "the burbs" we call it. We will be married in early September. And now you are the first of our friends to know.

Gertrude: Congratulations. What a happy surprise. How stupid of me to make the wrong inference. Oh, I'm not really saying the right words. Pearl and Earl, Earl and Pearl — my head's in a delightful whirl. A late summer marriage! May I share the wonderful news?

Pearl: Of course you may and I know you will. Now you help us to pray for fair weather for our nuptial get-together.

/ʌ/ (ŭ) As in *Cup*

/ʌ/ is produced with a relatively relaxed tongue arched a little bit toward the middle or the back of the palate. If it is produced with the middle of the tongue arching, it is a midvowel. Many persons, however, produce the sound with the back tongue arching as for a back vowel rather than a midvowel. Either way, the mouth is open fairly wide *without* lip rounding. The tongue should be arched higher for /ʌ/ than for /ɑ/, so that a clear distinction is made between these vowels and between words such as *sup* and *sop*, *suck* and *sock*, and *nut* and *not*.

The vowel /ʌ/ is represented by several letters in spelling, including *u* as in *cup*, *ou* as in *double*, and *o* as in *done*.

Except for the tendency of some speakers to produce an /ɑ/ instead of /ʌ/, the vowel causes little difficulty. For those persons who may be inclined to make the /ɑ/ substitution, it might be of help to know that /ʌ/ is the vowel that we are alleged to make when we supposedly grunt, "Ugh."

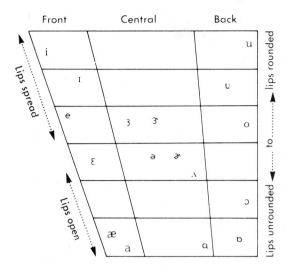

Figure 13–4 Tongue and lip positions of the American English vowels. The front vowels /i/ (ē), /e/ (ā), and /ae/ (ă), are produced with tongue and associated articulatory tension; the vowels /ɪ/ (ĭ), /ɛ/ (ĕ), and /a/ (ȧ) are relatively lax. The back vowels /u/ (o͞o), /ʊ/ (o͝o), /o/ (ō), /ɔ/ (ô), /ɒ/ (ŏ), and /ɑ/ (ä) are produced with relatively lax tongue positions.

Non-native speakers of American English may produce a vowel close to /ɑ/ when /ʌ/ is appropriate. This may be heard in the speech of persons for whom German, Russian, or Italian is the first language. Hispanics may produce a vowel closer to /o/. These productions are a reflection of a general tendency for those learning a second language to produce a sound of the first language close to the sound of the language being acquired. An inspection of the vowel diagram (Figure 13–4) indicates why this is so. Incidentally, the same tendency for sound substitution holds for consonants.

PRACTICE MATERIALS

The first set of exercises should help to establish the distinction between /ʌ/ and /ɑ/. Be certain to raise your tongue slightly higher for /ʌ/ than for /ɑ/. The mouth is somewhat more open for /ɑ/ than for /ʌ/. Note that /ʌ/ appears only in stressed syllables.

/ʌ/	/ɑ/	/ʌ/	/ɑ/
come	calm	gut	got
done	don	color	collar
sup	sop	chuck	cock
cut	cop	hut	hot
muck	mock	fund	fond
dull	doll	bubble	bobble
ruck	rock	bum	bomb
shut	shot	lug	log

slug	slog	buddy	body
nut	not	rump	romp

In the sentences that follow, the first italicized word contains the vowel [ʌ] the second the vowel [ɑ].

a. Do *come* and be *calm.*
b. A job that's *fun* is what *Ron* sought.
c. The *pup* belonged to *Bob.*
d. It was bad *luck* to lose the key on the *dock.*
e. Jim *shut* his eyes when he heard the *shot.*
f. The bear *cub* was fond of corn on the *cob.*
g. Sue *wondered* why *Don* wandered.
h. The *rut* was dried by the *hot* sun.

a. The woods are made for the hunters of dreams,
   The brooks for the fishers of song;
   To the hunters who hunt for the gunless game
   The streams and the woods belong.
                              —Sam Walter Foss, *The Bloodless Sportsman*
b. By gum and by golly,
   Fun's not always folly;
   By golly, by gum,
   Folly's not always fun.
c. Asked Bumpers of Lumpers,
   "Will you carve this big cod?"
   Replied Lumpers to Bumpers,
   "I will, but don't prod."

Contrast for /ʌ/ and /o/

/ʌ/	/o/	/ʌ/	/o/
bun	bone	hull	hole
cot	coat	mull	mole
fun	phone	nut	note
gut	goat	rug	rogue
hum	home	stun	stone

ADDITIONAL PRACTICE MATERIALS FOR /ʌ/

us	must	usher	lush
up	other	udder	upward
under	onion	utter	ulcer

cut	ugly	uncle	Ulster
upper	usher	oven	ultimate
hustle	bustle	numb	dumb
blubber	chunk	cucumber	discussion
blood	lunge	asunder	mud
blunder	mumble	assumption	much
brother	mutton	begun	rugged
bud	once	benumb	stuck
cub	rubber	instruct	tuck
club	supper	lump	wonder
done	punish	hungry	thunder
cuff	rough	enough	thumb
love	monkey	honey	funny
buck	bubble	trouble	rubble
buckle	double	thrust	rebuttal

lucky hunch   hungry for money
rugged brother   month of Sundays
supper club   country cousin
ugly tough   stunned hunter
double fun   blunt instructor
muffins for lunch something for nothing

a. Something's baking in the oven that smells like munchies.
b. Bud's Uncle Hudson smeared his well-done mutton with onion-flavored mustard.
c. "If that's your assumption," the judge instructed, "you are making an utterly foolish blunder."
d. Dudley hadn't had so good a supper in a month of Sundays.
e. Buckley had muddled her way out of dozens of troubles.
f. Duncan's uncle has ulcers.
g. The umpire raised his thumb and sent one of the benumbed players to the clubhouse.
h. Rough, troubled seas can make landlubbers blubber.
i. Father sewed another button on his young son's cuff.
j. General "Blood and Guts" Patton was considered a blunt, rugged officer.

a. It's a song of a merryman, moping mum,
 Whose soul was sad, and whose glance was glum,
 Who sipped no sup, and who craved no crumb,
 As he sighed for the love of a ladye.
      — W. S. Gilbert, *The Yeoman of the Guard*
b. Life's a pudding full of plums;
 Care's a canker that benumbs.
       — W. S. Gilbert, *The Gondoliers*

c. Not a face below the sun
   But is precious — unto one.
                                                    — Sir Edwin Arnold, *Facies Non Omnibus Una*

d. Double, double, toil and trouble;
   Fire burn and cauldron bubble.
                                                    — William Shakespeare, *Macbeth*

e. The camel's hump is an ugly lump
   Which well you may see at the Zoo;
   But uglier yet is the Hump we get
   From having too little to do.
                                                    — Rudyard Kipling, *How the Camel Got His Hump*

f. Love in a hut, with water and a crust,
   Is — Love, forgive us! cinders, ashes, dust.
                                                    — John Keats, *Poems, Lamia*

BUD AND THE UNBELIEVABLE CHUCK

"Mum's the word," said Chuck to Bud, giving him the hush-up sign. (Chuck was sitting in a lotus position on an unswept floor.)

"Mum," replied Bud. Then he waited for nuggets of wisdom to come tumbling from Chuck's mouth. But a minute went by, and nothing came. Bud counted to one hundred, but still nothing, not even one crumb of wisdom. Again Bud counted to one hundred, and once again nothing but a dull hum and the hush sign.

Bud, somewhat frustrated, decided that he may not have understood what he was supposed to say, so he uttered, "Mum's the word." But nothing changed. The prolonged hum was beginning to upset him. After counting to three hundred, Bud mumbled to himself, but he hoped that Chuck would hear, "You must think I'm dumb. You're making like a guru, but I think you're just a muddled numbskull. If you're playing a game, it's not much fun. As for me, I'll mush on to Humphrey's Hut. With luck, I'll meet my trusty pal Buck and other members of my club. Humphrey's Hut always has nuts and munchies to go with their soft suds."

CHAPTER 14

DIPHTHONGS

===

Diphthongs are vocalic glides (a blend of two vowels) that are uttered on a single breath impulse within a single syllable. A superficial analysis of the diphthong as well as a literal interpretation of the term suggests that a diphthong is a combination of two sounds. Ladefoged took exception to the notion that a diphthong is a blend of two vowels:

> Each of these sounds involves a change in quality within the one vowel. As a matter of convenience, they can be described as movements from one vowel to another. The first part of the diphthong is usually more prominent than the last. In fact, the last part is often so brief and transitory that it is difficult to determine its exact quality. Furthermore, contrary to the traditional transcriptions, the diphthongs often do not begin and end with any of the sounds that occur in simple vowels.[1]

Actually, a diphthong is the product of a continuous change of articulatory movement, and so of sound, beginning with the initial vowel of the blend and culminating in the second vowel. The first phonetic symbol of a diphthong really represents the *approximate initial position* of the articulators, and so of the first component sound. The second symbol represents the *approximate final sound*. Thus, the diphthong /ɔɪ/ (oi) is initiated with the sound /ɔ/ (o). The organs of articulation are then modified to produce a continuous change of sound until the diphthong is completed with what approximates the vowel /ɪ/ (ĭ).

First, we will consider three American-English phonemic diphthongs. Each represents a distinctive sound unit, and each serves as a basis by which we distinguish between spoken words not otherwise determined by context. The phonemic diphthongs are /aɪ/ (ī) as in *I* and *my*; /ɔɪ/ (oi) as in *boy* and *toy*; and /ɑʊ/ (ou) as in *house* and *out*.

In the last chapter, in our study of individual vowel sounds, we briefly considered nonphonemic variants of the vowels /e/ (ā) and /o/ (ō). Another group of sounds that might also be considered diphthongal variants are the "blends" produced by persons, mostly from the Northeast regional areas, who do not pronounce final *r*'s except in contexts in which the letter *r* is immediately followed by a vowel in the next word of the phrase, as in *supper is ready* or *dear aunt*. The nonphonemic variants include /iə/, /ʊə/, /ɔə/, and /ɛə/ as pronunciations for words such as *hear, poor, store,* and *care*.

---

[1] P. Ladefoged, *A Course in Phonetics* (New York: Harcourt Brace Jovanovich, 1975), p. 69.

/aɪ/ (ī) As in *Ice* and *Nice; Arrive* and *Reply*

The diphthong /aɪ/ is initiated with elevation of the tongue in the front part of the mouth. It ends, as indicated, with the vowel /ɪ/.

The most frequent spellings for /aɪ/ are *i* at the beginning and in the middle of the words and *y* as the final letter of words, as in *ice, spice, entice, my,* and *cry.*

The Vowel /ɑ:/[2] as a "Nonstandard" Substitution for /aɪ/. Many persons in the Southern dialect regions substitute a lengthened /ɑ:/ (**ah**) sound for the diphthong /aɪ/ or may produce the diphthong with the second component barely perceptible. In effect, the pronoun *I* is pronounced as /ɑ:/ (**ah**) and *mile* as [mɑ:l] (**mahl**). If you are from the South, and do not wish to maintain this pronunciation, the practice material should help you to make the shift. If you are so motivated, practice with intentional exaggeration of the length of the /ɑ:/. An immediate contrast with the /aɪ/ should increase your awareness of the difference between the two phonemes.

In the practice material that follows you should also check and correct any tendency to substitute the diphthong /ɔɪ/ for /aɪ/.

═══

PRACTICE MATERIALS

I	fine	bright	fired	apply
iambic	pipe	China	fight	astride
icicle	viaduct	cider	fly	beguiling
I'd	abide	citation	high	deny
Idaho	alive	cry	hind	espy
ideal	arrive	dice	mine	pantomime
identity	archive	dine	quite	remind
iodine	bias	dire	side	reply
ion	Bible	devise	pyre	required
ire	biceps	entire	strive	unsightly
ivy	by	file	style	untiring
slice	fried	blight	dive	shine

dry ice	spicy dining
type style	butterfly light
bright smile	ironic hindsight
iron biceps	refined designs
right height	rhyming iambs
sly guile	dire signs

---

[2] In phonetic transcription, the symbol /:/ indicates lengthening of a sound.

drive by night	slice of pie
light eyes	admire kindness
frightful crime	iodine ions
highly spiced	quite nice
sly and snide	inspiring sight
wise foresight	feisty feline

a. On Fridays, Myra and Miles liked to eat fried rice and spicy soup at a restaurant that specialized in Chinese diets.

b. McBride invited Lyons to look at his diagram for his device for increasing the size of his biceps.

c. The night riders were not frightened to drive by daylight.

d. Cyrus McCormick took great pride in his invention of the combine.

e. Writers should not require reminding that the use of irony is as likely to be unwise as it is unkind.

f. A tiger without at least nine stripes is a dire sight, but a white tiger is a zoo's delight.

g. Our guide reminded us that it was twilight and high time for us to glide our shiny canoe quietly to the island dike.

h. By midnight, Riles still had a five-mile drive before the lights of his goal would be in sight.

i. The mighty Lord High Executioner aspired to his objective sublime, that each punishment would be equal to the crime.

j. Myra and Ida, both from Idaho, were delighted that their citations for fine poetry would be filed in the state's archives.

k. I reminded Eli that pie in the sky is not a goal to which either he or I should aspire.

l. After high court drama, Lyman and Wright were convicted of conspiracy to bribe Tyson to organize a riot.

m. To be idle or to pretend that out of sight should be out of mind was not Ima's way of dealing with life.

n. Wright's kite spiraled higher and higher until it was out of sight, hiding behind a bright cloud in the twilight sky.

a. There is a smile of love,
   And there is a smile of deceit,
   And there is a smile of smiles
   In which these two smiles meet.

   —William Blake, *The Smile*

b. Tiger! Tiger! burning bright
   In the forests of the night,
   What immortal hand or eye
   Could frame thy fearful symmetry?

   —William Blake, *The Tiger*

c. My object all sublime
   I shall achieve in time —
   To make the punishment fit the crime.
   —W. S. Gilbert, The Mikado

d. A silence in thy life when, through the night,
   The bell strikes, or the sun, with sinking light,
   Smites all the empty windows.
   —Edward Robert Bulwer-Lytton, The Wanderer in Holland

e. When I was five
   My father was the wisest man alive;
   At ten and five
   I wondered he had wits enough to thrive;
   At five and twenty
   He had acquired new brains a-plenty.
   —J. E., Intellectual Evolution

f. Virtue itself turns vice, being misapplied;
   And vice sometime's by action dignified.
   —William Shakespeare, Romeo and Juliet

g. Light seeking light doth light of light beguile.
   —William Shakespeare, Love's Labour's Lost

h. When your Imp of Blind Desire
   Bids you set the Thames afire,
   You'll remember men have done so — in the Files.
   —Rudyard Kipling, The Files

i. Though in silence, with blighted affection
      I pine,
   Yet the lips that touch liquor must never
      touch mine!
   —George W. Young, The Lips That Touch Liquor

j. She walks in beauty, like the night
      Of cloudless climes and starry skies;
   And all that's best of dark and bright
      Meet in her aspect and her eyes;
   Thus mellow'd to that tender light
      Which Heaven to gaudy day denies.
   —George Gordon, Lord Byron, Hebrew Melodies

/au/ (ou), /ɑu/ As in *How, Now, House*

Whether you produce the diphthong /au/ or /ɑu/ in the listed words depends phonetically on whether the front or the back of your tongue is elevated in the first component of the blend. Most likely, your articulatory habit is determined by what you hear in your community. Both pronunciations are used by cultured speakers throughout the United States.

Avoid or correct the tendency to substitute the vowel /æ/ (ǎ) for the first component of the diphthong. Another tendency to avoid or correct is the production of a triple vowel combination /æau/ or /æɑu/ for either /au/ or /ɑu/.

The most frequent spellings of the diphthong are *ou* as in *out, house*, and *mouse* and *ow* as in *cow, bow*, and *now*.

PRACTICE MATERIALS

ouch	cloud	douse	gout	anyhow
ours	clown	dowel	house	announce
hours	clout	down	howl	rebound
oust	couch	drought	jowl	allowance
outer	council	drown	mound	endow
blouse	county	flounder	mount	impound
bough	coward	flour	mouse	disavow
bounce	cowl	foul	mouth	uncrowded
chow	astound	arouse	redound	flout
gouge	powder	resound	ounce	powwow

powdery flour	carouse and shout	brown blouse
mound of flowers	crowd of thousands	down's not out
hound's jowl	astounding rebound	floundered about
drowning flounder	about to announce	loud shouts
stout plowman	tower of power	proud clown
towering cloud	scowling mouth	howling hound
fouled out	mounted the bough	stout roustabout
powerful clout	county council	aroused crowd

a. The round ball bounced off Powell and rebounded out of bounds as a called foul.
b. Lowry was proud to announce that he had caught about a thousand flounders.
c. The hound, astounded by a mouse, aroused us with his howling.
d. Parts of the Southwest suffer from repeated drought and powder-dry soil.
e. The count, who made an astounding announcement that he stood for the crown, flouted his power before the stout councilors who disavowed and renounced him.
f. Mowry frowned at the scoundrel lounging on her brown couch.
g. When asked, "How now, brown cow?" she did not know how to take her allowance of bows.
h. The hour-long shower almost drowned the bower of flowers.
i. Bowers denied that he was the glowering coward who shot Mr. Howard.
j. The home crowd cheered long and loud when Rowly's powerful drive went over the tower onto the downtown mall.

a. While from a proud tower in the town
   Death looks gigantically down.

—Edgar Allan Poe,
The City in the Sea

b. Ye rigid Plowmen. Bear in mind
      Your labor is for future hours.
   Advance! Spare not! nor look behind!
      Plow deep and straight with all your powers!

—Richard Henry Horne, *The Plow*

c. He who doubts from what he sees,
   Will ne'er believe, do what you please,
   If the Sun and Moon should doubt,
   They'd immediately go out.

—William Blake, *Auguries of Innocence*

d. Time writes no wrinkle on thine azure brow—
   Such as creation's dawn beheld, thou rollest now.

—George Gordon, Lord Byron,
Childe Harold's Pilgrimage

e. With ruin upon ruin, rout on rout
   Confusion worse confounded.

—John Milton, *Paradise Lost*

f. In his poem *The Cloud* Shelley wrote:
      I bring fresh showers
      For the thirsting flowers.

g. Lord Howard wanted out,
   Of this there was no doubt,
   But he shouted, "I am no coward."
   And so fought on Lord Thomas Howard.

—J. E., Suggested by Tennyson's
Flower in the Crannied Wall

h. In for a penny, in for a pound—
   It's Love that makes the world go round!

—W. S. Gilbert, *Iolanthe*

/ɔɪ/ (oi) As in *Boy, Soil,* and *Noise*

The diphthong /ɔɪ/ is appropriately produced by beginning with the back, rounded vowel /ɔ/ and ending with the front vowel /ɪ/. The most frequent spellings include *oi* and *oy*, as in *oil, boil, toy,* and *boy*.

Some speakers tend to substitute /ɜɪ/ (ûr) for /ɔɪ/. This tendency is generally considered nonstandard, and we recommend that it be avoided or corrected. Another tendency to be avoided is the substitution of /oɪ/ for /ɔɪ/.

PRACTICE MATERIALS

boiler	hoist	noisy	anoint
boisterous	hoyden	oily	annoy
boycott	join	ointment	despoil
cloister	joist	point	embroil
coin	loin	quoits	employ
coy	loiter	roister	recoil
foible	moist	royal	exploit
goiter	loyal	soy	rejoice

boisterous roisterers   soiled coin
loyal to royalty   poisoned oyster
soybeans and poi   toy boycott
noisy boys   annoying foibles
broiled loin   exploited loyalty
moist ointment   joyful noise

a. McCoy ran a noisy, boisterous joint near Point Troy.
b. Roy exploited the oil that lay beneath his soil.
c. Doyle's voice sounded as if he were poised, but his words were annoyingly poignant.
d. Royal heads were anointed with oil.
e. Lloyd joined the floorboards to the joists.
f. She may look coy when embroidering doilies but she is often a roisterous hoyden.
g. Spoiled oysters are poisonous.
h. Joyce warned her little boy to avoid stepping on the toys he left in the foyer.
i. Though loyal, the envoy did not enjoy being employed as a foil or a decoy.
j. Boyle was never known to boycott a choice broiled loin chop.

Distinguishing /ɔɪ/ from /ɜ/ or /ɝ/

/ɔɪ/	/ɜɪ/ or /ɝ/	/ɔɪ/ or /ɜɪ/ or /ɝ/	
coil	curl	choice	"cherce"
boil	burl	voice	verse
oil	earl	noise	nurse
toil	turn	poise	purse

a. Royce enjoyed a game of curling.
b. Joy puts up her hair in curls.

   c. With surprising poise, Doyle emptied his purse.
   d. Toys should not be embedded with pearls.

Selections for /ɔɪ/

   a. She was a hoyden,
      Yet could play coy
      As a cloistered maiden
      Or a boisterous boy.

—J. E., *Tried and Untrue*

   b. The long guns poised,
      Exploded and recoiled
      From fire and burst of noise
      And what they had despoiled.

—J. E., *Annoying Toys*

   c. Asked Doyle of Boyle,
      "What is your ploy;
      What are the rewards
      You seem to enjoy?"

      Said Boyle to Doyle,
      "There is no ploy,
      Except the rewards
      Of honest toil."

/ɛə/ (âə) As in *There*

The diphthong /ɛə/ is used instead of the more frequently heard /ɛr/ or /ɛɚ/ by persons who omit *r*'s in their pronunciation except immediately before vowels in the same syllable. It is heard in such words as *air, their, fair, care, dare, chair,* and *pear.*

/ɛə/ is also heard as a not entirely approved substitution for the vowels /æ/ or /a/ in words such as *ask, last, class,* and *bath.*

Speakers who generally pronounce their *r*'s when the letter *r* occurs in the spelling are likely to use the combination /ɛr/ or /ɛɚ/ rather than /ɛə/ in the words that follow:

PRACTICE MATERIALS

air	lair	compare	repair
bear	fair	declare	unaware
care	their	chair	heirloom
dare	wear	forbear	heiress

flair	affair	prepare	impair
hair	beware	welfare	despair
spare	scarce	square	scared

air fare	undeclared warfare
scared hare	their welfare
scarce hair	dared to forbear
pared pears	bears and mares
their chair	cared and despaired
scary lair	unaware of the dare

a. When in its lair, it is wise to be wary and not do anything that might impair a bear's welfare.
b. With a flair, Mary wore her heirloom jewels wherever she went.
c. Claire showed her pair of mares at the county fair.
d. "Adair, beware! Mind your own affairs," Blair warned with a cold stare.
e. Despite an air of devil-may-care, the daring are often scared.
f. On an antique hunting tear, the pair exchanged their wares for an heirloom chair that needed repairs.
g. McNair's drive seemed to go squarely down the fairway, but his caddy could not spot just where it went.
h. Astair was in economic despair because his business affairs were beyond repair.

a. Fair tresses man's imperial race ensnare,
   And beauty draws us with a single hair.
   —Alexander Pope, *The Rape of the Lock*

b. Said Dairlington to Fairlington,
   "However various,
   You're reliably nefarious."

   Said Fairlington to Dairlington,
   "Were you not undarious,
   You too might be nefarious."

   —J. E., *Point Counter Point*

c. Shall I, wasting in despair,
   Die because a woman's fair?
   Or make pale my cheeks with care
   'Cause another's rosy are?
   Be she fairer than the day,
   Or the flow'ry meads in May,
   If she be not so for me,
   What care I how fair she be?

   —George Wither, *Fair Virtue*

/ɔə/ (ôə) and /oə/ (ōə)

The diphthongs /ɔə/ and /oə/ are used by persons who are inclined to omit the /r/ from their pronunciations except before vowels. Practice in regard to /ɔə/ and /ɔr/ or /oə/ and /or/ varies along the following lines (the transcriptions (ɔɚ) and (oɚ) are alternatives for (ɔə) and (or)).

In words such as *horse, lord, accord,* and *north,* usage is fairly uniform throughout the United States. The pronunciation is /ɔr/ for most Americans and /ɔə/ in the "r-dropping" sections of the country.

Usage varies between /o/ and /ɔ/ pronunciations for the words *board, mourning, course,* and *more.* These words are pronounced with either /o/ or /or/ by most American speakers. In the New York City area, these words are pronounced with /ɔ/ by "native" speakers. Thus, except for the New York City area, most Americans make distinctions between the words *horse* and *hoarse, for* and *four,* and *cord* and *cored.* The sound /ɔ/ is more likely to be used for the first word of these pairs and the /o/ for the second.

PRACTICE MATERIALS

Determine your own practice by comparing the pronunciation of the following pairs of words.

aural	oral	morning	mourning
border	boarder	war	wore
soar	sore	coarse	course
pour	pore	for	fore
horse	hoarse		

born to mourn	north of the border
explore the fort	forty horses
Formosan export	boring course
store of lore	courtly sport

a. Large-bored guns were stored at Fort North.
b. Each pull on the oars brought Lord closer to the shore.
c. Four hours of riding on his horse and Croydon reached the border.
d. The lion roared himself hoarse for more food.
e. McCord, the owner of a resort inn, was noted for managing to be in accord with forty different points of view, each according to that of his boarder.
f. Dora explored the organ for a lost chord.
g. More and more, Nora found sweeping the porch to be a boring chore.
h. Moore, the matador, saw the roaring bull burst through the door.

a. Cruel Remorse! where Youth and Pleasure sport,
   And thoughtless Folly keeps her court—
                                    —Anna L. Barabauld, *Ode to Remorse*

b. Come in the evening, or come in the morning,
   Come when you're looked for, or come without warning,
   Kisses and welcome you'll find here before you,
   And the oftener you come here the more I'll adore you.
                                    —Thomas O. Davis, *The Welcome*

c. He will hold thee when his passion shall have spent its novel force,
   Something better than his dog, a little dearer than his horse.
                                    —Alfred, Lord Tennyson, *Locksley Hall*

d. Three poets, in three distant ages born,
   Greece, Italy, and England did adorn.
                                    —John Dryden, *Under Mr. Milton's Picture*

e. Society is now one polish'd horde,
   Formed of two mighty tribes, the *Bores* and *Bored.*
                                    —George Gordon, Lord Byron,
                                         Don Juan, Canto XIII

f. **A Unique Discourse**

   Unicorn One (Given to being mournful)
        Though I was born
        A unicorn
        I would dearly adore
        A second horn.

   Unicorn Two (Not inclined to be scornful)
        I will not scorn
        But I love you
        As you were born,
        Unique, with a single horn.
                                    —J. E., From *Lines That Could Be Verse*

/ɪə/ (ĭə) As in *Dear* and *Year*

The diphthong /ɪə/ (ĭə), as noted earlier, is used by persons who omit medial and final /r/ sounds from the pronunciation of such words as *dear, fear, hear, beard, cheerful,* and *earful.* Throughout most of the United States, all of these words are more frequently pronounced with the combinations (ɪr) or (ɪɚ) rather than with the diphthong /ɪə/.

PRACTICE MATERIALS

Determine your own pronunciation of the following words and compare them
with the pronunciation of respected speakers in your community.

beard	pier	gear	piercing	earwig
beer	cheer	queer	seared	nearly
dear	arrear	cheerful	fierce	sincere
fear	mere	earful	spear	tearful
hear	drear	fearful	bier	Shakespeare
merely	clear	we're	year	hearsay

fearfully dear	steer clear
eerie bier	year's arrears
we're here	tearful earful
queer gear	fiercely pierced
near and dear	appeared sincere
sincerely cheerful	dreary pier
daring pair	spare chair

a. Geary sneered through his seared beard.
b. The daring hunter's gear included a fearful-looking spear.
c. Because of their sere leaves, the trees looked dreary.
d. Blair saw a fierce fire destroy the nearby pier.
e. Because of his habit of crying in his beer, Beardsley was clearly not a
cheerful person.
f. Claire has no fear of flying, but does not consider the experience to be a
sheer delight.

a. The skies they were ashen and sober;
   The leaves they were crisp and sere—
   The leaves they were withering and sere;
It was night, in the lonesome October
   Of my most immemorial year.

—Edgar Allan Poe, *Ulalume*

b. No! let me taste the whole of it, fare like my peers,
   The heroes of old,
Bear the brunt, in a minute pay glad life's arrears,
   Of pain, darkness, and cold.

—Robert Browning, *Prospice*

/ʊə/ (o͝oə) As in *Poor*

The diphthong /ʊə/ is likely to be used by speakers who are inclined to pronounce /r/ only in contexts in which the letter *r* is immediately followed by a vowel. These speakers would probably use /ʊə/ rather than (ʊr) or (ʊɚ) in words such as *poor, sure,* and *tour.* Others may use /ʊr/ in all of these words.

≡

PRACTICE MATERIALS

Determine your own pronunciation of the words and phrases that follow and compare each with what is current in your community.

poor	allure	assure	fury
sure	moor	jury	endure
tour	boor	ensure	touring

toured on the moor   poor but demure
boorish jurist   ensure the jury

a. Be he rich or poor, there is little that is alluring about a boor.
b. What we cannot cure we must learn to endure.
c. If you're surely poor, you can hardly afford to tour among the Moors.
d. The jury had to control their fury to ensure a fair and enduring verdict.
e. Though Moore was a poor woman, she felt socially secure.
f. The cat's nine lives were no insurance against curiosity.
g. The tourists were glad to have their ship securely moored after enduring the fury of the storm.
h. As the touring boorish actor sawed the air in fury, the director told the producer, "Rest assured, this ham will never by cured."

a. "I'll be judge, I'll be jury," said cunning old Fury.
>   —Lewis Carroll, *Alice's Adventures in Wonderland*
b. I'll make assurance doubly sure,
   And take a bond of fate.
>   —William Shakespeare, *Macbeth*
c. How small of all that human hearts endure
   That part which laws or kings can cause or cure.
>   —Samuel Johnson,
>   *Lines Added to Goldsmith's Traveller*

≡

/eɪ/ (ā) As in *Gale*

Earlier, we discussed /eɪ/ as a nonphonemic variant of the vowel /e/. At this point, we merely present additional practice materials that include words that may be appropriately pronounced with the diphthong /eɪ/.

PRACTICE MATERIALS

aid	blade	nail	wane	aerie
ale	blaze	pace	weight	reclaim
aim	braise	skate	await	disdain
bail	cape	tame	detain	aerosol
bait	hail	taint	dismay	airway
bane	mail	trait	waiver	aeronaut
Dane	fame	drain	refrain	unstained

a. After his zany escapade as an aerialist, Raymond was detained in jail without bail.
b. Brady labored at the mason's trade but aspired to be an aeronaut.
c. May Blaine cautioned her famous playmate, Davis Dane, that fate was about to play a painful hand if he did not waive his wayward ways.
d. Blaine advised Gail to take the late plane to Spain before the onset of rain in the plains.
e. The stranger paid the bill that the waiter had placed on the table and went on his airy way.
f. Hale could not refrain from weighing his airmail on the available scale.
g. Crayton did not hesitate to use the radio-telephone to relay each day's weighty news.
h. Kate waved to Daisy as they made their way to the shady dale.
i. In a quaint way, Lade Jany Grey betrayed her famous status.
j. Rain came with daybreak, as if nature wanted a delay in the croquet game to be played on the newly graded field.

a. Said Grayson to Payson,
"By the way that you behave
I cannot help but assay you
As primate trained to shave."

Said Payson to Grayson,
"The way in which you rave
Makes primates seem ascendant,
However you behave."

—J. E., *Evolution*

b. All human things are subject to decay,
And, when fate summons, monarchs must obey.
—John Dryden, *Mac Flecknoe*

c. What of the faith and fire within us
Men who march away
Ere the barn cocks say
Night is growing gray,
Leaving all that here can win us?
—Thomas Hardy, *Men Who March Away*

d. And the jocund rebecks[3] sound
To many a youth, and many a maid,
Dancing in the checkered shade
And young and old come forth to play
On a sunshine holiday.

—John Milton, *L'Allegro*

/ou/ (ō) As in *Bone* and *Prone*

Earlier we discussed /ou/ as a nonphonemic variant of the midhigh, rounded, back vowel /o/. We now present some additional practice materials in which /ou/ may be appropriately used. We should have in mind, however, that words such as *bone, home,* and *grow* do not change in meaning whether they are pronounced with the vowel /o/ or the diphthong /ou/.

Speakers for whom Spanish is a first and dominant language are likely to use the vowel /o/ rather than the diphthong /ou/. Those who do may not distinguish between the vowel in the salutation "Como esta" and the usual American-English diphthong pronunciation of the words and practice material that follows.

PRACTICE MATERIALS

boast	slope	focus	novice	Rome
bone	goal	alone	acetone	host
bonus	gold	although	bestow	coast
bowl	knoll	cyclone	regrow	groan
cone	loan	Dover	resole	ohms
drone	moan	below	unknown	sonar
ghost	prone	enroll	homely	pony
crocus	broach	postal	romance	ogre

[3] A rebeck is a medieval bowed, string instrument, somewhat like a violin.

Roman yeoman	sown oats
home grown	coterie of bowlers
ocean road	bouquet of posies
showboat	blown over

a. Joan made her home in the adobe hut on the knoll.
b. The troll was prone to fall into the old moat.
c. Although he kept his hold on the controls, the captain broke his nose when the ship almost rolled over.
d. Greta Garbo boldly chose to lead her own life over the moans of nosy reporters.
e. The rogue stole the brooch and the old robe from Toni's home.
f. The old rover warmed his hands over the coals glowing in his host's golden bowl.
g. The wind blows and moans across the road to Nome.
h. Rosa told Mona that she preferred older and homely men because they were supposedly easier to control.

a. Asked Dover of Rover:
   "By the smile on your face
   You must have just won
   A pot-of-gold race;
   Are you roving in clover;
   Old friend, may I know?"

Said Rover to Dover:
   "I wish it were so;
   I'm not roving in clover
   But this I now know,
   My wild oats now sown
   It's high time to grow."
                                              —J. E., *Wishful Dialogue*

b. I know a bank where the wild thyme blows,
   Where oxlips and the nodding violet grows.
                        —William Shakespeare, *A Midsummer Night's Dream*

c. I'm growing frugal of my gold;
   I'm growing wise, I'm growing—yes—
      I'm growing old.
                                   —John Godfrey Saxe, *I'm Growing Old*

d. Mark how my fame rings out from zone to zone:
   A thousand critics shouting: "He's unknown."
                                         —Ambrose Bierce, *Couplet*

CHAPTER 15

CONSONANTS: THE LIP (BILABIAL) AND GLIDE SOUNDS

=====

Consonants are speech sounds that we produce as a result of the way we modify the outgoing breath stream by our organs of articulation. The specific way we modify the outgoing breath produces the characteristics (features) peculiar to the individual consonants. Unlike vowels, which are all voiced sounds unless we intentionally whisper, consonants are either appropriately voiced or unvoiced. Those consonants such as /p/ and /b/, and /t/ and /d/, which differ only by the feature of voicing are known as *cognate sounds*.

The description and manner of production of each of the consonants are considered individually. Precautions to be observed and the pitfalls to be avoided are indicated for those sounds that some American-English-speaking adults find difficult. Tendencies and substitution errors of persons for whom American English is a second language will also be noted.

===== THE FAVORED ARTICULATORY CONTACT =====

Most languages seem to have a favored place of articulatory contact. In French, Spanish, and Italian, many sounds are produced by contact between the tongue tip and the upper teeth. In German, the point of contact is a bit lower. In American English, the favored contact area is the upper gum ridge. At this point, by contact with the tongue tip, the sounds /t/, /d/, /l/, and /n/ are articulated. A fraction of an inch behind the gum ridge, articulatory placements are made for the sounds /s/, /z/, /ʃ/ (sh), /ʒ/ (zh), /tʃ/ (ch), /dʒ/ (j), and one of the varieties of /r/.

Because of the proximity of articulatory positions of American-English sounds and those much like them in Spanish, French, Italian, and German, the tendency to carry over foreign-language speech habits is understandable. We should also be able to appreciate the need for special precautions and considerable practice to overcome these foreign-language influences. A good beginning in correcting such influences, and in establishing an awareness of the favored place of American-English articulation, is to study the diagram of Figure 15–1.

The consonant sounds are presented approximately according to the place of major articulatory activity, proceeding from the front to the back of the mouth (see Table 15–1). This order of presentation is not to be interpreted as necessarily the most desirable or the prescribed one to be followed. We believe that the specific order of consonant study should be determined by the instructional needs of the students or the philosophy of the teacher. An individual student, aware of his or her own limitations in diction, or striving for improvement in a given direction, might well begin with the sound, or one of the sounds, requiring attention. An instructor might determine the order of consonant study based on a screening of the group of students. The sound most in need of improvement for the largest number of students in the class may then be selected as the one with which to begin. If the instructor believes that it is better to teach a relatively difficult sound by contrasting it with another, easier sound for the student, then this may become the proper initial sound to be studied. An instructor who has many students coming from a given speech region and who, on the basis of experience, is able to anticipate frequent consonant difficulties may choose to begin the improvement program in the light of these anticipations. The instructor will soon learn whether the students are living up to expectations or whether his or her own program for this particular group of students is in need of modification. Such an approach will

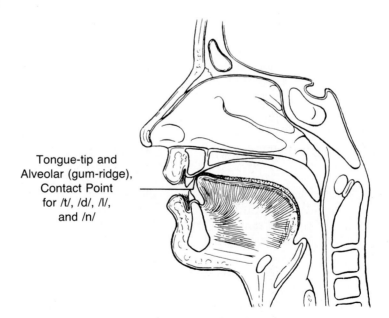

Tongue-tip and
Alveolar (gum-ridge),
Contact Point
for /t/, /d/, /l/,
and /n/

Figure 15–1 Diagram indicating the favored contact area for American-English consonants. The upper gum ridge is the contact point for /t/, /d/, and /l/. Essentially the same tongue-tip and gum-ridge contact is made for /n/.

Table 15–1   Classification of the Consonants of American-English Speech

Manner of Articulation	Lips (Bilabial)	Lip-teeth (Labio-dental)	Tongue-teeth (Lingua-dental)	Tongue-Gum-ridge (Alveolar)	Tongue-Hard-palate (Post-alveolar)	Tongue-Blade-palate (Palatal)	Tongue-velum (Velar)	Larynx (Glottal)
Voiceless stops	p			t			k	ʔ
Voiced stops	b			d			g	
Voiceless fricatives	ʍ (hw)	f	θ (th)	s	ʃ(sh)			h
Voiced fricatives		v	ð(th)	z	ʒ (zh)			
Nasals (voiced)	m			n			ŋ (ng)	
Lateral				l				
Glides								
(vowel-like)					r¹	r		
(consonants)	w					j (y)		
Voiceless affricate					tʃ (ch)			
Voiced affricate					dʒ (j)			

¹In our discussion of the /r/ phoneme, the variable characteristics of /r/ are considered.

afford the individual student and the class as a whole the greatest amount of instructional time and the opportunity for work on common problems and for frequent review during the course of a term.

An alternate rationale for the order of presentation of the consonants is one based on a knowledge of normal speech-sound acquisition in children. This approach would call for approximately the following order:

1. /m/, /p/, /b/
2. /n/, /f/, /h/, /ŋ/ (ng)
3. /w/, /j/ (y)
4. /k/, /g/
5. /t/, /d/, /l/, /r/
6. /s/, /z/, /ʃ/ (sh), /tʃ/ (ch)
7. /θ/ (th), /ð/ (th), /v/
8. /ʒ/ (zh), /dʒ/ (dz), /hw/

═══ THE BILABIAL SOUNDS ═══

/p/ As in *Pea, Soap, Separate,* and *Spy*

/p/ and /b/ are bilabial, closed-lip, stop consonants. These sounds are produced as a result of a lip-closing action that momentarily stops the flow of breath. Both of these sounds require a raised palate so that after the lip action, the sound produced is emitted orally rather than nasally, as indicated in Figure 15–2.

All but three American-English sounds are normally produced with an elevated soft palate. Except for the three nasal consonants /n/, /m/, and /ŋ/ (ng), the reader should assume that the directions for the production of a sound include the one to *elevate the soft palate*.

The sound /p/ in initial or stressed positions, as in *pea* and *plate*, requires considerable breath pressure. The lips must be tightly compressed to permit the production of a vigorous /p/. In unstressed positions there is considerably less breath pressure and less vigorous lip action. In all positions, /p/ is a voiceless sound. When /p/ is followed by a vowel, a distinct puff of breath (plosion or aspiration) should accompany the completion of the sound. In final positions, /p/ may not be "exploded."

The /p/ in Spanish is produced with minimal or no aspiration. If this tendency is carried over into American English, the result is a sound that is almost like /b/. In practice, to make certain that the /p/ has the required aspiration /pʰ/, hold the palm of your hand about six inches directly in front of your mouth and produce a series of three aspirated /pʰ/ sounds as if you were blowing out a small candle.

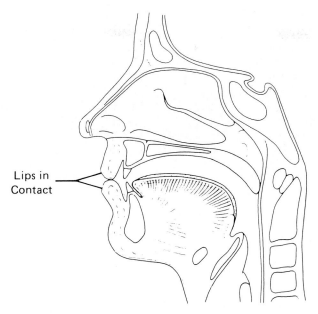

Figure 15–2 Articulatory positions for /p/ and /b/. The lips are tightly compressed and the soft palate is raised.

The practice material that follows includes notes as to the degree of appropriate aspiration according to context.

===

PRACTICE MATERIALS

pea	pool	person	pound
peat	pull	pert	pout
peel	poor	purse	powder
pill	poke	pun	power
pit	pole	put	peace
paid	paltry	pike	pitch
pay	paw	pile	peg
pen	park	pine	patch
pat	pond	point	pack
path	pot	poise	poem

When a medial /p/ is followed by a stressed vowel, a distinct puff of air should accompany the completion of the /p/. In combinations preceded by an /s/, however, the aspirate quality is considerably reduced.

Medial (Stressed Positions)

appeal	rapport	apart	rupee
appease	repair	repay	turnpike
repeat	repartee	upon	repugnant
repeal	impact	apology	umpire
unpin	report	deport	suppose
repaid	repatriate	despair	epistle
repent	repose	support	inspire
repel	oppose	superior	inspect
repast	appoint	superb	respite

For a medial /p/ in unstressed positions, the lip activity is less vigorous, and there is less accompanying breath puff in anticipation of the sound following the /p/.

Medial (Unstressed Positions)

deepen	stupor	rapier	napping
happy	sweeping	steeple	chopping
carpet	champion	taper	clapped
typify	grapple	stepping	flippant
tipped	hoping	clipping	wrapper
depot	vapid	reaper	slipper
tepid	gaping	taping	rapid
harpy	beeper	chaping	vapor

[p] in Final Position — Weakly Aspirated

keep	hoop	nap	leap
hip	hope	nape	reap
cape	cup	mop	hope
map	cop	mope	wipe

[pl] and [pr] Blends — Reduced Aspiration for the [p]

plea	plume	plight	place
please	Pluto	pliant	play
plenty	plot	plow	pleasure
plate	plum	applaud	plural
plain	plug	aplomb	plunder
plan	pluck	plausible	plunge
preen	prune	price	spread
pray	reprove	pride	sprite
prick	proof	proud	sprawl
press	prawn	prow	sprain
prank	prod	praise	spree
prattle	prolix	approve	prized

[p] Followed by [t] — Little or No Aspirate Quality for the [p]

aped	escaped	hoped	rapped
apt	gaped	lapped	reaped
capped	gapped	leaped	roped

caped	heaped	loped	soaped
draped	hipped	mapped	yapped

[p] Followed by [s] — Little or No Aspirate Quality for the [p]

apes	flaps	jumps	pops
beeps	flips	lapse	pups
capes	gaps	loops	raps
cops	hopes	mops	ropes
dips	hops	napes	tapes
keeps	weeps	sleeps	chaps

a. Pam and Peter, two respected Ping-Pong players, took a catnap before they started to play.
b. Pickled jalapeno peppers were too potent for Paul and Roper.
c. Prescott put a pippin apple into the piglet's mouth in preparation for baking.
d. Peterson produced a sample of prize-winning paint that he promised would never chip.
e. The Plimpton Company employs Pinkerton operatives to prevent plundering of their premises.
f. Springer polished the pistons of his "chopper," which he calls "Pie in the Sky."
g. "Spot" is not an appropriate appellation for springer spaniels, poodles, or Pekinese, but it is perfect for plain, dappled pups.
h. Patty wrapped the snappers she caught off the pier in a clean piece of brown wrapping paper.
i. Percy was pleased and proud to see his ships pulling out of the port to the open sea.
j. In his prime, Plunkett, the pride of Stanford, could put his powerful passes precisely where they were supposed to go.
k. The proud but impolitic prince placed too low a price on the approval of his people.
l. Browning's poem "Pippa Passes" is spirited verse about the approach of spring.

a. "I fly from pleasure," said the prince, "because pleasure has ceased to please."

—Samuel Johnson, *Rasselas*

b. When the hounds of spring are on winter's traces,
   The mother of month's in meadow or plain
   Fills the shadows and windy places
   With lisp of leaves and ripple of rain.

—Algernon Charles Swinburne, *Atalanta in Calydon*

c. Now when a doctor's patients are perplexed,
   A consultation comes in order next—
   You know what that is? In a certain place
   Meet certain doctors to discuss a case

And other matters, such as weather, crops,
Potatoes, pumpkins, lager-beer, and hops.
> —Oliver Wendell Holmes, *Rip Van Winkle, M.D.*

d. With me poetry has been not a purpose, but a passion; and the passions should be held in reverence: they must not—they cannot at will be excited, with an eye to the paltry compensations, or the more paltry commendations, of mankind.

> —Edgar Allan Poe,
> *The Raven and Other Poems*

Dialogue for /p/

"NO SOY RICO, SOY PICO"

Parish Priest: Parishioners repent! A few paltry pennies for the paupers is pathetic. When I pass the plate this Palm Sunday please, I implore you, plunge into your pockets! The pope can pray for prosperity, but you must provide for the impoverished—or they will perish!

Parishioner: Padre, we are not penurious cheapskates, just prudent. The plant on Carps Parkway employed us to program, repair, pack, and ship Pippin Computers. When the plant was wiped out, paychecks to employees stopped. Your appeal is simply impossible. Our pockets and purses are empty. We are the poor people! But we still aspire to help the impoverished. Please, padre, I, Pepito, can tell you, "No soy rico, soy pico."

/b/ As in *Bean, Rabid,* and *Robe*

/b/ is a voided, lip-stop, unaspirated consonant produced with less lip and breath pressure than /p/. Lip activity should be precise so that there is a clear-cut stop and release action for the /b/, even though it is less vigorous than for the /p/.

By way of review, /b/ is articulated with (1) a firm closing of the lips, (2) a compression of air behind the lips, and (3) a sudden parting of the lips to release the *vocalized sound*. Final /b/ may be articulated without the explosive or release phase.

PRACTICE MATERIALS

Make certain that you show a clear distinction between /p/ and /b/ in the following words, phrases, and sentences.

peak	beak	prick	brick
pay	bay	peen	bean
pane	bane	punk	bunk
paste	baste	plank	blank
pare	bare	planned	bland
paid	bade	pass	bass

pace	base	pat	bat
hup	hub	mop	mob
cup	cub	cop	cob
rip	rib	lope	lobe
fop	fob	rope	robe

staple	stable
ample	amble
rapid	rabid
napped	nabbed
nipped	nibbed

pass the bass	cup for a cub
barely paired	planned to be bland
peaked beak	patted the baseball bat
Pluto and Beelzebub	complain without blame

a. Pete Bailey bastes his beef patties with tomato paste.
b. Patty bailed the leaking punt with a pink pail.
c. Paul punted the football, which unhappily bounced off the goalpost.
d. Pamela packed her bags before she paid her bill.
e. The best peach pies are baked with the pits removed.
f. Benton's belt was made with a supple leather pelt.
g. Bertha was pleased to see Pat hang his pea jacket on a brass peg.
h. Before parachuting from the parapet, Piper bowed slowly and nobly.

ADDITIONAL PRACTICE MATERIALS

Initial

bean	boon	burn	broom
bill	bull	bud	bruise
bale	boor	breach	brought
beg	boat	bring	brain
back	ball	bread	brine
bask	bog	brass	brown
busy	bulk	bleed	bloom
bunch	burrow	blink	blue
base	bird	black	block
blame	burst	breath	blurt

Medial

about	table	somebody	disturbing
abate	feeble	habit	rubber
abbey	stable	noble	ribbon
abet	number	tumble	tribute
abhor	lumber	fumble	robust
Abner	obtain	trombone	thimble

Final

rib	tube	disturb	curb	tribe
crab	nub	cube	jibe	disrobe
web	rub	hob	daub	suburb
stab	robe	sob	cob	bulb
dab	lobe	rob	mob	cherub

fumbles and mumbled	everybody is somebody
borrowed robe	numbered crabs
pale banner	about to bloom
rupees for rubies	ambled in the bog
habitual busybody	broken bower
hobnob with Bea	beaned by a baseball
bunch of posies	table of plenty

a. Bill is fond of ripe berries and baked bass.
b. Buck abhorred boasting and preferred to be busy.
c. Bacon and beans are a breakfast habit with Bess and Pete.
d. Ben played a big brass tuba in the Pierpoint Boys Band.
e. Somebody permitted the black pony to break out of the barn.
f. Few buds bloom in February to attract bees and hummingbirds.
g. Paul swept the patio with a bulky brown broom.
h. Benton and Paula brought in lobsters and crabs in their old flat-bottom boat.
i. Bricks, boards, and plaster are basic building materials.
j. Brad slammed the ball for a three-base hit.

In your practice with the word lists and other material that follows, pay special attention to the items that have /bl/, /br/, /pl/, and /pr/ blends to avoid any suggestion of a /w/ sound after the stop consonant. Review the immediately preceding pages for this purpose. Additional practice material for these blends follow.

/bl/	/bl/	/br/	/br/
bleep	block	breeze	bride
blip	bluff	brim	broad
blade	bloody	brake	brow
blank	blow	brand	brute

brutish brow	brought brunch
broad bluff	broken brooch
brown blade	embroidered blanket
brought to the brink	blurb of blarney
brainy bride	blameless blip
bland blend	blocked the blow
blithely blundered	bluebells in bloom

/pl/	/pl/	/pr/	/pr/
please	plate	prance	prelude
plinth	placate	prim	approve
play	pliant	prod	approach
plant	plug	prickly	apprise

purple plums   approach with pride
primped for approval   practice the prank
prior to pleading   prawns and pralines
pleased to play   precise premise

a. Bryan called the gambler's bluff.
b. Blanche was pleased to accept Bliven's invitation to brunch.
c. The playful breeze blew brine over the decks of Priam's boat.
d. Although Blake was not a blue-eyed brute, neither was he a placid playmate.
e. Brenda and Bryce were mutually pleasing and proud to be blissful buddies.

a. But far on the deep there are billows
   That never shall break on the beach.
   > —A. J. Ryan, *Song of the Mystic*

b. This truth within thy mind rehearse,
   That in a boundless universe
   Is boundless better, boundless worse.
   > —Alfred, Lord Tennyson, *The Two Voices*

c. I am weary of days and hours,
   Blown buds of barren flowers,
   Desires and dreams and powers
   And everything but sleep.
   > —Algernon Swinburne, *The Garden of Proserpine*

d. Beauty can pierce one like a pain.
   > —Thomas Mann, *Buddenbrooks*

Dialogue for /b/, /br/

BREAKFAST AT BUBBA'S BAKERY

Boyd: Mr. Bubba, bag me six buttermilk biscuits, a bran roll, a blueberry muffin, and a buttery hot-cross bun. Because you have no tables, I'll grab a bite of breakfast on my bicycle.

Mr. Bubba: Buddy, for breakfast at Mr. B's you get bagels. Everybody buys boxes of them—nobody bugs me for biscuits!

Boyd: But . . . what's a bagel?

Mr. Bubba: It's a humble, chubby ball of bread with a hole like a doughnut. I boil then bake it until it's lightly browned. For breakfast, you break it in half, brush on a bit of butter, then eat it with a glob of blueberry jam. It's beautiful to your taste buds! Please, be my guest—take a jumbo bite!

> Boyd: Mr. Bubba, I don't want to bruise your feelings, but a bite of your beloved rubbery bagel brought on heartburn. Maybe I'll break my habit and skip breakfast today.
>
> Mr. Bubba: Boy, you've got a feeble belly, but you're no namby-pamby. You boldly braved the unknown and took a bite of my bagel. So I'm going to bend the rules and bring you a piece of my best, freshly baked banana bread. We'll just call it brunch, not breakfast. Boyd, it's blissful!

The Bilabial Glide Consonants: /ʍ/ or /hw/ (hw) As in *What* and *When*, and /w/ As in *Will* and *Wit*

The consonants /ʍ/ or /hw/ and /w/ are *glide sounds*. Such sounds are produced with the organs of articulation in movement from an initial, determinate position to a final position determined by the sound that immediately follows. The sound /ʍ/ or /hw/ is voiceless; /w/ is voiced. Both are initiated with the lips rounded in a close, pursed position as for the vowel /u/. The tongue is raised in back toward the soft palate. Study Figure 15–3 for the initial position for the lip glide sounds. Note that the lips do not touch the teeth, as they necessarily do for the sounds /f/ and /v/. The palate is raised for the bilabial glide sounds, and the sounds are emitted orally.

/ʍ/ (hw) occurs in words spelled with *wh* initially or medially. However, many persons use the voiced /w/ rather than the unvoiced /hw/ in contexts following a /t/, /s/, or /k/ sound as in *twin, swim,* and *quiet.*

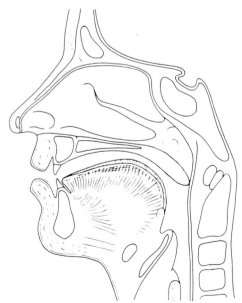

Figure 15—3 Initial articulatory position for the glide sounds /hw/ and /w/. Note that the back of the tongue is raised.

Caution is to be observed by persons whose native languages have neither /w/ or /hw/ sounds but which do have a /v/ sound (for example, Germans and Hispanics). They may substitute a /v/ sound for both /w/ and /hw/. As a result, *wake* may be produced as *vake*, and *where* as *vare*. (See pages 272, 276 for a description of the production of the lip-teeth sounds /f/ and /v/.) For a start, be sure to make clear distinctions in the production of the words in the following list.

/wh/	/v/	/w/	/v/
while	vile	wane	vane
wheel	veal	wow	vow
whale	veil	wince	Vince
wine	vine	west	vest

─────

PRACTICE MATERIALS

To determine whether you use a /hw/ or /w/, place your hand in front of your mouth for the trial words *what* and *where*. The /hw/ should begin with a definite stream of unvocalized breath. In contrast, /w/ is vocalized and there is no obvious stream of breath. The word pairs that follow should help to make the distinction between the two sounds.

/hw/	/w/	/hw/	/w/
whither	wither	while	wile
where	wear	white	wight
wheel	weal	whether	weather
whet	wet	whacks	wax
what	watt	whirled	world
which	witch	whine	wine
when	wen	Whig	wig
whirred	word	whish	wish
whale	wail	whist	wist
whey	way	whoa	woe

Initial /hw/

wheat	whistle	wharf	whiting
wheedle	whelp	whimper	whittle
wheeze	whence	whimsy	whipsaw
whiff	whirl	whiskey	whang
whim	whistling	whiffle	wheal
whip	whop	whinny	whetstone
whisper	whorl	whisker	whelp

Medial /hw/

pinwheel	somewhat	meanwhile	unwholesome
anywhere	awhile	bobwhite	buckwheat

nowhere	somewhere	freewheeling	erstwhile
elsewhere	bullwhip	flywheel	everywhere

/hw/ and /w/

where and when	wet weather
which way	whet your whistle
wore a watch	whispered wishes
whimsical words	witch or wight
wild wormwood	winding byway

a. Do you prefer the song of the bobwhite or of the whippoorwill?
b. What was Wilson's whispering to Watson?
c. Though Walt Whitman was somewhat wordy, he was always worth reading.
d. The wiley Whig thought it whimsical to wash the Tory's wig in white wine.
e. Wallace yelled "Whoa!" and whistled, but his freewheeling horse went for the bale of wheat.
f. The bewhiskered old man whet his knife and then whittled away on a piece of waxed wood.
g. The engines of the *White Witch* whirred as the steamer went off on the whaling voyage that would take her around the world.
h. With white-collar workers on one side and labor on the other, the management felt whipsawed because there was no way that either could win or persuade the other of what was really wanting in the contract.
i. Winton wished to return to Wichita to hear the wind wail through the Western Union wires.
j. Wiggins whispered to Wendy that he was ready to go somewhere, anywhere, just to be away from where he was.
k. Don't wail about the weather in San Francisco, because if you wait it will be either better or worse within the hour.
l. Mark Twain observed that the coldest winter he ever went through was one summer in San Francisco.

ADDITIONAL PRACTICE MATERIALS FOR /w/

wad	walk	web	wide
wade	wall	we'd	wield
wafter	wan	wed	wife
waffle	wander	week	will
wager	want	weigh	window
waif	ward	weird	wing
wail	wash	weld	woman
wait	wean	wen	won't
waive	wear	wet	wood
wake	weave	wick	worst

Medial /w/ (*note that the spelling may be* u *and* o *as well as* w)

biweekly	await	inward	unworthy
unwieldly	reweigh	unwavering	rewed
bewitch	away	awoke	earthworm
unwitting	awake	unworn	reworked
unwary	bewail	rewarned	anyone
unwept	byway	onward	everyone
unwelcome	unwilling	reweave	everyway
unwise	unworldly	reward	inquire
bewilder	unwanted	unwind	liquid
unwell	unwonted	reweb	require

a. Wales has many rewarding and wonderful vistas.
b. Kingsley wrote that "men must work, and women must weep."
c. Wilton walked west through the quagmire to earn one reward.
d. New York's Broadway, once a cowpath, is now known as the Great White Way.
e. Woodrow Wilson was president when the United States entered World War I, "the war to end all wars."
f. During World War II, General Dwight Eisenhower once was reputed to have wept while reviewing his troops.
g. Willy walked away into the woods, unaware that wolves and quagmires lay that way.
h. In weaving, the woof thread goes between the warps to form a web.
i. Watson wondered whether the equation would work out.
j. The lawyer winked unwisely at the bewildered witness.
k. The westerner wasted his wages on unwise wagers.
l. Whiskey is a liquid that can bewilder one in the worst way.
m. Welch wound up and swatted the wasp on the window.
n. Wanda tripped over a wet twig and twisted her ankle.
o. The once-bright flame waxed and waned and withered into nothingness.

a. We look forward to a world founded upon four essential human freedoms. The first is freedom of speech and expression — everywhere in the world. The second is freedom of every person to worship God in his own way — everywhere in the world. The third is freedom from want — anywhere in the world.

> — Franklin D. Roosevelt,
> Message to Congress, January 6, 1941

b. The Whence and Whither give no rest,
   The Wherefore is a hopeless quest.

> — Sir William Watson, *An Epistle to N.A.*

c. Those who have wealth must be watchful and wary.

> — Thomas Baily, *I'd Be a Butterfly*

d. Who splits his own wood warms himself twice.

> — *Saying*

e. In a wordy chat with the Carpenter, the Walrus wanted to know:
   "Why the sea is boiling hot and whether pigs have wings?"
   —Adapted from Lewis Carroll,
   Through the Looking Glass

f. Against the Word the unstilled world still whirled
   About the center of the silent Word.
   —T. S. Eliot, *Ash Wednesday*

g. A wail in the wind is all I hear;
   A voice of woe for a lover's loss.
   —W. C. Channing, *Lament for Thoreau*

h. Oscar Wilde and James Whistler were members of a group of wonted wits. Wilde admired Whistler, who was quick-witted in social repartee, whereas Wilde's wit was more apparent in his writing. One day, according to Ingelsby, the biographer of Wilde, Whistler said something that was extraordinarily witty, even for him. Wilde, overwhelmed with admiration, said, "Oh Mr. Whistler, I wish I had said that."

   Whistler, in return, replied, "Don't worry, Wilde; you will, you surely will."

THE WHISPERING WIND

Wendy Willard: My story, *The Whispering Wind*, is about Edweena, a wacky whiffet, who is whisked away from her squalid life by Ward, the son of a wealthy whiskey merchant. He woos Edweena, twirling her through the social whirl in Wichita. Everyone whispers that she's unworthy, but Ward worships her. Their love is almost quashed when Ward's whaling boat is whipped by the waves of a winter storm and lost in a whirlwind. Woebegone, Edweena watches the water from the wharf, wailing over the lost whaling boat, awaiting word of Ward's whereabouts. Meanwhile, Ward, washed ashore in the West Indies, whiles away the hours whittling a white water canoe and waits for Edweena. His unwavering faith is rewarded when Edweena sails a sea-worthy vessel through an estuary and finds him, swimming while he whittles wood. They wed and have a wonderful life, full of unwieldy wealth. Well, Professor Winchell?

Professor Winchell: Wendy, this is not the work I required. I wanted you to work on self-awareness. To acquire the wherewithal to create, you must look inward.

Wendy Willard: I wonder whether you can understand, Professor Winchell. Edweena *is* Wendy Willard—or what I wish I were. I'm from Whittier, California. I've never quivered or wasted away in the heat of a wicked passion nor waltzed across Wichita. I won't whine in my wine, but I could win awards for warming and rewarming bottles, diaper washing, and nose wiping.

Professor Winchell: I don't want to whipsaw you, Wendy, but nowhere do you write how you feel about your withering existence.

Wendy Willard: Within weary housewives everywhere lives an Edweena. She is a freewheeling wanderer, wise yet bewildered. She never whimpers or bewails her fate. She says "Whoa!" to her woes and hides her weariness. When will you see she is as real a women as Wendy Willard?

Professor Winchell: Edweena, as woman to woman, I will ask you just where and how did you get your window on the world? Well, you have a weird wit, but it is not unwelcome. You win! Don't waste your time reworking the whimsical *Whispering Wind*! We can't all be as witty as Mark Twain, or as sophisticated if not as wise, as Oscar Wilde or Dorothy Parker. Try to be the best possible Edweena Willard and learn to write with gentle wit. Let Elinor Wylie be your model.

/w/ and /v/

Some persons, probably because of foreign-language influence, tend to confuse the bilabial /w/ with the labiodental (lip-teeth) /v/. The following word pairs should help to establish the distinction between these two sounds. Observe the lip action in a mirror, and make certain that there is no contact of the teeth and lips for the /w/.

PRACTICE MATERIALS

/w/	/v/	/w/	/v/	/w/	/v/
wane	vein	wend	vend	ways	vase
wary	vary	worse	verse	wince	Vince
west	vest	wine	vine	weep	veep
weld	veld	wiper	viper	while	vial
wiser	visor	wow	vow	wise	vise
went	vent	wile	vile	Walt	vault
wet	vet	wail	veil	winery	vinery

/w/ and /v/ Within a Word

weevil	woven
weave	vowed
wave	vowels
wolves	wives

a. Wanda advised Wendy that it is wise never to be caught in a vise.
b. Wine is made from the fruit of the vine and stored in a winery.
c. Wilma West was fond of her velvet vest and her velour coat.
d. As the vain writer grew older, his ability was on the wane and his verse became obviously worse.
e. To vend his various wares he had to wend his weary way and be wary of wily customers along the wayside.
f. The knight looked wiser behind his visor.
g. We were puzzled at the witch's vow nevermore to use her wiles for vile purposes.

h. Vince Walters vowed that he would never give in to the boll weevils in their voracious attacks on his cotton.

a. There is not in the wide world
   A valley so sweet
As that in whose bosom
The bright waters meet.
                                      — Thomas Moore, *The Meeting of the Waters*

b. No longer mourn for me when I am dead
Than you shall hear the surly sullen bell
Give warning to the world that I am fled
From this vile world, with vilest worms to dwell.
                                      — William Shakespeare, *Sonnet 71*

Vending Wedgewood Valley Wines

Vintner: Vernon, I'm very wary of wordy verses that veil the truth. Wedgewood Valley varietal wines are good values, and our vintage wines are wonderful. I'm warning you, it's wise to stay away from vulgarity.

Vernon the Advertiser: Very well. "I vow you'll go 'wow' when you wise up with Wedgewood Valley Wines! They are virtually the best in the west!"

Vintner: That's vulgar in the worst way! I can't vie with your wit, but your verse couldn't be worse. "Wedgewood Valley vintage wine goes well with veal and vegetables." Now, my words have vim and vigor!

Vernon the Advertiser: What about, "Don't waste your wages on vinegary wines. Win a victory with Wedgewood Valley!"

Vintner: Vern, your wit is withering on the vine. Go visit the Wedgewood Valley Winery for a week. Wend your way through the vast woods, and wander with your wife through the wet vineyards. Witness the vaults, where the wine in vats is like washed velvet. Water your wit with visions of verdant woods and velvety wines. Then you'll find the words to vend my wares.

Vernon the Advertiser: Sir, I'm weary of your wordy verbiage and vain ways. Your vision of the world is veiled in the worst way. We vend your wines with vulgar words because the wines you vend are vile!

THE PALATAL GLIDE /j/ (y) AND THE LARYNGEAL FRICATIVE /h/

/j/ (y) As in *Year, Unite, Humid,* and *Argue*

/j/ (y) is a vocalized, palatal glide sound. In acoustic effect, it is vowel-like in quality because it is an unobstructed and continuant sound. /j/ glides or moves from the initial position of the vowel /i/ to a final position determined by the sound that immediately follows it. The initial articulatory position calls for the tongue to be arched toward the front of the hard palate and for the lips to be parted and retracted as though for a smile. The soft palate is raised and the vocal folds are in vibration throughout the production of the sound.

When the /j/ sound is represented by a single letter in spelling, it is by the letter *y*. In medial positions, /j/ may be represented in spelling by the letters *io*, *ie*, and *ia*. Frequently, however, in both initial and medial positions, there is no spelling representation for the /j/. The sound often becomes part of vowel blends, as in *unite* and *unify*.

PRACTICE MATERIALS

yield	yak	yoho	Europe
yeast	Yankee	yacht	young
yearly	you	yonder	yowl
yes	youth	yard	yucca
yen	York	yule	yesterday
yet	yawn	yearn	usual*
yellow	yawl	use*	usurp*
yank	yoke	unit*	eulogy*

Check your pronunciation of [hj] in the following words.

huge	humid	humility	Hugo
human	humidor	humor	humus
humane	hue	humanoid	hubris
Hubert	Hughes	hews	humerus

Medial [j]

Daniel	companion	accuse	volume
genial	familiar	refuse	collier
genius	billiard	confuse	review
senior	canyon	amuse	stallion
vineyard	million	onion	beauty
lanyard	abuse	bunion	opinion
Communion	galleon	beyond	bemused

[j] (y) Preceded by an Initial Consonant

The inclusion of a /j/ after an initial consonant varies according to context and regional practice. It is optional in words such as *Tuesday, tune*, and *new* and in many other words that begin with the sounds /t/, /d/, or /n/. If there are no special influences to direct your choice, regional usage should be followed.

---

* In these words, the /j/ may be considered part of the diphthong /ju/. Other words of this type include *unite, union, Ural*, and *euphony*.

PRACTICE MATERIALS

/j/ is regularly included after the first consonant in the word list that immediately follows. It is optional in the second word list and mixed in the phrases, sentences, and selections that follow.

I

cube	pure	fuel	cute	music
putrid	pupil	few	future	futile
Houston	beauty	feud	huge	fusion
puberty	muse	humane	view	mule
humid	mute	humorous	cupid	puny

II

Tuesday	due	knew	nuisance
new	tube	nuclear	nude
tune	numerous	duke	Nubian
tuba	duty	tumult	newt
constitute	reduce	institute	gratuity
destitute	annuity	plume	restitute
induce	platitude	acumen	enduring

inhuman abuse	pure and beautiful
fueled the feud	view of the future
refused to be amused	humorous muse
musical tune	puny tuba player
due on Tuesday	huge institute
familiar opinions	destitute seniors

a. The feud began on Tuesday over a puny gratuity.
b. Daniel's attitude indicated that he had no use for platitudes.
c. The dude took a dim view of his own future.
d. A united Europe has not yet been achieved.
e. The youth yearned for baked yams.
f. Cupid sometimes seems amused by those he seems to confuse.
g. The pack mule carried a huge load through the canyon.
h. William, a senior Yale student, enjoyed yesteryear's music.
i. Newton, a Yankee, enjoyed sailing his yawl.
j. Eugene, a Yorkshire millionaire, was fond of playing billiards.
k. Was Yarnell astute in refusing to believe that no news was good news?
l. The yet-to-be-completed institute was mute evidence that many were taking refuge from their duty.

a. Hugo, while still a youth, realized that it is futile to yearn for yesteryear or to take emotional or intellectual refuge in the past. All our yesteryears are continuous with the years ahead; all yesterdays constitute a prologue to the future tomorrows.

  b. Yates, though not a genius, argued that in his view of the nature of things, it is the peculiar duty of human beings to endure what, individually or collectively, they cannot at a given moment cure.

  c. The captain and senior officer of the *Pinafore*, who enjoyed platitudes and was not beyond appreciating gratuities, refused to yield to the temptation of using bad or abusive language.

  d. Beauty needs no excuse for being.

BEAUTIFUL MUSIC

Danielle: How do you view your future companion?

Hugo: I yearn for a pure and beautiful muse who is unusually genial. She must be a pupil of life who approaches each new day with amusement. And you?

Danielle: I have no yen for yachts or huge annuities, but I'd love to see Europe while I'm young. I want no mute with few opinions for a companion, but our arguments must not turn into feuds. I want Cupid to bring me a human being with a sense of humor and humility.

Hugo: I want someone who approaches her numerous duties cheerfully and is useful in her youth.

Danielle: I want a genius who never speaks in familiar platitudes.

Hugo: My wife's voice should be soft in volume and sound like flute music. I want someone with business acumen to invest wisely so that our yearly yield will take us to Europe annually.

Danielle: I want to be united in a love that will endure a million years!

Hugo: Would it amuse you to join me in the tumultuous institution of marriage, Danielle?

Danielle: Yes, Hugo, I yearn to assume this joyous responsibility. Will Tuesday be too late?

THE LARYNGEAL (GLOTTAL) FRICATIVE

/h/ As in *He* and *Who*

The sound /h/ lacks fixed or distinctive articulatory position and so may be considered a glide. The sound that immediately follows the /h/ determines the position assumed by the lips and the tongue for this usually voiceless fricative.

    /h/ consists of a stream of breath made discernible by the degree of contraction and vocal-fold vibration in the larynx.

    Few persons are likely to have difficulty in the actual production of the /h/. The most likely basis for difficulty is that of determining whether, despite or because of the spelling of the word, an /h/ is to be produced or omitted in the pronunciation. It may be of help to know that in American-English speech the /h/ is appropriately included chiefly before vowels in stressed syllables such as *he, hot,* and *hate.* Some speakers also include the sound in words that begin with a *wh,* as in *which* and *whale.* /h/ is usually not pronounced in medial, unstressed syllables.

In words such as *human, humid, huge,* and *humor,* some speakers blend or merge the initial [h] with the immediately following [j], so that a "new" and distinctive voiceless palatal fricative sound is produced that may be represented by the symbol [ç]. If the blending is not complete, the result may be represented by the symbols [hj], as in [hjudʒ] for *huge.* However, because there is no change in meaning that would result from the shift from the symbol representation [hj] to [ç] we will limit ourselves to [hj].

In words in which the [h] occurs between vowels, as in *reheat, behave,* and *behead,* the [h] may be produced with partial voicing. The IPA symbol is [ɦ].

Again, because there is no change in word meaning whether or not there is partial voicing in words such as those indicated above, we shall use the symbol /h/.

PRACTICE MATERIALS

Initial

he	help	hoof	harm
heed	ham	home	harsh
hit	hatch	hope	her
hilt	hoot	haughty	hurl
haste	who	halt	hurt
hate	whom	hog	heard
head	hood	hot	heart
hull	height	house	humid
hump	hide	howl	huge
hungry	hoyden	human	humor

Medial (*note the position in stressed syllables before vowels*)

unheeded	behind	unharmed	coherent
reheat	behold	unheard	dehydrate
inhabit	inhuman	rehearse	inherit
inhale	overhaul	uphold	upheaval
behave	rehash	rehouse	prehistoric
behead	cohort	somehow	enhance
reheard	perhaps	prohibit	apprehend

The following word list should help to create awareness of the [h] for persons inclined to drop the sound in the initial position. The [h] should *not* be heard in the second member of the word pairs.

hair	air	heart	art	heal	eel
hit	it	hear	ear	hike	Ike
heal	eel	her	err	hold	old
home	ohm	haul	all	hoe	owe
hire	ire	hurl	earl	hailed	ailed

a. Henry paid little heed to heights, but Hilda was apprehensive about hills.
b. Hazel was so hungry that she enjoyed Harry's reheated hamburger.
c. Horton and Helen enjoyed living in high mountain areas that had low humidity and little hot weather.
d. The hen was heard to cackle and looked haughty after she hatched her egg.
e. Hate can be inherited if it is not inhibited.
f. The hog who had a habit of entering the new house was cured as a ham.
g. Hiram's heart and his sense of humor were humane.
h. The hyena held up her head and howled to the heavens.
i. Harriet's uninhibited behavior won her a reputation as a hoyden.
j. The rehearsals for *Hamlet* were held in a house held to be haunted.
k. Arthur Schopenhauer held that hatred comes from the heart and contempt from the head.
l. Hildred happily announced that Hope had found a home in her new heated and humidified house.

Harry Helton, who lived in Soho, came from a part of London where human beings were somewhat variable about their *h*'s. Harry himself was a harried husband because he could not always make it clear whether ham was something he *ate* or something he preferred to *hate*. When you heard Harry, you could not be sure whether *honey* was what he *had* or what he would like to *add* to his butterhorns. The result was that Harry often went hungry. Unhappily, Helen his wife, was somehow never sure whether it was time to heed Harry or to humor him. One might say, "Poor Harry, poor Helen." Yet, despite it all, they had a happy home and enjoyed their habits.

SELLING HOUSES THE HARD WAY

Harry the Realtor: I hate to help people like the haughty Harpers find a house. They act as if I'm a prehistoric hunter who inhabits a cave!

Hope: Mr. Harper was hot to do a hasty overhaul of his interior so the selling price of his house would be higher. When I told him he could not hope for more, he hurled the harshest insults at me that I ever heard.

Harry the Realtor: Had I heard his harangue, I would have had his head!

Hope: I told him there was an art to putting your heart in a house and making it a home. He told me that with his money he would enhance his house to the hilt. He's a horrible human being!

Harry the Realtor: Heed my advice and don't humor him. Rehearse hard-hitting retorts and hurl them back at him. I wish I could somehow prohibit those who behave inhumanly from owning homes in Henderson Heights.

Hope: Let's not rehash our humorless day. Perhaps you would join your hungry companion for a ham sandwich. How about Hugo's? Let's be hale and hearty!

Harry the Realtor: Ms. Hope, I'll be happy to join you. And my hearty thanks for your good humor. Let me assure you that I will not err in the next house we see. I'll find one on nearby Haley Heights that should heal your hurts from the horrid and harsh Harpers.

CHAPTER 16

THE LIP-TEETH SOUNDS

The lip-teeth (labiodental) consonants /f/ and /v/ present little or no difficulty for persons who are native American-English speakers. Hispanics for whom English is a second language, especially those who are learning or have learned English as adolescents or adults, may carry over a tendency from their first language to use the sounds /b/ and /v/ interchangeably or to substitute a sound intermediate between /b/ and /v/.

Persons who have a Germanic background may confuse /v/ and /w/ because the letter w is pronounced /v/ in German. Fortunately, the pronunciation of the letter v as /v/ is consistent in English, so that the spelling serves as a reliable guide to its sound. Persons whose native language is German may also need to overcome an inclination to pronounce the letter *f* as /v/.

/f/ As in *Feed, Fame, Fun, Offend, Afraid*, and *Enough*

/f/ is a voiceless, fricative, lip-teeth (labiodental) consonant. You make this sound by pressing your lower lip against the upper teeth or between the lower lip and the upper teeth. The soft palate is elevated to prevent nasal emission of breath. (See Figure 16–1.)

In spelling, the sound is most frequently represented by the letter f. Other spellings include *ph* as in *phase* and *gh* as in *enough* and *rough*. This sound may occur in initial, medial, or final positions in a word.

PRACTICE MATERIALS

/f/

feed	fad	fob	fire
feel	fan	fog	fowl
fib	food	fox	foible
fin	fool	firm	foil
fit	full	first	foist
fail	phobia	fudge	feud
fame	photo	fuss	fume
fed	falter	fight	fuse
felt	fork	file	future
fence	fought	find	few

272

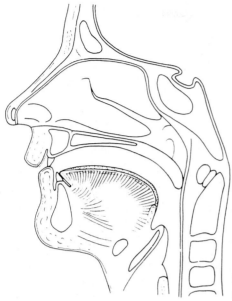

Figure 16–1 Articulatory position for /f/ and /v/. Note lower lip contact with upper incisor.

coffee	defeat	afford	afar
enfeeble	after	effort	stuffing
effete	aft	soften	rifle
sphere	raft	affirm	trifle
efficient	raffle	refurbish	stifle
sphinx	laughed	unfurl	sapphire
swift	refuse	roughen	refute
chafed	effuse	shuffle	prophet
effect	careful	sofa	reference
defend	barefoot	loafer	breakfast

beef	skiff	chafe	half
chief	cliff	deaf	staff
reef	whiff	chef	graph
belief	stiff	chaff	enough
thief	strafe	laugh	tough
tiff	safe	calf	golf

[fl]

flee	fluke	flirt	flutter
fleet	flute	flourish	flight
flip	flood	flurry	fly
flame	flaw	flub	flounder
flu	floral	flunk	flour
float	Florence	flush	flout

[fr]

free	fret	frozen	afraid
frill	frank	fraught	affray
fray	France	frolic	affricate
freight	frugal	front	affront
freckle	fro	fry	infringe
frisk	frame	Fred	effrontery

coffee at four	flight of fancy	fearfully funny
fit as a fiddle	defective fuse	fancy fluff
fraught with fear	fluttery flower	fifth flight
flow of traffic	fickle finger of fate	feudal fief
fancy-free	frozen flounder	a fine fettle
defuse the feud	frenetic flight	faded fancy
refuted the prophet	cheerful earful	fifteen figs
graphic offer	laughter from afar	fillet of flounder

a. Despite Phillip's fickleness, he gave no obvious offense to Fran or to any of her fifty friends.
b. Though fearless and tough, Fred Philbrick was considered by friends to be a diamond in the rough.
c. After the fog lifted, the fast planes took off for five foreign lands.
d. Although not efficient as a food, coffee is a favorite breakfast fluid for many of us.
e. Frank and his father are fond of golf and fishing and of food that is not fluff.
f. Florence and Phineas, who were born in France, made a swift visit to their favorite fishing village in Finland.
g. Truffles are fleshy, edible fungi that grow underground.
h. François, the chef, served the roast pheasant on a fancy chafing dish.
i. Fluke is a flatfish, a member of the family of flounders.
j. The flat-footed thief came to grief over the theft of a sapphire that had been cut without facets.

a. "Fair and foul are near of kin,
And fair need foul," I cried.
"My friends are gone, but that's a truth
Nor grave nor bed denied."

—William Butler Yeats,
Crazy Jane Talks with the Bishop

b. Time stoops to no man's lure;
And love, grown faint and fretful,
With lips but half regretful
Sighs, and with eyes forgetful
Weeps that no loves endure.

—Algernon Charles Swinburne,
The Garden of Proserpine

c. A faithful friend is a strong defence: and he that hath found such an one hath found a treasure.

—Ecclesiasticus, 6:14

d. Fare thee well! And if forever,
   Still forever, fare thee well.

—George Gordon, Lord Byron, *Fare Thee Well*

e. When tillage begins, other arts follow. The farmers therefore are the founders of civilization.

—Daniel Webster, *Remarks on Agriculture*

Dialogue for /f/

FAMOUS AND FORTY

Freelance Journalist: Fame is fickle and fleeting, but you refuse to fade! At forty, you are a full-fledged film star. Your faithful fans want to know if the fight for fame and fortune is rough and frustrating.

Film Star: I did not fly, swift and unfettered, into my elevated sphere. I floundered and faltered and fell time after time. But I was tough enough to laugh at the foibles of fate, and deaf to the prophets of doom. I was careful to feel my feet firmly on the ground as I forged ahead. Frankly, because of my belief in the future, I refused to be fazed by the frustrations of fate, and my life flourished.

Freelance Journalist: Father Time is a thief. But at forty, you are a phenomenon! Fit as a fiddle, your sapphire eyes shine forth from a face that is firm and flawless. Did you fly to France to have fun and frolic?

Film Star: I took a flight to France to breakfast in my favorite café and to flit barefoot among the flowers. I can afford to fly to France for a refreshing little frolic, and fun will outfox Father Time.

Freelance Journalist: Does fame infringe on your family life?

Film Star: Fortunately, my family is deaf to foolish gossip. Frannie, my daughter, is freckled and effusive and laughs at my folly. My boy, Raphael, is not afraid to offend any oaf who tries to fuel the fires of discord with foul lies. Finally, we don't flaunt our fortune, but financial freedom keeps my family cheerful and safe from strife.

Freelance Journalist: Are you having an affair with an old flame? A famous fellow who frets because you're forgetful?

Film Star: If you are referring to Phantom Phil, we are now fast friends. I prefer to forget we had a tiff.

Freelance Journalist: What free-floating thoughts do you have for females who want to follow in your footsteps? Feel free to pontificate.

Film Star: It's a stiff climb up a rough cliff to fame and fortune. If you have the stuff to tough it out, don't freeze out of fear. Laugh, stay cheerful, and never loaf. Finally, don't be afraid to fail! Fear of failure can stifle your finest efforts!

/v/ As in *Vie, Provoke,* and *Live*

/v/ is the voiced cognate of /f/. It is, of course, produced like the /f/, except that the /v/ is voiced and requires less breath pressure than the /f/.

Except for the f of *of*, /v/ is spelled as it is sounded.

The sound /v/ causes little or no difficulty for American-English speakers. As we have noted, some foreign-born speakers may have difficulty because they confuse the /v/ and the /w/. (See discussion and practice material for /v/ and /w/, pages 265–266.)

In context, when it is immediately followed by a voiceless consonant, as in "I've ten cents" or "Give Tom the book," the /v/ is normally produced with partial devoicing. It is also partially devoiced when it occurs at the end of a phrase or a sentence such as in "I had five" or "We enjoyed the drive."

=====

PRACTICE MATERIALS

Venus	valley	vault	visit
veal	van	vaunt	vile
venal	value	varnish	vine
veer	vend	varlet	vital
vigor	very	verse	vulgar
vim	vary	virtue	vulture
victor	voodoo	vernal	volume
vein	vogue	voice	volunteer
viper	verb	verify	verge
vale	vote	void	Volga
vapor	voracious	vice	vowel
evening	paved	proven	reverse
Eva	shaved	grooved	nervous
even	revel	hooves	convert
believing	event	roving	jovial
given	prevent	clover	revile
livid	having	Dover	trivial
evil	gavel	marvel	avoid
devil	travel	carving	invite
raving	ravel	starving	lover
staved	avid	avert	cover
deceive	delve	mauve	dive
receive	shelve	starve	strive
heave	have	carve	alive
sleeve	salve	nerve	hive
give	move	curve	naive
live	groove	swerve	resolve
gave	prove	glove	revolve
knave	rove	above	twelve

slave	stove	shove	love
stave	strove	dove	trove

evenly divided	convivial vendor
vile varlet	village on the Volga
vaunted virtue	nervous in the service
varied voices	swerved at the curve
jovial rival	carving of veal
avid knave	twelve drivers
vigorous and vital	violin virtuoso
vain victories	marvelous maneuvers
vernal voice	vital visit
clover from Dover	beloved trivia

a. Nervous and fearful of becoming a victim, Val would not volunteer to test the veracity of the village voodoo.
b. Vivian and Eve, avid travelers, undertook a voyage from Dover to Victoria.
c. The devil can be marvelously convivial, as well as a scrivener and a quoter of chapter and verse from the Bible.
d. Vince warned Vera that it is naive to approach a beehive without a veil for covering.
e. Jovial conversation went on while Violet carved the turkey for her five vocal guests.
f. Some have tried to improve the figure of Venus with velour drapes, but none has tried velvet gloves.
g. Twelve Javanese were found roving through the caves along the river valley.
h. Valentina banged her gavel to stop the vague and voracious verbalizations at the convention.
i. The villainous thieves found it to their advantage to cultivate a Harvard accent.
j. Vinson resolved to give up his vain ways and to live a life of proven value.
k. Volta, for whom the term *volt* is named, was an Italian physicist who taught at the University of Pavia.
l. Van de Veer and Viola Vanderbilt were jovial tennis rivals who once had a volley going from five minutes before five to twenty-five after the hour.

Selections for /f/ and /v/

a. From too much love of living,
From hope and fear set free,
We thank with brief thanksgiving
Whatever gods may be
That no life lives forever;
That dead men rise up never;
That even the weariest river
Winds somewhere safe to sea.
—Algernon Charles Swinburne, *Atalanta in Calydon*

b. At thirty, man suspects himself a fool;
   Knows it at forty, and reforms his plan;
   At fifty chides his infamous delay,
   Pushes his prudent purpose to resolve;
   In all the magnanimity of thought
   Resolves, and re-solves; then dies the same.
   —Edward Young, *Night Thoughts*

c. Nothing is given so profusely as advice.
   —François, Duc de La Rochefoucauld, *Maxim 110*

d. All civilization has from time to time become a thin crust over a volcano
   of revolution.
   —Havelock Ellis, *Little Essays of Love and Virtue*

e. All is ephemeral—fame and the famous as well.
   —Marcus Aurelius, *Meditations*

Dialogue for /v/

RELATIVE VALUES

Evelyn: Above all, value is relative. If you believe virtuous living is the best revenge against civilization, you will revile all trivial striving. You will find a village home off an unpaved gravel road near a river to be a treasure trove. A person who values nature would love to spend an evening watching the mauve sky, listening to the clever voice of an unshaven lover echo in the private void. Just reveling in the naive pleasures of being alive makes life worth living!

Victor: But a man who is a slave to his voracious appetite would starve at that river. His life revolves around a meal of marvelous veal. No matter how heavy, he never volunteers to diet. Above all, he loves invitations to the much-vaunted events at restaurants that are in vogue. Jovial and gentle as a dove when the food is good and the service invincible, he is livid when prevented from eating his victuals!

Evelyn: A man of vain victories must live above the law and give less than he receives. He will ravish varlets and invest in movies simply to prove his unswerving nerve. He loves to move in the groove with venal men who vanquish their more virtuous rivals. He is driven and reveals himself in vigorous activity. He must believe that nothing can prevent his victories, but he is not easily deceived. He invests and reinvests in proven ventures. To spend an evening watching a vale of fog slowly cover an unwavering river would make him very nervous.

Victor: I've talked to avid travelers who live to visit every spot on earth. They move from a village on the Volga to the Cliffs of Dover. They venture into casinos in venal Las Vegas, then drive through the vernal Everglades in a Rover.

Evelyn: Victor, I revel in our conversations. We delve into what it means to be alive. But I need a reprieve from this clever unraveling. Please, Vic, let's drive to the movie on Vincent Avenue.

CHAPTER 17

THE TONGUE-TEETH SOUNDS

The tongue-teeth consonants /θ/ (th) and /ð/ (th) present some difficulties for native speakers of English as well as for persons with foreign-language backgrounds. The causes of these difficulties and exercises for overcoming them are presented in individual considerations of these sounds.

/θ/ (th) As in *Thin, Thank,* and *Theory; Anything* and *Truthful; Faith* and *Earth*

The /θ/ is a voiceless fricative. It is produced by placing the tip of the tongue lightly against the back of the upper teeth or slightly between the teeth. Air is forced through the place of contact to produce the characteristic fricative quality. In spelling, the sound is represented by the letters *th*. The sound /θ/ may occur initially, medially, or finally.

/θ/ tends to be a somewhat troublesome sound for many speakers. Native-born Americans exposed to substandard or dialectal speech influences may substitute a /t/ for the initial /θ/, so that words such as *thin* and *three* are pronounced as though they were *tin* and *tree*. Foreign-born speakers who do not have the /θ/ in their native language tend to substitute their nearest approximation for it. Frequent substitutions include a dentalized /s/ (Japanese and German) and a dentalized /t/ (German, Italian, French, and Hispanic). A comparison of Figures 17–1 and 18–1 for the /θ/ and /t/, and practice with the material that immediately follows, should help to establish distinctions between /θ/ and /t/ and between /θ/ and /s/.

PRACTICE MATERIALS

Distinguish between /θ/ and /t/.

thank	tank	theme	team
thin	tin	thought	taught
through	true	deaths	debts
thread	tread	ether	eater

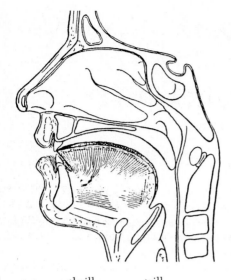

Figure 17–1 Representative articulatory positions for /θ/ (**th**) and /ð/ (**th**) as postdental sounds. Note the contact of the tongue tip with the upper teeth.

thrill	trill	sheaths	sheets
thick	tick	forth	fort
thrips	trips	bath	bat
thorn	torn	oath	oat
wrath	rat	hearth	heart
wraith	rate	Gertha	Gerta
faithful	fateful	ruthless	rootless
myths	mitts	booth	boot

Distinguish between /θ/ and /s/.

theme	seem	thought	sought
think	sink	thumb	sum
thick	sick	thigh	sigh
thing	sing	thin	sin
thank	sank	kith	kiss
thaw	saw	myth	miss
thong	song	thane	sane
faith	face	moth	moss
wraith	race	wroth	Ross
truth	truce	bath	bass
mouth	mouse	math	mass
worth	worse	fourth	force
north	Norse	path	pass
youthful	useful	something	some sing
pathway	passway	Kathy	Kassy

path to the pass	month for moths
Beth and Bess	lethal dose of ether
truthful truce	third and seventh

Sentences for /θ/, /t/, and /s/ Contrasts

a. Thelma and Selma were thrilled to hear the first trill of the thrush.
b. Matthew regarded Theodore as a man, true blue, all through.
c. Bess found a tick in the thick North Woods.
d. Thaddeus, a good student, thought that he had been well taught.
e. After Bertha heard the story through, she was thankful that it was true.
f. Katherine could sing mirthfully about almost anything.
g. The ache in the thick of Gertha's thigh brought forth a deep sigh.
h. Kenneth became sick when he breathed the thick, acrid smoke.
i. Thornton was wroth and declared that history, as it is taught, is mostly a myth.
j. There are now few traces of what was once the region of Thrace.

Some black English dialect speakers substitute an /f/ for the /θ/ in the final position in words such as *bath, mouth,* and *both.* Speakers who do this and who wish to change their pronunciation of final /θ/ words may use the practice materials that follow. They should make certain that the final articulatory position is postdental, and not labiodental.

breath	math	forth
cloth	path	wreath
faith	north	uncouth
growth	south	truth
health	teeth	Ruth
mirth	both	dearth
pith	broth	Beth

The following sentences provide the opportunity for establishing final /θ/ and /f/ sounds.

a. The sad fact is that Muff has little faith in Godfrey for telling truth from fiction.
b. The rough road went north and south from Fourth to Forty-Fifth Avenue.
c. Both Biff and Jeff bought long cloth coats.
d. Though math is a tough subject it almost always has a payoff.
e. Theo thanked the sleuth for catching the uncouth thief.

ADDITIONAL PRACTICE MATERIALS FOR /θ/

three	through	thud	thousand
theme	throe	thunder	thymus
thesis	throat	thump	theory
thimble	throne	third	threat
thicken	thrall	Thursday	throttle
theft	thought	thirst	thrust

thalamus	thwart	thirteen	thicket
thank	thaw	thigh	theology
thread	thrash	thrush	thyroid
thrips	thrive	thrum	Thrace
ether	pathos	enthusiasm	lengthen
breathy	pathetic	author	strengthen
anything	bathtub	orthodox	earthy
nothing	wrathful	orthopod	forthright
healthy	ruthless	slothful	toothless
wealthy	truthful	mirthful	atheist
stealthy	ethyl	toothache	method
rethread	birthday	mythical	lethargy
deathly	earthquake	synthetic	panther
youthful	hawthorn	arithmetic	Cathay
frothy	fifths[1]	sixths[1]	months[1]
wreath	booth	month	hearth
beneath	uncouth	mouth	sleuth
myth	both	warmth	troth
pith	oath	south	froth
kith	fourth	growth	length
faith	north	eighth	fifth
death	moth	ninth	breath
zenith	cloth	path	truth
wrath	dearth	mammoth	Ruth
stealth	earth	worth	Beth

faithful youth	thankless theory
wrathful truth	third Thursday
warmth of the south	enthralled with the myth
north of Cathay	thwarted atheist
fifth birthday	ruthless threat
oath unto death	zenith of growth
south of Fourth	youthful stealth
thick as thieves	mammoth toothache

Dialogue for /θ/

YOUTHFUL ENTHUSIASM

Atherton: Our orthodox theology class was enthralling on Thursday. We studied Hegel, a sleuth who ruthlessly searched for the truth. His dialectical method, where synthesis is created through thesis and antithesis, is a thumping thrill! At the end of his pithy speech, Mr. Wingsworth pointed out that to lengthen a theory does not give it strength. Where were you this Thursday? Were you held in thrall of your mammoth atheist Southern authors?

---

[1] Be on guard against a tendency to substitute a /t/ or omit the /θ/ in these words.

Theodore: Atherton, I thirst for a more earthy truth. Thursday, as stealthy as a
   thief, I threaded my way up the path that leads through the thick hawthorns to
   the mouth of the northern lake. There I saw a panther thrashing about in the
   thicket, caught in the throes of a rage. I held my breath and faced the threat of
   death from this beast with the frothy mouth. But as he was about to throttle
   me, the earth beneath my feet quaked, and the panther lost his teeth!
Atherton: Theodore, it's the ninth time this month that you missed theology.
   Your lethargy is both slothful and pathetic. This birthday you'll be thirty. You
   do nothing to justify your youthful existence, nor to acquire wisdom and wealth.
Theodore: Atherton, sloth is therapy for my soul. Your youthful enthusiasm for
   theory is fine, but I do not thrive on myth or the teachings of the faithful.
   Thursday I took a bath in the lake and baked in the warmth of the southern
   sun. Sitting by the hearth for months and studying theories will threaten your
   health. Take my path to the northern lake, listen to the thrush, and watch the
   fog thicken. Don't throw away your youth!
Atherton: I'll spend my youth in thought, thank you. The zenith of growth is to
   know truth from myth — something thoroughly worth all my enthusiasm!

Contrast in /θ/, /t/, and /s/

   a. Thirty faithful and enthusiastic elders meet on the third Thursday of every
      month.
   b. Samantha taught Matthew that one can be forthright in telling the truth
      without being ruthless.
   c. Although Thornton was proficient in arithmetic, he was fearful of higher
      forms of mathematics.
   d. Theodore blamed his lethargy on the warmth of the day, but his friend
      Thaddeus could be lethargic without concern about the weather.
   e. Thelma and Theo strengthened their friendship when they found that they
      shared a birthday.
   f. Shaw, famous author and first man of the theater, thought that youth is
      wasted on the young.
   g. Ruth considered it no myth in her belief that the eighth day of the month
      was thoroughly lucky for her.
   h. Roth spotted the panther creeping stealthily through the thicket.
   i. Nathaniel Hawthorne, whose father spelled his name as Hathorne, was a
      contemporary of Thoreau and more prolific as an author.
   j. There is no dearth of growth from the fertile soil of the South.

The youthful Keats was the author of many famous lines. Among the best
known are the following from *Endymion* and *Ode on a Grecian Urn*:
   a. A thing of beauty is a joy forever:
      Its loveliness increases; it will never
      Pass into nothingness.

      "Beauty is truth, truth beauty" — that is all
      Ye know on earth, and all ye need to know.

In *My Lost Youth*, Henry Wadsworth Longfellow, often called the poet of the hearth, wrote:

    b. A boy's will is the wind's will,
       And the thoughts of youth are long, long thoughts.

    c. On the thirty-second day of the thirteenth month of the
         eighth day of the week,
       On the twenty-fifth hour and the sixty-first minute, we'll
         find all things that we seek.

               —Sam W. Foss, *The Eighth Day of the Week*

    d. Said Bertha to Gertha,
       "You seem full of mirth;
       Does your ungentle laughter
       Endanger your girth?"

       Said Gertha to Bertha,
       "I am full of mirth,
       And my broad, healthy laughter
       Is good for my girth."

    e. It is of itself that the divine thought thinks (since it is the most excellent of things), and its thinking is a thinking on thinking.

               —Aristotle, *Metaphysics*, Book 9

Theme for Thanksgiving

Ms. Matthews: Today's theme for our diet team is "It's no sin to be thin—think before you sink a tooth into that chocolate mousse." Face the fact that it will be hard to keep the faith over Thanksgiving. You big eaters might need ether. It's a myth that you must miss the whole meal. Just don't kiss your kith for baking cakes. Learn to sigh and fuss over Gran's turkey thigh. It's no myth that you have to keep your mitts off the pie to get thin as a tin pin.

Gertha: Ms. Matthews, the theme here seems to be that you deserve a wrathful fate if you thrill to eat cake. But I saw you thaw a torte and cut a slice so thick it made me sick. How can you thumb your nose at the sum of those calories?

Ms. Matthews: Gertha, I thought I taught you that I sought eternal youth—and found it! You must make a truce with the truth. I'm a wraith half your size who rates a size six dress. Now, it's not worth a worse deprivation than dieting to get thin. Don't miss Thanksgiving altogether. But until then, take an oath to eat nothing but cooked oats! That's what Theodore and I have done. Truthfully, I suspect that Theodore may be cheating.

/ð/ (t̶h̶) As in *That* and *Those; Either* and *Weather; Bathe* and *Breathe*

/ð/ (t̶h̶) is the voiced cognate of /θ/. It is represented by the letters *th* and may occur initially, medially, or finally, as in *these, bathing,* and *wreathe*. The /ð/ is produced with light tongue-tip contact either behind the upper teeth or between the cutting edges of the teeth. Air is forced through the place of contact while the vocal folds are in vibration.

There is no certain way of determining whether a particular word should be pronounced with a /θ/ or a /ð/. We may note a tendency—in initial positions, at least—for words that are stressed and significant in a sentence, such as nouns, verbs, and adjectives, to be pronounced with the voiceless /θ/. Pronouns, articles, and conjunctions, which are more likely to be unstressed and weak in sentence context, tend to be pronounced with a /ð/. As a result, the /ð/ tends to occur more often than the /θ/ in our speech.

Persons who are inclined to substitute a /t/ for a /θ/ are also likely to substitute a /d/ for a /ð/. The first set of practice materials should help to establish a clear distinction between the /d/ and the /ð/. (See pages 299–300 for a description of /d/.)

PRACTICE MATERIALS

Distinguish between /ð/ and /d/.

breathe	breed	tithe	tide
thee	dee	their	dare
they	day	thence	dense
then	den	lather	ladder
than	Dan	lathe	laid
though	dough	loathe	load
those	doze	seethe	seed
thy	dye	other	udder
thine	dine	worthy	wordy
teethe	teed	lithe	lied

loathed the load   wordy but worthy
their foolish dare   writhed on their ride
then to the den   the other udder

a. Dan was taller than his brother but not as tall as his father.
b. Though Mathers was loathe to carry a heavy load, he did not bother to make his loathing evident.
c. There are few children who can say "no" to a dare.
d. Though David and brother Dan devoted the day to thinking worthy thoughts, they did not find time to perform worthy deeds.
e. Ben Rather thought that even though he could not help to make the dough, he was not loathe to breathing the aroma of the baking bread.
f. Mother and father went thence, further and further into the dense forest.
g. Though Carruthers and his brother had coffee with their doughnuts, nevertheless they both dozed off.
h. Farthington rode all day to dine with his wordy but worthy brother.

ADDITIONAL PRACTICE MATERIALS

these	than	the	thine
this	those	thus	them
then	though	thy	therefore
they	there	that	therein
either	weather	although	mother
neither	feather	loathing	bother
heathen	lather	brother	logarithm
leather	rather	father	further
breathe	soothe	scythe	swathe
bathe	scathe	writhe	teethe
wreathe	blithe	tithe	with

a. Although she was loathe to speak her mind, Mother thought that occasionally Father knew best.
b. Neither mother nor brother enjoyed foggy weather.
c. The word *thine* is the possessive form of *thou*.
d. *This* and *that* are demonstrative pronouns.
e. Mother is fond of feathered creatures but Father loathes bats.
f. The ghosts gathered among the other blithe spirits.
g. Leather is being replaced by plastic in the making of clothing.
h. The heather withered in the field.
i. The heathen considered it a bother to bathe.
j. Although the birds were of a feather, they preferred not to flock together.

Selections for /θ/ and /ð/

a. George Santayana, author and philosopher, advised that because there is no cure for birth and ultimately for death, a worthy use of time is to enjoy the interval between the two.
b. Said Theo to Brothers,
    "You are a bit mad,
    Your logarithmic theory
    Is mathematically sad."

Said Brothers to Theo,
    "Hold back on your wrath-o
    If you fathomed my theory
    You'd not think me patho."
c. But he who loveliness within
    Hath found, all outward loathes,
For he who colour loves, and skin,
    Loves but their oldest clothes.

—John Donne, *The Undertaking*

d. Rather than love, than money, than fame, give me truth.

—Henry David Thoreau, *Conclusions*

e. Those who would survive in the "game" of counterintelligence must be thorough in their projections and capable of thinking out what others may think that they think. They must be able to think ahead of their opposite numbers and think things through to their conclusion. Those who fail so to think are not likely to think whatever they may be thinking for very long.

f. At the door of life, by the gate of breath,
   There are worse things waiting for me than death.

—Algernon Charles Swinburne, *The Triumph of Time*

g. Why is this thus? What is the reason of this thusness?

—Artemus Ward, *Moses, the Sassy*

Dialogue for /ð/ and /d/ Contrast

WORDY QUESTIONS AND WORTHY DEEDS

Dan the Farmer: I will answer any worthy questions as long as they're not wordy, Dave.

Dave: Why did those workers doze off at dinner?

Dan the Farmer: They started their day at dawn. They laid that heavy drainpipe, after using the lathe to cut it. Then they replanted seed that was scattered by the seething winds. Then they went into the dense woods to clear a path through the dense thicket.

Dave: Why will no one dare ride that dark horse over there?

Dan the Farmer: If you writhe when you ride a horse of that breed, you may never breathe again!

Dave: Why don't you milk that other cow, the one with the heavy udder? It must loathe its milky load!

Dan the Farmer: Dave, rather than asking these wordy questions, do a worthy deed. Though you're small, you can knead dough for Dee. Or climb the ladder for the soap and lather the leather saddle. Then meet me in the den. Just remember, your mother bade you bathe before you dine with your father.

Dave: You win, Dad. I thought that if I asked worthy questions it would be too late for me to bathe. Oh well, Mother does know best.

CHAPTER 18

THE TONGUE-TIP TO GUM-RIDGE STOP PLOSIVE SOUNDS AND THE VELAR STOPS

═══

A glance at the consonant chart (page 251) will reveal that the tongue-tip to gum-ridge (lingua-alveolar) and the postalveolar sounds include a third of the American-English consonants. The lingua-alveolar and the postalveolar articulatory positions are distinctive in our language. For this reason, the sounds in these groups are given detailed consideration.

═══ THE TONGUE-TIP TO GUM-RIDGE SOUNDS ═══

The Phoneme /t/

We begin our study of the tongue-tip to gum-ridge consonants with the [t] as in *tea, ton,* and *too.* If the contact point and manner of articulation for this [t] are mastered, you will have an excellent point of reference for the production of other American-English alveolar speech sounds.

In this section, devoted to the phoneme /t/, we present separate materials for several of the allophones of /t/. In keeping with phonetic practice, the allophones are indicated in brackets [ ]. Allophones, we recall, are variants of phonemes and are the actual sounds that we produce in contextual speech. Allophones may be "defined" as the nondistinctive features of phonemes, the features that do not result in differences in our perception of words and their meanings.

[t] As in *Ton, Until,* and *Utopia.* To produce the [t] as in *ton* or as an isolated sound, the tongue is raised so that the tongue tip comes in contact with the upper gum ridge (see Figure 18–1). The soft palate is raised to prevent nasal emission of breath. The

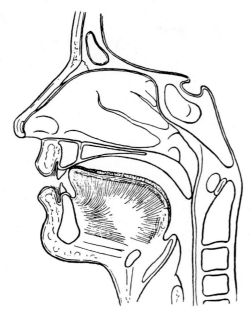

Figure 18–1 Articulatory position for /t/ and /d/. Note the contact between the tongue tip and the alveolar (gum) ridge.

sides of the tongue near the tip are in contact with the upper molars. The tongue, tense and extended, is held in this position for a fraction of a second. Then, quickly, and as completely as possible, the tongue is retracted, with a resultant slight "explosion" of air at the tongue tip. This should be felt as a puff of breath if you hold your hand in front of your mouth.

The [t] as just described occurs whenever the sound appears in a stressed syllable and is immediately followed by a vowel. The [t] in such contexts is a lingua-alveolar (gum-ridge), stop-plosive consonant. In producing this [t], observe the following cautions:

1. Make certain that the tongue tip is in contact with the gum ridge and *not the upper teeth*. The contact, when broken, should be quick and complete.

2. Do not permit the tongue to slide so that contact is made between the front surface of the tongue and the gum. If this happens, a [ts] blend is likely to be produced.

Practice Materials

Establish the contact position for the stressed [t] by practice with the material that follows. Repeat each of the words in the lists at least three times.

Initial

tea	take	too	tole
tee	ten	tube	talk

tip	tall	took	taught
tell	tag	tomb	tog
tape	tap	toe	top
turn	type	town	tone
Turk	time	tower	team
tub	tide	toy	teach
ton	tile	toil	tease
tie	tire	towel	tool

Medial (*followed by a vowel*)

attend	intern	Utopia	partake
atone	iterate	Utah	pitied
attack	deter	intake	rotate
attempt	deduct	eternal	entire
attach	until	retool	historical
attain	utensil	retook	intone
entire	intense	return	intend

talented team	ton of tin
take your time	talk and tell
tip to top	took the tea
ten and ten	ten times ten
twenty and two	turn the tape
tap the top	take a turn
twin tykes	timely talks
town tower	tie the tag
tall but tame	twice tested

a. Tongue twisters are sometimes used as tests of articulation.
b. Tim played a solo on his tuba to tease Tess.
c. Tammy set the timer at fifteen to two in order not to be late for her appointment.
d. Because they wanted to be entirely alone, Tina and Tom went to the next town for their important date.
e. Tarkington turned amateur detective to test his new attainments at detection.
f. An accepted verity is that time and tide wait for nobody.
g. The state of Utah is named for the Ute Indians.
h. The alert intern detected an infectious Rocky Mountain tick.
i. Todd hurt his left toe which had to be taped.
j. Two antiquity hunters broke into a tomb and fortunately were caught in the act.

═══

Final [t]. A final [t] is exploded (aspirated) when it is followed by a vowel in the next word within the same phrase, as in *the cat is here*. Most persons either do not aspirate the final [t] at the end of a sentence, as in *I'll come at eight*, or produce this [t] with little aspiration (a slight puff of breath). The same tendencies hold for final [t] at the end of a phrase within a sentence, as in *it might be right for now*.

PRACTICE MATERIALS

ant	fate	late	effete
bait	fat	dote	but
eat	bat	note	cut
it	boot	bought	hut
ate	emit	blot	hurt
might	foot	right	naught
out	flout	night	suit
quoit	incite	sought	root
sight	blight	fort	shoot
sweet	discreet	elite	defeat
wheat	height	mite	requite
debt	rant	doubt	refute

a. Pat and Matt eat breakfast at eight.
b. Whether football or basketball is the favorite American sport is a matter of frequent debate.
c. Art was hurt when he split his bat in his first time at bat.
d. Mint and fruit juice are ingredients for a pleasant drink.
e. The craft was lost in the thick mist that crept in at sunset.
f. When finished with the concert, naught could persuade Chet to emit another sound from his flute.
g. Dot was lost in thought, innocent of what she had wrought.
h. Hutt was adamant that a well-footed boot should not hurt even a tender foot.
i. Kit beat twenty contestants in the quoit contest.
j. Out of sight need not be out of mind.

[t] As in *Safety*. The sound [t] in an unstressed syllable followed by a vowel is produced in a less vigorous manner than when it occurs in a stressed syllable. The contact between tongue tip and gum ridge is not held as long as for a stressed [t], and there is less of a breath puff following the breaking of the contact. Avoid assimilating the unstressed [t] in the direction of either substituting a [d] for it or omitting the sound entirely.

PRACTICE MATERIALS

The words that follow provide practice for the unstressed [t].

pity	hatter	hefty	jetty
city	latter	utter	tempted
plenty	faulty	bitter	twenty
better	mountain	fifty	written
letter	scatter	thirty	litter
kitty	witty	fretted	patted

Practice in discriminating between the unstressed [t] and [d] in the following pairs of words.

dotter	dodder	matter	madder
latter	ladder	wetting	wedding
betting	bedding	written	ridden
heated	heeded	butting	budding
bitter	bidder	tenting	tending
rating	raiding	contented	contended
shutter	shudder	writer	rider

The exercises that follow provide practice for [t] immediately succeeded by a vowel and/or in the final position.

teen	tame	atone	tome	tout
tell	waste	fateful	bit	tat
ten	last	inter	flat	tent
till	quite	contain	flute	taste
time	after	rotary	hoot	tight
told	comet	twine	root	taught
tab	lout	twist	tote	toot
tangle	between	twig	wart	tort
toll	return	palliate	what	twist
at	continue	unite	flirt	twit
boat	atone	beet	wheat	tossed
totem	tact	tutor	tilt	two-time

a. Tiny Tom Tucker was fond of eating toasted white bread with a lot of butter.
b. Timton was alert to avoid having his tongue articulate faster than prudent thinking would dictate.
c. Is it always tedious to hear a well-told tale told twice?
d. If added correctly, ten and ten and two add up to twenty-two.

e. The tidings of the times portended that temptation was to be avoided at all cost.

f. On his recent trip to Utah, Thomas was seated next to a taciturn traveler from a town in East Texas.

g. Tess taught Toni that it is easier to start than to stop an argument.

h. Antoinette and Scot were upset because they had to wait at least twenty minutes between the acts.

i. The poet Donne lamented that too few appreciate in time that it is for them for whom the bell inevitably tolls.

j. Thomson could not take to being twitted, although he was quite proficient at teasing and taunting others not his weight and six-foot-two height.

a. Temptation can be many different things to different people. It has been a time-honored subject for the poet, the moralist, the dramatist, and the philosopher. Some views of temptation are presented in the quotations that follow.

   1. "I can resist everything except temptation," Oscar Wilde had one of his characters protest.

   2. In contrast, the ever-optimistic Robert Browning asserted in his *Ring and the Book*:

      Why comes temptation, but for man to meet
      And master and make crouch beneath his foot,
      And so be pedestaled in triumph?

   3. Mark Twain observed that there are several good protections against temptations, but the surest is cowardice.

   4. Finally, at least for the moment, we have the terse statement of the British poet and humorist, Douglas Jerrold, who in his writing *Cat's-paw* contends, "Honest bread is very well — it's the butter that makes the temptation."

b. Take hand and part with laughter,
      Touch lips and part with tears:
   Once more and no more after,
      Whatever comes with years.
                              — Algernon Charles Swinburne, *Rococo*

c.   O, it is excellent
   To have a giant's strength; but it is tyrannous
   To use it like a giant.
                              — William Shakespeare, *Measure for Measure*

d. In this essay *Sartor Resartus* (The Tailor Retailored), the famous British essayist Thomas Carlyle noted that "man is a tool-using animal. . . . Without tools he is nothing."

---

[t] As a Final, Morphemic Sound As in *Chased* and *Lunched*.   Note its consistent representation in spelling by the letters *ed*.

PRACTICE MATERIALS

based	diced	spiced	polished
raced	placed	creased	pounced
chased	branched	lunched	grossed
faced	lanced	munched	crossed
graced	bunched	tossed	nursed
laced	hunched	bossed	trooped

a. Tina munched as she lunched on the spiced meat.
b. Tom hunched in pain when his finger was lanced.
c. They trooped to the right of the triple-branched route.
d. Tom placed third when he raced in a leased car.
e. The haunched tiger pounced on its timid prey.

Other Varieties of /t/

As indicated earlier, the consonant /t/ varies somewhat in its manner of production and the acoustic end result according to speech context. Some of the more frequent variations are now considered.

[t] Followed by /θ/ (th) or /ð/ (t̶h̶) As in *Right Things* and *At The*. In combinations such as *at the, hit that, light things,* and *eighth*, the [t] is produced by contact between the tongue tip and the upper teeth rather than at the gum ridge. The dentalized [t] in these combinations is produced as a result of the assimilative influence of the next sound, /θ/ or /ð/, which is articulated dentally.

This variety of /t/ is least likely to be produced defectively by persons with foreign-language backgrounds. It is the variety most likely to be produced habitually by persons whose English speech is influenced by French, Spanish, Italian, or German.

PRACTICE MATERIALS

wet thaw	fat Thane
eighth time	sweet thoughts
hit the ball	right thinking
swat the fly	bright theorist
light the lamp	light theme
stout thump	correct theory
went there	hurt thumb

at third   meet at the tank
not at three   promised thanks

a. Bright theories by intelligent theorists result in right thoughts.
b. In this eighth and last time at bat, without thinking, Tom hit the ball over the thatched fence.
c. Did Nat Thatcher really hurt Thelma's little thumb?
d. Scott Thornike, who thought of himself as a poet, wrote in slight themes.
e. Ken thanked Thelma for her forthright thinking.
f. Thelma, in turn, thanked Kenneth for not thwarting her in writing her complete thesis.
g. After the first thaw, the wet thatched roof leaked all through the night.
h. At eight-thirty, just three hours before exam time, Pat Thurber went through his notes.
i. At the third try the arrow hit the target.
j. In his attempt to put out the light, Matt knocked it over and felt thwarted by his not-so-bright thought.

===

[t] Followed by /l/ or /n/ As in *Little* and *Button*.   When the [t] sound is immediately followed by an /l/ or an /n/, it is not necessary to remove the tongue tip from the gum ridge to complete the sound. Instead, the sides of the front part of the tongue break contact with the side teeth to permit a *lateral* escape or explosion of breath. When the [t] is followed by [l], as in *little, battle, settle, kettle,* and *mortal,* the breath of the explosion is emitted laterally.

In words in which [t] is followed by /n/, as in *written, button, cotton,* and *rotten,* the tongue position is maintained in going from the [t] to the /n/. When the velum is lowered for the /n/, a nasal rather than an oral explosion takes place. If you place your hand just below the nostrils, you should be able to feel a nasally emitted puff of air.

There is a marked tendency to substitute a throat or glottal (laryngeal) click sound for the [t] when it is followed by /l/ or /n/. This substitution, in American speech, is generally considered substandard. You may check your tendency toward glottal substitution by placing your hand at your larynx while speaking the lists of words and sentences that follow. If you feel a click, it is likely that you are using a glottal (laryngeal) "catch" sound instead of the [t]. To avoid this tendency, pay special attention to the prescribed manner of articulation for the [t] in [tl] and [tn] combinations.

===

PRACTICE MATERIALS

cattle	fettle	fatten	wanton
beetle	mortal	bitten	rotten
battle	glottal	button	fountain

metal	bottle	cotton	written
whittle	scuttle	gotten	fatten
settle	rattle	mutton	mountain
mental	spittle	subtle	mitten

a. Myrtle was in fine fettle as she filled the kettle and mentally anticipated the toast.
b. Burton's ill-gotten gains were hidden in a mountain cache.
c. Benton complained that the mutton chops were too tough to be eaten.
d. Little by little Fenton tested the contents of the bottle.
e. Preston whittled the ornamental buttons out of wood.
f. Sheldon's kitten played with his cotton mitten and soon, to Sheldon's dismay, there was neither mitten nor kitten.
g. By writing well-written words, Skelton hoped to become immortal.
h. The town fountain was dominated by a metal figure of Triton.
i. Trenton would not eat the mutton that his friend Martin had fed and fattened.
j. When he reached the top of the mountain, Denton took a long drink from his metal thermos bottle.

[t] Followed by [r] As in *Tree, Train*, and *Attract*. When this [t] is immediately followed by an [r] allophone, both are produced with tongue-tip activity. To produce the [t], your tongue tip makes and breaks contact with the upper gum ridge; for the [r], your tongue tip is curled close to but not in contact with the gum ridge. (See Figure 22–2, page 376 for a diagram of this [r].) However, unlike the [t] which is a stopplosive sound, this [r] is a fricative glide sound in that the tongue continues to move in anticipation of the next sound.

It is important to avoid substituting a [w] for the [r]. (See also Chapter 22, pages 379–81, for additional discussion and practice materials for this [r].)

Practice Materials

tree	treble	try
treaty	trill	triad
tryst	truth	tripe
trip	trailer	tread
train	trump	trifle
track	true	trout
tramp	trolley	trowel
trot	trophy	trivial
tropic	trudge	attract
trade	Trojan	atrium

trip by train	troubled tram
true but trivial	trio of tropes
tried and untruthful	treated to tripe
attractive atrium	truncated trial

a. Trisha would not trifle with the truth.
b. The international trade treaty was signed on a train.
c. Troy was fond of trinkets and other trivial objects.
d. The fall leaves trembled and fell from the tree.
e. Trenton found it attractive to trump his rival's ace.
f. Trusdale, after three tries, won a trophy as a member of his track team.
g. Tracy trudged along the train tracks until he reached his favorite trout stream.
h. An *atrium* is an anatomical term for one of the chambers of the heart through which venous blood is transmitted to the ventricles.
i. Trippler vowed that however long and troubling the trail, he would arrive at the truth.
j. Henry L. Stimson, who was secretary of war under F.D.R., held that "the only way to make a man trustworthy is to trust him; and the surest way to make him untrustworthy is to distrust him and show your distrust."

[t] Followed by /s/ and Preceded and Followed by /s/ As in *Pets* and *Posts*. In contexts in which the [t] is immediately followed by an /s/, the tip of the tongue is permitted to slide forward in anticipation of the [s]. Care should be taken not to omit the [t] entirely, especially in combinations in which the [t] is medial between two [s] sounds. The fine articulatory movements required for the [sts] combination increase the tendency to omit the [t].

PRACTICE MATERIALS

Practice with the words, phrases, and sentences that follow should help to focus attention on the precise articulation that is required for [ts] and [sts].

baits	eats	roasts	toasts
pets	pots	insists	pests
lots	flights	breasts	ghosts
gates	paints	posts	resists
facts	mists	rests	persists
lasts	jests	masts	tests
waits	guests	hosts	tempests

eats sweets	first sights
nuts and bolts	bats and ghosts
paints the posts	resists the pests
posts the gates	persists and insists
lots of facts	flights of bats
trusts students	instant protests

a. The last act of a play demands a playwright's best efforts.
b. Esther placed her stored painted pots next to the fence posts along First Street.
c. The still gray mists stopped the planes' flights from the state's airports.
d. Is it true, as Stanley insists, that the hard facts of life often interfere with the attainments of the heart's desires, or do persistent facts just test them?
e. Stoutly built birds' nests were found in nets hanging from the masts.
f. Stone persists in stating lists of facts at times when jests or stories of ghosts are more acceptable to most listeners' tastes.

a. Hope springs eternal in the human breast:
   Man never is, but always to be, blest.
   —Alexander Pope, *Essay on Man*
b. Now cracks a noble heart. Good night, sweet prince,
   And flights of angels sing thee to thy rest.
   —William Shakespeare, *Hamlet*
c. Even with the utterly lost, to whom life and death are equally jests, there are matters of which no jest can be made.
   —Edgar Allan Poe, *The Masque of the Red Death*
d. He leaves for America's history and biography, so far, not only its most dramatic reminiscence—he leaves, in my opinion, the greatest, best, most characteristic, artistic, moral personality.
   —Walt Whitman, *Death of President Lincoln*

[t] Followed Immediately by Another [t] Within a Phrase, As in *Hit Twice, Felt Tired*. In such contexts we have only one tongue-tip to gum-ridge contact and so only one [t] is produced. However, the contact is maintained a moment longer than it would be were a sound other than a [t] to follow. Because it is held longer than for a single [t], we perceive it as two [t] sounds. Following is some practice material for this variety of [t].

PRACTICE MATERIALS

post ten	eat toast
twilight time	set tasks

flight tower   best times
hot twist   bait traps

a. Pat twice asked Dot to fix the roast turkey.
b. The test tube contained a bright tan-tinted tincture.
c. Twilight time may be the best time to trot to town.
d. The guest took leave because he had a tryst to see a ghost.

And for a pleasant interlude:

On a tree by a river a little tomtit
Sang "Willow, titwillow, titwillow!"
And I said to him, "Dicky-bird, why do you sit
Singing, 'Willow, titwillow, titwillow!'
"Is it weakness of intellect, birdie?" I cried,
"Or a rather tough worm in your little inside?"
With a shake of his poor little head he replied,
"Oh, willow, titwillow, titwillow!"

—William S. Gilbert, *The Mikado*

BURT THE BASEBALL STAR

Sports Announcer: Burt, that ball you batted is still in flight. It's the eighth time you hit the ball and landed a man at third. Is it right thinking that busts those bats?

Burt the Star: I had gotten fat on mutton and had to whittle down. I got thin as I ate the leanest little roasts and turkey breasts. That is cause for lots of toasts!

Sports Announcer: There's a lot of rotten tripe written about you. What they say is that your wanton drinking persists.

Burt the Star: Those pests should button up about my battle with the bottle until they get the facts straight. If I was drunk, I could not hit that mosquito right there with a kettle. Write the facts and scuttle the rumors. My busted bats prove I'm in fine fettle.

Sports Announcer: Burt, I'll write a story for the *Afternoon Town Gazette* and try to put the tattling to rest. Keep hitting the ball over the twenty-eight-foot fence in left field, and the entire town, including the teetotalers, will be toasting you for your mighty bat and your timely hits. In the meantime, Burt, my best to you.

/d/ As in *Done, Ado,* and *Glad*

The consonant /**d**/ in *done* is articulated in essentially the same manner as the /t/ in ton, except that the /**d**/ is voiced. The /**d**/, like the /t/, is a variable sound. The varieties of /**d**/ parallel those of /t/. Faults in the articulation of /**d**/ also parallel those for /t/, the chief one being the tendency toward dental articulation. A second tendency to be avoided is the substitution of a /t/ for a /**d**/ in words in which the final /**d**/ should be voiced. This fault may be especially noted in the speech of German-born persons or of persons for whom German was a first language and continues to be a strong influence in speaking American English. Thus, because the final [d] does not occur in German, the tendency to produce a [t] in a final position is carried over to American English.

PRACTICE MATERIALS

The first set of materials should help establish a clear distinction between /t/ and /d/. Make certain that the /t/ is voiceless and the /d/ is voiced.

Distinguish between initial [t] and [d].

tame	dame	tuck	duck
teem	deem	tune	dune
tip	dip	tomb	doom
tense	dense	toll	dole
tamp	damp	tummy	dummy
tail	dale	toe	doe
ten	den	taunt	daunt
tan	Dan	tot	dot
time	dime	town	down
too	do	touch	Dutch

Distinguish between medial [t] and [d].

kitty	kiddy	writing	riding
fated	faded	wetted	wedded
knotted	nodded	butted	budded
utter	udder	grated	graded
rated	raided	otter	odder

a. The kitty delighted the kiddy.
b. A rose is fated to become faded.
c. Dan contended and seemed contented to come second in the duel race with Tania.
d. Dotty heeded the advice to keep her den heated.

Distinguish between final [t] and [d].

seat	seed	brute	brood
bit	bid	note	node
ate	aid	naught	gnawed
late	laid	not	nod
mat	mad	coat	code
let	led	writ	rid
bat	bad	cart	card
set	said	stunt	stunned
cat	cad	hurt	heard
beat	bead	curt	curd

    a. Dot said, "I'm set Rod, let's get going with our visit to Burt and Ned."

    b. Brad was pleased that his right hand had recovered from the slide and that he could now eat without aid.

    c. Brad and Pat were not able to get rid of the writ served on them without legal aid.

    d. Fred was in a state of fret because the mote in his eye obscured his vision and his mode of thinking.

    e. A Cavalier poet, truly unworthy of note, wrote an ode entitled "To My Lady's Beaded Coat."

PRACTICE MATERIALS FOR /d/ IN VARIOUS POSITIONS

Initial [d]

deal	daze	dart	dire
deep	duel	dark	dear
din	dough	dirt	dean
day	dote	dearth	dream
debt	dawn	dub	drip
dance	dock	dike	drain
dew	dog	doubt	draw
dale	damp	dull	does

deep in dew	dull and damp
dance till dawn	daily dozen
day by day	duel in the dew
dark and dreary	due date
din at daybreak	dull ditty
dry desert	denizen of the deep
dog at the dock	delicate dough
dearth of dough	dire dream
dime a deal	doubtful Dan
down the drain	deep in daisies

Medial [d]

adder	adduce	bedding	grander
admit	fading	bedlam	hinder
ardent	hidden	candor	needed
oddly	eddy	splendor	indoor
edict	adverse	random	odious

Final [d]

add	amid	said	spade
crowd	old	lead	code

rude	bald	heed	abode
hoard	fraud	reed	node
heed	curd	rod	aloud
ode	brood	toad	cloud
mode	druid	mood	mold

Medial and/or Final [d]

amid the crowd	druids of old
needed a code	dignified abode
oddly odious	heeded the edict
splendid brood	wedded to David
rained and thundered	diddled and dawdled
moody and rude	random blunder

a. Undaunted by earlier failures, Diane and Ted led a dozen determined ladies to begin a ten-day diet.
b. Dan claimed that frequently he could not distinguish between Dick's candor and his rudeness.
c. As the day was dying, a deep-red cloud rested on the mountaintop.
d. The dog's barking at dawn warned Daniel and helped him to undo a dastardly plot.
e. Duncan brooded over the fraud that deprived him of his gold and his abode.
f. Daybreak is considered the correct if not the good time for undertaking duels.
g. The crowd did not heed the warning to disperse.
h. London is reputed to be a city of dense fog and bright-minded traders.
i. The drug made Dick's head droop as he dropped off to sleep.
j. Matilda married her doting admiral, who wrote an ode to his bride.
k. David took heed of every detail as he decoded the note.
l. Druidism is a religion that was once prevalent in the lands that are now England and Ireland.

[dz]

adds	cards	reeds	fords
beads	fades	steeds	raised
beds	heads	rides	hazed
aides	hides	reeds	meads
brides	minds	lads	nodes
buds	roads	girds	rods

[d] Followed by [θ] (th) or [ð] (th)

had that	herd the cattle	ride through
hid the ball	sad thoughts	width and breadth
heard the call	rid the land	ford the stream
amid the crowd	hoarded things	heed the leader
odd theory	delivered Thursday	dreamed through the day

Selections for /t/ and /d/

a. Bernard De Voto, the American writer and editor, wrote, "History abhors determinism but cannot tolerate chance."

b. Cowards die many times before their death;
The valiant never taste of death but once.

— William Shakespeare, *Julius Caesar*

c. When Adam was created,
He dwelt in Eden's shade,
As Moses has related,
Before a bride was made;
Ten thousand times ten thousand
Things wheeled all around,
Before a bride was formed
Or yet a mate was found.

— George Pullen Jackson, *Wedding*

d. No living man can send me to the shades
Before my time; no man of woman born,
Coward or brave, can shun his destiny.

— Homer, *Iliad*

e. Said Trixon to Dixon,
"You look full of thought;
I'll offer you tuppence
Though it may be worth nought."

Said Dixon to Trixon,
"Your offer's quite tempty
But not for ten tuppence,
Would my mind for you empty."

— J. E., *A Thought's a Thought for All That*

f. According to Mark Twain, Adam was the only person who could know for certain that when he said a good or witty thing nobody could have said it at any time before him.

g. Mark Twain also advised that we try to get out of an experience only the insight and wisdom that is in it and stop there. He cautioned us not to be like the cat that, after sitting down on a hot stovelid, never again sits down on a hot lid. That is all to the good unless the cat also decides never again to sit on any lid, hot or cold.

/t/ and /d/ Review (including contrasts between /t/ and /d/)

DIALOGUE FOR A SATURDAY NIGHT

Tilden: You know football is my favorite sport. Saturday night I want to attend an out-of-town game in Utah. I bought tickets on the twenty-yard line. Our talented University team, with its budding players, could get hurt butting heads with Utah. But in our entire history we have not been defeated on a Saturday night. We'll beat those ten-ton trucks that consider themselves hot-shot athletes.

Edweena: But what about the women's tennis tournament tonight? Last Saturday we attended the football game, where overgrown adolescents tackled, attacked, pounded, and punched each other. Tomorrow night I want to root for our tennis team. Our team placed in the top ten. I took Tina to tryout, and even when she chased the ball, she graced the court with beauty. In tennis, the competition is intense but seldom does one get badly hurt.

Tilden: Once most women seemed content to be volunteers, to give freely of their time. Now they are setting things to right. They compete in bidding for hefty salaries along with the male stars. Of course, if we like to watch tennis, we pay at the gate. Tomorrow, let's take the tube downtown and watch the track meet, just for a change.

Edweena: It's a pity to stay in the city and waste the last night of August. Let's wash the boat from top to toe, retool, and take it out on the water. We can suit up at night and tread water in the moonlight. We will have tea for two, listen to the flute concert at the jetty, and flirt. The night will take a fateful twist as we are tossed about on the tide. We'll return Tuesday and continue to teach the delights of poetry to the elite.

Tilden: Edweena, dear, instead, why don't we mountain-climb outside of town and partake of Utopia away from the city litter. We can pitch a tent on a flat rock and quote from letters that poets have written to their loved ones.

Edweena: Tilden, that's a delightful idea! We can blot out all thoughts and talk of nothing. There's no sight as sweet as the scattered clouds above the city.

===

THE VELAR-PALATAL SOUNDS
/k/ AND /g/

In going from the tongue-tip to gum-ridge sounds we are moving from the front to the back of the mouth for articulatory position. The velar-palatal stop sounds are included in this chapter because they share the features of breath stop and, usually, breath plosion with the /t/ and /d/.

/k/ As in *Key, Because,* and *Luck; Quite, Quick,* and *Quart*

/k/ is a voiceless, velar, stop sound. It is produced by raising the back of the tongue to the elevated soft palate so that a firm contact is made between these articulators (see Figure 18–2). In contexts in which the [k] is followed immediately by a vowel, air is impounded at the place of contact and suddenly and completely released when the contact is broken. The sound is then said to be aspirated.

The sound of /k/ has several representations in spelling. The most frequent include *k* as in *key, c* as in *cat, ch* as in *chasm, qu* as in *quick,* and one element of the sound blend (**ks**) represented by the letter *x* as in *fix* and *six.*

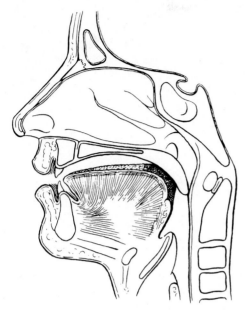

Figure 18–2 Articulatory adjustments for /**k**/ and /**g**/. Note the contact of the back of the tongue with the elevated soft palate.

The /**k**/ sound must be produced with energetic action of the articulators. Persons with normal control of their articulatory organs should find the /**k**/ sound an easy one to make, regardless of contextual position.

Persons with weak palates and those with cleft palate, often even after repair, may have nasal emission when the /**k**/ is produced.

PRACTICE MATERIALS

cape	kale	come	coat
keep	could	came	cough
key	coach	cap	cod
queen	cope	calf	chord
chemical	chorus	character	quash
ken	caught	cool	curb
kit	call	coop	curt
bacon	became	token	minks
beacon	because	blacken	Manx
weaken	recourse	reckon	thanks
bicker	require	booked	attacking
wicked	requite	looking	blocked
checker	enquire	turkey	boxed

ache	stake	rake	fork
beak	stork	lake	forsook
meek	talk	take	mistook
sick	Turk	back	stock
tick	spike	rack	dike
fake	amuck	hook	like
cake	cock	chaotic	kapok

kick	quack	kirk	coke
kink	cook	quirk	comic
quick	cosmic	konk	cork
coca	cockle	cocker	cackle
cockney	coconut	cocoon	cockcrow
conclude	concourse	connect	coccyx
consequence	concave	Quaker	quackery

keen conclusion	Manx cat
keep clam	honking turkey
keen kitten	basket of biscuits
camp cook	murky liquid
calm cow	mocked uncle
queer cat	quick kick
quaint chorus	cock crow
quiz kid	sick calf
call Kate	cook book
six knocks	thank Carl

Blends: [kl] and [kr]

clean	class	clot	climb
cleat	clue	clergy	cloud
click	close	clerk	clown
clip	claw	club	cloister
cleanse	clod	clump	Klondike
clash	clog	clutch	clause

cream	credit	crew	crust	krill
crease	credulous	crude	crouch	krone
creed	crest	crow	crowd	kraut
creek	crane	crawl	crown	krylon
crib	crag	crop	crime	Kriss
crisp	crack	cross	cry	krypton

critical crowd	clean cloth
crusty crown	clumsy clown
crude crystal	clatter and clash
crossed crop	cloistered clergy
Kris Kringle	clever clue
crackle and crunch	clippety clop
creep and crawl	cluttered closet

[ks]

leaks	rocks	makes
peaks	socks	talks
wax	bucks	mosque
attacks	fakes	extra
packs	folks	bakes

leaks in the dikes	picks and packs
lax folks	peaks and rocks
racks of socks	wicks and wax
stacks of sticks	Max and Jack's

In rapid speech or in colloquial speech there is a tendency to omit the [k] in words that are usually spelled with the letters *cc*. For instance, the word *accept* may be pronounced as if it were spelled *assept* [æsɛpt]. Practice with the following material should make you aware of and help you correct any such tendency.

accent	excuse
accept	accident
expose	eccentric
explain	Occident
express	occipital
expert	accessory

exciting expectation	accidental succession
expose the excavation	Occidental accent
acceptable experience	successful vaccination

a. Max would not risk climbing the hill for fear of an accident.
b. Jack's eccentric friend always had excuses for his actions.
c. Jacques' accent was beyond explanation.
d. The excavating team had sufficient experience to find a ready access to the unexposed cave.
e. The hawks alighted on the high peaks.
f. Folks who are lax may fall into cracks.
g. Clara Burks, an architect, presented the specs for the new mosque.
h. The hikers packed extra socks into their packs.
i. Jenks, who lives in Bucks County, has no use for fakes or quacks.

[kt]

Note the frequent *ed* spelling as a past-tense indicator.

acted	pact	cooked
peaked	snacked	hooked
racked	snaked	liked

mocked the pact	smoked and joked
lacked tact	cooked and stoked
whacked and decked	provoked and smacked

a. At his peak, Pluncket could kick or throw the ball wherever he liked.
b. Kathy was piqued because Kevin snacked as she worked.
c. Cranston broke the pact with Krissy when he hooked the cookies.
d. Raskin lacked tact when he whacked and decked Paxton.

[kw]

Most words with the [kw] blend are spelled with *qu* as in *queen, quite*, and *quaint*. Exceptions are words for place names such as *Quito* and *Quezon*, which are pronounced without the blend, and *quiche* and *quay*, which maintain their French pronunciation with [ki]. The Canadian city Quebec is pronounced with the [kw] blend by most English speakers and with a [k] by French Canadians.

In words such as *squash* and *square* we have a triple blend [skw].

PRACTICE MATERIALS

[kw]		[skw]
quad	acquire	squash
quack	acquit	squid
quiet	acquaint	squish
quid	equate	square
quail	equip	squire

a. Quentin had an unquenchable thirst for the juice of well-squeezed kumquats.
b. Quartz is a mineral acquired from silicon dioxide.
c. Squire enjoyed dancing the quadrille and other square dances.
d. A quadrant is a quarter part of a circle.
e. Quito is the captain of Ecuador.

Review of [k] in Various Phonetic Contexts

a. Much to his dislike, Keen had to keep his collie in a kennel.
b. The tick-tock of the clock had a calming effect on Kate.
c. Drake was lachrymose because his crock was empty.
d. Quinn enjoyed skiing in Colorado.
e. Kendall claimed that nothing was as calming as basking in the sun on warm, flat rocks.
f. The schooner carried a cargo of crackers, cookies, and kindred cakes for tykes.
g. Connie liked percolated coffee and scones for breakfast; Kurt elected bacon and eggs.

h. The choir sang quaint songs in the Scottish kirk.

i. Kitson was the captain of the cruiser that carried a cargo of Turkish goods to the Congo.

j. The blackhearted cook was caught in the crowd with his basket of biscuits and a cooked turkey.

a. Themistocles, being asked whether he would rather be Achilles or Homer, said, "Which would you rather be — a conqueror in the Olympic Games, or the crier that proclaims who are the conquerors?"

— Plutarch, *Themistocles*

b. H. L. Mencken, a crotchety journalist whose views were frequently contaminated by prejudice, held that "all successful newspapers are ceaselessly querulous and bellicose."

— *Prejudices, First Series*

c. By the pricking of my thumbs,
Something wicked this way comes.
    Open, locks,
    Whoever knocks!

— William Shakespeare, *Macbeth*, Act IV

d. Harlequin without his mask is known to present a very sober countenance, and was himself, the story goes, the melancholy patient whom the Doctor advised to go and see Harlequin.

— William Makepeace Thackeray, *The English Humorists*

e. I know the Kings of England, and I quote the fights historical,
From Marathon to Waterloo, in order categorical.

— W. S. Gilbert, *The Pirates of Penzance*

f. Edgar A. Robinson described Lincoln as a man uniquely capable of meeting rancor with laconic and cryptic humor.

g. Jack was nimble,
Jack was quick,
Yet came a cropper
Over a candlestick.

Dialogue for /k/

CLARK THE CRITIC

Clark the Critic: I did quite like your quirkish play *Junior's Revenge*. It crackled with crisp comic wit. The unrequited love between the key characters has a nice tragic quality.

Regina the Writer: Thanks, Clark. My agent Jack deserves the credit for the musical chorus and the cosmic conclusion.

Clark the Critic: My only critical comment is that the chaotic plot ran amuck, which weakened the story.

Regina the Writer: We booked the play in Cape Cod so we could quickly work out the kinks before taking it to Broadway.

Clark the Critic: Would it crush you if the crowd were to mock Junior and conclude that the play was a fake?

Regina the Writer: If this college crowd were to attack the play, I could cope.

Clark the Critic: How do you keep cool when your career as a playwright is at stake?

Regina the Writer: I walk down by the creek because it calms me. I try to keep my perspective, but talking like this makes my head ache. Let's walk across town to the lake, where the clean air will clear my mind. You can continue your inquiry and probe my weaknesses while I catch some haddock for dinner.

/g/ As in *Go, Forget, Aghast, Egg,* and *Rogue*

/g/, the voiced cognate of /k/, is a velar, stop sound. It is produced in the same way as the /k/, except that a less vigorous contact is required for the /g/.

/g/ is usually represented by the letter g or the letters gg in spelling; less frequently, it is represented by gh. The sound is also part of the consonant blend represented by the letter x in words such as *examine* and *exact*. The sound may occur initially, medially, or finally as in the [gz] blend for plural and tense endings (the spelling may be the same): *digs, tags.*

PRACTICE MATERIALS

gear	gale	gherkin	gird
geese	gape	goat	girth
gift	gaff	gall	gull
give	gap	gauze	goiter
guilt	ghoul	got	gown
guest	ghetto	guard	guide
meager	vaguely	embargo	beguile
begin	began	regard	disguise
digging	aghast	engulf	misguided
signal	again	laggard	tiger
forget	lagoon	beggar	bogus
regale	regulate	haggard	dugout
league	Hague	rogue	bug
fatigue	plague	morgue	snug
intrigue	vague	hog	shrug
dig	has	log	dug
rig	snag	iceberg	flog
egg	fugue	erg	vogue

[g] Blends: [gl] and [gr]

glean	glad	glob	mingle
glib	gland	glum	single
glisten	glass	glut	haggle
glitter	gloom	glide	tingle
glaze	gloat	glower	tangle
glen	globe	eagle	struggle

greed	grand	grope	grind
green	grass	groan	gripe
grid	grew	grow	egress
grip	groom	gross	angry
grade	group	growl	engrave
grain	groove	ground	ingrate

grape grower	great engraving
grin grimly	growl and gripe
green glade	greasy ground
glitter and glisten	grind grain
angry ingrate	glum glower
glad groom	global struggle
green grass	engrossed group
grim greeting	graph diagram
begrudging growl	grumble and grunt

[gz] in Medial and Final Position (*often as a plural or tense marker—s*)

leagues	nags
legs	togs
rigs	rugs
wigs	begs
rags	snags
lags	flags
lugs	exact
twigs	examine
ergs	example

lugs the rugs	exalted rigs
examined the rags	exert ergs of energy
exact examination	exotic wigs
bags of eggs	grinds and grins

Contrasting /k/ and /g/

There are two elements of contrast in the /k/ and the /g/. The first is the readily apparent element of voice that is present in the /g/ and absent in the /k/. The second is the less obvious aspect of vigor of articulation that characterizes the /k/ more than the /g/.

PRACTICE MATERIALS

cam	gam	pick	pig
cat	gat	rack	rag
kill	gill	hack	hag
cap	gap	peck	peg
coat	goat	tack	tag
coast	ghost	sack	sag
cool	ghoul	buck	bug
cull	gull	tuck	tug
cut	gut	chuck	chug
came	game	stack	stag
crass	grass	krill	grill

coat of goatskin	nagging backache
bagged a buck	pecked at the packed pig
calm ghost	bags on their backs

a. Chuck and Kathy liked to hear the chug-chug of locomotives.
b. The half-empty ragged sack was inclined to sag.
c. An old ghost haunted the Gold Coast.
d. Goatskin makes a crude but warm coat.
e. A tack was used to hang the rag tag on the rack.
f. A gull can cull food along a seacoast.
g. When Buck was tucked into his sleeping bag, he felt as snug as the proverbial bug in the rug.

ADDITIONAL PRACTICE MATERIALS

a. Morgan, a good cook, gained a reputation for his baked goose.
b. Margo, a gourmand, was glad to be married to Morgan.
c. An embargo was placed on the cargo of sugar from Granada.
d. Greta was aghast when, in an unguarded moment, she forgot to stop for a traffic signal.
e. Gordon's luggage had an engraved name tag.
f. Despite his name, Goodfellow was a rogue whose beguiling smile ensnared the misguided.
g. Despite his great hunger, the beggar would eat nothing but frogs legs.

h. The fog lingered on and grounded the planes in Gander and Goose Bay.
i. Peg and Gilda were eager to get to the football game.
j. The gargoyle appeared to have a vague grin.

a. Here Skugg lies snug
   As a bug in a rug.

   —Ben Franklin, *Letter to a Friend*

b. Algernon Charles Swinburne argued that a poet who begins no bigger than a tadpole cannot grow into anything bigger than a frog.

c. The gift of gaiety may itself be the greatest good fortune.

   —Irwin Edman, in *The Bookman*

d. "All that glitters (glisters) is not gold" is a line that most English-speaking boys and girls regard as Shakespeare's. Yet, a bit of digging reveals that the "gold glitter or glisten or glister" theme is repeated in English as well as in non-English literature. Cervantes wrote, "All is not gold that glisters." From Chaucer, in his *Canterbury Tales*, we gather that "but al thyng which that shineth as gold, Nis nat gold." Spenser in his *Faerie Queene* also, with regret, recalled that "gold all is not that doth golden seem."

Dialogue for /g/

THE MAJOR LEAGUE GAME

Grant the Sportscaster: Meg, you're a great slugger! You gripped that bat and hit a ground ball that gave your team the game! Congratulations!

Meg: I just guided that grounder toward the gate and ran myself ragged. I don't mean to be glib, but what a hit.

Grant the Sportscaster: Was it a grueling struggle to achieve your goal of playing in major league baseball? Did the other guys on the team grumble and glower at you in the dugout?

Meg: At first the guys were angry that I had the gall to dig in my heels and grapple with the game. There was a lot of griping, and I got a grim greeting from them. They begrudged me every grand homer I hit and greeted my gaffs with glee. But now they're glad I hung in there and made the grade.

Grant the Sportscaster: How did your intriguing career begin?

Meg: I grew up in the ghetto, where I was grateful for a meager egg for breakfast. I was single-minded and disguised myself as a guy to make Little League. I was so good that when they got a glimpse of me as a girl, they forgot the regulations and let me in the group.

Grant the Sportscaster: What advice would you give a woman who is gifted and eager to grab a little glory in the major leagues?

Meg: Don't let the growling and grunting of the players plague you. Gird up, ignore fatigue, and give it all you've got!

CHAPTER 19

THE TONGUE-TIP FRICATIVES

===

In this and the next chapter we will consider the tongue-tip fricative sounds and the blends of fricative and stop sounds. These sounds are /s/, /z/, /ʃ/ (sh), /ʒ/ (zh), and /tʃ/ and /dʒ/ (j).

/s/ As in *Sea, Asleep, Icy, Best,* and *Less*

The consonant /s/ is a high-frequency, voiceless, tongue-tip fricative that requires careful and precise articulatory action for its production. The adjustments involve the following:

1. The tongue is raised so that the sides are pressed firmly against the inner surfaces of the upper molars.
2. The tongue is slightly grooved along the midline. Air is forced down along this groove.
3. The tip of the tongue is placed about a quarter of an inch behind the upper teeth. The tongue tip is almost in position for a /t/. (Persons not able to attain this adjustment will probably find it easier to place the tongue tip close to the lower gum ridge.)
4. The teeth are brought in line, with a very narrow space between the rows of teeth.
5. The breath stream is directed along the groove of the tongue toward the cutting edges of the teeth.
6. The soft palate is raised to prevent nasal emission of the sound.

Use a mirror to see the articulatory adjustments for the /s/. The recommended articulatory position is represented in Figure 19–1.

In producing the /s/, exercise special care to avoid having the tongue tip touch either the upper teeth or the gum ridge. Neither should you permit the tongue tip to slide down so as to protrude between the rows of teeth. The first articulatory error will result in the production of a [ts] blend or in a lateral sound resembling a voiceless [l]. The second fault will result in the production of an infantile lisp resembling a [θ] (th).

Persons who habitually produce /t/ and /d/ sounds with dental rather than gum-ridge contacts are likely to lower the tongue tip for the production of /s/. The result, in most instances, is the production of a dull, low-pitched sibilant.

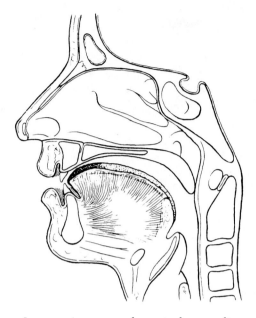

Figure 19–1 Articulatory adjustments for /s/ and /z/. Note that the tip of the tongue is slightly retracted from the upper gum ridge.

In some instances, the articulatory adjustments just described do not help to produce the desired result of a high-frequency, sibilant sound. Occasionally, the person, possibly because of an unusual mouth structure, must make individual adjustments to arrive at the same acoustic end result. With some articulatory adjustments, a low-pitched sound may be the best that the individual can achieve. Most persons, however, regardless of their articulatory mechanism, can learn to produce an /s/ that acoustically resembles the high-pitched fricative just described.

Apart from the manner of articulation, the sound /s/ in American-English speech may present some difficulty for the foreign-born speaker because of the varied spelling representations of the sound. The most frequent representation is the letter s; other representations include ss as in *less,* sc as in *scene,* c as in *race,* and x as in *hoax.* (The letter x in these contexts = the blend [ks].) The foreign-born speaker of English may be forgiven her or his failure to know when to produce the sound /s/ if we realize the many ways in which the letter s may be pronounced. In addition to the /s/, we have /ʒ/ (zh) as in *treasure,* /ʃ/ (sh) as in *sure,* and /z/ as in *his.* To add to the consternation of the foreign-born speaker, we also have the "silent" s as in *island* and *aisle.*

Practice Materials

Because of the frequency of the /s/ in American-English speech, we recommend that a considerable amount of attention be given to this sound. Practice first to produce the sound in isolation until a clear, high-frequency sibilant can be articulated at will. Then, incorporate the sound into nonsense syllables. The advantage of nonsense-syllable practice in the early stages of establishing or correcting a sound lies in the avoidance of habits of articulation that may be faulty. Suggested nonsense-syllable combinations precede the word lists.

seef	sif	sef	saf	sek
sah	sof	soo	sook	sawp
sut	sug	sul	sool	sipe

ahsah	ahsaw	eesaw	aysaw
ohso	ohsoo	ooso	oosoo
eensay	unsaw	akso	amsoo

Initial

see	sew	suck	circuit
seat	soak	seal	cease
say	saw	sale	citric
sane	sought	ceiling	cinch
sin	sog	sigh	scenic
sit	sop	cite	scent
set	song	civil	scepter
sell	sock	cider	science
sat	sir	cigar	scion
sag	certain	cinder	screen
sue	soil	cipher	screw
soot	sun	circle	scratch

Medial

aster	insist	aspect	pursue
asset	insert	lessen	insignia
asleep	boost	essay	tracing
mist	rooster	icy	trousseau
hasten	boast	pressing	bracer
pest	bossy	blessing	hoist
last	twosome	history	peaceful

Final

bless	remiss	peace	rehearse
crease	loops	choice	loss
leaps	loose	voice	dross
miss	dose	terse	hiss
kiss	horse	verse	hex
pace	Norse	curse	fix
race	bus	fuss	tricks
bets	truss	mouse	cheeks
debts	puss	house	plates
pass	worse	dress	waits
caps	hearse	niece	fleets
farce	entice	boss	keeps
nervous	goodness	famous	purpose

[s] Preceded and Followed by a Vowel

deceive	casing	assume	gusset
acetic	assay	twosome	russet
precede	resale	isobar	assign
acid	assemble	isolate	nicety
assimilate	assent	isotope	oscillate
asymmetry	asset	assault	ossify
aseptic	brassy	assort	ascent
essay	glassy	asunder	assail
lacing	messy	assert	asylum
assonant	Bessemer	basic	mason

[s] in Initial, Medial, and/or Final Positions

safe and sane	list of assets	Norse horse
civil suit	peacefully asleep	rehearse the verse
sagging sales	prestigious essay	dress nicely
science series	boastful insignia	acetic acid
soggy soil	passive resistance	terse essay
sad scene	swift pace	sweet syrup

a. Six swift horses started in the historic race at Seaside.
b. Sue, a suave, slim lass, wore a silk scarf and blouse.
c. Simon Sweet fussed about the small, squeaking mouse.
d. Selma insisted that clever verse must be terse but not assonant.
e. Simson had a steady fondness for sweet cider and salted nuts.
f. The storm-tossed sloop sank beneath the spray off Salem Sound.
g. Stevenson was a scientist who liked to be certain of his evidence and facts before making statements about his observations.
h. Stella was enticed by the high ceilings of the house.
i. "Puss in Boots" is a story for small children who like to listen.
j. Some historians say that there is no such thing as a bad peace.

If the /s/ sound cannot be mastered directly, it may help you to begin with a /t/ and to work initially for a [ts] blend. This is especially helpful for persons who have no difficulty with the /t/ but who do have some with the /s/. The following exercises should be useful for this approach.

Additional Practice Materials

cleats	meats	fats	kites
heats	mats	yachts	riots
beats	cats	divots	blunts
bits	hoots	blots	nights

gets	notes	ruts	blights
debts	floats	hurts	weights
hits	thoughts	flights	quoits
fights	lights	nuts	rates

bits of sweets	gets into fights
notes the beats	stunts in flights
hits the lights	heats the meats
ruts and divots	cheats the quoits
nuts and bolts	pats the pets
Pete's pots	studied for tests

a. Betsy's debts were incurred because of high interest rates.
b. Patsy enjoyed lifting weights and flights of fancy.
c. The nets were thrown from the yachts.
d. He who gets into fights must expect hurts.
e. Rivets and nuts and bolts of various weights were used to install the posts.

Dialogue for /s/ (emphasizing ci and ce spellings)

TALKING IN CIRCLES

Lucille: Let's describe life in terms of circles, using simple sentences.

Vincent: That's a cinch. The tents in a circus sit in a circle balancing on cinder blocks.

Lucille: My niece speaks in circles when she tries to be civil.

Vincent: You can race around the ice-skating rink because it is round rather than hexagonal.

Lucille: I'm certain your voice will sound twice as loud in a round room with a high ceiling as it does outdoors.

Vincent: Orange juice is a choice drink made from round citrus fruit.

Lucille: The round band that encircles a cigar costs less than a cent and has a nice tobacco scent.

Vincent: My sister is at the center of her circle of friends, and they surround her like a cement fence.

Lucille: Constance deceives herself that she is well-rounded in the art of romance.

Vincent: I could cite more examples, but let's cease playing this silly game and step into the manse.

Lucille: That's an enticing offer if it includes a nice glass of icy apple cider!

/θ/ (th) and /s/

Some persons must exercise caution not to confuse the voiceless /θ/ (th) with the /s/. The /θ/ is properly produced with the tip of the tongue in contact with the back of the upper teeth or slightly protruded between the teeth (see Figure 17–1, page 280). This contact is to be avoided for the /s/.

═══

PRACTICE MATERIALS

The following pairs of words should help to establish the difference between articulatory positions and acoustic results.

thin	sin	think	sink
theme	seem	thaw	saw
thick	sick	thuds	suds
thank	sank	thought	sought
thigh	sigh	thong	song
thumb	sum	third	surd
thane	sane	thunder	sunder
path	pass	worth	worse
bath	bass	kith	kiss
truth	truce	myth	miss
math	mass	Beth	Bess
faith	face	wraith	race

Make certain that the distinction between the /θ/ and the /s/ is made clear in the following material.

truce with truth	sought a thought
faith saved face	saw the ice thaw
kiss for kith	a sane thane
math for the masses	sang bass in the bath
pass to the path	worse than worthless

a. In counting the sum, the boy used his fingers and his thumb.
b. The thick smoke made us feel sick.
c. The lightning that tore the sky asunder was followed by thunder.
d. Because the cook did not think, he clogged the sink.
e. No thinking person can win a race with a wraith.
f. Though not a sin, it is a thin faith that is limited to saving face.
g. Although Sam did not catch the bass, he enjoyed a bath in the sunny stream.
h. The thane sanely took the path that led over the mountain pass.
i. Bess Ross and Beth Roth are kissing kith and kin.
j. Theodore did not seem to be able to find a theme or think of a thing to say or sing to Thelma.
k. Stewart was wroth with Ross and sought words for the thought to explain his annoyance.
l. Tom Thumb refused to pull out a plum no matter the promised sum.

Frequent [s] Blends and Clusters

Initial [sk]

scheme	scalp	score	sky
skiff	scab	scorch	scare
skin	scan	scorn	scallop
skill	scandal	skirt	scamp
skip	scant	scar	skewer
skit	scatter	Scot	sketch
schedule	school	skull	skeptic
scale	schooner	skunk	squire

Medial [sk]

risking	discount	Alaska	Ruskin
discuss	ensconce	basket	landscape
asking	Muskogee	escape	musket
casket	masked	inscribe	ascorbic

Final [sk]

brisk	whisk	bask	task
disk	desk	flask	tusk
frisk	musk	mask	rusk
bisque	husk	ask	mosque

Initial [st]

steam	stay	sterile	stark
steel	stain	stirrup	start
steep	station	stew	starve
steer	stealth	stole	style
stiff	step	stone	store
still	stem	stove	stork
stick	stigma	stack	stock
sting	stool	stamp	stop
stint	stout	stub	storm
steady	stoop	stunt	story

Medial [st]

Easter	roster	wasteful	basting
feasting	mastiff	coaster	toasted
blister	tasty	costly	castor
master	blasted	frosted	castaway
monster	aster	musty	punster
boasting	oyster	pasted	hoisted

Final [st]

beast	mist	past	host
east	best	roast	cost
least	rest	post	frost

whist	moist	bossed	joist
priest	pest	roost	lost
yeast	guest	just	first
fist	cast	rust	nursed
list	last	toast	oust
kissed	mast	most	Faust

Initial [skr]

scream	script	scrap	scrawl
screech	scrutiny	scramble	scrub
screen	scribble	scroll	scribe
scrivener	scrape	scruple	scrabble
scrimp	scrod	scruff	scrawny

Medial [skr]

discredit	miscreant	descry	unscrew
discreet	proscribe	describe	prescribe
discriminate	discretion	enscribe	inscrutable

Initial [str][1]

streak	strain	straw	strut
stream	strength	strong	stripe
strip	strap	strop	strive
stricken	strew	struck	strident
string	stroke	struggle	striate
stray	stroll	strike	structure

Medial [str]

restrict	instruct	upstream	distrust
construe	restraint	district	distress
constrain	unstrung	destroy	dystrophy
constrict	hamstring	distraught	frustrate
construct	restrengthen	distract	prostrate

Initial [sm]

smear	smack	smart	smug
smithy	smooth	smolder	smudge
smitten	smote	smother	smile
smell	small	smirk	smite
smelter	smock	Smyrna	smirch

Initial [sw]

Sweden	swing	swoon	swan
sweep	sway	swoop	swamp
sweet	sweat	swollen	swallow
swig	swelter	swarm	swine
swim	swear	swirl	swipe
swivel	swag	swap	swindle

[1] Avoid a tendency for the [s] in the [str] blends to approximate or actually to become an [ʃ] (sh).

Initial [sn]

sneak	snap	snare	snatch
sneer	snoop	snort	snipe
sniff	snow	snub	snicker
snip	snob	snuff	snug
snail	snarl	snake	snore

Final [ns]

wince	fence	glance	romance
pence	quince	lance	prance
hence	mince	manse	enhance

Medial [ns]

answer	balancing	instead	punster
dancer	instant	install	bouncing
Frances	instill	ensnare	winsome
Anselm	Dunstan	Winston	density

Initial [sp]

speed	span	spore	spun
speak	sparrow	sparse	spunk
spill	spat	spark	spy
spin	spew	spare	spike
speck	spool	Sparta	spine
spell	spook	spirit	spout
spade	spoof	spur	spoke
Spain	Spode	spurt	spoil
spent	spawn	sponge	spider
spaniel	spinal	sporadic	spiel

Final and Medial [sp]

lisp	crisp	despondent	despoil
asp	grasp	despair	despot
hasp	rasp	desperate	respect
clasp	cusp	aspire	respond
wasp	grasping	despise	respite
wisp	resplendent	bicuspid	perspire

[spl]

split	splendid	splurge	splotch
spleen	splice	splutter	splendor
splay	splint	splash	splat

[spr]

sprain	sprinkle	sprout	sprung	sprag
sprig	sprint	spruce	sprocket	sprat
spread	sprite	spry	sprig	spritz

PRACTICE MATERIAL FOR BLENDS

a. A sponge is the fibrous, porous skeleton of a species of plantlike sea animals.
b. The tasty scallop is a bivalve mollusk.
c. Scones are thin cakes made with masterful skill by the Scots.
d. The squid is a species of ten-armed cephalopods which have an ink sac and an elongated body that, according to its subspecies, varies in length from just four or six inches to sixty feet.
e. Skelton, lean but strong, swung his ax with concentration and skill to split his stack of spruce logs.
f. The Northwest coastal states, unlike those of the East, are sprayed by steady, moist winds called *chinooks*.
g. Stewart Scranton and six stalwart hunters set out to obtain scarce elephant tusks from their secret graves.
h. The swift schooner brought in a surprising catch of sea horses and starfish.
i. Stan Prescott always felt like strutting when he squired his sweet Stella.
j. Professors and other schoolmasters are likely to give scant positive attention to scribbled manuscripts.
k. The old scow was covered with seaweed and scale from stem to stern.
l. A sudden squall upset the skiff in the swift, swirling waters.
m. Spring rains may come in sprinkles or in torrents.
n. The sprite was a fanciful, spry spirit.
o. Smith was smitten the first time he glanced at Cecile in her artist's smock.
p. Sperry was smart, possibly a genius, but his presence did not suggest smugness.
q. Except when he sang bass, Stacy's voice seemed to suggest protestation by its stridency.
r. Scott Snead was famous, or perhaps infamous, for his stentorius snoring.
s. Struggle, if it is not fruitless, helps to make the struggler a strong person.
t. The scribe, a respected senior citizen, scrutinized his efforts and seemed to be satisfied with the results.

[sts] and [sks]

The combinations [sts] and [sks] are somewhat difficult because of the quick and precise tongue action needed in their production. Avoid a tendency to omit the first *s* in these clusters.

PRACTICE MATERIALS

The following word lists, phrases, and sentences should be useful as practice materials.

beasts	pests	boasts	toasts
feasts	rests	coasts	bursts

fists	casts	posts	firsts
lists	lasts	roasts	jousts
pastes	boosts	ghosts	musts
waists	roosts	hosts	rusts

discs	asks	tasks	whisks
risks	basks	husks	flasks
frisks	masks	tusks	casks

roasts for feasts	discs of tusks
musks for hosts	asks for risks
flasks for roasts	unmasks the boasts
lists of tests	hosts for ghosts

a. Stella expressed her regrets that the insect pests spoiled the outdoor feasts for her guests.
b. Two blasts signaled that the jousts were about to begin as tests for the knights.
c. Ghosts do not bother with boasts, nor do they respect toasts.
d. Six gun blasts were fired at the animal pests.
e. Good hosts demonstrate an air of unconcern about costs.
f. Risks must be assumed in many tasks, but risks must be worth the tasks.
g. Large oaken casks were used as tops for desks.
h. Wister beat his fists against the posts to scare the beasts from their roosts.

[skw]

Avoid approximating or substituting an [ʃ] (sh) in [skw] blends. Note the spelling of *squ* in the words:

squab	squamous	squeak	squirm
squad	square	squeal	squire
squalid	squat	squib	squirt
squall	squander	squint	squiggle
squalor	squeamish	squirrel	squaw

Initial [s] and Final [ʃ] (sh)[2]

Be sure to distinguish between the initial [s] and the final [ʃ] in the following words.

sash	squash	swash
smash	swish	squeamish
stash	squish	Swedish
splash	squarish	slash

---

[2] See pages 336–340 for production and practice materials for /ʃ/.

Initial and Final [s]

sacks	status	socks	sequence
sauce	source	slips	smacks
sense	seats	slants	streets
since	souse	spots	sinks
saints	sites	spurts	stunts
sweets	saps	speaks	squeaks
swaps	surfs	spouts	scuffs
sass	stoops	smokes	skirts

ADDITIONAL PRACTICE MATERIALS FOR [s] IN VARIOUS CONTEXTS

a. Genius without a sensible striving for work may be a waste of superior intelligence, at least, so Sylvia insisted.

b. Signs on the highways offer sage advice to passing motorists.

c. Simonson's satire was frequently indistinguishable from his attempts at farce; both efforts were fierce but seldom humorous.

d. Charles Dickens opens his *Tale of Two Cities* with the words: "It was the best of times. It was the worst of times."

e. Susan was pleasant and almost always easy to please. Sam was surly and almost impossible to tease.

f. Unseasonal scarcity of rains as well as inconsistent distributions have resulted in producing America's dust bowls.

g. Stanley observed that disease frequently attracts more attention than a healthy state of affairs, whether it be in persons or in nations.

h. Sooner's sullen silences spoke eloquently for his negativistic status.

i. Jurists are supposed to listen to all aspects of arguments and decide on issues presented to them.

j. The ascending moon cast a silvery light over the serene sea.

a. However erroneous, the assumption that genius is somehow associated with some signs of madness has a long history. Seneca, citing Aristotle, asserted that "there is no great genius without some sign of madness." Dryden, in the seventeenth century, stated, "Great wits are sure to madness near allied." In his preface to *The Man of Genius*, Lombroso, a nineteenth-century philosopher, said, "Good sense travels on the well worn paths; genius, never." And so, according to Lombroso, most of us who consider ourselves sensible persons do not understand the deviancies of genius and consider the superior and outstanding intellects as insane, at best harmlessly insane. Mark Twain, in his essay *Genius*, described the state of genius as "supreme capacity for getting its possessor into trouble of all kinds." Edward Young, in his essay *Night Thoughts*, written in the eighteenth century, may have anticipated and summed up our beliefs in associating genius with insanity in these lines:

Ah, how unjust to Nature and himself
Is thoughtless, thankless, inconsistent man!

b. H. L. Mencken, the so-called sage of Baltimore, enjoyed having people think of him as an acidic and outrageous person. He sometimes earned this right by sentences such as "Philosophy consists very largely of one philosopher arguing that all others are jackasses."

c. The rest to some faint meaning make pretence,
But Shadwell never deviates into sense.

—John Dryden, *Mac Flecknoe*

d. A nap . . . is a brief period of sleep which overtakes superannuated persons when they endeavor to entertain unwelcome visitors or to listen to scientific lectures.

—George Bernard Shaw,
Tragedy of an Elderly Gentleman

e. How *Homo sapiens* arrived at speech is lost in prehistory. Speaking humans speculate about the onset of speech and through speech conjecture and rationalize, and according to their needs, present interests, prejudices, and inclinations. The mystery and beginning of speech may be repeated in the cycle of infant development, but the infant forgets how it acquired speech as soon as it becomes a speaking child. Once again, adults speculate about the onset of speech in children and about their prelingual states of development. This is history, fascinating speculative history, with testimony abstracted from those who speak without telling us how or why. The task of learning to speak is immense. The immensity of the task, fortunately, is unconsciously and unwittingly assumed by the child. Before he or she knows the size or significance of the responsibilities to be assumed, the normal child has accepted and practiced the verbal habits—the ways of speaking—of her or his special culture and thus becomes a transmitter of the verbal habits of those with whom she or he lives. Speech is considered by most linguists a human species-specific function.

—J. E.

Dialogues for Frequent [s] Blends and Clusters

I. RESTAURANT BLUES

Customer: I want to splurge tonight to impress Frances my fiancée.

Waitress: It's not hard to squander a fortune in a costly restaurant like Sparrow's.

Customer: For my first course, I want pasta with steamed clams. Frances will start with your splendid watercress soup.

Waitress: On Sunday, we serve only a spinach salad, which I can sprinkle with bean sprouts.

Customer: Then let's skip right to the second course. I'm squeamish about squid, so I'll settle for scallops broiled on a skewer. Frances has discriminating taste, so bring her a rare skirt steak that is smothered in crisp onions. Don't forget the bread sticks.

Waitress: The best I can do is beef stew or scrambled eggs with squash.

Customer: This restaurant boasts the highest prices in town! We came here to celebrate with a feast, not to eat kitchen scraps!

Waitress: I can serve you a sticky baked Alaska with a thick sweet sauce. If you prefer a sponge cake, we have one left over from Easter.

Customer: I'm no snob, but I could not resist the status of Sparrow's. Now the lack of style in this scandalous place has ruined our celebration.

Waitress: Why don't you just take a brisk, swift stroll on the east side of the street to the Punster. It is a small and respectable place with simple food. Sparrow's is fancier, but at the Punster you won't be swindled. Frances will admire your style.

II. THE SLIPPERY SLOPE

Selma: Stu, your sly and slinky behavior tells me that you'll soon be on a slippery slope to the upstate slammer.

Stuart: Selma, don't be so snappish. Yes, I'm no slouch at deception, though once I was. To be sure, it's not easy to stop being smooth. But, honestly, I'm no longer deceitful and certainly not sly.

Selma: OK, Stu, I won't snap at you if you desist from giving me a snow job. Remember, I'm a social scientist and not a soft-soaper. Smooth is acceptable if you are scrupulously honest. I can accede to an occasional snafu, but not a spellbinding, sickly sweet song and dance. I prefer an honest sputter to a practiced stage performance.

Stuart: Dearest Selma, if you promise to stay by my side, even at the risk of my becoming a stuffed shirt, I'll promise to be stalwart in my unceasing efforts to attain your social and ethical standards. Selma, if you assure me of your support, I will forsake, skirt, and sidestep all asocial tendencies and inclinations in all seductive situations.

Selma: Stu, you have my promise. From this day on, let our dance together be a sign of masterful bliss.

Stuart: I'm ecstatic. May we make it spousal bliss?

====

/z/ As in *Zoo, Cousin, Azalea,* and *Buzz*

Except for the accompanying vocalization of the /z/, the sound is produced like the /s/. /z/ may be described as a lingua-alveolar, voiced fricative. Generally, it is produced with somewhat less tongue-muscle tension than is necessary for the /s/.

The spellings for /z/ are varied and include z as in *zero*, s as in *rose* and *nasal*, and zz as in *buzz*.

Persons who have difficulty with the articulation of the /s/ are also likely to find the /z/ troublesome. Vocalization, however, may conceal some of the acoustic faults that become apparent when an /s/ is not properly produced. If your best /s/ is articulated with the tongue tip behind the lower teeth rather than behind the upper gum ridge, the same adjustment should be made for the production of /z/.

PRACTICE MATERIALS

Initial

zebra	zest	zircon	zeal
zee	zephyr	Zouave	Zeno
Zeeland	Zachary	Zurich	zone
zinc	zoo	zither	zip
zinnia	Zeus	zyme	zoology
zany	zoom	zealous	zounds
zenith	zodiac	Zion	zygote

Medial

teasing	spasm	designate	design
pleasing	plasma	nozzle	desire
blizzard	music	cousin	enzyme
lazy	using	dozen	raising
daisy	dozing	used	noisy
pleasant	causing	desert	reason
resin	buzzer	deserve	appeasing
hazard	poser	preserve	resign

Final

ease	whose	because	toys
please	choose	repose	annoys
tease	doze	crows	boys
his	woes	yearns	ties
fizz	hose	spurns	replies
raise	grows	burns	dyes
maize	goads	buzz	rhymes
days	claws	eaves	wise
has	flaws	cows	surmise
lads	calls	browse	symbols

Morphemic /z/

A morpheme, we recall, is a minimal unit of meaning in a language. A morpheme may be a single word or a part of a word. *Buds* is a two-morpheme word: *bud* plus *s* to indicate plural.

The list for the final /z/ included several examples is which the sound had morphemic significance as a plural marker and/or as an indicator of grammatical tense. These examples include the words *claws, calls,* and *toys.* In the following words the final *s*, pronounced /z/, is part of a separate, final syllable. Many of the words may serve either as nouns or verbs.

PRACTICE MATERIALS

aces	doses	exposures	lunches
bunches	dozes	hunches	plunges
buzzes	eases	hunters	raises
chooses	entices	inducers	reposes
advises	bridges	praises	splices
masters	plunders	plasters	stencils

a. Zebras are pony-sized striped mammals, native to the plains of Africa, which can be found in most zoos.
b. The museum was open eight hours a day in all seasons.
c. Zoë wisely dozed off when others fell victim to their desires and yearnings.
d. Symbols are human beings' way of preserving and communicating the values, dreams, and ideas of their cultures.
e. Zachary was not able to afford diamonds and so presented zircons to his best girls.
f. Snows make the mountains near Zurich ever-pleasant views to beholders.
g. The Mormons converted thousands of acres of Utah deserts into green pastures and farming lands.
h. Girls and boys soon learn that some words can tease and others can please or appease.
i. Zinnias bloom late in the summer season, but daisies are early flowers.
j. The blizzard caused the travelers hours of delay in their journeys.
k. Zymes are disease germs that cause zymotic diseases.
l. Maize grows in many farms and fields throughout our lands.

[dz]

Persons who have difficulty with the articulatory position for /z/ might find it helpful to begin with /d/ and to "move" from /d/ to /z/. Be sure that you start with a tongue-tip to gum-ridge contact for the /d/ and then retract the tongue tip slightly for the /z/. Practice with the following.

Additional [z] Blends

Many of the words of the practice lists for medial and final /z/ contain blends of /z/ with a preceding [m], [b], [v], [n], [l], or [d]. The word lists and materials that follow feature these combinations.

PRACTICE MATERIALS

[dz]

adds	fads	fades	woods
weeds	cads	chords	cards
beads	lads	fords	rods
lids	moods	hoards	brides
bids	foods	birds	chides
maids	toads	herds	tides
raids	loads	builds	grounds
brads	seeds	reads	cords

Final [mz]

beams	gems	brooms	alms
creams	frames	combs	clams
reams	names	domes	charms
teams	crams	homes	harms
rims	lambs	storms	qualms
whims	booms	forms	alarms
hems	tombs	norms	farms
stems	chums	climbs	germs
clams	crumbs	chimes	firms
hams	numbs	dimes	terms

Final [bz]

Thebes	webs	dabs	tubes
cribs	ebbs	stabs	absorbs
fibs	jabs	tabs	cobs
nibs	cabs	cubes	nobs
robes	fobs	lobs	probes
swabs	jobs	nubs	herbs

Final [vz]

believes	delves	wharves	shoves
deceives	shelves	carves	drives
eaves	elves	starves	hives
thieves	calves	curves	knives
gives	halves	nerves	strives
lives	grooves	serves	thrives

braves	moves	swerves	wives
knaves	proves	doves	leaves
staves	roves	gloves	weaves
waves	stoves	loves	saves

Final [nz]

beans	stains	ruins	darns
screens	remains	fawns	burns
bins	dens	mourns	turns
fins	glens	dawns	spurns
grins	bans	groans	guns
brains	clans	owns	runs
trains	loons	stones	tons
lanes	boons	barns	gowns
refrains	tunes	earns	clowns
mines	signs	coins	joins

Final [lz]

deals	gales	coals	boils
keels	jails	coles	coils
wheels	nails	foals	spoils
hills	bales	moles	tiles
tills	duels	goals	miles
frills	fools	falls	wiles
mills	spools	appalls	jowls
stills	tools	stalls	cowls
gills	pulls	lolls	towels
wills	bulls	hobbles	owls

Final [dz] (*additional words*)

heeds	heads	goads	reminds
bleeds	weds	loads	herds
reeds	dads	frauds	curds
deeds	lads	swords	words
weeds	goods	towards	abides
bids	hoods	hods	hides
rids	foods	nods	glides
aids	moods	pods	abounds
fades	broods	floods	hounds
wades	intrudes	buds	rounds

a. Jones had qualms about touching coins because they might be covered with germs, but his phobias did not include bills.

b. Ben's wife believed that homes are kept clean by new brooms and zealous sweepings by husbands who take turns with wives.

c. Zale, a business executive, ordered frames for his wife's glasses that were encrusted with diamonds and other gems.

d. Zach Grimes had whims that resulted in his telling many zany fibs.
e. Hundreds of corncobs were stored in cribs on farms.
f. The thieves wore gloves when they stole the wares from the wharves.
g. Human brains are able to deal with symbols and signs.
h. The young of horses and asses are called foals.
i. Trains still carry goods to and from farms, as do planes and buses.
j. The storm's fury left many of the town's homes in ruins.
k. Sandra's dreams always were to write her country's refrains.
l. Ted's moods led him to take long walks down country lanes, and he seldom used roads or bypasses.

/z/ and /s/

Some persons with foreign-language backgrounds may have difficulty in distinguishing between /z/ and /s/ and substitute a sound in their first language that is close to it. Hispanics and Scandinavians may substitute an /s/; Germans may produce a [ts] blend for the [z]. If the element of voicing is not distinctive, then both phonetic and semantic differences (contrasts) in word pairs such as *zoo* and *sue, raise* and *race* should help, as in the materials that follow.

PRACTICE MATERIALS

Practice with the word pairs, phrases, and sentences that follow to make certain that the /z/ is clearly voiced and that the /s/ is voiceless.

zee	see	lose	loose
zeal	seal	prize	price
zip	sip	doze	dose
zinc	sink	pads	pats
zoo	sue	sends	cents
zone	sown	bids	bits
peas	peace	codes	coats
rays	race	kids	kits
maize	mace	beds	bets
his	hiss	knees	niece
pays	pace	fuss	fuzz
bays	base	rise	rice

lose what is loose   sown in a zone
price of the prize   sip with zip
kits for kids   a dose to doze
notes of nodes   bids for bits
plays first base   prize for a price

a. A seal eats fish with considerable zeal.
b. The bids ran high for the bits of gems.
c. The prize was won at a sizable price.
d. Selma and Zelda went to see the Zuyder Zee.
e. Zinc was used to line the rusty sink.
f. Cousin Sue enjoyed her trip to the zoo and the close-by Towns Museum.
g. The lost codes were found in the pockets of the coats.
h. The maize was pounded with a mace.
i. Grace and her husband, Zeke, disliked seeing their cattle graze in rented fields.
j. The racer was given a razor as a prize, though he preferred bronze coins.
k. Simpson, although not a psychologist, astutely observed that the things persons say to themselves constitute the basis for deciding what they will say to those who supposedly are listening to them.
l. When Susan sighed, there was little need to explain her sighs by spoken words.
m. Sylvia was statuesque and stately, and yet blissfully unconscious of these signal attributes.
n. The twins insisted that all the tales to which they listened be twice-told tales.
o. The American Psychological Association includes a division called the Society for the Psychological Study of Social Issues.

a. In his *Unsocial Socialist*, George Bernard Shaw argued that "a day's work is a day's work, neither more nor less, and the man who does it needs a day's sustenance, a night's repose, and due leisure whether he be a painter or a ploughman."
b. *Sneer words* are defined by William Safire, a columnist for *The New York Times*, as "adjectives that put some distance between the speaker and the subject by saying 'I'm using the next word under protest.'" Safire gives several examples of sneer words, such as *self-proclaimed, self-styled,* and the much-used *so-called*. It seems that feelings of displeasure and disdain now have their own punctuation, mostly featuring the use of hyphenated words and quotation marks.
c. There are some societies in which sloth is considered amongst the deadliest of sins; in others, sloth, in the guise of indolence, is considered a symbol of status and affluence.
d. Most sociologists assess social class on the basis of a person's years of education, his or her vocation or profession, and his or her place of residence.
e. The cosmologist Rees has observed that the absence of evidence does not constitute evidence of absence.
f. The world is still engaged in a massive armaments race designed to insure continuing equivalent strength among potential adversaries. We pledge perseverance and wisdom in our efforts to limit the world's armaments to those necessary for each nation's own domestic safety, and we will move

this year a step toward our ultimate goal—the elimination of all nuclear weapons from this earth.

—President Jimmy Carter, Inaugural Address, 1977

g. We never know how high we are
Till we are called to rise
And then, if we are true to plan
Our statures touch the skies.

—Emily Dickinson, *No. 1176*

h. There is a silence where hath been no sound,
There is a silence where no sound may be,
In the cold grave—under the deep, deep sea,
Or in wide desert where no life is found,
Which hath been mute, and still must sleep profound.

—Thomas Hood, *Silence*

i. Terms ill defined, and forms misunderstood,
And customs, where their reasons are unknown,
Have stirred up many zealous souls
To fight against imaginary giants.

—Martin F. Tupper, *Of Tolerance*

j. Good laws lead to the making of better ones; bad ones bring about worse. As soon as any man says of the affairs of the State, "What does it matter to me?" the State may be given up for lost.

—Jean Jacques Rousseau, *The Social Contract*

k. In this best of all possible worlds, the Baron's castle was the most magnificent of castles, and his lady the best of all possible Baronesses.

—Voltaire, *Candide*

l. It is indeed a desirable thing to be well descended, but the glory belongs to our ancestors.

—Plutarch, *Of the Training of Children*

m. Of all the causes which conspire to blind
Man's erring judgment, and misguide the mind,
What the weak head with strongest bias rules,
Is pride, the never-failing vice of fools.

—Alexander Pope, *An Essay on Criticism*

n. At least a quarter of a century ago, the British scientist Launcelot Hogben wrote an essay suggesting choices and procedures for intrastellar communication. The essay, "Astroglossa or First Steps in Celestial Syntax," proposes that signals—the units of the language, or glossa—be based on concepts of numbers. This suggestion derives from the assumption that numerals are the most universal of all symbols. So humans who wish to establish intrastellar correspondence must do so through numerals, serving as signals, with these properties: (1) by sequence or order, the signals become symbols; (2) by rules of usage, the signals constitute a snytax.

o. While running for the presidency of these United States, Adlai Stevenson advised his San Francisco listeners that wise persons do not try to hurry history.

p. "Hope" is the thing with feathers
   That perches in the soul —
   And sings the tune without the words —
   And never stops — at all —

— Emily Dickinson, No. 256

q. There has never been time or season
   When Stephens could aspire to reason;
   Reason to him was cerebral treason:
       A state of mind;
       Esoteric, unkind;
   To which his perceptions
       Were stoically blind.

— J. E., Retrospective Appreciation

SILLY SUE AT THE ZOO

Zane: I took Sue to the zoo today. I was afraid I would lose her if I let her run loose.

Melissa: The zoo is so much fun! Just to stand and gaze at the prize gorillas is worth the price of admission.

Zane: First, I took Suzie to see the zebras. The mother zebra fends off threats to her young by keeping them away from the fence. The babies just zip around and sip water all day, gazing at the spectators.

Melissa: Did Sue burst out laughing when she saw the birds with the bizarre feathers?

Zane: Your niece fell to her knees and tried to squeeze an ostrich! I raised her to her feet, and we raced over to the seals before the zookeeper had us arrested.

Melissa: When you take Sue to a place like the zoo, she plays hard.

Zane: Sue fed the seals with lots of zeal because it was illegal.

Melissa: The only thing that will faze Suzie is coming face to face with a tiger. She's scared he will lose his temper and hiss at her. Zane, Suzie is fast asleep now, so we can eat our steak and peas in peace.

Zane: After a dose of your crazed niece on Sunday, all I want to do is doze until Tuesday! I'll freeze the steak and peas and save them for Wednesday or Thursday. Tonight let's have steamed clams surrounded by a dozen other seafood goodies. That's my antidote for Sue.

CHAPTER 20

THE POST-ALVEOLAR SOUNDS

The post-alveolar sounds are /ʃ/ (**sh**) and /ʒ/ (**zh**) and the affricate blends /tʃ/ (**ch**) and /dʒ/ (**j**). All of these phonemes have a fricative quality (second component of the blends) and are produced with an initial tongue-tip position for a stop sound, immediately followed by a fricative component with the tongue tip contracted a fraction of an inch behind the gum ridge.

/ʃ/ As in *She*, *Ashore*, and *Mash*

We will begin with the phoneme /ʃ/. With the sound /s/ as a basis for comparison, the near-to-/s/ sound /ʃ/ should be easy to master. The /ʃ/ is produced with the tongue retracted, the groove wider, and the tongue as a whole broader than for the /s/. The stream of breath is forced through the groove of the tongue and emitted between the rows of teeth. The /ʃ/ is usually produced with slight lip rounding. Acoustically, the /ʃ/ is lower in pitch than the /s/. Phonetically, the /ʃ/ is described as a voiceless, orally emitted, blade-tongue, post-alveolar fricative sound, as shown in Figure 20–1.

The sound /ʃ/ is represented by several spellings in English. The most frequent are the letters *sh* as in *she*, *ship*, and *shy*. Other frequent spellings include *ti* as in *nation*, *ration*, *patient*; *si* as in *pension*, *tension*; *ci* as in *precious*, *delicious*; *ch* as in *machine*, *chef*; and *s* as in *sure*. We also have *c* as in *ocean* and *ss* as in *passion*.

For some persons with foreign-language backgrounds and for others who may have high-frequency hearing losses, the similarities in spelling and in manner of articulation may cause confusion between the /ʃ/ and the /s/. Emphasis on lip rounding and on the more retracted and relatively larger-grooved tongue for the /ʃ/should help to contrast it with and distinguish it from the /s/.

PRACTICE MATERIALS

Practice before a mirror with the word pairs that follow should be helpful.

she	sea	shoe	sue
sheik	seek	shoot	suit

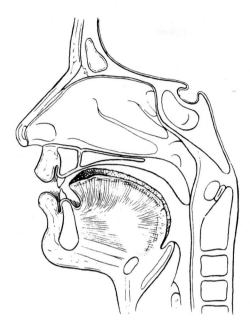

Figure 20-1 Articulatory adjustments for /ʃ/ (**sh**) and /ʒ/ (**zh**). Note that the tongue tip is retracted more than it is for /s/ and /z/. Compare with Figure 19-1 (page 315).

sheep	seep	show	sew
shield	sealed	shawl	Saul
ship	sip	shore	sore
shin	sin	shop	sop
shay	say	shot	sot
shake	sake	shock	sock
shad	sad	shy	sigh
shall	sal	shed	said
brash	brass	gash	gas
clash	class	plush	plus
mesh	mess	rushed	rust
leash	lease	fashion	fasten
mash	mass	crash	crass

Maintain the difference between the /ʃ/ and /s/ in the following phrases and sentences.

Shad looked sad	clash in class
a sealed shield	she went to see
shipped to be sipped	no shoe for Sue

a. Sue held that it was no longer in fashion to use buttons to fasten shoes or shirts.
b. The brass instruments clashed with a sound that was brash.
c. The mess of mash was shipped by sea.

d. Sam enjoyed steamed shad that he bought in a shop near the seashore.
e. Was it Celia or Sheilagh who sold sea shells along the Bayshore near Ocean Shores?

ADDITIONAL PRACTICE MATERIALS FOR /ʃ/

she	shoe	shirt	shriek
sheen	shoot	shirk	shrimp
ship	should	shut	shred
shin	shook	shun	shrewd
shay	shone	shout	shrub
shame	show	shower	shrine
shell	shawl	shine	shroud
shed	shore	shy	shrank
shall	shop	sugar	shrink
shaggy	shock	shark	shrug
leashing	lashes	pressure	fission
wishing	passion	quashed	hushing
ashamed	fashion	machine	Flushing
glacier	pushing	pension	national
nation	cushion	delicious	fractious
patient	lotion	conscience	crashed
precious	ocean	anxious	rushing
dashes	caution	mission	washed
leash	hash	hush	Danish
wish	crash	harsh	blemish
fish	bush	marsh	English
dish	push	rush	garnish
mesh	burnish	tarnish	Flemish
flesh	furnish	varnish	brandish
flash	punish	Amish	gnash
cash	blush	vanish	lush

flush with cash	Danish dishes
shrank in shame	passion for fashion
ship to shore	shocking crash
burnished dishes	showered good wishes
shouted impatiently	Flemish shrine
shunned the shay	tarnished machine
motion of the ocean	delicious portion

a. Ocean fishing furnishes a livelihood for many British fishermen.
b. The shaggy Prussian brandished his tarnished sword.

c. Hamlet had an anxious and disturbed conscience blemished by indecision.

d. Shaw was not ashamed to be fractious, snappish, or querulous, but was seldom perverse.

e. The chef earned a pension for his well-garnished dishes aesthetically served to society.

f. "Pshaw," said Sheila, as she shrugged her shoulders and added two portions of sugar to her milk shake.

g. The motion of the ship on the ocean made a patient of the man from South Flushing.

h. A flash flood transformed the shrubless field into a marsh suited for the birds.

i. Some nations have a passion for peace; others seem to have a passion for aggression.

j. Ship-to-shore communication is available for most of our nation and those overseas.

k. Do you anticipate a clash among the boys in the class?

l. Sam Sherman shunned the sun even when smeared with squash sun lotion.

a. I think that, as life is action and passion, it is required of a man that he should share the passion and action of his time at peril of being judged not to have lived.
> —Justice Oliver Wendell Holmes, Memorial Day Address, 1884

b. For he might have been a Roosian,
A French, or Turk, or Proosian,
Or perhaps Itali-an!
But in spite of all temptations
To belong to other nations
He remains an Englishman!
> —W. S. Gilbert, *H. M. S. Pinafore*

c. Friendship is a sheltering tree;
Oh the joys that came down shower-like,
Of friendship, love, and liberty, . . .
> —Samuel Taylor Coleridge, *Youth and Age*

d. Daniel Shays was a captain of the militia during our Revolution against the British. Later, during the period of the Confederation and in a time of financial depression, Shays led an armed insurrection against the Massachusetts government. The insurrectionists were made up substantially of farmers. They protested that the salaries of public officials were too high. In addition, they petitioned against the imposition of high taxes. Shay's petitions, protestations, general dissensions, and finally his insurrection are believed to have hastened the ratification of the Federal Constitution by Massachusetts.

e. They shall beat their swords into plowshares, and their spears into pruning hooks; nation shall not lift up sword against nation, neither shall they learn war any more.
> —Isaiah 2:4

Dialogue for /ʃ/ (emphasizing contrast between /ʃ/ and /s/)

SHIP TO SHORE

Sheila the Salesperson: That's no shoe for an ocean voyage, Sue. The plush in-soles are a plus, and many women have rushed in to buy the rust-colored pair. But there is no rubber sole to cushion your step and take the pressure off your shins. It would be a shame if your feet got sore the minute you stepped ashore to go sight-seeing.

Sue: The open mesh toe would be a mess the first time I was caught in a harsh rain shower. Still I want a shoe with some flash to wear to sip champagne with the ship's captain.

Sheila the Salesperson: Why don't you buy this pretty silk shirt? You can hand-wash it and it won't shrink. It's all the fashion to fasten your blouse with tarnished buttons made of brass.

Sue: Sheila, you know I have a passion for shiny silks, especially if they show up my shoulders. But I'm not flush with cash and I still have to buy a warm shawl from Mr. Saul, just down the street. I wish that you could show me how to sew.

Sheila the Salesperson: Sue, if I showed you how to sew, I would be short on sales. Suppose I sell you the silk blouse at a discount. You would then save enough to buy this swanky swimsuit. It's modest enough for a shy suitor who tends to be on the serious side.

Sue: Sheila, you're a savvy salesperson. It's a swift sale. But be sure our settlements include the discounts.

/ʒ/ (zh) As in *Azure, Treasure, Rouge,* and *Decision*

The sound /ʒ/ (zh) is a voiced, post-alveolar fricative. It is produced in the same way as the /ʃ/, with accompanying vocal fold vibration.

/ʒ/ occurs medially or finally in English words. The most frequent spellings for this sound are *z* as in *seizure, s* as in *treasure, si* as in *vision,* and *ge* as in *rouge.* The word *genre,* of French derivation, begins with [ʒ] as does the name Jacques.

PRACTICE MATERIALS

azure	intrusion	vision	persuasion
casual	measure	regime	incision
confusion	pleasure	glazier	derision
contusion	seizure	delusion	precision
decision	treasure	implosion	exposure
explosion	usual	erosion	illusion
conclusion	version	lesion	occasion
beige	corsage	garage	persiflage
camouflage	entourage	ménage	rouge

usual confusion	adhesion from a lesion
azure illusion	measure of pleasure
casual decision	seizure of a treasure
occasion for persuasion	visual delusion
sabotaged by abrasion	precision measurement

a. The Eurasian found nothing more pleasurable than an azure sky.

b. The collision was a result of one driver's poor vision and another's unusual decision.

c. The physician had to make an incision to cut through the adhesion.

d. A mirage is a visual delusion causing mental confusion.

e. Because Borgia was given to persiflage, his decisions always seemed unusually casual.

f. The invasion by an infantry division was preceded by an explosion of the camouflaged airfield.

g. The glazier won prestige by the precision of her work.

h. Confusion resulted in numerous contusions among members of the treasure-hunting entourage.

i. The intrusion of the police prevented the seizure of the gold.

j. Persuasion brought about legislation to prevent soil erosion.

a. He weaves, and is clothed with derision;
   Sows, and he shall not reap;

His life is a watch or a vision
   Between a sleep and a sleep.

— Algernon Charles Swinburne,
Atalanta in Calydon

b. Rich the treasure,
   Sweet the pleasure,
   Sweet is pleasure after pain.

— John Dryden, *Alexander's Feast*

c. Frazier, an expert glazier, was given to visual illusions and to occasional delusions. Unfortunately, he also acted in the light of these visionary aberrations. Frazier's demise was a result of this inclination. On the final and fatal occasion, Frazier was confronted with an escaped tiger that had hidden in his garage. Because of a visual illusion, Frazier insisted that the tiger was his cat, *Felis domestica*, a member of his own ménage. In the light of this decision, he began to pat the animal. The beast, not sharing the illusion and having no delusions about itself as a domestic treasure, attacked and devoured Frazier. The job was done with dispatch and precision. Thus, poor Frazier was consumed, a victim of a visual illusion and of delusionary behavior. Frazier was a culinary pleasure but no measure for this member of the genre *Panthera tigris*.

d. When a man's busy, why, leisure
   Strikes him as wonderful pleasure:

'Faith, and at leisure once is he?
Straightway he wants to be busy.

—Robert Browning, *The Glove*

e. Coleridge, a visionary poet, on frequent occasions welcomed illusions. He wrote of pleasure domes and of rivers that casually wound their way "through caverns measureless to man."

THE MEASURE OF A MAN

Woman: It's unusual to find you in this much confusion over the measure of a man.

Woman Friend: I treasure the pleasure of John's company and enjoy gazing into his azure eyes. But on occasion, his version of the truth does camouflage reality.

Woman: You mean that his persiflage is filled with casual lies.

Woman Friend: His vision is clouded with delusions of his own worth. He demands that we travel with an entourage to establish his prestige. If I suggest that his friends are an intrusion, I invite derision. No form of persuasion will change him.

Woman: It sounds to me as if you've already come to a conclusion and made a decision.

Woman Friend: The more exposure I have to John, the greater is my disillusionment. The goodness I see reflected in his azure eyes is merely a mirage. I have come to a decision, and no new version or persuasion will change my vision or alter my conclusion.

/tʃ/ (ch) As in *Chest, Orchard,* and *Hatch*

The sound /tʃ/ (ch) is a blend of /t/ and an immediately following /ʃ/ (sh). It may occur initially, medially, or finally. The blend, a combination of a stop and a voiceless fricative sound, is classified phonetically as an *affricate*. This voiceless affricate is regularly represented by the letters *ch* in spelling.

   The sound may be troublesome for speakers for whom English is not a first language and in whose native language the /tʃ/ does not occur. For example, it may be troublesome to native French speakers because it does not occur in French. For such persons, the most frequent tendency is to substitute the second element, [ʃ], for the blend /tʃ/.

PRACTICE MATERIALS

The exercises that follow should be of help in differentiating between /tʃ/ and /ʃ/.

cheer	sheer	hatch	hash
cheat	sheet	latch	lash
choose	shoes	march	marsh
chairs	shares	match	mash

chin	shin	much	mush
catch	cash	witch	wish
crutch	crush	watching	washing
ditch	dish	catching	cashing
leech	leash	hutch	hush
batch	bash	charred	shard

too much mush   choose new shoes
shares the chairs   wish of a witch
march in the marsh   slashed chin and shin
chores at the shores   cash for the catch

a. Chip by chip, while singing chanteys, the unshaven sailors removed the charred paint from the ship.
b. Fido, a shaggy dog, liked to chew on an old shoe.
c. The sheik had a scar on his cheek.
d. On chosen occasions, it may be pleasant to share a chair.
e. Cheryl, a chanteuse, bruised her chin and her shin.
f. Charles insisted that one spoonful of mush is much too much.
g. The cheerless marine went on a march through the marsh.
h. Lady Macbeth hoped that the witch would help her realize her cherished wish.
i. After a tennis match, Chuck almost always chose a dish of pistachio ice cream with a large portion of mashed cherries.
j. The fishermen went ashore with a good fish catch they sold for spot cash.

ADDITIONAL PRACTICE MATERIALS FOR /tʃ/

cheese	chance	churn	chore
chief	chant	chug	change
chill	chewed	chum	Charles
chimp	choose	chunk	chirp
chain	choke	chowder	choice
chafe	chose	chide	chat
check	chalk	China	chicken
chess	chuck	chive	chin
channel	chop	chime	Chester
champ	char	child	chap
reaching	brooches	marching	bachelor
beeches	broaching	urchin	batches
pitcher	coached	birches	paunches
kitchen	encroaching	lurching	parched
exchange	orchard	searching	righteous

hatchet	launched	bunched	preaching
each	match	staunch	couch
teach	dispatch	porch	slouch
speech	blotch	scorch	pouch
ditch	watch	torch	touch
witch	pooch	lurch	clutch
fetch	encroach	birch	such
wrench	coach	bunch	research
detach	reproach	hunch	squelch

pitcher of punch	teaching and research
charred chops	staunch bachelor
righteous preaching	watchful pooch
squelching speech	enriching change
branches of birch	churning in the channel
chess champion	unlatched the kitchen

a. Charles was taught by those he coached to observe the difference between teaching and preaching.

b. After searching in the orchard, Chester found the chart under the beech tree.

c. Chuck liked cheese and chives as well as chutney with his sandwiches.

d. Research results need to be checked so that conclusions will be beyond reproach.

e. The child was chided for chewing her chocolate-colored chalk.

f. Chambers had a hunch that the peaches in his orchard needed watching because of poachers.

g. In a close match, the Chilean champion, after a checkmate, won the chess contest.

h. Some choose to eat their steak charred, but Charles and Charity chose marinated chunks.

i. Birches are a climbing challenge for many children.

j. Chilton was partial to choice, slightly scorched chops.

a. When I was a child, I spake as a child, I understood as a child, I thought as a child, but when I became a man, I put away childish things.
$$\text{— 1 Corinthians 13:11}$$

b. In his essay, *Time and Change: The Gospel of Nature*, John Burroughs stated, "Nature teaches more than she preaches."

c. I'm not a chicken, I have seen
Full many a chill September.
$$\text{— Oliver Wendell Holmes, } \textit{The September Gale}$$

d. Said Chester to Chase,
"You chew as you race;
Though chewing's a chore,
A choice chop's not a bore."
Said Chase to friend Chester,
"As a child it was best, sir,

To chomp as I'm able
Or I'd have no choice at the table."

—J. E., *The Race Is to the Quick*

THE STAUNCH BACHELOR

Rachel: Why does a charming chap like yourself remain a staunch bachelor?

Charles: I choose to remain unattached because I am my own perfect match. There's too much mush written about the richness of marriage. I don't need someone to choose my shoes or chide me when I grow a paunch. I don't want to see my hutch filled with bone china or be reproached for the way I chugalug a pitcher of beer.

Rachel: How do you stay free of those who would latch onto you? Your cash makes you a good catch.

Charles: I check my dates carefully and watch out for fortune hunters.

Rachel: Do you know that most of the men I've researched sit in a chair and watch TV on Sunday rather than share the chores with their wives?

Charles: Exchanging chitchat with the wife while watching the washing machine choke on batches of dirty laundry is not my idea of an enriching afternoon.

Rachel: Would a woman's touch in the kitchen encroach on your lifestyle?

Charles: I can chop a bunch of chuck meat and turn it into cheeseburgers myself. I can also charbroil chops, and my chilled cucumber chowder achieves perfection.

Rachel: Is there a chance that a fetching wench can change your single status?

Charles: Rachel, not much chance. Why is it that righteous people like you are always preaching about choice, then chastise me because I choose to be alone?

═══

/dʒ/ (j) As in *Age, Adjust,* and *Budge*

/dʒ/ (j) is the voiced cognate of /tʃ/. This voiced sound blend may occur initially, medially, or finally. In *judge* and *George*, it occurs both initially and finally. In *agent* and *engine*, the affricate /dʒ/ occurs medially. The most frequent spellings for /dʒ/ are *g, j,* and *dg*, as in *wage, jam,* and *ridge*.

Many American and English speakers tend to unvoice /dʒ/ when the blend occurs in final positions. French, Spanish, and German speakers may have difficulty with the voiced affricate because the sound does not occur in their native languages.

Those who have difficulty in deciding whether a given word calls for /dʒ/ or /tʃ/ should be helped by the relative frequency of the *ch* spelling for the unvoiced sound and the inclusion of the letter *j* or *g* for the voiced affricate.

═══

PRACTICE MATERIALS

The purpose of the first set of exercise material is to establish the distinction between the two affricates.

| gin | chin | jigger | chigger |

jar	char	jug	chug
jeer	cheer	bridges	screeches
jest	chest	badge	batch
jump	chump	ridge	rich
jeep	cheap	surge	search
joke	choke	liege	leech
Jane	chain	singe	cinch
Madge	match	purge	perch

chug of the jug	chump to jump
batch of badges	a match for Madge
jeers not cheers	change of range
chili for Jill	lunge for lunch
etched edges	jumped the ridge
ridged rich	charming Jane

a. The region was rich in majestic visions.
b. Charles and Marge marched over the bridge.
c. Jim found a batch of badges in the gem-studded chest.
d. The orange-painted carriage carried Jim and Jane to their marriage.
e. Gene's dog, Jigger, was full of itches because he had been a host to chiggers.
f. The judge would not budge from his injudicious judgments.

=====

ADDITIONAL PRACTICE MATERIALS

jeans	jewel	germ	junior
jib	June	jar	jury
giraffe	judicial	journey	just
Gipsy	joke	jowl	jute
jig	jovial	jug	jade
jail	Jonah	jump	jilt
jay	jaunt	giant	general
jet	jaw	jibe	germane
gem	job	joint	genius
jack	jog	join	gentle

besieged	agent	adjust	larger
regent	changed	adjourn	margin
imagine	ranging	surgeon	region

regenerate	major	urgent	disjoint
hedging	stranger	merger	enjoin
wedged	ajar	legion	lounging
ledger	rajah	soldier	gouging
badger	plunged	budget	rejoin
liege	huge	nudge	sponge
siege	sledge	grudge	bilge
ridge	forge	oblige	discharge
bridge	engorge	gouge	dirge
rage	barge	singe	grange
stage	large	fringe	strange
edge	urge	surge	derange
pledge	merge	emerge	average
carriage	bulge	orange	peerage
marriage	fudge	revenge	steerage

besieged agent   marriage merger
huge sledge   gentle genius
just jurist   large stranger
plunged over the ridge   avenged a grudge
jibes and jeers   enraged rajah
hedge on the ridge   ledger for a budget
major pledge   adjustment agent
giant merger   jailed jester

a. After landing on the ridge, a legion of soldiers was discharged from the giant jet planes.
b. Janice Jones, an imaginative lawyer, jovially engaged the judge and with germane arguments, urged both judge and jury to be judicious.
c. Dr. James, a diligent surgeon, adjusted Joe's disarranged jaw.
d. Jonah had a strange journey in a giant whale which, after three days, disgorged him.
e. Gerald, a gentleman of the peerage, once traveled by steerage.
f. Justice cannot always be determined by jurists who occasionally make strange judgments.
g. Jargon is a strange form of language usage enjoyed by children.
h. June was in a rage because she was rudely nudged by Julian, who generally was considered to be of near genius intelligence.
i. Jane was both just and gentle in making germane judgments.
j. Sturgeon is a major Russian item exported in jars and small jugs.
k. The hedge under the bridge was edged with gentians, violets and geraniums.
l. Even though it was a semiprecious gem, Joyce enjoyed the jade.
m. Julie thought it a joke for James to adhere rigidly to his budget.
n. Jenny and Jed searched for sponges along the rock ledges under the huge bridge.
o. Marge and Jane joined a jaunty group for a trip on a barge.

[dʒ] and [tʃ]

The sentences that follow should be practiced with a view toward maintaining vocalization for the final [dʒ]. Make certain that vocalization continues so that there is no substitution of [tʃ] for the voiced affricate.

   a. The judge enjoined George and Marge from marriage.
   b. Madge would not budge from her strange position.
   c. John stood at the edge of the ridge but did not jump.
   d. Jones yielded to his urge and ate a large orange.
   e. At two years of age, the average child can speak her or his language.
   f. A large suspension bridge was built over the huge gorge.
   g. The grange was the scene of a battle of revenge.
   h. The stage was set for a strange play of maladjusted giants.

[dʒ] and [ʒ]

In the following sentences, make certain that you distinguish between the [dʒ] and [ʒ]. The first italicized word(s) will include the blend [dʒ]; the second will have the voiced fricative [ʒ].

   a. A *general* commands a *division*.
   b. Charles *pledged* himself to a life of *pleasure*.
   c. A *jury* found Wilson guilty of *usury*.
   d. *Agile* Peter climbed a hill to admire the *azure* sky.
   e. *Drudgery*, in *measure*, is part of living.
   f. Ben *rejected* attempts at *collusion*.
   g. *Judge Johnson* carefully announced her *decision*.
   h. Charles liked to *imagine* finding rich *treasure*.
   i. Chet *enjoyed* his *ménage*.
   j. *Jill* drove her car into the *garage*.

   a. Casey Jones, born John Luther Jones, was a railroad engineer and a personage legendary for courage but not necessarily for exercising good judgment. Through a deluge of rain, C.J. cannonballed his passenger train around a curve into a freight train on a siding, resulting in a fatal collision. C.J. ordered his fireman to jump, but he himself died an engineer's death with one hand on the brakes and the other on the whistle cord. The following verse was written for Casey Jones, or perhaps for the legend about him.

   > On a Sunday morning it began to rain,
   > 'Round the curve sped a passenger train,
   > Under the cab lay poor Casey Jones,
   > He's a good engineer, but he's dead and gone.
   >   —John A. Lomax and Alan Lomax (Eds.), adapted from
   >   "The Legend of Casey Jones," *American Ballads and Folk Songs*

   b. Max Bohr, a German-born physicist and a Nobel Laureate, received his doctorate at the University of Göttingen. Nazi policies compelled him to leave Germany for England where he became a lecturer at Cambridge University. In a paper published in 1957 he warned that the human race is in danger of self-annihilation either through the misuse of atomic technology or through poisoning of the environment that would result in deterioration of genetic structure.

   c. And what's a life? — a weary pilgrimage,
       Whose glory in one day doth fill the stage
       With childhood, manhood, and decrepit age.
                                — Frances Quarles, *What Is Life?*

   d. George Jenson generalized that judgments are generally made most judiciously when the judger does not jump too hastily to conclusions. This generalization, Jenson acknowledged, was a subjective judgment, but one about which he could feel objective because it had germinated slowly after genuine and judicious study.

   e. Although psychology had its genesis in philosophy, many psychologists as well as sociologists are urging that psychology emerge as a genuine science. Through technology and research, the general public may be the large gainers from the marriage of technology with scientific psychology.

   f. In *Antigone*, Sophocles held that it is both dreadful and unjust "when the right judge judges wrong."

TO STAGE A MERGER

Jud the Stage Producer: Do you think the average Joe can relate to your imaginative stage play, *Junior's Revenge*?

Reginald the Writer: The audience is generally just. Junior is jilted by his fiancée Jade and becomes a jewel thief who forges checks. It's a story of rage, revenge, and regeneration.

Jud the Stage Producer: But Junior is a strange and deranged joker who somehow manages to stay out of jail.

Reginald the Writer: He hides the gems in a barge and journeys down the mountain in disguise, doing odd jobs.

Jud the Stage Producer: It's a huge budget for a regional play set in the Blue Ridge Mountains of West Virginia. There's a giant cast with major roles for largely overpaid stars. We need to adjust the scope of the project so there is a larger margin for failure.

Reginald the Writer: My agent is besieged with urgent offers for this play. He wants me to jump a jet and join him in California. There are legions of producers who want to arrange a deal with me.

Jud the Stage Producer: Reggie, that's bilge. This play's too regional and disjointed to generate a surge of interest. I want to oblige you because you are a genius and I genuinely like your play.

Reginald the Writer: I guess the bulging budget demands a joint venture. Let's join my agent Jack in California and make a merger with a person who is outrageously rich. Only don't ask me to take a knife to my pages like a surgeon just to adjust the budget!

CHAPTER 21

THE NASAL CONSONANTS

═══

The three nasal phonemes /**m**/, /**n**/, and /**ŋ**/ (**ng**) are quite different in regard to tongue-mouth contact position, but share the essential features of nasal cavity reinforcement. All three are also continuant sounds. The position of the articulators within the mouth for the /**n**/ and /**ŋ**/ and the lips in gentle contact for the /**m**/ produce differences in oral cavity resonance and, thus, identifiably different characteristics of the sounds. See Figures 21–1, 21–2, and 21–3. Also review the discussion of nasal reinforcement in Chapter 8.

We begin our consideration of the nasally reinforced sounds with the bilabial phoneme /**m**/.

/m/ As in *Me, Summer,* and *Plum*

/**m**/ is one of the three nasal, continuant consonants. As such, it is produced with a lowered soft palate, nasal cavity reinforcement, and nasal emission. /**m**/ is articulated with the lips in relaxed contact and the teeth slightly parted. Vocal fold vibration is a necessary accompaniment for the /**m**/, as well as for the other two nasal sounds. As indicated in Figure 21–1, the tongue usually lies at the bottom of the mouth in the production of the /**m**/.

The sound /**m**/ is usually represented by the single letter *m*. Occasionally, the *m* is followed or preceded by a "silent" letter, as in *lamb* and *dumb, psalm* and *calm*. The sound is found in initial, medial, and final positions. Unless hurried, slurred, or produced with the lips too tight, the /**m**/ is a relatively easy sound to produce. As suggested in our discussion on nasal reinforcement (see pages 129–132), the /**m**/ lends fullness and roundness to the voice. The material and exercises for /**m**/ in the section on the voice should now be reviewed (see pages 131–132).

═══

PRACTICE MATERIALS

Initial

me	main	most	mirth
meek	mend	mode	murky
meal	met	mote	murder

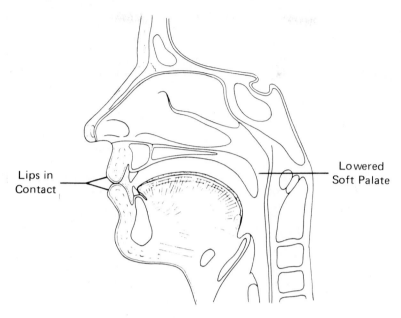

Figure 21–1   Articulatory positions for /m/. Note the lip contact and the lowered soft palate.

mean	mess	motive	mud
meat	man	motor	moist
middle	map	mourn	mouth
milk	mash	mortar	mount
mist	mask	mauve	mouse
make	mass	mock	my
mate	match	month	might
mail	mood	mob	mine
made	moon	monk	mile

Medial

demean	ember	foaming	human
seemly	emanate	reformed	humor
seamstress	embank	informing	grimy
dreaming	embassy	armor	slimy
remit	embattle	termed	omit
permit	cement	termite	remind
simple	amnesty	terminal	remedy
amity	Ambrose	remove	unmake
emblem	emotion	almond	amazed
immerse	permit	rhyme	crime

Final

beam	game	groom	worm
seem	gem	tomb	term
team	stem	tome	drum
theme	phlegm	comb	hum
dream	lamb	dome	I'm
dim	ham	home	dime
trim	tam	form	climb
slim	sham	dorm	grime
aim	slam	calm	crime
same	doom	farm	prime
tame	room	alarm	column
blame	broom	bomb	autumn

In a final, unstressed position, the final [m] may sometimes have syllabic value. What is your pronunciation of the words that follow?

chasm	schism	spasm	bedlam
bottom	rhythm	theism	bosom
prism	atom	truism	column

Is your pronunciation the same for the words in the following phrases?

bottom of the chasm	columns of prisms
schism in theism	rhythm of spasms

In the following material, work for a light, sustained [m]. At first, exaggerate the length of the [m] and avoid carrying over the nasal quality to proximate nonnasal sounds.

mumbled monologue	man-made mountain
monotone music	Mammon's money
mimicked mania	minimal number
modicum of modesty	

a. Murmuring pines and hemlocks and moss-covered bottoms of maples are to be found in the Maine woods.
b. Miniver mourned mightily for memories of days that might have been.
c. Termites, in numbers innumerable, undermined a mansion in Miami.
d. Melanie grumbled because she stumbled over Mamie's mauve-colored umbrella.
e. Morton was phlegmatic about many matters that make most ill-humored men and even some women storm in manifest anger.
f. Amanda's prime way of staying calm was mending and making neat seams in her garments.
g. The monk remained in good humor as he informed the mourners about the grimy tomb.
h. Mortar, a material employed in masonry, is made by mixing lime or cement with sand and a measured amount of water.

i. Humanity maintains its continuity through selected esteemed memories.

j. Broom in hand, Amelia was not in a mood or state of mind to be stymied by a mouse in either animal or human form.

k. Human beings, men and women alike, share a mighty capacity to transform molehills into mammoth mountains.

l. Emerson maintained that each mind has its own method.

m. The moon may look on millions of men and women, but they have but one moon.

n. Remembrance and repentance may come simultaneously in the morning.

o. Rhyme and rhythm alone do not generate a poem or a truism.

a. In *Man and Superman*, George Bernard Shaw made these observations:
  1. "The more things a man is ashamed of, the more respectable he is."
  2. "An Englishman thinks he is moral when he is only uncomfortable."
  3. "Marriage is popular because it combines the maximum of temptation with the maximum of opportunity."

b. Neil Armstrong, on landing on the moon, summed up his thinking and his mood with the statement: "One small step for man, one giant leap for mankind."

c. Terence manifested his understanding of humanity and his insight into himself when he noted that "nothing which is common to mankind is foreign to me."

d. I have thought some of Nature's journeymen had made men and not made them well, they imitated humanity so abominably.

  —William Shakespeare, *Hamlet*

e. Go! You may call it madness, folly;
    You shall not chase my gloom away!
  There's such a charm in melancholy,
    I would not, if I could, be gay.

  —Samuel Rogers, *To* ——

f. In his *Maxims*, Nietzsche remarked, "Many a man fails to become a thinker for the sole reason his memory is too good."

g. The fancy is indeed no other than a mode of memory emancipated from the order of time and space.

  —Samuel Taylor Coleridge, *Biographia Literaria*

h. They drew all manner of things—everything that begins with an M . . . such as mousetraps, and the moon, and memory, and muchness—you say things are "much of a muchness."

  —Lewis Carroll, *Alice's Adventures in Wonderland*

FOOTBALL AND THE MARRIED MAN

Marvin: Tampa Bay meets Miami in Tampa's home stadium today. After the monsoon, the summer air is humid and moist, and the field is a muddy swamp. Remember, Emma, the Rams from Anaheim creamed Tampa Monday, so they've got murder on their minds. It might be a smashing game!

Emma: Those men can't maneuver in that grimy slime. They stumble and tumble and get mired in the muck. What a mess.

Marvin: Emma, watch the TV! Tampa fumbled and the team's found themselves stymied at the midfield marker. Those dumb bums! Now Miami's man crams the ball under his arm, slams through the columns of his enemies, making a run for it. They meet like two embattled armies. That's drama, Em!

Emma: Marvin, it's bedlam! The game was made up by moral and mental amputees. The team members remind me of lumbering mammoths, animals mashing each other into mincemeat. They merely imitate human emotions.

Marvin: Woman, you misunderstand! Football imitates modern dance. It has theme, form, rhythm, and meaning. The moves are diagrammed. It's a mass rhumba or samba—quite harmless.

Emma: You mean a rumble, not a rhumba. Miami's man was bashed, rammed, and mangled on that marshy field. He's crumpled, his helmet is mashed, and he limps to the ambulance. That's some mean samba, Marv! The game is plumb dumb. Mayhem for money—that's criminal!

Marvin: Emma, lamb, I am dim. But you, like a beam of light or a flaming ember, illumine my mind. Football is competitive, combative, remorseless, and embittered. A man can compare it only to a mismanaged marriage!

/n/ As in *No, Any,* and *Again*

To produce the /n/, the tongue should be elevated and the entire tongue tip should be in contact with the upper gum (alveolar) ridge. The soft palate is relaxed (see Figure 21–2).

In spelling, /n/ is represented by the letter *n*. In some words, a silent letter precedes the n, as in *know, gnat,* and *pneumatic.*

The sound /n/ presents little difficulty except that it may be slurred or replaced by a nasalized vowel in medial positions, especially in unstressed syllables, as in *contact, infer,* and *inform.* The /n/ is likely to be treated with greater articulatory respect in initial and final positions. Because of the high frequency of occurrence of the sound in American-English speech, careful articulation of the /n/ is strongly recommended.

PRACTICE MATERIALS

/m/, we recall, is produced with the lips in gentle contact and, like [n], with the soft palate lowered. For /m/, the tongue usually lies relaxed at the floor of the mouth. You may increase your awareness of the difference between the /n/ and the /m/ by practice with the word pairs that follow.

knit	mitt	knock	mock
knee	me	knob	mob
need	mead	note	mote

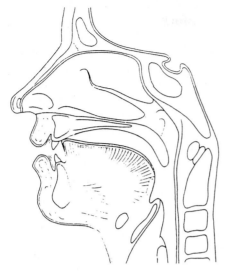

Figure 21–2 Articulatory adjustments for /**n**/. Note the relaxed (lowered) soft palate as well as the contact of tongue tip and the gum ridge.

knock	mock	null	mull
nude	mood	neat	meat
nail	mail	night	might
net	met	nice	mice
name	main	Norse	Morse
Nile	mile	new	mew

PRACTICE MATERIALS FOR /n/ IN VARIOUS POSITIONS AND CONTEXTS

Initial /n/

knee	natal	node	nut
niece	knell	notary	knuckle
neat	neck	gnome	number
kneel	nebula	gnaw	knife
near	knack	naughty	nice
knit	gnash	nautical	noise
nip	narrow	knob	now
nimble	natural	nocturn	notch
nape	nasty	nurse	pneumonia
name	nook	nerve	knew
nail	noose	nurture	knoll
nasal	nose	nub	knowledge

noise in the night	near the nook
gnawing note	now or never
number nine	nimble gnome
narrow notch	knew the knock

Make certain that an articulatory contact is made between your tongue tip and your upper gum ridge for the medial and final /n/. Failure to make this contact will result in the substitution of a nasalized vowel for the nasal consonant. Prolong the contact in the lists and phrases that follow.

Medial [n]

anneal	grinning	plaintive	fender
menial	spinet	fainting	rented
screening	sinful	feigned	banded
dinner	hinted	fence	handed
sinner	tainted	fend	landing
thinner	saintly	defense	standing
blandish	demanded	intoned	spondee
vanish	cannibal	morning	respond
candy	stoned	dawning	despondent
dandy	telephoned	bonfire	fonder
bundle	bind	joining	pinch
trundle	kindly	connect	bench
cunning	miner	intact	branch
hunted	finer	instead	launch
gunner	ground	confer	munch
burning	hound	consume	lynch
turned	pound	confess	binge
furnace	frowning	definite	strange
burnish	lounge	inflect	lounge
furnish	coined	infest	sponge

Andy Dandy	fender bender
ineffective defense	feigned a faint
plaintive sound	intoned the lines
pounded the ground	turned around
sounds of a hound	fond of munching
intact connection	turned cunningly

Final [n]

bean	amen	cone	spurns
lean	main	hone	stern
scene	lane	drone	burn
dean	grain	moan	run
mean	can	roan	done
sin	fan	brawn	stun
win	plan	faun	fine

tin	began	scorn	dine
hen	span	barn	down
ten	spoon	darn	frown
again	loon	gone	crown
when	dune	turn	brown

The consonant /n/, like /m/ can sometimes have syllable value without the "help" of a vowel. /n/ is or may be pronounced as a syllabic sound when it occurs in a final unstressed position. This is the case in the words that follow.

button	kitten	mutton	seven
cotton	leaden	open	sudden
deaden	maiden	oven	token
heaven	mitten	rotten	leaven
reason	ribbon	poison	fatten

ADDITIONAL PRACTICE MATERIALS

main avenue	mutton dinner
strange scene	cunning hunter
dine at seven	fine and dandy
eleven turns	morning news
again and again	tin horn
barn dance	change of plan
munch lunch	cotton mittens
ground sirloin	pound of beans
intuition and knowledge	nine tokens

a. Diana and Dan were fond of meandering in the garden.
b. Nathaniel wondered why his friend Ron, the owner of a ninety-foot launch, could ever find reason to frown.
c. The missionary endeavored to teach the cannibal the difference between having a friend for dinner and having dinner with a friend.
d. Nona, as a sign of affection for her husband, began baking in her oven, set at seven in the morning.
e. Frances looked stunning in her ten-pointed crown.
f. Minton confessed that he was inclined to strange hunches.
g. Nine sloops were anchored at Blanding's Landing.
h. Nettleton insisted that today's apparently insane notions may be the next day's brilliant insights.
i. Spencer and his son used a bundle of branches for their bonfire.
j. Every morning Nadine intoned nine plaintive tunes to the ascending sun.
k. A neologism is a new, or invented, word needed for a novel event.
l. The new highway connected nine old towns in Northern Maine.

m. Mauldin was smitten by the antics of the kitten with a ball of yarn.
n. Cotton was inserted between the partitions to insulate and deaden the sound.

a. In his paper, *Our Knowledge of the Causes of the Phenomena of Organic Nature*, Thomas Henry Huxley noted that "the method of scientific investigation is nothing but the expression of the necessary mode of working of the human mind."
b. In his essay, *The Idea of a University*, John Henry Cardinal Newman wrote, "It is almost a definition of a gentleman to say he is one who never inflicts pain."
c. There were gentlemen and there were seamen in the navy of Charles II. But the seamen were not gentlemen, and the gentlemen were not seamen.
    —Thomas Babington Macaulay, *History of England*
d. In *Design Science*, Buckminster Fuller cautioned us, "Change the environment; do not try to change man."
e. Beginnings and endings:
    1. In the beginning was the word.
    —The Gospel According to John, 1:1
    2. How many times it thundered before Franklin took the hint! How many apples fell on Newton's head before he took the hint! Nature is always looking at us. It hints over and over again. And suddenly we take the hint.
    —Robert Frost, *Comment*
    3. The beginnings and endings of all human undertakings are untidy, the building of a house, the writing of a novel, the demolition of a bridge, and, eminently, the finish of a voyage.
    —John Galsworthy, *Over the River*
    4. The time to stop a revolution is at the beginning, not the end.
    —Adlai Stevenson, Speech,
    San Francisco, September 9, 1952
    5. More than an end to war, we want an end to the beginnings of all wars.
    —Franklin D. Roosevelt,
    Address written for Jefferson Day broadcast,
    April 13, 1945 (Roosevelt died April 12, 1945)
f. Samuel Johnson, the eminent eighteenth-century English writer, cynic, and brilliant conversationalist insisted that most persons' minds are persistently involved in avoiding the present. In Johnson's own language, "No mind is much employed upon the present; recollection and anticipation fill up almost all our moments."

    Johnson "edited" a dictionary with many entries that were expressions of his own sentiments. For example, he defined *oats* as "a grain, which in England is generally given to horses, but in Scotland supports the people."
g. When Dan was young and had no sense,
    He bought a horn for eighteen pence,
    But the only tune that Dan could learn

Was "High on a Hill and Around a Turn."

—J. E., Adapted from an old English ballad

DONNA AND THE CHILDREN

Mrs. Nelson: Donna, I'm annoyed that you telephoned me at Anna's dinner party to complain about the antics of my children. Another night, it might not matter, but Anna served a main course that I enjoy. On the phone, you hinted that Cain, Melanie, and Nigel were naughty. Now kindly explain.

Donna: Mrs. Nelson, you know I never moan or groan unless I am nearly despondent. This morning Cain and I painted the fence green. Nigel made notches in the newly painted fence with his knife, and nailed the mailbox shut. Meanwhile, Melanie pretended to down the can of thinner. I nearly went insane. I bundled her up, ready to trundle her off to the emergency room. Then she confessed she was only pretending.

Mrs. Nelson: That's only a minor inconvenience and no reason to interrupt my dinner. I never hinted that my children were saintly.

Donna: I'm not finished. When I demanded that they munch some lunch at eleven, the children vanished. I found Melanie and Cain in the garden consuming a pound of candy.

Mrs. Nelson: It's rotten to binge on fattening candy, but it need not concern you.

Donna: After lunch, Nigel tried to poison the kitten with rancid food. He tied it up with a ribbon and built a bonfire with a bunch of branches. I managed to untie the kitten in the nick of time.

Mrs. Nelson: I confess Nigel has a strange imagination. But he never intended to injure the kitten.

Donna: I heard a noise earlier tonight and found Nigel standing next to the station wagon. He had driven the car and knocked down the fence. When I asked your fourteen-year-old son about the bent fender he had no defense.

Mrs. Nelson: Never mind, the car was rented. Donna, you have reason to want to punish the children, but give them another chance! Next week I want to go to the barn dance in Newtown.

Donna: Change that plan, Mrs. Nelson. I'll never tend your nasty children again—not for all the money in the universe!

The Velar Nasal /ŋ/

The third of the nasally reinforced phonemes is the velar nasal /ŋ/. As indicated in Figure 21–3, this sound is produced by elevating the back of the tongue so that it makes contact with the lowered soft palate (velum) while the vocal folds vibrate. /ŋ/ is a continuant sound that is reinforced and emitted nasally. In American-English speech, the /ŋ/ occurs either medially or finally, but never initially as it may in Chinese and in Southeast Asian languages.

The /ŋ/ is represented by the letter n or the letters ng. The sound usually occurs in words in which the letter n is followed by either a k or a g in the same syllable. /ŋ/ is generally not heard in standard speech in combinations where the n and the g that follows are in different syllables, as in *ingrate, congratulate,* and *engross.*

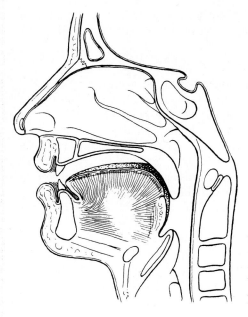

Figure 21–3 Articulatory adjustments for /ŋ/ (ng). Note the relaxed (lowered) soft palate and the lowered front portion of the tongue. The back of the tongue is in contact with the soft palate.

Except for possible confusion between the /n/and the /ŋ/, there is seldom any difficulty in the actual articulation of the velar nasal sound. There is some tendency, however, for some speakers to add either a /g/ or a /k/ following the /ŋ/, so that all words containing the velar nasal sound are pronounced either /ŋg/ or /ŋk/. (In context, a [g] or [k] regularly follows an [ŋ].) This tendency may frequently be traced to the influence of a foreign dialect. A second influence may be attributed to failure to remember the pronunciation of the particular word relative to the omission or the inclusion of the [g] or the [k]. A third influence is a direct result of the manner of articulating the /ŋ/. If the soft palate is raised before the contact between the tongue and the palate is broken, a [k] or a [g] sound is produced. To avoid adding either of these sounds when only the velar nasal is required, you must watch your articulatory timing. Specifically, you should make certain that the back of the tongue is moved away from the soft palate before raising the soft palate to block off the entrance to the nasal passage.

To know how to produce an /ŋ/ is not enough. We must also know whether the velar nasal is to be followed by a velar stop [k] or [g], or by some other sound. There is, of course, only one reliable way to learn the pronunciation of a word with velar nasal consonants. The reliable way is to study each word individually, using an up-to-date, large dictionary as a pronunciation guide. A second approach of general help is to learn the so-called rules for the use of the velar consonants in English speech:

1. When a word ends with the letters *ng* or *ngue*, the pronunciation calls for the [ŋ]. Examples include *wing, rang, tongue,* and *meringue.*
2. Usually, when a suffix is added to a root word that is pronounced with the /ŋ/, the pronunciation calls for the /ŋ/. Examples include *swings, rings, singer, longing,* and *stinging.* The exceptions to this general rule include the comparative and

superlative forms of the adjectives *long, young,* and *strong: longer, longest; younger, youngest;* and *stronger, strongest.* These are pronounced with [ŋg].

3. Where the letters *ng* are medial in a root word, as in *finger, tingle, hunger, extinguish,* and *single,* standard pronunciation calls for the use of /ŋg/. An exception is the pronunciation of *gingham* as [gɪŋəm].

4. In combinations in which the letter *n* is immediately followed by *k, c,* or *x* in the same syllable, the [ŋk] is used. Examples include *link, hank, bunk, distinct, anxious,* and *larynx.*

Note that not all words that include the letters *ng* in their spelling call for [ŋ] in their pronunciation. For example, words such as *range, binge, singe, tinge,* and *longevity* are pronounced with the combination [ndʒ] rather than with either the /ŋ/ or the [ŋg].
Apply these rules to the list of words that follow.

[ŋ]	[ŋg]	[ŋk]
wing	single	link
rang	spangle	anchor
young	younger	wink
harangue	elongate	sank
evening	anger	bunk
ringing	bungalow	trinket
longing	longest	sphynx
swings	tingle	length[1]
strong	stronger	strength[1]
singing	longest	larynx

Practice to Establish a Final /ŋ/ (ng)

If you tend to add a [g] or a [k] to words that should properly end with the [ŋ], you should be helped by contrasting the stops /g/ and /k/ with the nasal continuant /ŋ/. The stop sounds call for an abrupt stopping of the breath and frequently for the emission of a puff of air. The [ŋ] should be produced so that the nasally emitted sound dies away gradually. At the outset, exaggerate the length of the sound so that it is prolonged to two or three times what it might be in normal conversational speech.

PRACTICE MATERIALS

In your practice with the material that follows, establish your timing and control. Prolong the /ŋ/ and continue, without stopping, to complete the phrase.

holding it	speaking up	trying on	tongue exercise
hang on	reaching it	staying away	exciting events

[1] The words *length* and *strength* are acceptably pronounced with or without a [k] before the final sound.

young once	during an evening	charming all	dreaming all day
giving up	baking apples	running on	cutting up
swing it	exciting acts	standing up	cruising around
going on	being able	doing all	taking a break
teaching all	altering everything	letting it	sailing away
cooking oil	telling a truth		

a. Browning occasionally failed to see the distinction between teaching and preaching or knowing when letting go is the way to go.
b. Cumming's loving husband was fond of baking and cooking.
c. Blanding explained his behavior by reminding all who observed his fooling that one can be young only once.
d. Maturing is often more painful than growing older and growing up while so doing.
e. During his childhood, young Bennington learned that telling a truth or admitting a fault may solve as many problems as running away.
f. Waring always longed for things that past hoping did not give him.
g. A waiting throng assembled at the Long Island train station.
h. "Long ago" is a fond and indefinite time for recalling and reliving old dreams.
i. Young Arthur, the future king, did not know the source of his strength for pulling the sword from the stone.
j. Baring unfortunately learned that to be smiling and beguiling is not easy for one lacking in aptitude for acting or for being truly charming.
k. Passive observing is not satisfying for those who have a yearning for participating and acting.
l. Springer was better at haranguing others than at correcting errors of his own making and thinking.

Final [ŋ]: Additional Materials

Practice the following final [ŋ] words and then incorporate them into phrases in which each word is followed by one beginning with a vowel (e.g., *among us, ambling along, owning up*).

ambling	laughing	trying	staying
among	morning	asking	rang
bang	owning	boring	swing
bring	pacing	chanting	tong
doing	putting	fading	yearning
everything	sing	gasping	zooming
fling	sting	handing	daring
hang	throng	humming	darling
king	wrong	landing	fang
long	young	moaning	amazing
mining	looming	nothing	being
seeing	yelling	flying	pretending

Medial [ŋ]

The words that follow conform to Rule 2: a suffix is added to a word ending in the letters *ng*.

bearings	longs	borings	clanged
beings	mornings	fangs	endings
bringing	paintings	gaspings	firings
darlings	pronged	hanged	gangster
evenings	questionings	longing	drawings
flinging	songbird	throngs	strongly
hangmen	tracings	twangy	tongueless
kingly	wrongly	youngster	winged

Medial and Final [ŋ]

    a. "Shooting the stars" enables navigators to get their bearings when sailing.

    b. Young Loring banged on the door because there was no response to his shouting and ringing.

    c. Many Swiss youngsters belong to bellringer societies.

    d. The mockingbird can imitate the songs of other songbirds but has no identifying song of its own.

    e. The king's minstrel sang a song portending exciting events in Nottingham.

    f. Billings, in a complaining but not a whining voice, asked her husband to stop rearranging the furniture without first warning her of what he was intending.

    g. As a youngster, Sterling learned that telling the truth was more than a tongue exercise.

    h. Topping specialized in raising longhorn cattle.

    i. Ingrid Corning enjoyed teaching all she knew to her aspiring and admiring young students.

    j. Livingston Channing thought his children to be darlings whenever they listened to his tear-jerking singing.

Final [n] and [ŋ]

In easygoing, informal speech, many speakers use an [n] rather than [ŋ] as the last sound in words that end with *ng* in their spelling, as in *going, running, speaking,* and *eating*.[2] The same tendency holds for many southern and black-English dialect speakers in both formal and informal speech. However, most American-English speakers do make distinctions in their pronunciations of words such as *bin* and *bing, sin* and *sing,* and *run* and *rung*. The following material should help to establish the distinction between final [n] and final [ŋ] for speakers who wish to accept our recommendation to observe the difference.

ban	bang	bin	bing
fan	fang	gone	gong
kin	king	lawn	long

---

[2] It may be of interest to note that in Elizabethan English, words spelled with final *ng* were pronounced with [n] rather than [ŋ].

tan	tang	ton	tongue
pan	pang	sun	song
sin	sing	dun	dung
run	rung	tin	ting
stun	stung	hun	hung
bun	bung	Jan	jang
win	wing	ran	rang
clan	clang	din	ding

[n] Versus [ŋ] Distinctions

a. Sterling rang the bell as he ran along the road.
b. Fan removed the fang from the snake.
c. Lord Baring was kin to the king.
d. Golding was the first to run up each rung of the ladder.
e. The tan fluid had no tang.
f. Starling, a fledgling stunt pilot who was determined to win, took to wing with a prayer.

[ŋg]

When the letters *ng* occur within the root of a word, the pronunciation includes [ŋg], as in *angle*.

anger	fungus	languish	tangle
Anglican	ganglion	languor	tingle
anguish	gangly	mangle	wrangle
Bangor	hunger	mingle	distinguish
bungle	ingot	Mongol	Rangoon
Congo	jangle	mongrel	sanguine
dangle	jingle	penguin	singular
dungaree	jungle	shingle	triangle
England	kangaroo	single	linger
finger	language	spangle	elongate

The following suffix words are pronounced [ŋg] and are exceptions to the *ng* rule.

longer	stronger	younger	prolongate
longest	strongest	youngest	diphthongal

[ŋk]

The following words are pronounced with [ŋ] followed by [k].

anchor	dank	Manx	slink
ankle	drink	mink	spunk
anxious	banquet	plankton	tranquil
banker	dunk	monk	tank
bankrupt	flunk	monkey	trunk
blank	frank	pink	twinkle
brink	hanker	plank	uncle
Bronx	ink	rank	lynx

bunker	jinx	rink	larynx
clink	junk	sank	pharynx
crank	lanky	sink	conquer

[ŋg] and [ŋk]

English language	Uncle Frank
singular Anglican	trunk of junk
anger and anguish	ranking banker
elongated wrangle	dunk in the tank
hungry mongrel	blink and wink
single spangle	Bronx conqueror
Congo jungle	pink mink
linger longer	larynx and pharynx
dangling dungarees	lanky Yank
mangled ganglion	slinking lynx

Although rules have been suggested for determining the pronunciation of words spelled with *ng* and *nk*, there are many words that do not conform to the rules and have current pronunciations that are a result of assimilative influences or of the influences of analogy. Thus, a word such as *hangar* is now likely to be pronounced no differently from the word *hanger* (influence of analogy); *income* is likely to be pronounced with a velar adjustment /ŋ/ rather than the alveolar /n/ (influence of assimilation). In the final analysis, if you are not certain of the pronunciation of an *ng* or *nk* word, you should check the pronunciations either by listening to other respected speakers or by consulting an "authoritative" current dictionary. It is suggested that you check the following words if you are at all uncertain about the pronunciations.

banquet	fishmonger	rancor
Binghamton	gingham	tranquil
congress	inquest	wrangler

[ŋg] and [ŋk]

a. Although Waring was the youngest sibling, he was more daring than Hank, the oldest and strongest brother.
b. Franklin irritated his larynx and pharynx by making throaty, angry noises.
c. Despite their natural carrying cases, it seems unlikely that kangaroos will replace donkeys or elephant trunks for bearing our burdens.
d. Fielding wanted to become a distinguished linguist but, frankly, without much studying.
e. If vowels are elongated, they tend to become diphthongized.
f. Blandings had cause for agonizing while plank by plank he was overseeing the building of his dream house.
g. Golding, a lanky New England Yankee, became an outstanding wrangler.
h. Sterling's young wife could not decide whether the trimming for her coat should be of lynx or mink, so she settled on fake monkey fur.
i. Browning enjoyed dunking doughnuts and eating languidly, thinking of every meal as a banquet.

j. Bingham, emulating Lincoln, wanted to be considered a tranquil person who held no rancor.

———

ADDITIONAL PRACTICE MATERIALS FOR [ŋ] IN VARIOUS CONTEXTS

a. The competing youngsters enjoyed singing "The Daring Young Man on the Flying Trapeze."
b. Movements of the tongue modify breath from the lungs in creating articulate speech.
c. Wilding learned that listening for longer periods than speaking was earning him a reputation for conversing.
d. After long years of waiting and striving, Browning's yearnings were rewarded by his Uncle Frank.
e. Planes flying at ever-increasing speeds are making small ponds of our oceans.
f. All morning the angry waves pounded the New England shore.
g. The word *wrangler* has distinctly different meanings in England and in the United States.
h. Loring was no stranger to angling in swift-running waters.
i. Although she was dressed in gingham, the maid from Birmingham caught the eye of the young king.
j. The bellringer needed all his strength to keep the bells clanging.
k. Many banquets are spoiled by long harangues.
l. Bob enjoyed filling his lungs with the fresh morning air before undertaking the day's chores.

a. He's a wonderful talker, who has the art of telling you nothing in a great harangue.

—Molière, *Le Misanthrope*

b. Sad was the ending of Mike O'Day,
Who died maintaining his right of way.
His right was clear, his will was strong,
But he's just as dead as if he'd been dead wrong.

—Anonymous, Epitaph (twentieth century)

c. Walt Whitman believed that no matter how many songs have been written or sung, "the strongest and sweetest songs yet remain to be sung."
d. On deck beneath the awning,
I dozing lay and yawning;
It was the grey of dawning,

Ere yet the sun arose;
And above the funnel's roaring,
And the fitful wind's deploring,
I heard the cabin snoring
  With universal noise.
—William Makepeace Thackeray, *The White Squall*

e. Deep into that darkness peering, long
  I stood there, wondering, fearing,
Doubting, dreaming dreams no mortal
  Ever dared to dream before.
—Edgar Allan Poe, *The Raven*

f. As I went out one morning to breathe the morning air,
  I heard a dear old mother saying, "O my daughter fair,
You better go wash them dishes and hush that flattering tongue,
You know you want to marry and that you are too young."
—Adapted from *Lolly-Too-Dum*, American Ballad

g. A little learning is a dangerous thing;
  Drink deep, or taste not the Pierian spring.
—Alexander Pope, *An Essay on Criticism*

h. A very merry, dancing, drinking,
  Laughing, quaffing, and unthinking time.
—John Dryden, *Alexander's Feast*

i. Human beings have many reasons for feasting and eating, most having little
   or nothing to do with hunger or the body's continuing need for being fed.

j. A man—I let the truth out—
Who's had almost every tooth out,
Cannot sing as once he sung,
When he was young as you are young,
When he was young and lutes were strung,
And love-lamps in the casement hung.
—William Makepeace Thackeray,
Mrs. Katherine's Lantern

TEACHING GENIUSES

Painting Teacher: The young geniuses among us think nothing of staying up all
   evening and working on drawings or paintings. You find them going on and
   seldom, if ever, giving up. They are the ones you find laughing in the morning
   at the exhausting amount of effort it takes for their ongoing endeavors. Their
   yearning to see their own drawings and paintings hang in the wing of a gallery
   is all-consuming. Nothing will stop these young artists from attaining their
   goals.

Young Hopeful: Are you telling us that we never have fears of failing? All artists
   are given to self-questioning and entertain doubts about their talents. I have a
   hard time believing that a genius never fails or never feels like cutting up a
   drawing and flinging it into the nearest spring. There are mornings when doing
   a sketch and reaching for glory are frustrating when not outright boring!

Painting Teacher: Despite what I seem to be hearing, my general finding is that these amazing youngsters find painting to be an exciting art. They do spend long hours in the evening asking me if they are wrong, and often they are actively doubting everything in their thinking and attempts at creating art. But in the dawning of a new and shining morning, their negative feelings fade away. As long as the songbirds sing their hopeful songs, these young geniuses will be found working to bring us a kingdom of things that are beautiful. Teaching these youngsters is demanding, but it is also satisfying and thrilling.

[ŋg] *and* [ŋk]

TALES OF UNCLE FRANK

Uncle Frank: In the Congo jungle, I learned to play the bongos and monkeyed around in dungarees with the kangaroos.

Dinky: How did you distinguish yourself in England, Uncle Frank?

Uncle Frank: In the dank fog I tangled with a hungry lynx who hankered after the junk food in my trunk. With a single shot, I sank him.

Dinky: In Anchorage, where they speak the English language, you did more than attend banquets.

Uncle Frank: I drank until I was tranquil and watched the spunky penguins mingle in a freshwater tank. I wrangled with a fishmonger for the slinky birds and gave them to the Bronx Zoo.

Dinky: Why didn't you linger longer in Anchorage?

Uncle Frank: I'm a ranking banker who would go bankrupt if I stayed away from Bangor too long. I admit it's angering to languish away in a bank all day, ankle deep in paper and ink. Here my only challenge is to conquer the anguish of boredom.

Dinky: Uncle Frank, I don't think that you will ever linger long enough in whatever you may be doing to become bored. As for me, I hope that I can hold on to a job long enough for it to be boring.

CHAPTER 22

THE VOWEL-LIKE SOUNDS

THE LINGUA-ALVEOLAR LATERAL /l/

/l/ As in *Lake, Alone,* and *Bill*

The phoneme /l/ is a lingua-alveolar, voiced, lateral sound. This vowel-like consonant (semivowel) may occur initially, medially, or finally. As we may note from the spellings of several of the words in the opening sentences, /l/ is represented by the letters *l* or *ll*.

In common with the alveolar stop sounds /t/ and /d/, the /l/ is usually produced with the tongue tip in contact with the upper gum ridge. A difference, however, is that the blade of the tongue (the portion left and right just behind the tongue tip) is lowered and so permits vocalized breath to escape over the sides. The soft palate is raised (see Figure 22–1) to prevent nasal reinforcement and nasal emission. The result is a continuant and vowel-like quality which some phoneticians refer to as a liquid sound.

As we will soon note, the phoneme /l/ has several variants, or allophones, depending essentially on the position of the sound in context.

PRACTICE MATERIALS

In producing the sound /l/, make certain that the *tip* and *not the blade* of your tongue is in contact with the gum ridge. Avoid contact between the tongue tip and the teeth.

Initial

lean	loose	lock	lace
leap	lute	learn	lake
lip	loom	lug	lower
late	load	lie	lapse
let	lawn	like	lane
lack	lot	low	linger
laugh	lost	lout	loin

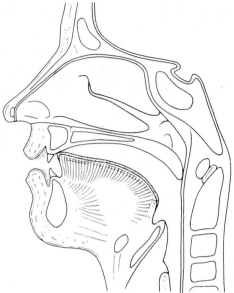

Figure 22–1 Most frequent articulatory adjustments for /l/. Note the tip-of-the-tongue contact with the upper gum (alveolar) ridge.

In some contexts, before consonants and in final positions, a variant of the /l/ sound may be produced with a quality referred to as *dark*. This results from a slight elevation of the back of the tongue. It may be heard in many of the words that follow.

Medial

elder	callous	gallop	elevate	elect
called	heels	pooled	alike	allow
boiled	hills	pulse	align	pallid
moles	hailed	cold	sleep	palace
smiles	held	stalled	ballad	tailor
fooled	gals	gold	elope	tilted
riled	bells	enfold	alter	build

Final

haul	deal	zeal	jail	kale
whale	keel	tool	earl	gale
drawl	till	full	gull	ball
style	pale	foal	foil	guile
angel	fell	hall	tile	eel
total	pal	doll	cowl	pearl
tonal	dale	roll	broil	hurl

Initial and Medial

labeled	lability	lollipop	literally
Lila	lively	listless	lifelong
lamely	lonely	lullaby	likely

| Leola | lowly | Lillian | leaflet |
| loudly | lately | lilting | liability |

Initial and Final

level	legal	lawful	Lionel
local	labile	lentil	loll
lapel	lethal	labial	lisle
liable	libel	liberal	logical
lateral	loyal	lonely	lightly

likely tale	lordly labor	hail and farewell
light laughter	tile floor	all, all alone
lie low	cold lair	lethal leap
learn a lot	clanging bells	lonely flyer
linger longer	build a wall	legal eagle
let live	gold and pearls	logically concluded
lovely lullaby	hill and dale	lilting lyric
sleep well	mail a letter	hold old Hal
dull tool	lower the load	pallid and lifeless

a. Lillian Lawton, a lawyer known for her cold logic, specialized in libel suits, which she seldom lost.
b. Lila sang a lilting lullaby to her lovely infant child.
c. Lou and Lisa picked flowers on the hill, close to the landfill.
d. Helen liked lentil soup, especially when prepared by Lionel.

Most of the /l/ sounds in the preceding practice material may be characterized as "light" and are produced, as indicated in the description of the sound, by tip-of-the-tongue to gum-ridge contact. Most final [l] sounds are similarly produced but have a "darker" quality. A different kind of [l], essentially a palatalized variety, occurs when the [l] is followed immediately by a [j] (y) sound, as in *million, billion,* and *value,* and *ball yard, Bill yearns,* and *will you.*

Initially, the same tongue-alveolar contact is made for this allophone of /l/ as for the "light" sound. However, there is a difference, in that the tongue blade rises toward the palatal portion of the roof of the mouth in order to produce a /j/ (y) sound.

The following sentences incorporate a palatalized [l] sound as well as the "light" and "dark" varieties.

a. William regretted his failure to make a million.
b. A billion is a thousand times a million.
c. The large lot was converted to a ball yard.
d. Leslie asked, "Bill, will you join me in billiards after you mail your letter?"
e. Although Malvina was normally a lighthearted lady, she occasionally played the role of a hellion.

[l] Preceded by [p] or [b]

Some persons produce an "infantile" sound in contexts in which the [l] is immediately preceded by [p] or [b]. This effect is frequently a result of failure to make the tongue-tip to gum-ridge contact for [l]. A [w]-like sound is produced as a carryover of the lip movement of the [p] or [b].

PRACTICE MATERIALS

For the following practice materials, avoid lip movement for the [l]. Make certain that there is a definite tongue-tip to gum-ridge contact for the sound.

please	plume	bleed	blue
Pliocene	pluck	blame	blood
pleasant	plausible	blink	bloat
play	plot	blend	bluff
plan	plunder	bland	blot
pledge	plight	black	blind

The following word pairs and sentences should help to establish a clear distinction between [l] and [w].

weep	leap	wade	laid
wack	lack	wit	lit
wag	lag	way	lay
wax	lacks	wear	lair
went	lent	wet	let
wick	lick	wane	lane
wad	lad	wean	lean
weak	leak	wife	life
Will	Lill	wink	link

a. Bly held that he was blameless for frequently feeling blue.
b. When Leola was with him Bliven enjoyed playing his violin by candlelight.
c. Blake was black and blue from his fall on Plum Hill.
d. Lona, a natural blonde, enjoyed strolling on the village mall with Billy Blackston.
e. Blaine and Wayne were called the lickety-split linesmen by their fellow players on the intramural football team.

ADDITIONAL PRACTICE MATERIALS FOR [l] IN VARIOUS CONTEXTS

lean	loom	glide	claw
lip	law	glaze	clue

lace	lock	glower	club
left	log	glimpse	cloy
lance	learn	glue	clan
glance	lunch	glutton	climb
loot	lion	clean	clutter
lose	glow	class	cluster
glen	glare	blip	blunt

lean and lanky	leg of lamb
grind the glass	stolen loot
clean but cluttered	claws of a lion
fell off a log	lying glances
blighted plight	lawful plot
Blueberry Hill	bloody but blameless
flowers in bloom	blend of fall colors

a. Delilah rarely listened to her lover's lilting lyrics, and so she lost her lovelorn lyricist.
b. The melodramatic play had an implausible, albeit compelling, plot.
c. Lila dreamed of a knight with a plume and a lance whom she longed to meet by plot or by chance.
d. Lyman planned to lead Linda to the altar and pleaded that she not lag on the way.
e. William built an olympic-sized pool in the middle of his large lawn.
f. A flock of gulls flew over the Great Salt Lake.
g. Hal and Lou were childhood pals and close friends as adults.
h. All too many politicians are long on palaver but usually short on lucid explanations.
i. If well timed, light laughter may be an eloquent, wordless declaration of approval.
j. Gold was discovered at Sutter's Mill in the Sacramento Valley early in 1848.
k. Lola learned to fly and planned to pilot her own plane.
l. The ballad related an unlikely tale of a beguiling prince and an artless, almost childlike princess.
m. Lucy scolded her girlfriend Lola for falling asleep in their after-lunch Latin class.
n. Beulah lost her gold locket on the lakeside lawn near the Old Lodge.
o. Walt was thoughtful and habitually slow at leaping to misleading conclusions.

a. In his *Popular Fallacies*, Charles Lamb held, "A pun is a pistol let off at the ear; not a feather to tickle the intellect."
b. The cruellest lies are often told in silence.
    —Robert Louis Stevenson, *Virginibus Puerisque*
c. Old and young, we are all on our last journey.
    —Robert Louis Stevenson, *Crabbed Age and Youth*

d. Blazing in Gold and quenching in Purple
    Leaping like Leopards to the Sky . . .
    And the Juggler of Day is gone.

    —Emily Dickinson, *No. 228* (c. 1861)

e. I do not love thee, Dr. Fell,
    The reason why I cannot tell,
    But this alone I know full well:
    I do not love thee, Dr. Fell.

    —Thomas Brown, *Paraphrase of Martial*

f. In his *Song of Myself*, Walt Whitman wrote:
        I think I could turn and live with animals,
            they are so placid and self-contained,
        I stand and look at them long and long.

g. Charles Lamb, a prolific letter writer and essayist, was versatile and eclectic
    in his interests. In his *Essays of Elia*, he lamented, "The red-letter days, now
    become, to all intents and purposes, dead-letter days." In a letter to poet-
    laureate Robert Southey, Lamb acknowledged, "Anything awful makes me
    laugh. I misbehaved once at a funeral."

    Lamb had a low opinion of people who borrowed books. He held them
    to be "mutilators of collections, spoilers of the symmetry of shelves, and
    creators of odd volumes."

    Recalling his childhood days, Lamb wrote sentimentally:
        I have had playmates, I have had companions,
        In my days of childhood, in my joyful schooldays—
        All, all are gone, the old familiar faces.

h. Claude Lucas, a loner but not a lonely man, held it to be folly to believe
    any statement with political implications until it is firmly denied. It is
    doubly so, Claude lamented, when the denial comes from a diplomat or a
    politician in a diplomat's clothing.

i. The world is a difficult world, indeed,
    And people are hard to suit,
    And the man who plays on the violin
    Is a bore to the man with the flute.

    —Walter Learned, *Consolation*

j. When the lion fawns upon the lamb,
    The lamb will never cease to follow him.

    —William Shakespeare, *King Henry VI*, Part III

k. A light year is the distance light travels in a single solar year. Translated
    into meters, a light year is 5.87 million million miles.

    In an address, the astronomer Frank Drake told his listeners that elec-
    trical bargains are still available. For the price of about a dime's worth of
    electricity, it is possible to send a ten-word telegram a full one hundred
    light years beyond our globe.

l. In his novel *The Way of All Flesh*, Samuel Butler wrote, "It is our less
    conscious thoughts and our less conscious actions which mainly mold our
    lives and the lives of those who spring from us."

m. Since time immemorial, and probably before recorded time, pictorial representation has been the means employed to communicate in the absence of a mutually understandable oral or verbal language system. Manual signing is an extension and elaboration of pictorial representation. Interestingly, manual signing has had limited success in the fulfillment of our trials to use visual language with high-level primates such as selected chimpanzees and gorillas.

n. The Order of the Dolphins is composed of persons whose scientific interests are in extraterrestrial communications. The name of the order was chosen out of respect for dolphins and the scientists' wholesome appreciation of their intelligence and gentleness, rather than as an indication of a high level of interest in dolphin "language."

o. All human behavior is the result of the way on which one nerve cell relates to another cell in the complex circuitry of the globular, alluring, cellular mass of billions of nerve cells we refer to as the brain. This oatmeal-colored mass of multibillion cells is the last and most highly developed part of the neurological mechanism.

WILLIAM'S BLUES

David: William, you are a lousy lout for leaving a lovely lady like Daisy at the altar. What made you lose your zeal and cool your heels?

William: I'm so lost and feel so blue I can't even sleep. My pledge to make Daisy my lawful wife was a heartfelt goal. Now all I have left of my pearl of a girl is a gold lock of her hair.

David: Did you get cold feet when you saw the bridal lace and heard the wedding bells toll?

William: Please believe me, I am not to blame! It was her blue-blooded family that foiled our plans. They are a clannish lot and thought me a social climber. They did not allow that our love was legitimate because I could not build her a palace. Daisy and I plotted to elope, but she foundered. Then I got a letter in the mail that pleaded with me to lie low for a while. I watch her play on her lawn a lot and listen to her laugh, but I know she is lost to me.

David: Daisy is really one in a million, but her family is lethal. I apologize for blaming you. Don't languish here alone any longer, old pal. Hurl the lock of hair into the cold, still lake. Then let's fill up on cool ale. With luck, you will forget the lovely lady!

THE VOWEL-LIKE SOUND /r/

There is considerable variation in the production and pronunciation of /r/ according to context and regional practice. In regard to the latter, as we indicated earlier, some persons in the areas of eastern New England, eastern Canada, New York City, and the

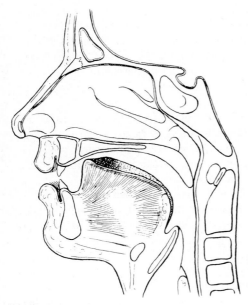

Figure 22–2 Articulatory adjustments for retroflex [r]. Note that the tongue tip is slightly flexed toward the back of the mouth.

southern coastal states pronounce an [r] only when it is immediately followed by a vowel, as in *reach, rise, grows, boring,* and *Marion,* and omit [r] in other contexts. Most Americans, however, pronounce an [r] sound whenever the letter *r* appears in the spelling of a word, regardless of whether the immediate next sound is a vowel or a consonant. The general tendency for most Americans is to produce an [r] in words such as *cart, bargain,* and *turn* as well as in contexts such as *around, through,* and *pour it.*

We consider three varieties of /r/. Two of these call for the production of the *r* as a semivowel or vowel-like consonant. The third is a fricative and, more characteristically, a consonant sound.

Allophones of /r/ are presented in brackets [ ].

[r] As in *Rise, Rose,* and *Around*

There are two ways of producing an [r] when the sound is immediately followed by a vowel in a stressed syllable. The first method is to raise the tongue tip toward the roof of the mouth. The tongue tip may be brought close to the gum ridge, but actual contact with the gum ridge should be avoided. The tongue tip may also be flexed slightly toward the back of the mouth. Compare Figure 22–2, demonstrating production of this type of [r], with Figure 22–1 for the /l/.

The second method of articulating an [r] before a vowel in a stressed syllable more nearly approximates the production of a vowel sound. The tip of the tongue is lowered and the central portion of the tongue is raised toward the roof of the mouth about where the hard palate ends and the soft palate begins. This position is illustrated in Figure 22–2. For both [r]s the sounds are vocalized.

If you have no difficulty with either [r] allophone, you have no need to concern yourself about being consistent as to manner of production. If, however, you do have difficulty with these [r] allophones, and especially if you tend to produce either or both so that the effect is much like a /w/, then you should analyze your efforts for the tongue-tip and central [r] and try to produce consistently your best [r] sound. Experience suggests that persons who tend to confuse /w/ and /r/ usually improve by establishing and regularly producing a tongue-tip [r]. Persons who tend to confuse /l/ and /r/, as native Oriental speakers sometimes do, may do better by establishing a central position for the [r] and a tip-tongue or blade-tongue position for the [l]. The contrast in positions may help to overcome confusion. Whichever variety you produce, do not hold onto the sound excessively and do not convert the sound into a distorted vowel or a growl.

PRACTICE MATERIALS FOR [r] FOLLOWED BY A VOWEL

Initial [r]

read	rail	room	roll
reach	rage	rude	rope
ream	red	rule	raw
rid	rest	rook	wrought
rim	rack	roof	rock
rate	rap	rote	rod
rug	rice	royal	wren
rough	rise	roam	wreck
run	rhyme	roost	roast
rout	ripe	raucous	wrangle
round	real	road	wrestle

Medial [r] (*followed by a vowel*)

around	erase	harangue	harass
arid	error	bearing	erode
Arabic	berate	bereave	surrogate
arable	barometer	beret	baron
arrange	barium	boron	theory
bureau	borough	oral	oracle
orange	bury	weary	thorough
orator	Orion	Byron	moron
marry	tarry	surely	purely
tarot	tearing	wiring	thereon
moral	thereabout	correct	morose

barium ore	Byronic oration
berate Boris	arid arroyo
Arabic oracle	correct the error

orange beret	moribund bureaucrat
Oriental arrangement	eroded borough
raw rope	enraged parent
royal road	rhythmic run
raucous wrangle	rain rinse
rough rider	rudely raging
rote memory	really rugged
wrought iron	rim of brine
roam forests	run around
rice recipes	wretched aroma
rise and run	wrecked lorry
ripe berries	arose in peril

For the medial [r] followed by a consonant, check your practice and pronunciation with what is current in your community. Do you include or omit this [r]?

Medial [r] (*followed by a consonant*)

pierce	art	smart	mourn
fierce	part	dart	dormitory
beard	warm	swarm	wired
seared	warn	forlorn	tired
chart	farm	orphan	hired
charm	unharmed	scarf	Martha
storm	absorb	dwarf	Marvin
alarm	fork	north	York
harm	pork	forth	inform
ark	hard	ward	torn
corn	adorn	Norman	Berlin
perform	torque	armor	scorned

northern storm	target for darts
partly warm	pierce the pork
horse and cart	started to arm
tired and forlorn	inform the partner
orphan of the storm	harmful warts
absorbing art	charming in parts
bearded dwarf	chart the course
fierce farmer	alarmed York

For the final [r], is your practice in the omission or the inclusion of the final [r] consistent with that for medial [r] followed by a consonant? It is, for most speakers.

Final [r]

sire	shore	queer	austere
dear	are	four	bother

hear	bar	more	mother
fear	car	lore	ignore
near	far	core	father
care	mar	soar	sister
dare	star	ire	tower
fair	boor	dire	shower
admire	adore	tour	store
lure	appear	sour	explore

pare the pear	winter shower
hear sister	ignore brother
near the bar	tour the moor
their paper	lair for the bear
dire cure	summer flower
dear mother	four to a car

For special medial [r] words, review the discussion of the /ɜ/ (ûr) and /ɝ/ vowels (see pages 222–225).

Special Medial [r]

earn	surf	verve	surly
birth	stern	turf	curl
mirth	burn	shirt	curtain
terse	girl	girth	certain
first	whirl	nerve	lurch
nurse	heard	serve	churl
purse	hurl	spurn	yearn

first thirst	churned and hurled
terse girl	burned earth
curved turn	swerve with verve
earn the purse	heard in church
lurch and whirl	burst with mirth
serve the nurse	uncertain person
first spurned	hurled to the turf

Distinction Between /r/ and /w/. Persons who tend to produce /r/ so that it resembles /w/ should work to establish a clear acoustic difference between these sounds. The /r/ should be produced without lip activity and, preferably, with the tongue tip raised toward the gum ridge. The /w/ should be produced with lip movement and without front-of-the-tongue activity.

=====

PRACTICE MATERIALS

The following materials should help to establish the distinction. Use a mirror to see what you do, and listen carefully to hear what happens with and without lip movement.

Suggestion: To become aware of unintentional lip movement, look in a mirror as you *intentionally exaggerate such activity.* This should increase your level of awareness and so help you to avoid producing a [w] sound when an [r] is intended.

Distinguish between /r/ and /w/ in the following word pairs.

rick	wick	rind	wind
rack	wack	rill	will
reap	weep	roof	woof
read	weed	run	won
reek	week	ring	wing
red	wed	rue	woo
wren	wen	room	womb
rest	west	row	woe
rag	wag	ride	wide
rage	wage	rise	wise
rate	wait	rare	wear
rain	wane	rile	wile

=====

Difficult [r] Combinations.   Words beginning with [p] and [b] followed by [r], as in *prize* and *breeze*, may be troublesome because of the lip activity required for the first sounds. The fault is similar to the one in our previous discussion of the [l] preceded by [p] or [b].

=====

PRACTICE MATERIALS

Avoid lip movement for the [r] as you practice with the materials that follow.

preach	praise	prude	sprawl
preen	press	prove	proud
prince	precious	probe	prow
print	prank	prone	pride
pray	prattle	prawn	price
pretty	prudent	spry	spring

breech	braise	brood	brought
breeze	breast	brew	broad
brick	break	broke	brow
bring	brain	broth	bride
bray	brash	brawn	brine
brass	abrasion	brief	upbringing

preen with pride	pressed for proof
preach prudence	princely prank
proved by the probe	prone to pride
praised by the press	pretty print
profound and prolific	proof of promise

broken brick	brain and brawn
brewed a broth	abrupt and brash
abrasively brief	bruised brow
bread for brunch	brother of the bride
brief brawl	brutal breach
abridged pride	briefly abroad

a. Reverend Brooks declared that it is easier to preach than to practice, but prudently more productive to practice than to preach.

b. The German-born psychologist Kurt Lewin presented his respected peers with the provocative assertion that there is nothing as practical as a really good theory.

c. Mary Richards observed that she frequently found it difficult to determine whether her philosophy professor was erudite and brilliant or broadly abstruse.

d. Rick Preston's behavior appeared to be crisp and abrupt, but his friends protested that it was surface pretense generated by insecurity.

e. In contrast, Pritchard's manners made it apparent that his abruptness was nurtured by pervasive rudeness.

f. Bryan Brice, who was first among umpires, prevented cries of outrage among veteran players and rookies alike by presenting them with a brief list of practicing ground rules in clear writing.

g. Jane Austen, the British writer and author of *Pride and Prejudice*, appeared to be seriously concerned with the then-ever-present problem of getting proper husbands for daughters of marriageable age.

h. Brenda's bright laughter brought warmth to mornings that might otherwise have been gray and dreary.

i. The crude bridge cracked and crumbled under the burden of the oversized and overloaded trailer truck.

j. Priscilla Brenton, a soprano virtuoso, earned three curtain calls after her brilliant rendition of her original lyrics.

k. General of the army Omar Bradley authored *Soldier's Story*, an autobiography of his military experiences.

l. Richardson was partial to prawns and lobster, but as a pragmatist did not ignore crayfish.

—————

[kr] and [gr] Blends.   The blends [kr] and [gr], which include a velar stop plus [r] as in *crumb, crease, krone* and *grim, grass, green*, are most easily and proficiently produced with a central tongue position as illustrated in Figure 22–3. Because the consonants [k] and [g] are produced by mid- or back-tongue contact with the palate, the blends with [r] are easier to produce with this articulatory movement than that required for a retroflex [r], as shown in Figure 22–2.

—————

PRACTICE MATERIALS FOR [kr] AND [gr]

cream	crest	crew	crock
creek	crept	crude	crowd
crib	cram	crow	crown
crayon	crash	croak	crime
cradle	craft	crawl	scribe
green	grew	grind	grist
greet	group	grape	grief
grin	grope	grime	grace
grit	grow	groom	grade
grate	gross	gruel	grant
grain	groan	groove	graze
grenadine	grog	grand	growl
grass	grotto	grunt	grudge
grapple	grub	grasp	gruff

green grass	grand grin
grind grain	crushed cranberries
grunt and groan	grinned and grimaced
greet Grace	crash the craft
ground grain	Cripple Creek
craved a crumb	grew grapes
green grub	greasy crock
griped about the gravy	overgrown grain

a. Granger ground the organically grown grain for breakfast bread.
b. Great pride may bring greater grief.
c. The gray horse was well groomed by Bruce.
d. The green car crashed into the gray cart on Bryant Road.

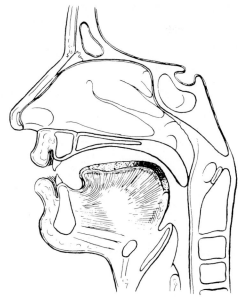

Figure 22–3 Articulatory adjustments for central [r]. Note the lowered front portion of the tongue and the raised central and back portions.

e. Grayson, a practical man, came to grips with his bristly problem.
f. More than grain may be grist for a mill.
g. Brian poured the grog out of the cracked crock.
h. The wrestlers grunted and groaned as if they carried a truly mutual grudge.
i. The proud groom grinned at his gracious bride.
j. Graceful Greta pruned the blue-green grape vine to ensure new growth.

[fr]. The blend [fr] may also pose some difficulty in production. The chief problem is a tendency to produce a sound approximating a [w] following the [f], possibly because of the lower-lip involvement for the articulation of this sound. See the discussion of establishing a distinction between [r] and [w] (page 379).

PRACTICE MATERIALS

frame	frappé	French	fringe	afraid
friar	freckle	fruit	from	affront
freeze	fresh	frugal	frock	affricate
frigid	friend	fro	front	affray
frail	fragile	froze	fry	confront
freight	frank	frog	fraught	infrared
fraud	freedom	fritter	frown	infrequent

a. Freya enjoyed fresh fruit and cream frappés, but not too frequently.
b. Fred and his French friend, François, enjoyed frogs' legs and crumbled crackers.
c. The fragile frame was shipped by air freight from France to Great Britain.
d. Freedom will survive only if it is nurtured and shared by those who are free.
e. The frantic general avoided the dangers of exposure at the front.
f. Friar Tuck was proud to be a friend of Robin Hood and his proud Merry Men.
g. Frugality is no insurance against fraud or confrontation with the fraudulent.
h. The frigid weather kept everything in a deep, prolonged freeze.
i. Francine, who was inclined to be frivolous, wore a French-designed frock to her friend Frank's wedding.
j. Frampton, a prolific writer, sued Frisby for copyright infringement.

[r] As in *True, Through,* and *Dry*

A third variety of [r] approximates a fricative sound in manner of production. It is articulated by placing the tip of the tongue close to but not quite touching the gum ridge. When air is forced over the tongue tip, a fricative [r] is produced (see Figure 22–4). When this variety of [r] occurs in the initial position, the sound is vocalized. When it occurs after a voiceless sound, as in *three* and *tree*, the [r] may be completely or partly unvoiced. This [r] is not as frequently produced by American speakers as the other varieties considered earlier.

This allophone of [r] is described as a postdental fricative. It is most likely to be produced after tongue-tip consonants such as [t], [d], and [θ] (**th**).

Practice with the material that follows.

PRACTICE MATERIALS

treat	tread	true	trot
tree	track	troop	trouble
trip	trap	truce	trunk
trigger	trash	trout	tripe
train	tram	trophy	try
trade	transit	tropic	trowel
three	thrash	throttle	throng
thrift	through	thrush	Thrace
thrill	throne	thrall	threaten
thresh	throw	thrive	throat

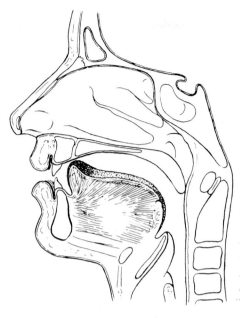

Figure 22–4 Tongue position for fricative [r]. Note the tongue position close to but not in contact with the upper gum ridge and the lowered position of the middle and back portions. This [r] is a postdental fricative.

thread	throb	thrombus	thrust
dream	draft	droop	dry
dread	dram	drum	drub
dray	drape	drop	drudge
dragon	Andrew	drawn	druid

droopy dragon	dreadful dream
drawn drapes	dreary drudge
thrifty trade	enthralled throng
three trout	trouble in transit
thrilled by the treat	thrush in the tree
thrived on tripe	tricky throttle
trips by train	dreamy trio

a. The weary troops arranged a morning truce.
b. Trenton enjoyed his train trips but tried to avoid street trams.
c. The fast-running stream was noted for its trout.
d. The triple-threat athlete won several trophies before retiring.
e. Dumas observed that truth is great because fire cannot burn nor water drown it.
f. Travis and Drake declared a brief truce in their recurrent quarrels and went fishing for trout in a nearby fast-running stream.
g. The throng cheered as the trotters raced around the track.
h. Throttle in hand, the engineer sped the train through the night.

i. A thrush built a nest in the branch of the tree.
j. Trash should not be thrown from moving streetcars or any other vehicle in transit.
k. Trenton, a drum major, drained every drop from the dram of cherry cordial.
l. Andrea dreamed that Andrew, her dear and reliable friend, would become her dragon killer and her true love.
m. Druids were priests in ancient Britain and Ireland who held their ceremonies among groves of trees.
n. Truston, a trained drover, carried his trunk on an old dray.
o. Therese Truman went through three drafts of her term paper before turning it in to Professor Frampton.

Linking [r] and Intrusive [r]

Earlier, we discussed the regional tendencies in producing and pronouncing words in which the letter r is final in the spelling. The [r] in contexts such as *far away, near us, for it, for old,* and *bear it* is usually heard as a linking sound between vowels. If you listen closely to the production of the linking [r], you will note that it is produced with less vigor and is of shorter duration than the initial [r] or the medial [r] in stressed positions. Acoustically, the sound is much like the [r] in unstressed syllables, as in the words *berry, marry, carry,* and *ferry.*

Occasionally, an [r] sound is intruded where the spelling of the word does not include the letter r. It is most likely to be intruded in combinations such as *law and order, idea of, America, is,* and *vanilla ice.* It is apparently easier to maintain speech fluency by inserting an [r] between words when one ends and the next begins with a vowel than to produce two successive vowels. The intrusive [r] is generally considered to be substandard, and its use is therefore not recommended.

Practice the following phrases and sentences. Read each with deliberate slowness to avoid the intrusive (intruded) [r].

PRACTICE MATERIALS

law of a country	saw a sight	Nora is alert
idea of it	Irma and Emma	Alaska is cold
Nebraska and Nevada	Stella, always Stella	saw a ghost
Victoria is regal	china is breakable	vanilla extract
Martha arrived	Rosa is eager	opera opening

a. North America and South America are in the Western Hemisphere.
b. I saw Edna order a vanilla ice cream soda.

c. Peterson liked his job as a law officer.
d. Barbara is fond of sliced banana in her breakfast cereal.
e. Unless the writer intends to be abstruse, the central idea of an essay should be readily apparent to an intelligent reader.
f. Grandmother almost always enjoyed reading stories to her grandchildren, Martha and Bruce.
g. Brenda and I saw a three-act drama at the Astor Theater.
h. Nora enjoyed resting on the sofa in the living room.
i. Sheriff Truman and his deputies established law and order in the area of Nevada and Northern California.
j. Rhoda always had bright ideas, but Ira almost always saw a flaw in them.

/l/ and /r/ Contrast

Some speakers for whom English is a second language seem to have difficulty in making clear distinctions between /l/ and /r/. The phoneme /l/ is not present in some Asiatic languages, and the phoneme /r/ is absent in others. The following pairs of contrast words and phrases should help to establish the distinction between the phonemes.

PRACTICE MATERIALS

leap	reap	look	rook
leaf	reef	law	raw
lend	rend	load	road
lid	rid	lock	rock
lip	rip	lot	rot
laid	raid	low	row
lap	rap	lie	rye
lack	rack	lies	rise
lug	rug	light	right
lung	rung	lice	rice
lack	rack	loom	room
lift	rift	list	wrist

lacked a rack	late for the rate
lot of rot	look for the rook
right sheds light	a load on the road
lie in the rye	loom in the room
a leaf of the reef	a wrap for the lap
rode the load	rife with life

ADDITIONAL PRACTICE MATERIALS FOR /r/ IN VARIOUS POSITIONS AND CONTEXTS

a. Brown showed no gratitude when the state provided him with free room and board for four years, and he broke out of the brig.

b. O'Brien took every possible opportunity to proclaim his Irish breeding and his proud name.

c. Random thoughts are the products of free reveries.

d. The mixture we breathe called air contains approximately four parts of nitrogen to one part of oxygen.

e. The timorous groom was afraid to carry his bride across the threshold into their new and very own three-room apartment.

f. Crisp and crackly leaves inform us of summer's end.

g. Contemporary weather forecasters are much more accurate than were their predecessors a generation ago.

h. Rabies are transmitted by animals that have contracted hydrophobia.

i. Vandenburg Air Force Base has rocket-firing apparatus.

j. Thoreau for long periods lived as a recluse near Walden Pond.

k. The crafty real estate broker appropriated the poor widow's property when she could not meet the mortgage requirements.

l. Theories should be supported by relevant data and proved by an application of experience.

m. In *Prue and I*, George Curtis remarked, "The pride of ancestry increases in the ratio of distance."

n. Three officers of the law arrested thirteen disturbers of the fragile peace.

o. The right to freedom of expression is a cherished part of the American heritage.

p. Aesop warned that most persons would be truly sorry if their wishes were gratified.

q. In a letter to an editor, Abraham Lincoln wrote, "I go for all sharing the privileges of the government who assist in sharing its burdens."

r. Contrary to Shakespeare's view of King Richard III, some historians reveal that the brief reign of Richard was remarkable for legislation that tried to safeguard the rights of poor persons against abusive barons.

s. According to Pindar, "The best of healers is good cheer."

t. In *Oedipus Rex*, Sophocles wrote, "The greatest griefs are those we cause ourselves."

a. *Hubris* is a word derived from the Greek meaning arrogance arising from overbearing pride or from uncontrolled feelings. The term *hubris* is used to imply that it is a supercilious, graceless state of wanton arrogance that properly precedes a person's fall.

b. In his writing *Of the Training of Children*, Plutarch clearly observed that though it is certainly desirable to be well descended, the glory really belongs to our ancestors.

c. Cryptography is the study of constructing and breaking codes. When cryptography is applied to code breaking rather than code creating, it provides an example of the human search for bringing order out of an apparently random occurrence of events.

d. How was the Devil dressed?
O, he was in his Sunday's best;
His coat was red, and his breeches were blue,
And there was a hole where his tail
   Came through.

   — Robert Southey, *The Devil's Walk*

e. I was angry with my friend:
I told my wrath, my wrath did end.
I was angry with my foe:
I told it not, my wrath did grow.

   — William Blake, *A Poison Tree*

f. Richard Rumbold's last words, according to the historian Macaulay, were "I never could believe that Providence had sent a few men into the world, ready booted and spurred to ride, and millions ready saddled and bridled to be ridden."

   — Thomas Babington Macaulay, *History of England*

g. Omar Khayyam, expressed the poet's wish to be freed from the trials and tribulations of yesterdays and tomorrows in these lines:

   Ah, my beloved, fill the cup
   that clears today of past regrets
   and future fears.

A more realistic versifier, without being cynical, might reply:

   There is no drug, no cup, no wine
   That will rid this day, this hour of time
   Of yesterday's regrets, nor provide a better tomorrow
   Free of its own measure, its burden of sorrow.

h. Robert Pryor was chronically perplexed with a perennial problem concerning his recalcitrant memory. "Frankly," he informed his dearest friend, Terence Bradfield, "I don't really know which is the greater of my problems: trying to remember what I forget, or trying to forget what my cerebral resources are able to remember."

   Bradfield, who had a well-earned reputation for practical realism, replied, "Don't worry, Robert. There is really very little that you forget that is worth your while remembering. If you learn to put your cortical cells to rest for brief periods, you will almost certainly recall what it is urgent for you not to forget."

   Pryor was not certain that he truly understood his friend's serious advice. However, Bradfield's words had such a profound ring to them that he did not inquire further about their meaning. In fact, he forgot what the problem was that he had presented to Terence Bradfield. But Robert Pryor felt better, more comfortable, almost serene, and, for reasons that he did not try to understand, considerably more secure about his tricky memory.

i. Leola Radcliff dolefully and probably realistically observed that it is difficult, and almost impossible, to alter beliefs with nothing more powerful than factual information. Leola regretted that what is all too often considered acceptable and believable is little more than wish fulfillment when it is confronted with cold and nonhistrionic truth. Nevertheless, Leola Radcliff refused to give up hope. She comforted herself with the reminder that eventually the truth does set us free, even though freedom is not realized until persons feel an urgency to greet it.

j. In his writing, *Masters: Portraits of Great Teachers*, Alfred North Whitehead observed, "There is danger in clarity—the danger of overlooking the subtleties of truth."

Dialogue for [l] *and* [r] *Contrast*

A RAW DEAL

Buyer: Look, you tried to rook me when you sold me this throw rug. You led me to believe it was red, but in the right light, it's a wretched orange.

Rug Salesperson: That is a lot of rot. You must have a wry sense of humor to say I lied. It's clearly red.

Buyer: Buddy, I had to lug this rug on a bike that lacked a rack. I rode with it wrapped in my lap. It was a heavy load to carry up this steep road!

Rug Salesperson: I'm sorry, but you returned this rug too late to rate a refund.

Buyer: Your lies make my temper rise. There must be a law against such a raw deal!

Rug Salesperson: I won't sink so low as to brawl with you. Leap into a lawsuit, and we will see who reaps the rewards.

Buyer: Now that I've collected myself, remember, "As you sow, so shall you reap." Lawsuit or not, you shall see me here no more. I'll lose no sleep while you wretchedly reap!

Dialogue for Distinction Between [r] *and* [w]

THE TOMBLIKE ROOM

Edweena: I rue the day I let you woo me into taking this trip. This hotel room is the size of a small tomb, and I heard something woof on the roof!

Marvin: I'll ring for the clerk and ask for a room in the other wing.

Edweena: The rest of the rooms in the West End Motel are full. Let's rest a while before we become too riled.

Marvin: If the rain would wane a bit we could pack the car rack and take a whack at another motel.

Edweena: At this rate we could wait forever. This room reeks as if the window has been shut for weeks!

Marvin: It's rare for you to wear a frown while we are on an adventure. You usually bear up no matter how rare and ridiculous the circumstances.

Edweena: It is wise to rise to the occasion when you travel. The wage you pay for frustrated rage is a sleepless night.

Marvin: Tomorrow the storm will surely dry up, and we will go down to the rill and read poetry.

Edweena: All right. But tonight I will reap the rewards of rightful anger before I will myself to sleep.

Selection: Review of [l] and [r]

Most persons, astronomists and extraterrestrial experts included, like others to think well of them. Scientists concerned with establishing extraterrestrial communication are confronted with a dilemma. If it does become possible to confirm that there are civilizations at least as intelligent as ours in outer space, we would want to impress our extraterrestrial neighbors with the quality of our intellects, to impress them so that they would think well of our thinking. This, however, may not be possible and perhaps may even prove to be embarrassing. If we consider the intellectual trash produced daily by our radio and television commercials and by the news media, it is altogether likely that the extraterrestrial civilizations already have a discouragingly realistic picture of civilization on planet Earth; extraterrestrialists have arrived at their own conclusions about the level and quality of our intellectual life. However bleak the thought, this may explain why we fail to receive any identifiable responses to our signals.

—Adapted from *How Real Is Real?*
by Paul Watzlawick, Vintage Books, 1977, p. 178

Epilogue

In the opening chapter I presented my premise that this edition of *Voice and Diction* is concerned with the effective use of your voice and your diction and, in a broad sense therefore, with enhancing oral speech communication. Another premise implicit in the exposition and in the practice materials is that knowledge should precede action, that to be aware of what our language is about should be directly relevant to what you are going to do about its use. Accordingly, as the author of this book, I accepted an obligation to share information about our language—American English—as well as the mechanisms for speech and some basic concepts about the sound system of our language. In keeping with these premises, an enlarged chapter, "Our Changing Speech Patterns" and a new chapter, "American-English Pronunciation," are included, which deal with standards of speech and dialect differences. I do not think that there is any doubt about my "nonprescriptive" preference for using an acceptable standard of speech, at least in formal situations.

Implicit in this text is the assumption that those who use it are motivated to improve voice and diction and thus, in these respects, to enhance their effectiveness as communicators. I hope that this expectation has been realized in explicit and desirable results.

If you will consider Chapters 1 through 22 to be a long prologue, this epilogue may serve as a brief text, taking the form of a few selected and pointed quotations.

A powerful agent is the right word. Whenever we come upon one of those intensely right words in a book or a newspaper the resulting effect is physical as well as spiritual, and electrically prompt.

—Mark Twain, *Essay on William Dean Howells*

Talking and eloquence are not the same: to speak, and to speak well, are two things. A fool may talk, but a wise man speaks.

—Ben Jonson, *Discoveries Made upon Men and Matter*

When you meet your friend on the roadside or in the marketplace, let the spirit in you move your lips and direct your tongue.

—Kahlil Gibran, *The Prophet*

The music that can deepest reach,
And cure an ill, is cordial speech.

—Ralph Waldo Emerson, *Merlin's Song*

Every vital development in language is a development of feeling as well.

—T. S. Eliot, *Philip Massinger*

VOICE IMPROVEMENT CHECKLIST

Before working on this checklist, review the section "Objective Self-listening" (pages 6–9).

Breathing

1. Is your amount of air intake adequate for your speech effort? _____
2. Is your breathing controlled and synchronized with your speech effort? _____
3. Is your flow of breath sustained for proper phrasing? _____
4. Is your breath expelled between phrases? _____
5. Is your muscular action basically abdominal-thoracic? _____ Clavicular? _____
6. Is there any evidence of excessive tension in the larynx or throat? _____

Pitch

1. Is your range narrow? _____ Wide? _____ Patterned (monotonous)? _____
2. Are your changes consonant with your meanings? _____ Feelings? _____
3. Is your habitual pitch the same or close to your optimum pitch? _____
4. Does the major part of your speech effort occur within the optimal range? _____
5. Are your individual inflectional changes appropriate to the meanings and feelings that you intended to communicate? _____
6. Is your overall intonation suggestive of a foreign pattern? _____ If so, can you identify the pattern? _____

Loudness

1. Is the loudness of your voice adequate for the size of your group of listeners? _____

2. Do any of your listeners have to strain to hear you? _____

3. May your voice be characterized as full? _____ Thin or weak? _____ Overloud? _____ Sufficiently varied and appropriate for meanings? _____

4. Are your changes independent of your variations in pitch? _____

5. Are the changes related to the meanings you wish to emphasize? _____

Quality

1. Is your voice hypernasal? _____ Denasal? _____ Breathy? _____ Husky? _____ Guttural? _____ Hard or metallic? _____

2. Is your voice reinforced only within part of the pitch range? _____

3. Is your voice varied according to the nature of the content? _____

4. Are you generally satisfied with your voice quality but would like to improve it in one or more aspects? _____
   Which? _____

Rate

1. Is your overall rate too slow? _____ Too rapid? _____ Unchanging? _____ Does your rate vary according to the relative importance of the units of your message? _____

2. Is your rate too rapid for effective articulation? _____ Does your overall rate include pauses between major units of meaning to permit your listeners to "digest" your meaning? _____ Are the pauses too short? _____ Too long so that you may lose your listeners? _____

Personality

1. Is the overall effect of your voice pleasing? _____

2. Does your voice reflect the person you think you are? _____ Want to be? _____ Any surprises? _____

PRONUNCIATION AND ARTICULATION CHECKLIST

Pronunciation

1. In your overall pronunciation, are you aware of any individual variations of vowels or diphthongs from those current in your community? _____

2. Are these variations ones you wish to maintain or modify? _____

3. Do you follow regional practices with regard to /r/? _____

4. Are you aware of any dialectal pronunciations? _____ Do you wish to maintain them? _____ List your variations from General American speech:
   _____

Articulation

1. What sounds or sound blends need improvement:
   a. Consonants? _____
   b. Vowels? _____
   c. Diphthongs? _____

2. Do you have any tendency to slur or to overassimilate? _____

3. Are your medial nasal consonants given full value? _____

4. Do you tend to give excessive nasal "coloring" to vowels or diphthongs that are in close proximity to nasal consonants? _____

5. Do you tend to unvoice final sounds such as /z/, /ʒ/, and /dʒ/? _____

6. Is your speech in general as intelligible as you would like it to be? _____ As intelligible as that of a speaker you admire? _____

7. Are you aware of any differences in your "formal" speech and your casual, conversational speech? _____ Are these differences comparable to those of your peers? To those of speakers you admire? _____

GLOSSARY OF TERMS

Abdomen The cavity below the thorax (chest cavity) that contains most of the digestive organs, including the stomach (see Figure 2–3); the belly.

Abdominal breathing Breathing characterized by controlled action of the muscles of the abdomen.

Accent Pattern of pronunciation, including stress and intonation, that characterizes the speech of an individual, group, or persons in a geographic area or region (regional dialect).

Adam's apple A projection of the thyroid cartilage at the top front of the neck, usually more prominent in men than in women.

Affricate The blend of a stop and a fricative sound. The phonemes /tʃ/ (**ch**) and /dʒ/ (**j**) are affricates.

Allophones Members or varieties of sounds within a phoneme; the sounds that are classified as belonging to a phoneme in a given linguistic system (see *Phoneme*).

Alveolar ridge The upper gum ridge.

Amplitude Extent of range. In vocalization, the greater the amplitude of the vocal bands, the louder the voice.

Articulation The modification of the breath stream by the organs of the mouth (the lips, tongue, and palate) and the laryngeal mechanism to produce identifiable speech sounds (phonemes).

Arytenoid cartilage A pyramid-shaped cartilage situated in the posterior portion of the larynx. There are two arytenoid cartilages in the larynx to which the vocal bands are attached. The movements of the arytenoids influence the position and the state of tension of the vocal bands.

Aspirate quality Breathiness that accompanies vocalization or articulation.

Assimilation The phonetic changes that take place in connected speech when one speech sound is modified as the result of a neighboring sound or sounds.

Audition The process or act of hearing.

Back vowels The vowel sounds produced as a result of the action (position) of the back of the tongue.

Bilabial consonants The consonants that are produced as a result of lip-closing action that stops or diverts the flow of breath.

Breathiness An excess of breath that may accompany vocalization.

Buccal cavity The mouth or oral cavity.

Cavity reinforcement   The building up of selected vocal tones resulting from the size and shape of the individual cavity; cavity resonance.

Central nervous system (CNS)   The parts of the nervous mechanism that include the cerebrum, the cerebellum, the medulla, and the spinal cord. The CNS is responsible for the coordination, control, and regulation of responses to stimuli and thus for the establishment of patterns of behavior.

Central vowels   Vowel sounds produced as a result of the action (position) of the central portion or midportion of the tongue.

Cerebellum   The "little brain," a part of the central nervous system, situated posteriorly and under the cerebrum. The cerebellum is importantly involved in the coordination of the motor activity needed for speech production.

Cerebral cortex   The gray outer covering of the cerebrum. The cortex contains billions of nerve cells. Some portions of the cortex have special functions that are significant in the understanding and the production of speech.

Clavicular breathing   Breathing characterized by action of the upper part of the rib cage and the shoulders.

Cognate sounds   Phonemes that are produced in the same place and with the same manner of articulation and that are differentiated by the presence or the absence of vocal-band vibration; /p/ and /b/, /t/ and /d/ are cognate sounds.

Consonants   Speech sounds produced as a result of either a partial or a complete (temporary) obstruction or modification of the breath stream by the organs of articulation.

Continuant consonant   A consonant sound that has duration and that is produced with the articulator in a fixed position (such as /s/ and /l/), in contrast to stop consonants that are short and that result from the interruption of the breath (such as /p/ and /g/).

Contour   The pitch pattern of a unit (phrase) in speech; the intonation pattern of identifiable pitch changes from the beginning to the end of a phrase.

Cricoid cartilage   The ring-shaped cartilage in the lower and back portion of the larynx. The posterior part of the cricoid serves as a base for the arytenoid cartilages.

Decibel   Measurement of the unit of hearing for the intensity (loudness) of a sound.

Denasality   A lack of appropriate nasal reinforcement (resonance) that may accompany a common cold or upper respiratory involvement (a stuffed nose), including allergy.

Diacritical symbols (marks)   A system of alphabet letters and a number of markings used by dictionaries to indicate phonetic values.

Dialect   Variations in pronunciation, word meaning, or grammar within a language system that are identified with a geographic region or a social group. Despite variations, speakers of different dialects of a language are able to understand one another. When differences become too great for mutual intelligibility, we then have different languages derived from a common language.

Diaphragm   The double, dome-shaped muscle of respiration situated between the chest and abdominal cavities.

Diction   The production of speech sounds in a given linguistic code; also the selection of words within a linguistic system.

Diphthongs   Vocalic glides of two vowels uttered on a single breath impulse within one syllable. The phonetic symbols of the diphthong represent the approximate initial and final sounds of the glide.

Foreign accent   The overall pattern of pronunciation, including stress and intonation, that suggests a foreign (in relation to American-English) language. Often a carryover of the phonetic characteristics of a first language.

Fricative   A consonant produced by forcing the stream of breath between the articulators with a resultant "noisy" sound.

Front vowels   The vowels produced as a result of the action (position) of the front, or blade, of the tongue.

Fundamental pitch   The pitch resulting from the frequency of vibration of the body as a whole; the lowest tone in a complex tone.

Glide sounds   Sounds produced as a result of the continuous movement of the articulators. The initial position of the articulators in the production of a glide is stable. The final position of the articulators is determined by the sound that immediately follows.

Glottal   Referring to sounds produced as a result of laryngeal tension and action, as by a sudden stoppage and release of breath by the vocal bands.

Glottal fry   A crackly, "bubbly," rough voice quality that is usually produced at the lower part of a speaker's pitch range.

Glottis   The opening between the vocal bands.

Habitual pitch   The pitch level at which an individual most frequently initiates vocalization.

Hard palate   The front (hard) portion of the roof of the mouth; the portion between the gum ridge and the soft palate.

Hz (hertz)   A unit of frequency of a sound wave equal to one cycle per second (100 Hz = 100 cycles per second). The Hz is named for the German physicist H. R. Hertz.

Idiolect   A speaker's individual variation of a dialect. Each of us speaks in an idiolect of one or more dialects of a language.

Inflection   Pitch changes that occur without interruption of phonation during the production of a syllable or word. Inflectional changes may be *downward, upward,* or *circumflex* (downward and upward or upward and downward).

International Phonetic Alphabet (IPA)   A system for representing the distinctive sounds (phonemes) of a linguistic code through special visual symbols.

Intonation   The pattern or contour of pitch changes for a spoken phrase or sentence (see *Contour*).

Labiodental sounds   Consonants produced as a result of activity of the lip (lower) and teeth (upper); lip–teeth sounds.

Laryngeal fricative   The sound /h/ made discernible as a result of laryngeal tension and vocal-fold activity.

Laryngopharynx   The portion of the pharynx nearest to the larynx.

Larynx   The uppermost part of the trachea; the structure that includes the vocal bands; the voice box.

Lateral consonant   The sound /l/ produced as a result of the emission of vocalized breath at both sides of the tongue with the tongue tip at the gum ridge.

Lingua-alveolar consonants   The consonants produced as a result of contact between the tongue tip and the gum (alveolar) ridge.

Midvowels   See *Central vowels.*

Morpheme   The most elementary semantically functional unit of a language. This may be a one-morpheme word, an affix (prefix or suffix), or a root.

Nasal cavities   The cavities in the head directly above the roof of the mouth.

Nasal consonants   The speech sounds produced with nasal reinforcement. In American English these are /m/, /n/, and /ŋ/.

Nasality   The quality of voice resulting from reinforcement in the nasal cavities.

Nasopharynx   The portion of the pharynx nearest the entrance to the nasal cavities; the uppermost portion of the pharynx.

Optimum pitch   The pitch level at which one can usually achieve the best vocal quality and the necessary loudness with the least expenditure of energy; the pitch level at which one can initiate the voice with the greatest ease and effectiveness.

Oral cavity   The cavity of the mouth; the buccal cavity.

Oral resonance   The reinforcement of vocal tones by the oral cavity.

Oropharynx   That portion of the pharynx nearest the oral cavity; the middle portion of the pharynx.

Palatal sounds   The sounds (phonemes) produced by intended activity of the middle or back of the tongue and the palate.

Paralanguage   The audible and visual components that accompany spoken language — voice quality, loudness, stress, pitch variation (inflection and intonation) and pitch range, rate, pause, and body language including gesture — that modify the meanings of the words; in essence, *how you say what you say.*

Pharynx   The cavity between the esophagus and the entrance to the nasal cavity; the throat.

Phonation   The production of voice; the vibratory activity of the vocal bands in the larynx.

Phone   A speech sound (see *Phoneme*).

Phoneme   The basic unit or sound family within a linguistic system; a group or family of closely related sounds that share distinctive acoustic characteristics; the distinctive phonetic or sound "elements" of a word. Phonemic differences permit us to distinguish between spoken words.

Phonetic alphabet   See *International Phonetic Alphabet.*

Pitch   The attribute of sound resulting from the frequency of vibration of the vibrating body; the attribute of auditory sensation in terms of which sounds may be ordered on a scale from high to low; our subjective reaction to frequency changes or differences.

Plosive sounds   The consonants produced by a stoppage and release of the breath stream.

Postdental sounds   The consonants produced as a result of contact between an anterior portion of the tongue and the area of the mouth behind the dental ridge.

Pronunciation   The articulation of meaningful units of speech; the combining of phonemes in meaningful contextual utterance; the utterance of appropriate sounds and the placement of stress in the production of contextual speech.

Resonance The strengthening or building up of sound either through cavity reinforcement or through the sympathetic vibration of a body in close proximity to the source of the sound (the vibrating body); the vibratory response of a body or a cavity to a sound frequency imposed on it.

Respiration The act of breathing. Controlled breath is the motor force for speech. Normally, we speak on controlled exhaled (expired) breath.

Schwa The weak vowel; a central vowel that occurs in a strong majority of unstressed syllables and in unstressed prepositions and conjunctions. The schwa is the most frequently used vowel in English.

Sinus A hollowed area (cavity) within a bone. There are several sinuses in the facial structure near the nasal cavity and the eyes.

Stop sounds Sounds produced by a complete closing of the breath channel.

Stress The degree of emphasis given to a morpheme or a word by the speaker's varying the loudness, the pitch, and/or the duration within a larger utterance.

Stridency A tense, "metallic" voice quality that usually occurs in the upper pitch range.

Thoracic cavity The chest or thorax.

Thyroid cartilage The large, shieldlike fused cartilage of the larynx.

Trachea The cartilaginous tubelike structure between the pharynx and the bronchi; the windpipe.

Velar sounds Sounds produced as a result of articulatory activity between the soft palate and the back of the tongue.

Velum The soft palate.

Vocal attributes The characteristics by which we distinguish vocal efforts: pitch, loudness, duration, and quality.

Vocal bands Two small, tough bands, or folds, of connective, or ligamentous, tissue situated in the larynx. The vocal bands are continuous with folds of muscle tissue and are connected to cartilages in the larynx. Pulsations of the vocal bands give rise to the voice.

Vocal cords See *Vocal bands.*

Vocal folds See *Vocal bands.*

Vocal fry See *Glottal fry.*

Vocal tract The continuous cavities above the vocal folds that include the larynx, pharynx, mouth, and nasal cavities. These cavities serve as both organs of articulation and speech sound reinforcement (resonators).

Voice Tones produced as a result of action of the vocal bands and reinforced by the resonating cavities.

Voice box See *Larynx.*

Vowels Sounds produced as a result of articulatory action without obstruction or interference of breath; unobstructed sounds produced by changes in the size and the shape of the oral cavity and by differences in the elevation of portions of the tongue.

Windpipe See *Trachea.*

INDEX